GW00367902

Education Matters

Education Matters draws together a selection of the most influential papers published in the *British Journal of Educational Studies* by many of the leading scholars in the field over the past 60 years. This unique collection of seminal articles published since the first issue of the *Journal* provides students and researchers in education with an informed insight and understanding of the nature of the development of the field of Educational Studies in the UK since the Second World War. It also assesses the current position of Educational Studies and explores the possibilities for the development of the field in coming years.

Compiled by the journal's editors, past and present, James Arthur, Jon Davison and Richard Pring, the book illustrates the development of the field of educational studies, and the specially written Introduction contextualises the selection, whilst introducing students to the main issues and current thinking in the field.

Each of the 18 articles includes a preface which highlights the changing conceptions and development of, or consistency in, educational thought over time, as well as debates and conflicts in the seminal articles by key educational thinkers that have been published in the *Journal*.

James Arthur is Professor of Education and Head of the School of Education, University of Birmingham, UK.

Jon Davison has been Professor of Teacher Education in four UK universities including the Institute of Education, University of London, UK where he was also Dean.

Richard Pring is Emeritus Professor of Education, Department of Education, University of Oxford, UK.

Education Matters

Sixty years of the *British Journal of Educational Studies*

**Edited by James Arthur,
Jon Davison and Richard Pring**

Routledge
Taylor & Francis Group

LONDON AND NEW YORK

First published 2012
by Routledge
2 Park Square, Milton Park, Abingdon, Oxon OX14 4RN

Simultaneously published in the USA and Canada
by Routledge
711 Third Avenue, New York, NY 10017

Routledge is an imprint of the Taylor & Francis Group, an informa business

© 2012 selection and editorial material, J. Arthur, J. Davison and R. Pring; individual chapters, the contributors

British Library Cataloguing in Publication Data
A catalogue record for this book is available from the British Library

Library of Congress Cataloging in Publication Data
Education matters : 60 years of the British journal of educational studies / edited by James Arthur, Jon Davison, Richard Pring.
p. cm. – (Education heritage)
1. Education–Great Britain. I. Arthur, James, 1957- II. Davison, Jon, 1949- III. Pring, Richard. IV. British journal of educational studies.
LA632.E396 2012
370.941–dc23
2011039363

ISBN: 978-0-415-50552-9 (hbk)
ISBN: 978-0-203-12382-9 (ebk)

Typeset in Galliard
by Taylor and Francis Books

Printed and bound in Great Britain by
CPI Antony Rowe, Chippenham, Wiltshire

Contents

vi   *Contents*

Contributors

James Arthur is Professor of Education and Head of the School of Education in the University of Birmingham. He is the current Editor of the *British Journal of Educational Studies*.

Jon Davison has been Professor of Teacher Education in four universities in the UK, including the Institute of Education, University of London, where he was also Dean. He is Chair of the Society for Educational Studies.

Richard Pring was Professor of Educational Studies, University of Oxford 1989–2003 and Director of the Department. He was Lead Director of Nuffield Review 14–19 Education and Training 2003–9 and editor of the *British Journal of Educational Studies* from 1986 to 2001. His most recent book, *The Life and Death of Secondary Education for All*, is published by Routledge.

Sixty years of the Society for Educational Studies

Jon Davison

> The concept of a Standing Conference was first aired at a meeting in St Catharine's College, Windsor, on research in Education, on the 10th and 11th of November 1950. After some discussion, Professors Judges, Niblett and Oliver were asked to draft proposals for the establishment of a new *Journal of Educational Studies*. (30, 2: 230)

The Society for Educational Studies began life as the Standing Conference on Studies in Education (SCSE) on Wednesday 19 December 1951, when former Director of the Institute of Education, University of London, Sir Fred Clarke chaired a conference of Professors of Education and Directors of Institutes of Education from across the UK in order to discuss what they believed to be the problems raised by the growth of educational research during the previous few decades. The prevailing belief held by those attending was that 'British studies in the various fields of education—philosophical, historical, social, psychological and pedagogic—need to be better organized and better known' (1, 1: 67).

Professors Judges, Niblett and Oliver reported to the Conference and their proposals for a journal were approved. A. C. F. Beales, King's College, London agreed to become Executive Editor (see Figure 1 *Editors of the British Journal of Educational Studies* on page xvi). The first edition of the *British Journal of Educational Studies*, which included a note of the untimely death of Sir Fred Clarke a month after the inaugural conference, appeared in 1952 and included a clear statement of intention. The statement was not made in an editorial – the *Journal* did not have one – but rather in a section entitled 'Notes and News':

> The new *Journal* will [therefore] give prominence to articles embodying research, and it will disseminate information about educational research in progress. The journals sponsored by the British Psychological Society already provide a medium for the publication of psychological and statistical research into some problems of education. The new *Journal*, while taking account of this work, will be mainly concerned with other aspects of the study of education. But it will not be narrowly specialist; on the contrary, it is intended to

serve the needs and interests of everyone concerned with education whom the implications of specialized research affect.

It will be different in form from existing educational journals in this country. Its 'Notes and News', for example, will not be a matter of editorial comment on topical events in education; they will indicate how and where these developments are being studied, and the trend of opinion upon them. The major articles will be contributions by experts, sometimes as surveys of work in progress up and down the country and abroad, sometimes as original contributions giving the results of the writers' own individual work. The broad objects of the *Journal* will never be lost sight of: viz. to explain the significance of new thought, to provide philosophical discussion at a high level, and to deepen existing interest in the purposes and problems of current educational policy. These objects will determine the selection of books to be dealt with in review articles and in reviews. There will also be, from time to time, contributions from the national Research Foundations of England and Scotland; and particulars of graduate research in progress in the Universities and elsewhere.

With the exception of the introduction of a more 'traditional' editorial from Volume 26 Issue 3 in 1978, the Society's *Journal* has held true to these objectives for 60 years. The *BJES* has had three publishers in its lifetime: Faber for the first 20 years; Blackwell from 1972 to 2009, and Taylor and Francis since 2010.

At the inaugural meeting of the SCSE, Professor W. R. Niblett, University of Leeds, became Chair of the Standing Conference (see Figure 2 *Chairs of the Society for Educational Studies* on page xiii) and Professor J. W. Tibble, University College, Leicester, Secretary-Treasurer. There were 74 members of the Standing Conference, 55 representing English institutions, 11 Scottish, 5 Welsh, one from Northern Ireland, and two from elsewhere (1, 1: 191–92). Founding members of the Standing Conference *inter alia* also included: Professors M. Read, W. O. Lester-Smith, L. A. Reid and P. E. Vernon of the Institute of Education, University of London; Professor W. A. C. Stewart, University College of North Staffordshire, Keele; Professor F. J. Schonell, University of Queensland, Australia; Professor S. D. Nisbet, University of Glasgow; Professor R. A. G. Oliver, University of Manchester; Professors A. V. C. Jeffreys and E. A. Peel, University of Birmingham; Professor J. Pilley, University of Edinburgh and J. F. Wolfenden CBE, University of Reading.

Writing in the *Journal* on the 30th anniversary of the foundation of the SCSE, Professor Roger Webster, Chair of SCSE 1973–1976, noted that the 1950s and 1960s were not good decades during which to take a holistic view of studies in Education:

This was the period when 'undifferentiated mush' was derided; when the sociology, history and philosophy of education were being established as studies in their own right, with their own associations and journals. However, despite the impressive advances made by the 'disciplines' of education, 'boundary maintenance' between them has considerably reduced the effectiveness of educationalists in influencing either teachers or policy makers. (30, 2: 230)

R. S. Peters had described educational theory as 'undifferentiated mush' in his inaugural professorial lecture at the Institute of Education, University of London in 1963 and in a keynote at the 1972 SCSE Annual Conference, Peters crystallised the problem facing educationalists: 'I take as my starting point that education, as a subject, is like politics in being concerned with problems which cannot be tackled, like mathematical problems or problems in physics, by reliance on just one way of thinking' (30, 2: 230). For Peters, 'education is not an autonomous discipline, but a field, like politics, where the disciplines of history, philosophy, psychology, and sociology have application' (50, 1: 100).

During its existence the SCSE held annual conferences on a variety of topics including, in the first four decades: 'A Central Agency for Educational Research' (1951); 'The Development of Educational Studies' (1952); 'Teacher Training in Scotland and England' (1953); 'The Teaching of the Philosophy of Education in Departments of Education' (1955); 'The University as an Instrument of Education' (1963); 'Education as a Subject in First Degree Courses' (1964); 'The Implications of Comprehensive Secondary Education' (1966); 'The Purpose and Structure of Higher Education' (1970); 'Education as an Academic Discipline' (1972); 'Educational Attitudes and Economic Survival' (1977); 'The Place of Research in Educational Studies' (1980); 'Quality Control in Education' (1991); 'The Idea of a University in the 21st Century' (1992); 'The Study of Education: Its Place in Professional Development' (1993), which included contributions from academics including, Professors Rosemary Deem, John Elliott, David Hargreaves, Maurice Kogan and Sally Tomlinson; 'Alternative Futures for Education' (1995), which included keynotes from Professors Anthony Giddens and Michael Barber.

By the middle of the 1990s the Standing Conference had enjoyed an international reputation for over 40 years. Subscribers to the *BJES* were located in universities and schools across the world. In the 1996 Standing Conference, *BJES* publisher Blackwell and the Centre for the Study of Comprehensive Schools sponsored a series of fourteen at the University of Oxford entitled *Affirming the Comprehensive Ideal*. The title generated a fair degree of controversy. As *BJES* editor of the time, Professor Richard Pring noted, 'Should a university be *affirming* something which "research has demonstrated to be a failure"? Should not a university be engaged much more impartially, through careful research, in the effectiveness or otherwise of the "comprehensive experiment"?' (44, 2: 140).

The Standing Conference's defence was simple and true to its core intention: the lecture series was affirming an ideal – not necessarily the system, which was but one attempt to implement that ideal. 'That ideal sets out a moral framework within which, as a result of research, experience, argument, philosophical reflection, all young people might receive an education according to age, ability and aptitude. Such a framework or set of ideals is necessarily controversial ... The lectures, therefore, within an affirmed moral framework, try to make sense of the research evidence, the experience of teachers, the diversity of arrangements, the values which sustain the system' (44, 2: 140).

Writing in the summer of 2001, the year of the 50th Anniversary of the founding of the Standing Conference, *BJES* editor Richard Pring pleaded, ' ... as my fifteen years of editorship – following the excellent precedents of Beales and Sutherland – approach their end, I make a special plea, namely, that the *Journal* abandons not its main and original task of applying the very best of historical, philosophical and sociological thinking to those questions of educational aims and value which permeate policy and practice' (49,1: 3).

At its Annual General Meeting in November 2001 the Standing Conference on Studies in Education decided to re-name itself the Society for Educational Studies (SES). The new name described far more clearly and accurately the aims and objectives of the Society and its associated *Journal* and provided a stimulus to re-consider the nature of the study of education. In line with its reconstitution, the Society changed its 'Annual Conference' to an 'Annual Seminar' that would be followed by a financially sponsored seminar series in universities around the UK in the following year, which focused on aspects of, or issues raised by, the Annual Seminar. The first of the Annual Seminars 'The Price of Performance: Emerging Evidence from Schools and Universities' was held on Thursday 13 November 2003 at the Royal College of Physicians at Regent's Park, London. Other Annual Seminars and seminar series followed that included: 'An Academic Life: The Next Ten Years' (2008); 'Engaging Young People in Civic Action and Learning' (2009); 'Beyond Impact: Connecting research to policy and practice?' (2010) and 'Disciplinarity, interdisciplinarity and educational studies: past, present and future' (2011).

As well as publishing the *Journal* and organising the Annual Conference since 1951, the Society has financed its Annual Book Awards for excellent publications in the field. Additionally, the Society has awarded sums of money to support educational research in UK educational institutions. At first these sums were small and during the 1990s the Society was awarding approximately £5,000 per annum in research awards. In 2003, the research awards were revised. A sum of £30,000, comprising a major educational research project award, was offered, as well as up to five awards of Small Research Grants of up to £2,000 to support small-scale projects. From 2009, the Society increased the sum for Small Research Grants to a maximum of £10,000 per grant and also instituted its National Award of £200,000. In order to address areas of major interest to the Society, the Research Sub-Committee of the SES Executive invites bids to undertake research on its behalf upon a prescribed topic. The first biennial award was made to a team led by Dr. Hilary Cremin from the University of Cambridge for the project *Engaging Young People in Civic Action and Learning*. Fittingly, in its 60th Anniversary year the Society's National Award was entitled *The Social Organisation of Educational Studies: Past, Present and Future*. The call for proposals attracted a great deal of interest and the National Award went to a team from the Institute of Education, University of London led by Professor Gary McCulloch.

In November 2011 a dinner was held to celebrate the Society's 60th Anniversary at The Athenæum Club, London attended by the current Chair, Professor Jon Davison, officers and Executive Committee members and previous Chairs of the Society. A similar dinner took place at The Athenæum Club, London in March 2012 to celebrate the 60th Anniversary of the *British Journal of Educational*

Studies. Guests included the current Editor, Professor James Arthur, and previous editors of the *Journal.*

Throughout its 60 years, the Society, in its conferences, seminars, through its research funding and in its *Journal,* has remained steadfast to its original aim of bringing together educationalists of varying viewpoints and skills to discuss educational problems and issues. Many of the Society's officers, members of its Executive Committee and general membership have not only contributed to the numerous debates about educational studies during the past six decades but have also written seminal and influential articles and books that have contributed to the development of the field: a fitting legacy to the integrity and foresight of the founders of the Society and *Journal,* in particular Professors Beales, Judges, Niblett, Oliver and Tibble.

Chairs of the Society for Educational Studies 1951–2012[1]

1951   Professor W. R. Niblett, University of Leeds
1956   Professor A. V. Judges, King's College, London
1960   Professor R. Wilson, University of Bristol
1968   Professor J. W. Tibble, Institute of Education, University of Leicester
1972   *Vacant*
1973   Professor J. R. Webster, University College of N. Wales
1976   Professor W. A. L. Blyth, University of Liverpool
1979   Mr. K. B. Thompson, North Staffordshire Polytechnic
1982   Dr. T. R. Bone, Jordanhill College of Education
1985   Professor M. B. Sutherland, University of Leeds
1988   Professor G. Batho, University of Durham
1991   Professor P. Croll, University of Reading
1994   Professor G. Littler, University of Derby
1997   Professor K. L. Oglesby, Manchester Metropolitan University
2000   Professor D. Lawton, Institute of Education, University of London
2003   Professor G. Nicholls, King's College, University of London
2006   Professor J. H. Davison, Institute of Education, University of London

1 Institutional affiliations of Chairs given are those at the time of their appointment to the position.

Introduction

Richard Pring

Sixty years of the *British Journal of Educational Studies* is an event worthy of celebration because no other journal of this kind in Britain has enjoyed such longevity – except the *British Journal of Educational Psychology*. And there hangs a tale.

Compared with universities in Europe, those in Britain were late in coming to recognise 'education' as an important area for study in the preparation for teaching – with the exception of Scotland where, at Aberdeen University, Alexander Bains, Professor of Logic, set a trend with his publication in 1879 of *Education as a Science* – showing how 'associationism' provided a psychological basis for understanding learning and thereby improving the curriculum.

Perhaps it was the dominance of the independent schools and the Headmasters' Conference that deterred at least the older universities from showing interest in educational theory. According to Herbert Warren, President of Magdalen College, Oxford, in his evidence to the Bryce commission in 1895, the student who has read Plato's *Republic* and Aristotle's *Politics* and *Nichomachean Ethics* has whatever theory is necessary for the practice of teaching. But in addition it would be helpful

> that a young man who has passed through an English public school, more particularly if he has been ... a prefect ... has had experience in keeping order and maintaining discipline ... Thus the average Oxford man, more especially the classical student, ought not to require so long an additional training, either in theory or practice, as is sometimes necessary for students elsewhere.[2]

Belatedly maybe, the University of Oxford finally agreed to establish a Chair of Education in 1989.

The early development of educational studies in the British universities, beginning with Aberdeen, focused very much on the benefits of psychological study. Not until much later was there seen to be the need for a wider base, and the *Journal* in 1952 set out to provide it. The *British Journal of Educational Psychology*

2 Bryce Report, v.257.

took care of psychological studies, and the *British Journal of Educational Studies*, therefore, widened the theoretical background beyond that. As might be expected from the first editor, A. C. Beales, Professor of the History of Education at King's College London, there was a strong emphasis on history. An early contribution was from Beales' predecessor, A. V. Judge, the first Professor of History of Education at King's, and it is fitting therefore that this selection has picked his contribution to the very beginnings of the debate on comprehensive schools.

However, the first issue showed this wider perspective on theory with William Stewart's paper on *Karl Mannheim and the Sociology of Education* and a paper by Louis Arnauld Reid, the first Professor of Philosophy of Education in Britain, on *Education and the Map of Knowledge*. Soon, too, psychology entered the pages of the *Journal*, for the prevailing interest in genetics had given rise to theories of intelligence which were to shape education and particularly selection for education at the age of 11. Hence, the early contribution from Cyril Burt reprinted here.

In this book, we have picked out 18 papers published in the *Journal*, not because they are necessarily more distinguished than the many other papers published, but because they reflect the broadening interest in the theory of education that would become the basis of the theoretical foundations of teaching. History and philosophy remained a continuing interest, especially before there arose specialist journals in these areas. Of particular interest therefore are Armytage's paper on the 1870 Act, and Robert Dearden's, Olive Banks' and Brian Simon's surveys respectively of philosophy, sociology and history of education from the time of the *Journal*'s inception until 30 years later. The new Bachelor of Education degree launched in the 1960s required a theoretical literature and the *Journal* provided it.

However, the changing interest in theory is reflected in these papers. John Nisbet and Patricia Broadfoot, it is true, wrote about the impact of educational research some years ago, but this became of increasing concern as time went on, stimulated no doubt by the importance of research assessment from the late 1980s onwards. Philip Davies was the first to write about the evidence-based approach with which we are now familiar, and the paper by the Torgersons provided yet more detailed technical account of the randomised controlled sampling which was crucial to this kind of research.

Another area of interest that developed, mainly from the philosophers, was the part which values and value judgment play not only in the underlying educational theory but also in the validity and shaping of research: hence, the choice of papers by Terence McLaughlin, John Hull and David Carr. But this interest permeates the paper on higher education by Alasdair MacIntyre on the historical ideal of a university. We need to be reminded of the latter in the current ferment of change. How could we have predicted the growth of for-profit universities, foundation degrees at colleges of further education and distribution of research money on the basis of the metrics of publications and their citation?

Throughout there is a reflection on the nature of educational theory, and it is fitting that we should publish the valedictory paper by the second editor, Margaret Sutherland, on her retirement from the *Journal – The Place of Theory of Education in Teacher Education*. After all, it was in the pursuit of exploring such a place that the *Journal* was established 60 years ago.

   Sixty years ago also, John Dewey, the American philosopher and educationist, died. His ghost appears quite rightly throughout the *Journal*, and it is fitting that in the most recent issue before the publication of this collection his ghost reappears in more definite form.

Editors of the *British Journal of Educational Studies* 1952–2012

Arthur Beales   1952–1974
Margaret Sutherland   1975–1985
Richard Pring   1986–1990
Richard Pring and David Halpin   1991–1999
Richard Pring and Geoffrey Walford   2000–2001
Paul Croll   2002–2004
James Arthur and Paul Croll   2005–2009
James Arthur   2009–2012

Selected Articles

Each of the selected articles that follows is prefaced by a brief biography of the author and a discussion of themes within the *British Journal of Educational Studies* exemplified by the article. The institutional affiliation of each author cited is that which was current at the time of publication. Each article is cross-referenced to other papers in this volume and in the *BJES* within the respective theme with commentary on the significance of the theme past, present and future.

A full archive of the *British Journal of Educational Studies* containing every volume published since 1952 is freely available online to members of the Society of Educational Studies. Details of how to become a member of the Society may be found on its website at www.soc-for-ed-studies.org.uk/

1 Karl Mannheim and the Sociology of Education

W. A. C. Stewart

Author

A former schoolteacher and research student of Karl Mannheim, William Alexander Campbell Stewart (1915–97) was the first professor of Education in the Institute of Education, Keele University (previously University College of North Staffordshire). Campbell Stewart wrote numerous books and articles on education and sociology, such as *Quakers and Education as seen in their Schools in England*, *Progressives and Radicals in English Education, 1750–1970*, *The Educational Innovators* and *Systematic Sociology: An Introduction to the Study of Society* (with Karl Mannheim), which he wrote and published in 1962. Karl Mannheim had been appointed to the Chair in the Sociology of Education at the Institute of Education, University of London, in 1946, but died the following year. Campbell Stewart based the book on Mannheim's manuscript and lecture notes. His last book, *Higher Education in Postwar Britain*, was published in 1989. He was Vice-Chancellor of Keele University 1967–79. Perhaps fittingly, Professor Stewart died while on a visit to Keele University on 23 April 1997.

Introduction

In *Karl Mannheim and the Sociology of Education* (1, 2: 99–113) Professor Campbell Stewart attempts to explain the nature of Mannheim's thought by exploring the main trends in the continuity of Mannheim's thought to see how these came to be expressed in his approach to the sociology of education. He does so by considering what he sees as two geographically distinct phases of Mannheim's work: *The German Period* and *The English Period*.

In his consideration of Mannheim's *German Period*, Campbell Stewart furnishes readers with detail of the background of the development of his thought from his doctoral thesis (1922) and his writings produced at the universities of Heidelberg and Frankfurt before he fled the Nazi regime in 1933 to come to England. The development of the general philosophic bases of Mannheim's sociology are considered in his key texts including *Analysis of Epistemology* (1922), *Interpretation of Weltanschauung* (1923), *Historicism* (1925), *The Sociology of Knowledge* (1925), *Conservative Thought* (1927) and the German edition of *Ideology and Utopia* (1929).

Campbell Stewart then moves on to explore Mannheim's *English Period* from 1933, when he worked at the London School of Economics and the Institute of Education, University of London until his death in 1947. A revised English translation of *Ideology and Utopia* was published in Britain in 1936 and *Man and Society in an Age of Reconstruction* (1940), which contains the often quoted,

> Sociologists do not regard education solely as a means of realizing abstract ideas of culture, such as humanism or technical specialization, but as part of the process of influencing men and women. Education can only be understood when we know for what society and for what social position the children are being educated. (p. 105)

and *Diagnosis of Our Time* (1943), in which, Campbell Stewart asserts, Mannheim

> ... develops the whole theme of a sociological approach to education. Aims and methods in education have to be understood 'in and for a given society'. Education is one of the means of influencing human behaviour, a form of social control which can be effective in maintaining emotional stability and mental integrity only if it has strategy in common with agencies outside the school. Education can no longer be considered mainly as an interchange between teacher and pupil. It is part of a broader process altogether. (p.106)

Campbell Stewart is clear in his admiration of Mannheim's contribution and critical of his detractors, such as G. H. Bantock. Although his intellectual contribution was cut short 'when he died in 1947, he had already had an important effect, not all of it good, because it was not difficult for shallow or prejudiced minds to distort or over-simplify his thinking for their own purposes' (p.99).

For Campbell Stewart, Mannheim's belief of the study of education is as a social science that involves 'a synoptic study for pursuing which data could be collected and collated from many different fields'. As Gary McCulloch (50, 1: 100–119) has noted elsewhere in the *BJES*, 'Mannheim's published work established a disciplinary heritage, an inspiration and source for continued sociological work'.

Other related articles in the *Journal* include: Professor Campbell Stewart's *Progressive Education – Past Present and Future* (27, 2: 103–10) as well as *Disciplines Contributing to Education? Educational Studies and the Disciplines* (50, 1: 100–119); *Utopianism and Education: The Legacy of Thomas More* (49, 3: 299–315); *Relativism, objectivity and moral judgment* (27, 2: 125–39); *Jung and the living past* (6, 2: 128–39) and *The sociology of knowledge and the curriculum* (21, 3: 277–89).

Karl Mannheim and the Sociology of Education

by W. A. C. Stewart, Professor of Education,
University College of North Staffordshire

Karl Mannheim came to England in 1933 as an exile from Germany. He was actually a Hungarian born in Budapest at the end of the last century and educated in his own country, where he had been trained in the German philosophic tradition. He taught sociology in German universities after the first World War, at Heidelberg and then at Frankfurt-am-Main, where he held the Chair of Sociology; and, before he left Germany, he had built up an international reputation for himself in academic circles. When he came to England he started to teach sociology at the London School of Economics, and, as his command of English improved and his writings were translated into the language, his ideas began to reach a wider circle.

We are not much inclined in this country to read systematic analyses of society, particularly when they were originally written in academic German and have had the variable advantage of being translated in America by those whose first language was not English. However, Mannheim's two main works, *Ideology and Utopia* and *Man and Society*, are of such importance for social philosophy and sociology that they deserve the hard work they demand. Besides, after he came to England, Mannheim turned to an analysis of the place of Britain in the emerging world picture, and in *Diagnosis of Our Time*, written in wartime, and in essays which were gathered together and published after his death entitled *Freedom, Power and Democratic Planning* he tried to show how Britain could take a unique place in the urgent conflict between what he called *laissez-faire* liberalism and totalitarianism. He brought to his examination of British institutions and ways of thinking a constructive candour and a massive learning, for which we have reason to be grateful.

In 1946 he was appointed to the newly created Chair of the Sociology of Education at the University of London Institute of Education, and he had then a field of study rich in possibilities and virtually unexplored in this country, where his discernment and his abilities for synthesis would have found scope. In his way, he would have deepened our thinking in education if he had lived. As it was, when he died in 1947, he had already had an important effect, not all of it good, because it was not difficult for shallow or prejudiced minds to distort or over-simplify his thinking for their own purposes.

It is the intention of this essay to try to show the main trends in the continuity of Mannheim's thought and to see how these came to be expressed in his approach to the sociology of education.

1. The German Period

Mannheim's doctoral thesis in 1922, *Structural Analysis of Epistemology*, though having obvious Kantian affinities (it was published as a Supplement to *Kant-Studien* in Berlin in 1922), finds 'meaning' not so much in the intrinsic properties of an object or a perception, as in relationship within a physical or psychological structure. In philosophy he specifically rejects absolutes of which we are, in some way, a part, and with which we can communicate. There can be no 'revelation' of knowledge through some pre-existing absolute, whether Christian or any other, nor do we grasp the reality of an object because the reality was there and is timelessly the same and happened to be revealed to our experience. The reality exists in the essential contact in our experience within time, with all its historical limitations and partial perspectives.

This rationalism is always present in Mannheim's thought, and he says that his emphasis on 'this-worldliness' prevents him from making any jump beyond, such as postulating a pre-existent realm of truth and validity. In all that Mannheim has written we find the idea of structure, of inter-connectedness within history, of what he himself calls 'relationism', present in simple or elaborated form. His sociology is rooted in philosophy, and the 'sociology of knowledge' grows out of his dissatisfaction with the final reference to absolutes in traditional epistemology. He recognized the metaphysical consequences in this attitude to truth in history and indeed to the concept of truth as a whole.[1] In his writings on the sociology of knowledge, Mannheim from the beginning differentiated between the ways of knowing and verifying appropriate to the natural sciences and mathematics, and those appropriate to the social sciences.

'It is well known that the Hellenic or Shakespearian spirit presented itself under different aspects to different generations. This, however, does not mean that knowledge of this kind is relative and hence worthless. What it does mean is that the type of knowledge conveyed by natural science differs fundamentally from historical knowledge – we should try to grasp the meaning and structure of historical understanding in its specificity, rather than reject it merely because it is not in conformity with the positivist truth-criteria sanctioned by natural science.'[2]

He gained no satisfaction from the approach to truth worked out by the Vienna school of logicians. As Bramstedt and Gerth say, he engaged in sociological study as a response to the challenging present. Positivism as it took shape in Vienna left too much out of the field of discourse. The general philosophic bases of his sociology were laid in *Structural Analysis of Epistemology* (1922), *Interpretation of Weltanschauung* (1923), and *Historicism* (1924). In *The Sociology of Knowledge* (1925) a change is apparent in that he does not now make the analysis in such general philosophic terms. Instead of interpreting past ages by bringing together as many 'adequate' views as possible in order to recreate something of the climate of the times, he applies a Marxian technique, unmasking thought systems and power devices in ruling groups. As always, Mannheim rejected Marx's reliance on the unique significance of the proletariat. In this essay there appears a readiness to see social and philosophic ideas expressed in actual social groups, and conversely, that membership of such groups tends to make certain ways of thinking more likely than others.

In *Conservative Thought* (1927) he took this further in an actual piece of historical analysis of the social consequences of the struggle in German class structure between 1800 and 1830. The earliest sketch of 'ideological' and 'utopian' ways of thinking appears in this essay. These characteristic polarizations of thought and attitude can be reliably detected, says Mannheim, in the last century of development of our western industrial society.

In 1929 the German version of *Ideology and Utopia* appeared.[3] The main thesis of this work represents a further refinement and expansion of his earlier sociological theory. He takes the general proposition that thought and attitude are circumscribed by our position in time and place, and he tries to show two main perspectives or viewpoints which have arisen in our past and present western situation.

Perhaps the best way to show the nature of the two perspectives from which the book takes its title is to quote Mannheim's own words:

'The term "ideology" reflects the one discovery which emerged from political conflict, namely, that ruling groups can in their thinking become so intensively interest-bound to a situation that they are simply no longer able to see certain facts which would undermine their sense of domination. There is implicit in the word "ideology" the insight that in certain situations the collective unconscious of certain groups obscures the real condition of society both to itself and to others and thereby stabilizes it.

The concept of "utopian" thinking reflects the opposite discovery of the political struggle, namely that certain oppressed groups are intellectually so strongly interested in the destruction and transformation of a given condition of society that they unwittingly see only those elements in the situation which tend to negate it. Their thinking is incapable of correctly diagnosing an existing condition of society. They are not at all concerned with what really exists; rather in their thinking they already seek to change the situation that exists. Their thought ... can be used only as a direction for action. (The collective unconscious) turns its back on everything which would shake its belief or paralyse its desire to change things.'[4]

He examines these two characteristic ways of thinking and evaluating, showing how an unreflective and traditionalist attitude, characteristic of the nobility in a feudal social structure, can harden into a conservative or reactionary style of thought when it is faced with an emerging middle class which has a liberal-democratic definition of the situation. As industrial society develops, another point of view becomes established, that of the working classes, the proletariat. This dialectical view of historical change Mannheim accepted from Marx and Hegel, more particularly from Marx, though he rejects the specifically economic basis of Marx's analysis, maintaining that there are many more sources for intellectual and political perspective than economic self-interest. 'The style of thought' of a group and persons who belong to it is far more complex, and to identify economic and political wisdom with the proletariat was, in his opinion, to shirk applying the dialectical principle to it. According to the historical period and the social position of the group (for example, whether in political ascendancy or struggling for it) the liberal-democratic and the Marxist perspectives contain both ideological and utopian elements in varying degrees. Each element distorts reality, since ideology is ana-chronistic, and utopia projects a wish-fulfilment. Such synthesis and balance as may be possible ought to inhere in a group which has not a firm status in the social order:

> 'This unanchored, *relatively* classless stratum is, to use Alfred Weber's termi-nology, the "socially unattached intelligentsia".'[5]

It is these and not the proletariat who should provide some synthesis of the conflicting ideas which might otherwise bid fair to disrupt such stability as society might have. How ineffective this synthesis would be in political fact has been dis-mally proved too often of late for Mannheim to have continued to accept this part of his analysis.

When *Ideology and Utopia* appeared in 1929 it was at once recognized as an important book, though it received much downright criticism.[6]

The subtitle to the book was 'An Introduction to the Sociology of Knowledge' and though it moves nearer to 'the emerging and the actual', its strength lies in its analysis of the characteristic distortion of each viewpoint more than in the slender hope of a clear and practical assessment of 'reality' by the socially unattached intelligentsia. He says:

> 'We are not concerned here with examining the possibilities of a politics exclusively suited to intellectuals. Such an examination would probably show that the intellectuals in the present political period could not become inde-pendently politically active. ... Most important ... would be the discovery of the position from which a total perspective would be possible. Thus they might play the part of watchman in what otherwise would be a pitch-black night.'[7]

Ideology and Utopia, by using the Marxist method, is in fact a devastating critique of Marxism. His more directly political analysis, however, began with *Man and Society.*[8]

******

This very brief introduction to Mannheim's work is intended to give some impression of the background of his thought before he came to England. The tradition of an island community with an empirical approach to problems based on a certain continuity and cohesion, where Marxist analysis was too stark even for most of the socialists, was very different from the chaos of the Weimar Republic and the pre-Hitler years. If we are to understand the fuller implications of Mannheim's thinking on education and to assess his flexibility of mind (which is not often considered) we must remember that he was a Jewish social philosopher reared in the German philosophic tradition of Kant, Hegel and Marx, sensitively aware of the trends in this century of philosophy, economics, political theory and psychology (especially psychoanalysis), who was in his early twenties when the First World War ended, who lived and taught and wrote as a Hungarian in Germany through the period of Weimar, whose study of society was given point and urgency by his exile from Germany. On the one hand we must expect that education is for him an aspect of social organization, in the sociological sense an institution, the product of, the perpetuator of and in some senses the critic of a political and class structure of a certain kind. On the other hand we must remember that he has 'incomparably sharp eyes for what can be called the ideological elements in social thought'.

2. The English Period

A. *General sociological analysis*

Mannheim wrote at the beginning of *Man and Society* that the book was an attempt to explain that this was an age of transformation:

> ' ... to the Western countries the collapse of liberalism and democracy and the adoption of a totalitarian system seem to be the passing symptoms of a crisis which is confined to a few nations, while those who live within the danger zone experience this transition as a change in the very structure of modern society.'

The German version of the book was written, as he says, in the conviction that the democratic system had run its course, that the Weimar Republic had revealed the helplessness of the old *laissez-faire* order to deal with modern mass society either politically or culturally. When he came to England he found a much more deeply rooted liberal democracy, which was working so satisfactorily that he was tempted, he says, to an optimism that would make him forget that we were all on the edge of crisis. The English version of the book was written, then, that the peaceful democracies might learn to control the future trend of events by democratic planning, avoiding the negative aspects of the process—dictatorship, conformity and barbarism. Later, in *Diagnosis of Our Time,* he called this the Third Way.

It is true that in England there was not the diversity of destructively hostile groups which had led to the disintegration of Weimar. People could tolerate a wide variety of political, religious and philosophic beliefs in practice because of a deeper stability. But with this went the lazy-mindedness and the moral torpor of 'appeasement', a form of isolationism more possible in an island country, the centre of a commonwealth. We can also remember without difficulty the anxiety and dejection, the political and intellectual conflict of the decade.

On coming to England Mannheim had to develop his knowledge of the language. We find in *Man and Society* a much greater infusion of English and American material from the fields of psychoanalysis, social anthropology and contemporary social theory and practice. There is even more in *Diagnosis of Our Time* (1943).[9]

The war-time situation brought about such radical changes in thinking and planning that the whole argument about freedom and control became urgently topical. We had to have total mobilization, and orders and priorities became a normal part of the organization. In this upheaval of institutions and established ways of thinking, could the distinctive features of British democratic life be made sufficiently explicit, so that even in the over-organized national life during a total war the principles of planning for freedom could be grasped and remembered in their essence when peace returned? Education was one of the central issues in such an enormous question.

B. Sociology and Education[10]

There is a didactic element in Mannheim's later writing which is implicit in the whole theme of the Third Way and planning for freedom. He saw more and more clearly that 'real planning consists in co-ordination of institutions, education, valuations and psychology'.[11] He naturally became interested in education both as a means of influencing ways of living and thinking and as an expression of the nation's institutional, social and philosophic values.

The first sustained mention of the purpose of education occurs, as an aspect of 'success' and incentives, in a paper *On the Nature of Economic Ambition and its Significance for the Social Education of Man* (1930). In it is this sentence:

> 'The task of education, therefore, is not merely to develop people adjusted to the present situation, but also people who will be in a position to act as agents of social development to a further stage.'

One recalls Sir Fred Clarke's fondness for W. E. Hocking's saying that education must provide for the growth of the type and for growth beyond the type. In *Ideology and Utopia*[12] Mannheim points out that a common educational heritage tends increasingly to suppress differences of birth, status, profession and wealth and to unite people on the basis of the education they have received.[13] Modern education gives a medium within which a preliminary trial of strength of the various differences of interest and status takes place. It is, he says, a replica on a small scale of the conflicts in society at large. Or again, in *Man and Society*[14] the much quoted passage:

> 'Sociologists do not regard education solely as a means of realizing abstract ideas of culture, such as humanism or technical specialization, but as part of the process of influencing men and women. Education can only be understood when we know for what society and for what social position the children are being educated.'

These extracts may give the flavour of his early pronouncements on education. In one section of *Man and Society* he was concerned with the problem of enabling man to understand and contribute to a changing society, and he finds an ally in 'recent trends in education' which, by doing away with grades and marks, were keeping in mind a co-operative and not only a competitive society. The strategy of the school aims at moulding the whole personality.

In *Diagnosis of Our Time* he develops the whole theme of a sociological approach to education with more assurance and no less vigour. Aims and methods in education have to be understood 'in and for a given society'. Education is one of the means of influencing human behaviour, a form of social control which can be effective in maintaining emotional stability and mental intregrity only if it has strategy in common with agencies outside the school. Education can no longer be considered mainly as an interchange between teacher and pupil. It is part of a broader process altogether.

This précis is what is commonly understood as the main residue of Mannheim's thinking on educational matters, and while many people accept the relevance of its emphasis others regard it as dangerously impersonal. It has been my purpose in the earlier account of his philosophic development to try to show the sweep and scope of his thought, into which this approach to education fits. It is not suggested that his analysis makes an easy appeal, is completely satisfying, or that it is not the better for careful valuation. However, a responsible author ought not to allow himself to write, on the basis of one essay by Mannheim on popularization:

> 'Professor Mannheim, whose mechanical outlook is in direct contradiction of all that wisdom has found previously satisfying, reflects the growing impersonality of human relationships.'[15]

More particularly since he says elsewhere in the same chapter, with his own italics:

> 'It is precisely because he tends to think on a certain level of abstraction that Professor Mannheim makes the mistake of imagining that any idea can be reduced to a simpler form than that in which it already exists and *still remain the same undiluted idea.*'

Two obvious things should be repeated at this point. The time that Mannheim had in direct relationship with educational theory and practice in this country was short, and that mainly during wartime. Secondly, he wrote as a Continental sociologist with a massive sociological experience behind him and all the training and personal experience that have already been mentioned. He knew how difficult it was for him to assimilate the British tradition, which is to such an extent inarticulate, and in some ways he never understood its gradualism, but it seems to me that some people criticize Mannheim because he did not live long enough to become an Englishman who would therefore know enough about the tradition to prevent himself from looking to see what it was doing.

His manuscripts on sociology and education show a remarkable range of reading, and a concern to shape and reshape the material many times so that the crucial aspects might be considered with his students. On many topics he has left comments as matters for later development or as subjects for research students—he has, for example, only general remarks on the composition and justification of curricula. He sees education as in need of explicit aims which should be defined as the result of sociological analysis of what is being and ought to be done now in a democratic society at a stage of crisis in its existence. One chief concern is to realize concrete purposes and methods for the education of the masses. This needs a policy as much for adult education as for the secondary modern school. It is concerned with the educative society. He is aware that many may think he over-estimates the intellectual capacity of the man in the street, and education as enabling judicious and intelligent participation in public affairs. He makes the point that this reproach is characteristic of the general mental climate of capitalism in the monopolistic stage. It is here that popularization is relevant, or as Bantock puts it, 'the dissemination of culture without diluting it'. Bantock goes on to suggest that Mannheim, by implication, has helped to create the contemporary myth of the noble scion of the masses appropriate to the superficial taste of our age. What Mannheim actually says is this:

'An age of mass-produced education ... may swamp all sense of quality which matures slowly in society. Mass production and standardization of goods to satisfy routine demands is one thing. In education, however, this principle can only make the lowest common denominator the universal norm. Reluctance to accept the tendency of the principle of levelling as a tendency to "level down" is far from being snobbish disdain of the lower strata as of inferior innate human quality; on the contrary, it is based upon realization that as the culture and education of the less privileged have been neglected down the centuries, they can now assimilate and appreciate only things of inferior quality.'[16]

Education will not accept any level as final, says Mannheim, but sets out to improve it. In his latest writing, as in his earliest, he sees the intelligentsia as the mainspring of productive cultural life, and he commented, in *Diagnosis of Our Time*, on his surprise and puzzlement on first coming *to* England *to* find a peculiar deprecation of theory and general ideas. One would have been interested to read his analysis of 'parity of esteem'.

However, it can be said that Mannheim went to the heart of democratic education—the education appropriate to the bulk of the populace, 'the lower strata'. It is the greater pity that he had no time to develop this in detail. A valuable essay might be written for this *Journal* comparing the explicit and implicit views of Mr. Eliot, Dr. James and Karl Mannheim on the education of the mass of the people.

Mannheim's viewpoint and method as a philosopher and sociologist have much in common with pragmatism which, for him, no longer made a distinction in kind between thought and action. Dewey, in particular, appealed to him, as did the psychological pragmatists in America, whose theory of the emergence of the self and the ways in which knowledge grows and coheres, derives from the meeting of a biological relativism such as Watson's with Dewey's philosophic and social relativism. Such authors as Baldwin, Cooley, G. H. Mead (an important thinker for Mannheim), W. I. Thomas, Park, Burgess, Fans and Kimball Young, are frequently found in Mannheim's bibliographies. It would seem at first sight that he accepted the doctrine of adjustment, that response and personality pattern develop out of the interplay between the organism and the environment. But he agreed too much with Gestalt and psychoanalytic theory for that.[17] He accepted much of Dewey and the others as an account of psychological and sociological change. He rejected their account of personality structure and the sources of motivation as being incomplete. He says that pragmatism makes the adjustment character of human behaviour quite plain, and such explicitness is to be welcomed, for it represents a conscious awareness of the process. However it does not take into account powerful basic experiences of life which become standards and give the personality a cohesion and unity which enable it to have 'initiative' in this process of adjustment. This is always a razor-edge for Mannheim, for he also wrote (in the 'thirties, it is true):

'Even though much still remains obscure and very many assertions problematic, nevertheless this approach has reached such a point that we can, logically at least, foresee our goal, which is the planned guidance of people's lives on a sociological basis and with the aid of psychology. ... The promising beginnings of psycho-analysis, together with subtler forms of pragmatism like that of Dewey, give a good start and may well lead to promising consequences, the nature of which we are not yet able to foresee.'[18]

Accordingly, he emphasizes the social structure of the school and accepts the definition of the school as 'an intermediary society between the family and the state, which serves to train children in the ways of adult life'.[19] Later he saw that it ought also to be a place where children were allowed to live as children, where, as Dewey put it, they were not only preparing for something farther on, but being and doing what was right for them at the various stages.

Since the family, the workshop and the community in industrial centres have lost or surrendered much of their educational function, the school will have to broaden its contacts with other areas of life and social institutions and lose the emphasis on bookish studies. The kind of school he seems to envisage is of the Dewey stamp. He mentions many times the 'progressive' theories of education as having the process of change in mind, and the 'traditional' theories as being rooted in the preservation of a 'static' society. But he did not work out a consistent criticism of 'scholasticism' in English schools. The criticism has been made that if Mannheim earlier on charged Marx with over-simplification, he might similarly be blamed for failing to experience the complexity of English gradualism in education, as in everything else.

Most of his educational thinking seems to proceed from the application of general principles and not from field-work in the schools as a sociological inquirer. He is not, therefore, a 'practical teacher's' thinker. However, he was becoming increasingly interested in social psychology as it applied to education. He is interested in the structure, inner relationship and functioning of the school situation both as it works out for the school and as it expresses ideas, attitudes and knowledge which are going to be carried into adult society. He is not concerned with what might be called the existential and inspirational aspects of the teacher-pupil relationship such as may be found in Buber or Highet—or, indeed, at some point or other in almost any English writer on principles and aims of education.[20] The infrequency of specific reference to the English situation is understandable both for reasons of limited practical background and because, as a sociologist, he was establishing a method of analysis which was new in English educational writing, and references to English written work were bound, therefore, to be few. There was more in the United States on which he could call.[21] Sir Fred Clarke wrote from a sympathetically similar viewpoint, without Mannheim's sociological range or systematics, but with the kind of empirical pregnancy which was in the native style. Mannheim's concern with systems and function and processes and change, and not so much with people, represents an omission (and from his point of view, in my opinion, an inevitable mission) of the possibility of the profoundly influential relationship between persons. He does not deny its importance—very much the opposite. It is simply not the aspect of education he is dealing with. He says in the introductory lecture to his course on the Principles of Education:

'In my opinion the study of Education has reached a stage when it is ready to be taught as a scientific discipline. There is so much accumulated knowledge both on the level of everyday experience and of tested scientific observation that it is no longer a bold venture to treat the problems of Education in a systematic, scientific fashion.'[22]

The rigour with which he holds to the principle of relationism with its philosophic corollaries precludes any 'eternal' aim for education. He found such aims too aloof from history to be really helpful in concrete situations. The needs of a democratic society, as sociologically alert people would come to diagnose them within a national tradition, would suggest the aims; and these would, by definition, be partial and tentative. This would seem to have some affinities with the recent emphasis in Christian theology on the sinful nature of man and the inevitably partial nature of his judgments.[23] There is in Mannheim's earlier writing, as has been shown, a kind of stoic trust in the total of history as being its own reward and its own justification. Christians believe in a God to whom history is subservient, who is concerned in individual and collective human destiny. At no time did Mannheim relate his view of history to any form of theism. Some who knew only his main English writings (*Ideology and Utopia, Man and Society, Diagnosis of Our Time*) have not thoroughly known his view of history, and have found his emphasis on what might be called social, political, psychological and educational engineering both distasteful and dangerous. Even one of his last essays, taking further the significant interest in religion seen in the last essay in *Diagnosis of Our Time*, still keeps true to his sociological position:

'If the sociologist realizes that for many reasons there is need of spiritual power to integrate people, this does not mean that he endorses clericalism or any superimposed creed. He merely recognizes that religion fulfils certain indispensable functions in this age of transition.'[24]

The stringency with which he keeps faith in educational aims with this view, without calling upon any metaphysic, has been a stumbling block to many.

In the two following quotations, how understandable it is to think that Mannheim only partially grasped the human predicament, and at the same time how easy to see that in his role as a sociologist he could not speak as a disciple:

'There is no help to be found today in such a paradigmatic experience as, say, the practice of the presence of God unless God truly exists and can in actual fact dwell in the human soul and unless experience and reason give increasingly irresistible testimony to this truth. The real issue, in other words, is that of the metaphysical truth *on* which the experience, if it is not an illusion, depends. Mannheim is writing on this as a man who is himself without religious faith and who rejects (or is agnostic about) a theistic metaphysic. As such he is unable to penetrate to the heart of the problem.'[25]

'The religious focus is not a moral or ethical experience, nor a way of regulating behaviour and conduct, but a way of interpreting life from the centre of some paradigmatic experience. One may discuss whether the basic Christian experience is original sin, redemption, the liberating and creative power of love, or the Cross, the deeper meaning of suffering. It is from these foci of experience that the adjustment patterns of right behaviour and conduct are always interpreted.'[26]

Mannheim approved of the functions which Warner, Havighurst and Loeb ascribed to the American educational system as applying substantially in England.

(1) It provided a basis of communication and a common core of values.
(2) It taught children to live and work together.
(3) It helped people to find ways of realizing their social ideals.
(4) It taught skills for carrying on the economic life of society.
(5) It selected and trained children for social mobility.

He was always aware of education as a selective agency and as providing social lessons of one sort or another. Few people have noticed his comments on privacy and inwardness, which he regards as the strongest means of individualization and a great, if not the greatest, asset in the growth of an independent personality.[27]

'This process of socializing our experiences is a healthy one as long as it is balanced by a sphere of privacy. Without it there is no power left in the self to resist continual change and the individual develops into a bundle of uncoordinated patterns of adjustment.'[28]

The curriculum in school must have *relevancy* as Dewey, Clarke and Mannheim all say. There is no denying that in Mannheim's writing this tends to mean relevance to contemporary needs and education for change, although he makes qualifying comments on the new order being built out of the past and in continuity with it. He has not written anything on the place and content of history in school. Nor has he much to say on aesthetic education and the sociological, psychological and philosophical issues involved. However, linked with the theme of privacy as a means of individualization he has written of the importance of 'paradigmatic experience' in personality structure. By this phrase he means those decisive basic experiences which are felt to reveal the meaning of life as a whole. Their pattern is so deeply impressed upon our minds that they provide a mould into which other experiences flow, and so they help to shape what later on we are able to experience. This is related to the sociology of knowledge, of course, but is of particular importance in moral and religious education. Mannheim in his lecture notes has developed these themes in connection with psychoanalytic and group therapy techniques. This is mentioned without further elaboration, simply to show that he was concerned with what is sometimes called 'the education of character' not simply as a series of contemporary adjustments, but as an aspect of personal psychology having relationships with and drawing strength from the archaic levels of experience.[29] Not only so, but bringing philosophic criteria within its ambit. One of his central aims for education is, time and again, training for group responsibility and, complementary to it, individual education.

Perhaps, in conclusion, something should be said of the study of education as he saw it. Education was, from his point of view, a social science. It was a synoptic study for pursuing which data could be collected and collated from many different fields. Just as the Modern Greats School at Oxford had to work out the content and relationship of the studies involved, so too Education, from the sociological point of view, would have to show how aspects of history, philosophy, psychology, anthropology, economics, political theory, aesthetics and pedagogy could be brought into some synthesis, or, in another fashionable word, could form some discipline. The best short account of what he thought the sociology of education might contain can be seen in his lecture *Sociology for the Educator and the Sociology of Education*.[30] In it he differentiated between the relevant preparatory setting, which he called 'Sociology for the Educator', and the directly applicable 'Sociology of Education'. In the first of the two he considered human nature and the social order, the impact which social groups had on individuals and on social structure. In 'Sociology of Education' he considered the school and society, the sociology of education in its historical aspects and the school and the social order. There is also a third general heading, 'The Sociology of Teaching', under which appears the sociological interpretation of life in the school, the teacher–pupil relationship and the problems of school organization. Here the personal issues in education, which he is commonly not supposed to consider, appear, though not at all in the way that is usual in English educational writings such as those of Nunn or Norwood. The original lecture expands these bare topic-titles with fuller indication of their content. The synoptic view that is characteristic of sociology in the study of education can then be seen.

Conclusion

After having become familiar with most of Karl Mannheim's writings, one has been struck by the vigour of his mind and his readiness to learn, and if necessary to modify. At no time was this more true than in his work in education during the last few years of his life, and one is left with the assurance that its development was continuing in a way that might well have been fruitful both for his own thought and for English education as a whole.

The books of Karl Mannheim so far published in English are:

Ideology and Utopia, 1936
Man and Society, 1940
Diagnosis of Our Time, 1943
Freedom, Power and Democratic Planning, 1951
Essays on the Sociology of Knowledge, 1952

Further volumes of posthumous papers are to be published.

Notes

1 'The historicist standpoint, which starts with relativism, eventually achieves an absoluteness of view, because in its final form it posits history itself as the Absolute; this alone makes it possible that the various standpoints, which at first appear to be anarchic, can be ordered as component parts of a meaningful whole.' (*The Problem of a Sociology of Knowledge,* an essay in *Essays on the Sociology of Knowledge*: Routledge and KeganPaul (1952), 172.)

   Two comments from Dr. Kecksemeti's introductory essay to this volume should be mentioned. First, Mannheim adopted the partly existential concept of truth as 'being in truth' as distinct from the Aristotelian concept of truth as 'speaking the truth'. This follows from his refusal to accept that there is a truth which is the same for everyone at all times. Second, that the view instanced in the above extract assumes that history has a progressive and humanly successful development and that this ignores that history may turn to negative ends. In *Competition as a Cultural Phenomenon* Mannheim analyses Hegel's view of history to which his own is related, showing the resemblances and the sharp points of difference.

2 *The Interpretation of Weltanschauung* (1923) in *Essays on the Sociology of Knowledge*, Routledge and Kegan Paul (1952), 61.

3 The English translation, with new additions, appeared in 1936.

4 *Ideology and Utopia*, Routledge and Kegan Paul (1936), 36.

5 *Ideology and Utopia*, 137.

6 See three later examples: Alexander von Schelting's review in the *American Sociological Review*, August 1936, 1, 4, 664–74, and the same author's criticisms of Mannheim's 'sociology of knowledge' in his book *Max Webers Wissenschaftslehre*, 1934. Also H. O. Dahlke's comments in *Contemporary Social Theory*, ed. Barnes, Becker and Becker, 1940.

7 *Ideology and Utopia*, 143.

8 The book appeared in a much shorter German form, *Mensch und Gesellschaft im Zeitalter des Umbaus*, published in Holland in 1935 after he had left Germany. The English version was published in 1940.

9 When I visited Germany at the end of 1952 I was fortunate to meet a number of scholars who had worked with Mannheim in Frankfurt and Heidelberg days. When I asked if they noticed any change in his writing after he came to England they all drew attention to the greater immediacy in its content and presentation. They considered that he had become less of a systematiser, more 'mellowed', more 'empirical', more 'English'.

10 I am glad to acknowledge the generosity of Dr. Julia Mannheim, Karl Mannheim's widow, in placing her husband's papers on educational sociology at my disposal. I hope to do fuller justice to them at a later time, but as may be imagined they have been of the greatest value to me in this essay.

11 His preface to *Freedom, Power and Democratic Planning* (1951), the first of the series of posthumous volumes.

12 pp. 138–39.

13 Readers may be interested to compare this idea with a similar theme in an essay by Mrs. J. Floud in the *Yearbook of Education* (1950), 117–35.

14 p. 271.

15 G. H. Bantock, *Freedom and Authority in Education*, Faber and Faber (1952), 36.

16 *Freedom, Power and Democratic Planning*, 263.

17 He thought that most of the above-named social psychologists paid too little attention to Freud's dynamisms.

18 *Man and Society*, 222.

19 W. L. Warner, R. J. Havighurst and M. B. Loeb, *Who shall be Educated?* Routledge and Kegan Paul (1946), 54.

20 All his earlier sociology is presented in abstractions based more on philosophic reflection than on empirical sociology, but because they arise out of the contemporary situation, his generalizations always have a concrete and topical relevance as well as historical perspective from the philosophic point of view.

21 *Diagnosis of Our Time* has most of what he has to say on English education in one form or another. The relevant chapters in *Freedom, Power and Democratic Planning* have more generalized reference. His manuscript notes have a good deal to add.

22 MS, sources.

23 See, for example, Barth, Brunner, Niebuhr. See also Clarke's appendix to *Freedom in the Educative Society*, U.L.P. (1948). This book is dedicated to Karl Mannheim. For a number of years before and during the war Mannheim was a member of a group of thinkers, mostly Christians, which met regularly, to which he gave much and of which he spoke warmly as having given his ideas sympathetic and critical appraisal. Dr. Oldham, Middleton Murry, T. S. Eliot, the late Lord Lindsay were among the members.

24 *Freedom, Power and Democratic Planning*, 313.

25 From a useful and fair-minded essay on Karl Mannheim by J. B. Coates in *The Crisis of the Human Person* (1949), 119.

26 *Diagnosis of Our Time*, 134–5.

27 Dr. Paul Halmos discussed a great deal of his book *Solitude and Privacy* (Routledge and Kegan Paul, 1952) with Karl Mannheim.

28 *Diagnosis of Our Time*, 157–8.

29 C. G. Jung has written a good deal on this theme, particularly (with R. Wilhelm) *The Secret of the Golden Flower*, 1931 and *Psychology and Religion*, 1938. More recently Erich Fromm has considered the topic from the psychoanalytic point of view in *Psychoanalysis and Religion*, 1950.

30 In *Sociology of Education*, LePlay House Press, 1944.

2 Tradition and the Comprehensive School

A. V. Judges   1953

Author

In 1949 Val Judges (1898–1973) was appointed as the first Professor of the History of Education in the United Kingdom, at King's College, London. He was a professional historian having previously been Reader in Economic History at the LSE. During the First World War, Judges served with the London Rifle Brigade and then with the Tank Corps. He joined the Home Guard and Ministry of Labour, ending World War II as Assistant Secretary and Labour Advisor in the Ministry of Production. He was also Chairman of the Southern Rhodesian Education Commission in 1962–63. Judges co-founded both the *British Journal of Educational Studies* and the Standing Conference on Studies in Education. A. C. F. Beales, the editor of the *British Journal of Educational Studies*, succeeded Val Judges in the Chair at King's College, London in 1965.

Introduction

This article represents one of the first academic discussions of the idea of comprehensive schools in England. Written in 1953 it came after the establishment of the first five experimental comprehensive schools in England set up by the London County Council in 1946. Judges refers to how discussion of comprehensive schools had already become 'common currency'. Certainly momentum for change had grown and parents and teachers were increasingly conscious of the great waste in working-class ability. In 1954, Kidbrooke School opened in the London Borough of Woolwich as the first purpose-built comprehensive school in Britain, although the teaching style remained traditional. Judges reviews both the strengths and weaknesses of a non-selective school programme from a historical perspective and ends the article with some of the more positive aspects of such a proposed change. He details the ideological, economic and political factors that influenced the development of the comprehensive school movement of his time. Professor Judges captures the debates of the time and places them within an historical context that is both interesting and significant.

Articles and reviews of books on comprehensive education are numerous within the pages of the *Journal* and include the following articles: *A case study in comparative education: Comprehensive education in the United States and Britain* (17, 1: 16–25); *Education in a post-comprehensive era* (29, 3: 199–208); *The comprehensive ideal and the rejection of theory* (35, 3: 196–210); *The present image and future of comprehensive schooling* (37, 4: 339–57), and *Revising the comprehensive ideal* (44, 4: 426–37).

Val Judges wrote a number of historical texts, including *Pioneers of English Education* (1952) and contributed both articles and reviews to the *British Journal of Educational Studies*, including an article on *The educational influence of the Webbs* (10, 1: 33–48).

Tradition and the Comprehensive School

by A. V. Judges, Professor of the History of Education, University of London King's College

Actually the best adjective at hand is *non-selective.* This word has fewer emotional overtones than are sounded by some other adjectives currently in use for the common school. Further, it does in an unequivocal way express the notion of a neighbourhood school for all children, in which, and in relation to which, the conventional processes of sorting and formal segregation are reduced to a minimum.

But the word *comprehensive,* with all its dubious shades of meaning, has now become common currency and must go into my title. I would emphasize that the distinctive characteristic which can be held to give a peculiar value to the kind of school under discussion, namely the provision of a common life to be shared under the umbrella of the curriculum of a single institution by every sort of child, must be present in unmistakable fashion to validate the conception. This would seem to exclude recent ideas of compromise or of approach by stages to the real thing. Examples of these are:

(a)   the building of country complements, i.e. schools of a 'modern' type, to be associated in some rather indeterminate fashion with existing grammar schools possessing rich corporate personalities of their own already;

(b)   the collection on one campus (school base) of separate schools in a kind of family gathering, each member possessing its own identity grounded on the early selection of children of a separate description;

(c)   truncated comprehensive schools which have their sixth-form pupils transferred elsewhere.[1]

These and their variants lack the essential requirements of the common framework and the common life. One must be an optimist indeed to believe that the attempted realization, in the forms thus proposed, of a comprehensive policy will not in nearly every case produce more frustration than satisfaction in terms of the genuine non-selective school for all children of post-primary age.

Whilst the latest sallies have been exchanged, we have been increasingly conscious of the absence from the scene of the non-selective school *in propria persona.* Does this explain why discussion of it, among both supporters and critics, has so far yielded remarkably little information, and why debate on its theoretical implications has indeed produced far more heat than light?

It can plausibly be objected that the finer implications of proposals so closely bound up with human organization cannot come to light until the ideas themselves have received concrete expression in form. So the observer, before showing impatience about details of school management which may yet expose vulnerable patches, must wait until the earliest of the schools designed to teach a true cross-section of a local community have had time to work out a viable programme.[2] In this age of blue-prints it seems none the less a little odd that the root-and-branch wing of the reformers, who after all represent a point of view associated with the calculated enlargement of a national scheme of social services, should not have been more willing to risk their reputations in showing precisely how the curriculum plan at the entrance level of the non-selective school will at the same time *(a)* do full justice to ambition and ability during the diagnostic years[3] and *(b)* provide enough opportunity for the integration in one community of disparate types by one species or another of class-room technique.

It seems needful that more constructive discussion on the classroom level should show whither theories are tending. Even at this stage, however—noting as we must the distortion of ideas by purposes which are clouded by political prepossessions—we can venture upon an examination of some of the commonly held axioms or assumptions on which the main weight of present-day theoretical discussion is supported. Such an examination demands amongst other things an inquiry into origins.

It is probably right to give close consideration to the belief, already sharply questioned by critics in one of its current manifestations, that in any structure of educational provision certain proper lines of cleavage in the vertical plane inevitably show themselves; such lines of division conforming to requirements based on fundamental realities of human nature and society. Accordingly, however convenient we may find it to assemble all kinds of children in non-selective primary schools for a common start, there comes a stage in life, so it is asserted, when a division of schooling into three types is required to meet the variant needs of three types of pupil. Argument along these lines proceeds to disclose the claims of the secondary *triad,* so well known to us in the present tripartite organization of the maintained and aided schools.

Now what is the inner reality of this triad? Whatever its pretensions to sanctity we must admit that, even to-day, ten years after the composition of the great war-time manifesto of children's rights,[4] one of the thing's three legs is frequently under-developed or atrophied, and that it is only in men's imaginations that the true triplex formation, with a real place for organic development on the technical side, is to be found.[5] Indeed the closer we look at it the more of an upstart the triad appears to be.

It was invented eighty-five years ago on the eve of the appointment of Gladstone's first administration. The State was trying for the first time to get some kind of picture into focus of the future of secondary education, whether private or provided. The belief was expressed by the Endowed Schools Commission (1867) that such education is most fitly organized by the recognition of three types of school. Some of the assistant commissioners (among whom was Matthew Arnold) seem to have recommended a solution of a tripartite nature, inspired partly no doubt by the example of Prussia, where, though a three-tier system was not yet officially in being, such a system seemed to be foreshadowed by experiments in short-course *Realschulen* for the burgher class. The commission was convinced by the evidence received that English parents desired three kinds of school outside the elementary sphere, namely a first grade, typified by the public school preparing boys for the university and for higher professional careers; a second grade, represented by the local endowed grammar school, catering for boys of middle-class upbringing preparing for business careers; and a third grade, for which in 1867 no satisfactory prototype was forthcoming, designed for boys with humbler pretensions who would leave at 14 years and pass into shop or warehouse or mill.

Had the constructive proposals of the Endowed Schools Commission been implemented by Parliament, our present state of public instruction would perhaps be vastly different. As it was, the commissioners only bequeathed a classification of schools and a novel machinery for reorganizing endowments.

The notional division of secondary schools on a tripartite model caught on. As the Bryce Commissioners observed in 1895, this classification 'was followed by subsequent writers, and indeed, has largely passed into common speech'. In making their proposals for the future of secondary education the Bryce Commissioners themselves adopted the triad of common usage, frankly noting the existence of an economic and social stratification, and accepting the view that the higher elementary schools,[6] which the school boards in the larger towns had been setting up for selected children beyond standard VI, had 'stepped into the educational void'. These institutions were carrying out almost precisely the functions in relation to the future employment of the boys and girls which the *schema* of the 1867 commissioners had prescribed on their lowest tier.

The importance for us of the Bryce Report (which went right in face of an earlier report from the Cross Commission on elementary organization) is that it proposed that these ambitious school-board enterprises should be treated as what they appeared to be, i.e. as secondary schools, and that they must be brought into organic relationship with other elements in the system to be managed by some future local authority for secondary education. The Bryce Report also made it very clear that, in the commissioners' view, technical instruction must not be treated as a separate type or grade, but could properly be embodied as part of the curriculum of any of the three secondary grades of the triad.[7]

Now we discover from their report that Sir James Bryce and his colleagues took over the three grades, 'with some reluctance', because convenient: there was admittedly no justification in educational principle, and it is to be remarked that, although the expression ' educational ladder' was already in frequent use, at the end of the last century there was little pretence that merit or ability played or ought to play an appreciable part in the 'allocation' process. The change in this respect hardly even began to come in with the implementation of the 1902 Act (which gave the new L.E.A.s. control of provided secondary education) or with the adoption of the free-place system that soon followed. As late as 1911 the Board of Education was opposed to the granting of free places as a means of sifting talent or intellectual quality. None the less the climate was gradually changing; and we look with interest to see what now happened to the contemporary model of the triad, and especially to its third element.

It is well known that most of the higher elementary schools, together with some municipal technical schools, were absorbed under the Act of 1902 into the new county secondary system. And of course they influenced its character, lending it a practical and earthy quality which the efforts of Robert Morant and the Board of Education's inspectors, who for some years were urging the endowed grammar schools (the type of the old second grade) as a scholastic model, only partly offset. For a time the conception of the triad disappeared from discussion; but the memory of the third grade, with its bluff unacademic simplicity and its 'elementary' associations, did not die: it remained very much alive in the minds of teachers, old students and administrators, as the type of an upper school for ambitious working-class children; and the tradition was partly kept alive too by the continuous experiments of the local authorities in the form of new central and day technical schools and the like, designed to give higher instruction, under the grant regulations of the Elementary Code, to children in the upper forms who would not be passing into secondary schools.

Thus, during the early decades of this century, whilst the triad, even as a formal description of the 'secondary' scene, was in a sort of eclipse, it was recognized that grades I and II did survive, and were distinct (although certainly not always logically distinguishable from one another in respect of either ownership or control), and that both flourished. The increasing anxiety among educational reformers that all children, and not only those who could contrive an entry into the existing secondary schools, should receive post-primary instruction, secured expression in many ways, but in no way more successfully or more coherently than in the response of the Board of Education's Consultative Committee to the pressure of opinion in its two famous reports in 1926 and 1938.

On the first occasion the terms of the Committee's reference, since they put the purposes of the existing grammar-type school virtually out of bounds, precluded the adoption of any solution on non-selective lines. Such inquiries as I have been able to make about the nature of the discussion in committee which lay behind the resulting ('Hadow') report confirm the view that the committee were almost entirely occupied with constructing an end-on system of junior and senior schools, *within the elementary code*, which should be universally available—a large enough investigation in all conscience. Their outlook as planners was in some degree limited by their recognition of 'the half-conscious striving of a highly industrialized society to evolve a type of school analagous to and yet distinct from the secondary school', which would fit children to begin as wage-earners at the age of fifteen (para. 38), and by the fact that a new wave of higher-elementary school foundations was actually moving across the country. To be sure, the committee wished all full-time post-primary education, with the significant exception of one sector they distrusted—the technical schools—to be accepted as 'species of the genus "secondary education"'; but their real concern was with the encouragement of all reputable *varieties* of higher-elementary schools, for convenience to be broadly classed as 'modern schools', and in practice to be allowed as broad an opportunity for independent growth as children's needs, local conditions and certain norms in curriculum planning would permit. There is nothing monolithic about the committee's model of the new schools for the adolescent of the future: it would seem that there were to be as many kinds of school as there were varieties of demand, and the first transfer at eleven plus might often be the prelude to further moves.[8]

The recommendation of eleven plus as the age of transition was claimed to have the support of experienced teachers and administrators and of some of the leading teachers' associations; it had been known to work well for many years in the sequel to that 'momentous invention, the Free Place system of 1907'.[9] Moreover, as the Committee were assured (para. 88), psychological science showed that 'a new phase in the life of children themselves' conveniently opened at this age.[10] Reading between the lines, we discover that the Committee were convinced that their projected adolescent schools would have very little chance to acquire any shape or character at all as scholastic communities unless they could receive the children for at least three years. Intake at a later age than eleven would spell disaster, even with the prospect looming up of a higher statutory leaving age than fourteen; and indeed the committee's warm advocacy of the raising of the age of compulsory attendance to fifteen rested largely on the belief that a four-year course was needed to make post-primary education a manifest reality. Here then is the most convincing explanation, in its correct institutional setting, of the origin of the clean cut at eleven plus which has come down to us with the statutory blessing of the 1944 Act.

The work of reorganization and regrading to which the 1926 report gave a stimulus and the 1936 Act a decided push was slightly hampered by doubts about the educational principles embedded in the former and seriously checked in its orderly progress by the great economic depression. It is not as widely known as it should be that over 5,000 all-age schools, accounting for not far short of a million children, have stubbornly survived from pre-Hadow days, have weathered the millennium of 1945, and are with us still to-day as a reminder of the recent character of the transformation of our schools.

Where the 1926 report stimulated the liveliest reactions was amongst those who wished to see the new 'secondary' schools for the masses approximate to an older ideal based on the liberal and academic traditions of Grades I and II. The rival spectre of a Grade III school resurgent seemed to be taking on flesh before their eyes, and it is clear from the pronouncements of bodies of teachers (including some secondary-school associations) that, admitting as they did that there was a great deal of unpromising material to be accommodated, they were none the less inclined to favour what was beginning to be called multiple-bias or multilateral schooling, namely the provision of neighbourhood schools for all types of ability with amenities well up to the type then provided in the county secondary schools.

We should be careful not to undervalue the strength of a suspicion of long standing which has made all reformers on the left restive in face of what they have believed to be attempts to introduce pre-vocational teaching for the children of the poor. The general impression given by critics of the Hadow 'system' is that they wished above all, by establishing 'one roof as well as one code', *to* ensure the fullest opportunities to the boy or girl who would otherwise miss contact with academic teaching and with it a chance of an equal start in life with the more fortunate child.

Although Labour Party elements and the Trade Union Congress were active on this front, the first phase of the non-selective school movement in no sense implied a socialist programme. The stress was upon the levelling-up of educational opportunities, even at the risk of providing the wrong fare for the dull and stupid, and hardly at all on the removal of class differentials.[11] It is well to remember that since those days the movement has lost support in many quarters through a switch of emphasis to the demands of social egalitarianism and that it has been weakened by the slackening of its old concern for the white-collar career open to talent.

During the middle years of the 1930s the Consultative Committee, having in the meantime reported on primary, infant and nursery schools, and in so doing somewhat revised their views about the psychology of child development,[12] turned their attention once more to the teaching of adolescents. On this occasion they were under instructions from the Board to exclude from attention schools of the types already reported on in 1926 and to think about children in grammar and technical schools. Here was an invitation to maintain the principle of grammar-type segregation; it conformed entirely with a conviction from which the central authority for education in England and Wales has never departed, whatever party was in power. None the less, although the committee obediently gave their detailed attention to grammar and technical school curricula, they remarked with obvious truth that reform in any type of school raises problems in relation to all the alternative ways of getting educated; and they did in fact go almost out of their way (i) to dismiss the claims (which were sympathetically but not quite accurately stated) of 'multilateral schools',[13] and then (ii) to furnish what, on looking back now, we see to be an astonishingly sensitive forecast of the principles and general configuration of the whole area of publicly supported secondary education which has since been developed.

No advisory document prepared for a government department has ever been more influential in guiding thought and action than this (the 'Spens') report of 1938. Its statesmanlike candour, its admission that there were two or more sides to every question, its determination to be positive and constructive whilst being fair, all helped to carry conviction. The proposal in the report to provide parity of status by assimilating the new modern types of school into the ampler provisions of the secondary code (with all that this implied in salary scales and school equipment) and thus to remove causes of jealousy and division, commanded respect. The hardening convention that worked on the belief that the kind of intelligence which could contribute to the success of a grammar-school education could in nearly all cases be picked out at ten or eleven years, received the blessing of the Committee. Finally justification was found for promoting a form of reorganized junior-technical teaching which, in order to provide a workable school life-span, should take its pupils in at the tender age of eleven plus. Thus, within the sphere of public action, *(a)* the grammar school (with increased provision so as to enable it to accept on an average some 18 per cent, of each year's eleven-year age-group), together with *(b)* the modern school, established on a more eligible footing and furnished with a streamlined appearance, *plus (c)* the Committee's 1938 surprise novelty, the technical high school, should between them provide for all requirements.[14]

In this way the idea of the triad which always lingered in men's minds was to be given form again in the institutional framework of the nation. But it was a triad with a difference. Gone with the old grading (so it was fondly hoped) was the taint of class distinction. And here at last, in an atmosphere of parity of esteem, had come vocational education, hitherto never admitted to be quite respectable and now abruptly raised, in the shape of the technical high school, to the position of an independent member in the family of secondary types. All that was now needed by the new pattern was some stronger support from educational theory; and within a few years this was forthcoming in a contribution from a Committee of the Secondary Schools Examination Council appointed by the President of the Board to consider the bearing of changes in secondary education on the School Examinations system. In a closely reasoned essay on educational reorganization, this (the 'Norwood') Committee volunteered (rather gratuitously, some critics have thought) their belief, or discovery, that the evolution of education in south Britain had thrown up three groups or varieties of capacity—each described in the report in words of measured assurance. Of these groups the third, constituting the great majority of the nation's children, did not show at an early stage in life 'any pronounced leanings'; whilst the other two did—in the direction respectively of grammar and technical education.[15]

A foreigner in this country, fresh to the predilections of our time, may find it is easy to smile at the way in which the three mental types of the Norwood Report in 1943 slide neatly into position in the 1938 pattern of the redesigned triad. Yet elsewhere the report is shrewd and practical enough, particularly in its attitude to the future of the schools themselves, as when it remarks that parity of *condition* may well be accorded by outside authority, but parity of esteem must be won by the schools themselves (p. 24).

Any damage which may be held to have resulted from the new inquiry was now done: this betrothal of utility and theory was announced to the public shortly after the white paper on Educational Reconstruction had accepted by implication the validity of the findings. The three types of school invented by the Consultative Committee and justified by a committee of experts were now enshrined in the statement of the Government's reconstruction policy. The Labour Party have indeed claimed[16] that they kept them out of the Act of 1944; but the Act merely left the legal initiative, in proper accordance with statutory precedent, to the L.E.A.s. The triad was indeed now very much alive.

Loyalty to it became manifest again in the instructions and guidance relating to county development plans issued in the form of circulars by the Ministry of Education, and in due course also in Ellen Wilkinson's vindication of her policy in *The New Secondary Education*[17] (1947), which hinted that, although in favourable conditions a combined school might be tolerated, still the difficulties must be viewed as formidable, and a compromise on the tripartite school-campus plan should be considered in preference to other models. *Circular 144*, issued in the same year, proceeded to give a novel official definition of a multilateral school as one containing the 'three elements in clearly defined sides', and seems to have successfully driven a wedge some way into the reformist ranks; while the Ministry's *Building Bulletin No. 2A* of 1951 went even farther in suggesting that a non-selective school on an acceptable model should be conceived of as virtually three organizations within one perimeter wall.

So far for the history of ideas on organization. To the lessons this offers we shall return in a moment. During these recent years, as pressure from the non-selective camp has been applied to the national authorities and fairly successfully resisted, three developments are especially noteworthy. First, the local authorities in their handling of their development plans have shown, as perhaps was right, far greater freedom in judgement and more generosity of mind towards experiment than has the Ministry. At least three of the largest authorities have, on grounds of principle, openly criticized the narrowness of government directives; London and the West Riding of Yorkshire have indeed published elaborate arguments and doctrinaire statements; one thickly urbanized county area authority has twice apparently changed its mind on comprehensive schooling, to the general discomfiture of its teachers and the bewilderment of its electors, as one ratepayer can bear witness.[18]

Secondly, the debate has been steadily shifting from the educational conference platform to the political arena. Professional associations, since 1943, have been much more careful in drafting public statements concerning their attitudes. The largest of them all, representing the mass of the teachers publicly employed, ceased some time ago to express any corporate enthusiasm for the comprehensive idea, and has contrived with rare ingenuity to issue two substantial reports on secondary curriculum planning and on techniques of transfer to the secondary school without even a cautious side-glance at the non-selective school.[19] Many secondary-school teachers working in areas like London, where more than a mild experimental interest in the subject is now displayed, are feeling anxious about their careers, and we may well ask whether in the present atmosphere these educational authorities are likely to recruit a personnel of sufficiently high quality into their great new schools to ensure the success of their first ventures into the unknown.

It is to be observed, thirdly, that as the points in debate have assumed political colouring they have been coarsened in texture and become oversimplified. The situation at Westminster has hitherto been such that the Conservatives have hardly needed to do more than take such shelter against the weather blowing from the comprehensive quarter as is provided by the Labour front bench, and have been content merely to appear to be tolerantly conciliatory towards experiment.[20] Outside the Labour Party no-one is very clear at the moment how far the intellectual support for a 'comprehensive' policy within that party is the concern merely of a vigorous minority and whether it is at all likely to influence the attitude of the political leaders. What seems to be undeniable is that the egalitarian demands of the reformers to use the school of the future as the crucible of a non-striated society have in recent years been linked up with the well-worn arguments for equality of treatment to the virtual exclusion of the old concern of the inter-war period about the coaxing forth of latent abilities in unpromising circumstances. The old hostility to vocational experiment has given way to hostility to grammar schools. And responsible political speakers and writers may even be heard calling for the annihilation of perfectly good existing schools because these would compete for custom with new experimental schools in their neighbourhoods.

In earlier paragraphs I have tried to suggest that in the scene around us there are far more artefacts of recent construction than most people are aware. It is clearly a mistake to regard the reform of schools on non-selective lines as an outrage upon the kind of settled principles and traditions which have a right to respect as part of our English heritage. Morant never succeeded, even if he really tried, in infusing the county secondary school with the spirit of the grammar-school tradition. The higher-elementary and technical antecedents, the new subjects, the developments of studio and craft work, the strong, thinly disguised commercial bias (in many districts), the dim cultural background of many of the fee-payers (to say nothing of most of the free-place pupils) all contributed to make a new kind of school, which in my opinion was one of the best kinds this country has ever known; and this, noting as we must the meagre dimensions of its 'C stream', might, without straining the words, be described as multilateralism of a qualified kind. Before the universal free place and the new common entrance examination made the county school 100 per cent selective, it was by no means a fenced enclosure for able children. As for the public schools, so much has been said recently about the 'comprehensive' make-up of the average establishment on the Headmasters' Conference list, between the wars and before, that no comparisons need be laboured here. Comprehensiveness is no stranger in Britain. We are however prone to forget that the grant-supported grammar school of to-day is a new product of our native ingenuity—vintage 1945.

What is now so interesting is not that school organization has become an element in political debate, for that has happened often enough before when finance or religious control were leading issues; it is that the concern of parents of all classes has for the first time been invoked, and, moreover, invoked on live matters of clear educational import; and, although their reasons for worrying must often seem discreditable to those who have no children, they are none the less real reasons which may have power to shape events. This, in one of its aspects, is democracy at work. Whether 'symptoms of snob psychology' or not, the anger of disappointed parents with no prospect for the child but a secondary modern school, still to be creamed and re-creamed by talent scouts, and the anxiety of 'grammar-school' parents in areas where, in a new chapter of reorganization, the doctrinaire reformers are going to do their best to obliterate the selective schools, are features of the present age of tension. Better this, it may be thought, than the apathy of the 'twenties and 'thirties!

Whether in regard to the proper shape and nature of secondary education there are axioms and affirmations of the kind which precede and underlie all appeals to argument, or only generalizations of a very insecure order, we must try to make up our minds, having some regard to historical evidence. If we look at the foundations of the present tripartite design, or examine the pretension that the pattern of provision should follow any narrow demarcation of psychological type-boundaries, and in doing so seek some established *scientia discernendi,* the cupboard will be found to be sparsely furnished and probably bare. Certainly there is nothing in the cupboard to sustain and fortify anyone who would seek to take a stand on the essential naturalness and propriety of the clean break at eleven. We are thus obliged to admit that within our present system there is no *logos,* no discoverable law, no principle or measure. And I would urge that we are justified in questioning first the belief in clean-cut types, so recently made respectable; secondly its peculiar manifestation in the doctrine of the reconstituted triad; thirdly the conviction that the selective grammar school, reserved for bright boys and girls, has any depth in traditional usage; fourthly the general assumption that the break at eleven has been dictated by any compelling reasons other than those of convenience; and fifthly the contention that a programme for schools which is designed to apply to a broad wave-band of aptitude and talent contains much that is novel and revolutionary.

So much for the principles of organization. Social policies, if implicit—or some would remark, if relevant—in an educational structure, are certainly open for critical examination in a similar way, although here, for obvious reasons, the historical approach has less of value to offer. When we come to the view that, as the result of equalized salary scales, curtailed holidays, common standards of re-equipment, and so on, parity of esteem can be brought into being, as it were, by decree, we are dealing with one of the most remarkable of all recorded attempts to force obstinate facts into the mould of principle. The deliberate harnessing of social to educational theory has admittedly produced some novel problems. But who would have believed that many honest people in positions of influence would be so easily self-deceived? Watch the system in operation, and it becomes plain enough that institutions and the wares they offer are assessed by consumers in the market: *their* esteem is only too nicely calculated. When entry into some establishments is selective, a rarity value somewhat out of proportion to merit, service or fittings, will, in the consideration of all within reach of the threshold, attach to the places available. We are surely entitled to place current assumptions about the meaning of parity of esteem in the sixth place in our gallery of suspects.

Much of that which we see around us does indeed support those who argue that the triad in action is breeding social discontent—a distrust of leaders, and a dislike among the less 'privileged' for the future leaders, the lordly ones who have passed their test—an attitude which is the result in part of sheer ignorance, in part of a real dislike for operations of the selective process. Although the success of some of the better secondary modern schools is unquestionable, many of us share the anxiety caused by the unmistakable fixation, on a prognostic calculus, of broad occupational types, and of their separation from each other at an absurdly early age.[21]

It is none the less conceivable that the rebels have been prone to overlook one interesting phenomenon of recent social change, a change which shows the old frontier of jealousies between the upper working-class layers and the lower middle class, in all their manifold complexity, to have been overtaken and almost submerged by events, and indicates the development of a new and more evident stress line between family groups of relatively secure and adequately nourished skilled workers, with their sharpened awareness of cultural values, and their capacity to provide quiet conditions for home-work, and on the other side of the invisible barrier the insecure and overcrowded homes of the lower income levels, with their feckless outlook, their sluttish economy and their high output of young delinquents. It is this new line of social cleavage which will correspond with the lower boundary of differential privilege from now onwards. Its existence signifies and reveals the power of the educational influence of the home in the clearest possible fashion as soon as the boy or girl comes up to face the sorting machinery at the top of the junior school.

To argue that effective class boundaries have changed is not to belittle their significance in an educational setting. Hardly less important, however, is it to realize how scarce are the indications and how weak the positive arguments in support of the harmonizing functions of the non-selective school, for the view, that is, that this school can function as a melting-pot of antagonistic social types. Indeed the claim that such a school must in the nature of things not merely provide the most satisfactory conditions of educational opportunity, but *also* in some way impose social unity, constitutes the seventh of the affirmations I wish to question.

As far as English practice is concerned, it is all of course plain conjecture. One observes that even so eloquent and persuasive an advocate as Mr. A. G. Hughes, of the L.C.G. inspectorate, is vague about the manner in which the expected result will be obtained, and that he rests his case on a condemnation of selective education as we know it.[22] Sir Michael Sadler never spoke with more considered emphasis than when he said fifty years ago:

> 'Social unity cannot be achieved by any mechanical means; still less can it be secured by compulsory attendance at certain day schools. Varieties of schools are more the effect than the cause of social differences. Day-schools can do little to establish social unity while the homes of the children are so different.'[23]

This judgement was made long before a considerable amount of experience had been gathered of the operation of comprehensive high schools in America. There are undeniable examples of almost complete social solidarity in quite a number of such schools, notably in the Middle West. Close inspection of such cases shows the adult background to be homogeneous. Elsewhere, conditions of racial and economic stratification can be vastly different, and in consequence the social situation in the high school may be deplorable. American school children in fact get on together just as well or just as badly as their parents do.[24]

Advocates of the non-selective school have perhaps been over-zealous in planning the use of educational instruments for purposes of social discipline and harmony. Society can indeed be transformed by schools, but in a less direct manner, in fact largely by the quality and depth of the education provided for those who need the services of the school most to redeem the bankruptcy of a mean culture in the home. It seems evident that if non-selective schools are to triumph in this less spectacular field of endeavour—and given able direction and good staffing they may well do so—they must, with attentive care, concern themselves with the cultivation of some of the rarer pedagogic virtues. On a further occasion I hope to discuss the ways and means, and to assess the prospects, of doing this in the new schools on the county programmes, schools with which willy-nilly we shall all have *to* achieve a working relationship in the next few years. In the previous pages the plan has been to undermine or destroy a group of received opinions most but not all of which hinder a sympathetic consideration of a non-selective school programme, or at any rate stand in the way of positive thinking. It would be courteous to the reader who has followed me so far to finish on a more constructive note.

Let us glance at the future. The non-selective secondary school of south Britain, carrying, as it usually will, disabilities of great size, involved time-tables and delicate staff relationships, may yet succeed, and perhaps may soon revolutionize our ideas on educational practice, if—and the proviso is a severe one—certain essential demonstrations of capacity can be furnished. These cannot, I would argue, be reduced to fewer than four.

First it must show that a cross-section of some eighty per cent of our children is actually getting a richer education (shown in the main by a wider vocabulary and the more sensitive use of words) as a result of living in community with the cleverest pupils and the most knowledgeable teachers.

Secondly, there must be evidence that the accursed fear of vocational studies has disappeared in the only school atmosphere which will tolerate an organic and happy combination of liberal and technical studies; the school must show up at last the bogus nature of this old antagonism.

Thirdly, the school must plainly have avoided loss of time and opportunity in discovering, and putting its best resources at the disposal of, the really able minority. If, during their first two years, these boys and girls can be enabled to keep pace with the grammar-school norm of attainment, there can be no doubt that an adequate upper school will develop on a firm basis, and there will be little trouble in ensuring the retention of those who should remain in the community beyond the compulsory school leaving age.

Fourthly, every child will have found the place in the curriculum at which he can saturate his abilities, and will have sensed the stimulus of achievement at his true level of performance.

Although no doubt the third of these requirements will be most in the public eye and will without question possess vital importance, the crux will be the fourth. It is hard to see how we shall ever be able to explore or understand the mysterious problems of latent ability and late development, or do even reasonable justice to children with a home background of frustration, until much more of the apparatus of controlled experiment is available within schools which conform to comprehensive requirements. The rose blossoms on the briar will not be counted until they have had their spring.

> Non sien le genti ancor troppo sicure
> A giudicar, si come quei che stima
> Le biade in campo pria che sien mature;

Ch'io ho veduto tutto il verno prima
II prun mostrarsi rigido e feroce,
Poscia portar la rose in sulla cima.[25]

Notes

1 *A Policy for Secondary Education* (The Labour Party, June 1951), pp. 9, 12.
The latest version of this appears in *Challenge to Britain* (The Labour Party,
June 1953), p. 21. ' ... those who remain at school after fifteen should move
on to high schools.' Here the true inwardness of a belief in horizontal
cleavage, entirely at variance with the trend of recent western European thought,
and curiously at odds with the desire to avoid the implications of a clean cut at
11 years, appears in a striking condition of simplicity. I have met no members of
the Labour Party with experience in teaching who pretend to understand the
practical implications, or to sympathize with the intentions, of this proposal for
future policy.
2 Admittedly there are already more than a dozen claimants to the name in operation,
but, short as they all seem to be of a full 'academic' stream, I should hesitate to
pick any one of them out as a good working model. The latest annual report of the
Ministry of Education (June 1953) shows a total of 2,241 pupils in 'multilateral'
schools and 8,536 in 'comprehensive' schools. In assessing the weight to be given
to the latter figure it is well to observe that less than 100 of these pupils had
reached the age of 16.
3 It should be noted that the policy of comprehensive secondary schooling adopted
by the Communist Party in Great Britain is opposed to any specialization or to any
form of streaming in vocational directions before the present statutory leaving age,
and virtually excludes the principle of grouping by aptitudes from the programme
of four-fifths of the school. This is entirely in line with recent theory and practice
in the U.S.S.R. and in her satellite countries in Europe, where forms of common
schooling for ages 7 to 15, without testing or differentiation of subject teaching or
any diagnostic pause between these ages, are the rule. After 15 years the functional
prognosis takes over, and there is an abrupt swing-over from comprehensiveness to
vocational division.
4 White paper on *Educational Reconstruction* (Cmd. 6458, 1943), paras. 27–35,
with its important condensation of doctrine in para. 31, beginning: 'Such, then,
will be the three main types.'
5 There is some regional bias in this statement. In some areas, especially in the north
of the country, it would rightly be repudiated.
6 To avoid confusion in the text of this article they are not called 'higher-grade
schools', the name which they so often took. The term 'higher elementary' did for
a number of years receive official recognition, and applied to a small class of institutions receiving grant under the Elementary Code of 1901. I am using it here in
a much more general sense.
7 *Report of the Royal Commission on Secondary Education* (C. 7862; 1895), I,
pp. 10, 138,143, 282, 285, 289–90.
8 ' ... it must correspond to the needs of the pupils, and if it is to correspond to
their needs, it must embrace schools of varying types. Progress must take place, in
short, along several different paths.' *Report on the Education of the Adolescent*
(H.M.S.O., 1936), para. 59.
9 R. H. Tawney, *Juvenile Employment and Education* (Barnett House Papers, No. 17,
1934), p.5. Sir Cyril Burt's ingenious explanation, in terms of I.Q. levels, of the
original acceptance of this age as the right one for scholarship entry is compared

with other ideas of historical causation by Mr. H. C. Dent in part II, ch. III of his *Secondary Education for All.*

10 'There is a tide which begins to rise in the veins of youth at the age of eleven or twelve. ... If that tide be taken at the flood,' etc., etc. *Report ... Adolescent,* xix. There can be no doubt of course that, on the occasions of the preparation of the 'Hadow' and the 'Spens' reports, the Consultative Committee believed, and rightly believed, that in choosing the age of 11 + for transfer, they were being guided by the best educational opinion available.

11 Miss G. M. Thomas, to whose work I am under an obligation, in her M.A. thesis (for the University of London) on 'The development of the idea of multilateral schools in England' has culled a number of significant quotations from the conference reports and pamphlet literature of this period.

12 Discussed by R. Morris in 'Twelve come Christmas' in *King's College* (Newcastle) *Education Papers,* VII, no. 3 (1953), pp. 29ff., where a case is argued for a reconsideration of the use of a standard age transfer.

13 On grounds of *(a)* size; *(b)* insufficiency of senior pupils to balance the school; *(c)* the belief that grammar and modern sides would need to be kept quite separate, and that no head could control both at the same time.

14 *Report on Secondary Education with special reference to Grammar Schools and Technical High Schools* (H.M.S.O., 1938), especially pp. xvii–xxxviii.

15 *Curriculum and Examinations in Secondary Schools* (H.M.S.O., 1943), pp. 2–4.

16 *A Policy for Secondary Education* (The Labour Party, June 1951), p. 5.

17 This ministerial statement of policy was issued after her death. Her successor George Tomlinson said that he accepted its policy without qualification.

18 'Then in 1949 our hopes were dashed. ... The Tories were returned to power following a campaign of wicked misrepresentation; they boasted that a major cause of their victory was their opposition to the comprehensive school in favour of the three distinct types.' *An Urgent Appeal to Middlesex* (London Labour Party, 1952), p. 4.

19 Reports of National Union of Teachers Consultative Committees, 1949, 1952.

20 'Certainly they may be given some trial. ... On the whole I regard these experiments with some anxiety. ... Those who advocate these schools do so very often on political rather than on educational grounds. The mover of a resolution supporting the policy of establishing comprehensive schools, which was carried at the Annual Conference of the Labour Party in 1950, said: "I believe that in the comprehensive system of education lies the basis of educating the next generation to form a Socialist society". I will be forgiven if I do not regard this as a very compelling argument.' R. A. Butler, 'Education: the view of a Conservative', *Year Book of Education* (1952), pp. 34–35.

21 ' ... given a segregated education, nothing can prevent them from developing the characteristics of a "managerial class".' G. D. H. Cole, 'Education, a Socialist View', *Year Book of Education* (1952), p. 57.

22 *Education and the Democratic Ideal* (1951), Ch. VII.

23 'The Unrest in Secondary Education', Board of Education: *Special Reports on Educational Subjects,* ix (1902), 26.

24 Dr. James B. Conant, a warm advocate of the comprehensive school as a social solvent, has lately admitted these facts. *Education and Liberty* (1953), pp. 63 etc. Foreign ideals (believed to be expressed in *Einheitsschulen, écoles uniques, common schools,* etc.) are often brought together with English needs and, as it were, conflated, in current discussion. It is done in the documents assembled in support of the *London School Plan* (1947). This method of demonstration, as used both by supporters of comprehensive schools and by their opponents, calls for the use of numerous qualifications, owing to differences in the patterns of society, in function and in organization, and even in the use of words; and may be held to be useless and indeed dangerous in any but skilled hands. As soon as one realizes, for example,

that the English secondary school system customarily performs many of the functions of 'college' education, the fruitless nature of comparisons drawn between normal practice and attainment in our secondary schools and those of the comprehensive high schools of Canada and the U.S.A. becomes apparent.

25 Dante, *Paradiso,* xiii, 130–35.

3   The Examination at Eleven Plus

Cyril Burt   1959

Author

Cyril Burt (1883–1971) was a leading proponent in the development of the '11 plus' examination and the inclusion of IQ testing. During his career at University College London, he was Professor of Education (1924), Professor of Psychology from 1931 and the first London County Council educational psychologist. In a radio interview in the late 1940s he proposed setting up a society for very intelligent people, which today is known as *Mensa*. Knighted in 1946, Burt had a background in research in behaviour genetics, which included twin studies focusing on the heritability of intelligence. Seven years after Burt's death, it was claimed that he had falsified some of his research data and had invented two non-existent research collaborators. However, the veracity of these claims continues to be the subject of debate.

Article

Published twenty years before the scandal surrounding his work broke, *The Examination at Eleven Plus* (7: 2, 99–117) acknowledges that the use of the examination to assign pupils to grammar, technical or modern schools had become a 'target of heated controversy and vigorous attack': attacks that Burt claimed were based not upon educational grounds, but on 'social and political arguments'. Burt's aim in the article is to clarify matters for supporters and critics, both of whom he believes 'often seem singularly ill-informed about the origin of the plan', by exploring: the original intentions of the 1944 Act to provide secondary education according to pupils' perceived 'ages, ability, and aptitudes'; the psychological basis of testing and the concept of General Intelligence; research evidence; the nature of the examination, and the 'need for selection':

> a division of labour is and must be the basis of every organized society; and for the immediate future our paramount aim must be to make far better use of the best human material than we have done up to the present, and to do this we must first discover it.

What perhaps comes through most strongly in the article is Burt's espoused commitment to the eleven plus and standardised testing on grounds 'of exploiting to the full our untapped sources of human ability', because 'it is essential, in the interests alike of the children themselves and of the nation as a whole'.

For the twenty-first-century reader Burt's written style may appear florid by comparison to the more measured (some have argued 'anodyne') contemporary written style of academic papers. Burt's article is very much a product of its time, written by someone whose work arguably shaped, for better or worse, the adult lives of countless children in the second half of the twentieth century. Half a century on from publication, Burt's claim in the article that 'Of the methods hitherto tried out the so-called 11+ examination has proved to be by far the most trustworthy' is unlikely to convince all readers. The fact that girls' 11+ scores were adjusted down compared to boys' results; Burt's citing of the work of Francis Galton as a justification of testing, his echoes of the eugenicist's fear of a national decline and a need to ward 'off the ultimate decline and fall that has overtaken each of the great civilizations of the past', all will raise questions in the minds of today's readers. Nevertheless, the issues raised in this article remain contentious, are still debated and to some extent echo in the arguments of educational policy makers in the Coalition government in the United Kingdom today.

Other related articles from the *Journal* in this volume are: *Tradition and the Comprehensive School* (2, 1: 3–18) on page 17; and *City Technology Colleges: an Old Choice of School?* (37, 1: 30–43) on page 16. Related articles to be found in the *Journal* are: *The Grammar School Through Half a Century* (5, 2: 101–118); *The Changing Idea of Technical Education* (11, 2: 142–146); *Lord Butler and the Education Act of 1944* (20, 2: 178–191); *Towards an Educationally Meaningful Curriculum: Epistemic Holism and Knowledge Integration Revisited* (55, 1: 3–20); *Selection by Attainment and Aptitude in English Secondary Schools* (57, 3: 245–264).

The Examination at Eleven Plus

by Sir Cyril Burt

I. The Origin and Background of the Scheme

Aims. The allocation of pupils *to* different types of secondary school by means of what is known as the 11 plus examination has of late become the target of heated controversy and vigorous attack. Much of the opposition is avowedly based on social and political arguments rather than on educational. But even those who are concerned primarily with its educational merits, whether as supporters or as critics, often seem singularly ill-informed about the origin of the plan—the practical problems which gave rise to it, the aims it was intended to achieve, and the facts and data on which its advocates chiefly relied.

The ultimate object of the proposal is summed up in the words of the Act of 1944, which directs that the extended scheme of secondary education, now to be provided for older pupils, shall have due regard to their 'ages, ability, and aptitudes'. But our English educational system, like our constitution and our cathedrals, has grown by a slow process of irregular accretion; and the real crux of the matter has been to reorganize the existing system, with its oddly assorted relics of unrelated efforts in the past, and reshape and readjust it so as to meet the complex needs of a new age which has already experienced a swift succession of social, industrial, and technological changes. The details both of the problem and of the proposed solution are admirably set forth in the reports of the Consultative Committee, appointed by the Board of Education soon after the first world war, on which the recent Act and the regulations that followed it were largely based. Of their three main publications the most influential and the most revolutionary was that entitled *The Education of the Adolescent* (1927), commonly known as the Hadow Report.

As the report points out, this country has for centuries been famous for its scheme of 'scholarships' and 'exhibitions', which were designed to aid children of promise to obtain a higher education at schools or universities, such as they would not otherwise be able to secure, and which were usually awarded on the results of a scholastic examination. But from the outset our educational tradition has been cast in the classical mould. As a consequence, towards the close of the nineteenth century Britain was starting to lag painfully behind countries like Germany and France in providing new types of education in order to keep pace with recent advances of industry and science. In 1889 the Technical Instruction Act was passed which empowered the new county and county borough councils to supply instruction in 'the principles of science and art, as applied to specific employments or industries'. But the final outcome of all this and other early efforts, both public and private, was a crude incongruous patchwork; and at the beginning of the present century English education still remained split into three ill-coordinated systems—elementary, secondary, and technical—each under separate control.

The first attempts at modernization were made by the Act of 1902. Its two chief aims were to unify the administrative arrangements, and to extend and encourage 'the supply of education other than elementary'. One immediate consequence was that education authorities themselves began to build municipal or county secondary schools of their own, and to develop plans for awarding scholarships and free places at secondary schools to the more deserving pupils. Originally what came to be known as the 'junior county scholarship examination' was designed, or at least described, as a qualifying examination, which all entrants, fee-payers as well as holders of free places, were expected to pass. But, since the number of candidates vastly exceeded the number of free places, it became in effect a competitive examination.

The Clean Cut. The proposals of the Hadow Report were still more revolutionary. It was taken as axiomatic that no child should be precluded by financial handicaps from securing an education appropriate to his merits: the problem was to devise a workable machinery for attaining this goal. The solution advocated was based, as the preface explains, on a plan put forward—chiefly on psychological grounds—by the Principal of the Institute of Education (Sir Percy Nunn), and endorsed by most of the leading directors of education of that day and by the various bodies representing the views and experience of teachers themselves. The essence of the scheme, as he explains, was 'to make a *clean cut* across our public educational system at the age of 11+': primary education should end at that stage and post-primary education start and then continue up to 15 or later. 'And', he adds, 'it is vital to regard all types of post-primary education as attempts to solve, by different means appropriate to the different cases, what is essentially a single problem—namely, the education of adolescent boys and girls.'[1]

The detailed recommendations envisaged the establishment of new post-primary or (as they were in future to be called) 'secondary' schools of many different types—a recommendation that is as yet far from fully realized. To begin with, 'many more pupils', it was argued, 'should pass to secondary schools of the existing type' (i.e., schools providing a literary or scientific type of curriculum for the ablest children): in future these were to be re-labelled 'grammar schools'. What the precise number should be the committee hesitated to suggest: Professor Nunn thought the average proportion might well be raised to about 25 per cent of each age-group, the percentage varying according to the needs and general level of the locality. Secondly, the committee urged the establishment of far more junior technical schools, 'to prepare children either for those industrial occupations which require manual craftsmanship or for those connected with the engineering and allied trades, and in addition a smaller number of schools with a commercial bias and junior art departments at schools of arts and crafts'.[2] Thirdly they proposed a wider development of schools of the 'central type', both selective and non-selective, with a realistic or practical trend (like that of the German *Realschulen* and *Mittelschulen*), to be known in future as 'modern schools'. Finally, for the dull and backward they contemplated 'the provision of schools where the pace will be slower and practical work will play an even larger part than in schools of the "central" type'. This was regarded as the ideal scheme. But in districts where the provision of more than one type of post-primary institution (in addition to the grammar school) is impracticable, they recommended that 'the necessary discrimination between pupils of different abilities should be made by a system of parallel forms'.

Admission to the grammar, technical, and other selective schools was to be decided by the results of an entrance examination, similar to the existing 'free-place' examination, in order to 'distinguish the more gifted from the general body'. The examination was to be compulsory (with certain minor reservations) and not, as had been the practice in many areas, purely voluntary. The final allocation was to be dependent, not on mere attainment but rather on ability—that is, 'on each child's natural endowment'; and to this end, it was suggested, 'a psychological test might be specially employed', particularly to deal with borderline cases and those in which there was a discrepancy between the teachers' estimates of the child's ability and his actual performance in question papers of the ordinary type (English, Arithmetic, or the like). All these reforms were to be introduced experimentally and progressively 'in accordance with that gradual evolution which is so marked a feature in our constitutional history'. And, long before the passing of the Act, many authorities had already initiated changes in the directions proposed.

II. The Psychological Basis

The Concept of General Intelligence. The details of the scheme were avowedly based on psychological considerations; and these, it was contended, were not only 'in keeping with the results of scientific research', but were also confirmed by teachers and administrators, who had arrived at similar views independently by dint of direct practical experience. The language in which the committee's witnesses expressed their psychological opinions was often vague and ambiguous. Accordingly in the reports on primary and secondary education the committee include separate chapters stating the conclusions which they themselves accepted in regard to 'the mental development of children' between the ages of 7 and 11 and 11+ and 16+ respectively. Hence, before examining current criticisms of the scheme thus outlined, it will, I think, be helpful to summarize the committee's arguments so far as possible in their own words, and then consider how far later experience and the results of more recent psychological investigations either tend to bear out the assumptions adopted by the committee or require appreciable changes in the views which they held.

The psychological issues are discussed most fully in the report on *Secondary Education* (p. 77). The committee begin by pointing out that 'the traditional psychology of the nineteenth century, with its emphasis on faculties and mental transfer, has played an important part in perpetuating the idea of a curriculum common to all pupils; it assumed that most boys and girls are equipped with the same natural endowments and develop at almost the same rate: little attention was paid to individual differences in abilities or interests'. This view the committee emphatically reject. 'Modern psychology', they declare, 'insists on the wide individual differences discernible in both intellectual and emotional characteristics'; and they aptly quote the injunction of Quintilian, which might almost serve as their motto: 'Proprietates ingeniorum dispicere prorsus necessarium est'.

In place of the doctrine of separate 'faculties' lodged in specific centres of the brain, they accept the conception of mental 'factors'. These are to be regarded rather like the 'hypothetical components of a resultant force' in physics. 'During childhood', they say, 'intellectual development progresses as if it were governed largely by a single central factor, usually known as "general intelligence", which may be broadly described as *innate, all round, intellectual ability*, and appears to enter into everything the child attempts to think, say, or do: this seems the most important factor in determining his work in the classroom.' Since 'the ratio of each child's mental age to his chronological age remains approximately the same, at least up to the pubertal period', it follows, that, 'as age increases, the mental differences between one child and another will grow larger and larger, and reach a maximum towards adolescence. And by the age of 11 they will already have increased so much that it will no longer be sufficient to sort out different children into classes within the same school.'

The committee then go on to discuss the importance of special abilities and special disabilities. Among those bearing directly on the work of the schoolroom they mention differences in sensory discrimination, in mental imagery, in observation, memory, and reasoning, and—most important of all from the standpoint of higher education—specific aptitudes for verbal, numerical, and manual or practical work. But the latter, they believe, do not, as a rule, emerge, or at least do not become conspicuous, until about the age of 11 or later. 'At or after that age different children will, if justice is to be done to their varying capacities, require types of education varying in certain important respects.' Hence the need for different kinds of post-primary schools.

They add that their psychological witnesses were especially insistent on two further points. First, 'there is no sharp line of demarcation, psychological or social, between pupils who attend grammar schools and those who attend modern schools'. Secondly, quite apart from any shortcomings in the method of examination or selection, it is impossible to forecast with absolute certainty at the age of 11 + how each child is likely to develop: time will therefore reveal a number of 'misfits'. On these grounds, it is contended, there is bound to be, and indeed ought to be, an appreciable amount of overlapping between the curricula of the two main types of post-primary school—namely, the grammar and the modern. For the same reason there should be, a year or two after the date of entry, 'a further review of pupils in the light of what has been observed of their progress and development, and opportunities for transfer should be freely used'. In the case of the brighter children of an academic type, i.e., those who seemed destined for further education in a university or similar institution, this review should take place at the end of the first twelve months, since 'pupils of this type would be gravely handicapped if they did not begin their second foreign language in their second year', and similarly with other subjects.[3] On the other hand, the committee lay equal stress on the need of 'facilities to enable exceptional pupils to proceed to grammar schools at 12 and at 13, and even later'.

Criticisms. It will be noted that many of the criticisms nowadays urged against the procedure thus put forward were already anticipated in the committee's reports, and would have been largely nullified had all their proposals been carried out with the same thoroughness by every educational authority. As it is, the provision of grammar school courses varies widely from one area to another; in some the percentage of grammar school places (or the equivalent) amounts barely to 10 per cent; in others it reaches nearly 45 per cent. Only about one quarter of the authorities provide G.O.E. courses in modern schools. And in almost every area there is a grave shortage of facilities for technical and other forms of higher education. Moreover, the committee, as we have seen, envisaged a process of allocation which should continue after the age of 11+. Yet in practice less than 2 per cent of the pupils get retransferred from modern schools to grammar schools, and less than 1 per cent from grammar schools to modern.

However, most of the attack on the 11+ examination has centred on the concept of 'intelligence', and particularly on the assertion that differences in intelligence are innate and more or less permanent. On these particular issues a vast amount of research has been carried out during the last thirty years; and the after-histories of many of the children who were tested between 1915 and 1925 are now available by way of a check. What then are the main results? And how far do they bear out the initial assumptions on which the whole scheme was based, and in what respects, if any, do they call for modifications or amendments in the way those assumptions were stated?

The committee, it will be remembered, used the word intelligence as a shorthand label for a quality that they defined as innate general intellectual ability. Our main task therefore will be to examine the precise meaning of these three descriptive terms. Each of them rests on an implied antithesis: 'intellectual' characteristics are contrasted with 'emotional'; 'general' ability with 'specific' aptitudes; and 'innate' capacities with 'required' knowledge or skill. Let us therefore take these several distinctions in turn, and ask what is the evidence on which they are based.[4]

III. The Evidence from Research

1. *Intellectual versus Emotional.* The distinction between intellectual characteristics and motivational (or as the committee prefer to say, 'emotional') is at least as old as Plato and Aristotle. With Plato, however, the contrast is viewed from a behaviouristic standpoint. Man is compared to a chariot borne along by two horses, 'appetite' and 'spirit' (i.e., the baser and the nobler emotions), but guided in its course by reason or 'nous'. The modern analogue would be a self-steering missile or an aeroplane with an automatic pilot: each of them needs *power* to start and sustain their movements and a built-in *mechanism* to regulate and guide them. Thus the basic distinction is between the *dynamic* and the *directive* aspects of the mind.

Individual psychology is, or ought to be, strictly behaviouristic. Unfortunately its terminology has largely been borrowed from general psychology, which, from Locke and Descartes down to Stout and McDougall, has been predominantly introspective. Hence the traditional names—'intellectual' and 'emotional', and their more recent substitutes 'cognitive', 'affective' and 'conative'—have preserved a strongly introspective flavour. As a result we find many modern psychologists defining 'intelligence' from a purely subjective standpoint: Terman describes it as 'capacity for abstract thought'; Spearman as 'the ability to educe relations and correlates'. Consequently, several critics have interpreted the word 'intellectual' in the narrower sense, as though it implied a contrast with, and so excluded, 'practical' ability.

The interpretation I have just proposed is entirely in accord with current views on the function and mode of operation of the central nervous system.[5] The 'brain', as it is popularly called, requires electrochemical energy to run it, and a modifiable structural mechanism to provide what may perhaps best be designated *organized guidance*. To avoid needless pedantry, however, I shall continue to refer to this element in the total process as the 'intellectual' aspect, but I shall trust the reader to understand the word in this somewhat Pickwickian sense.[6]

2. *General versus Specific Factors.* The distinction between 'general ability' and 'specific aptitudes' is due primarily to Galton, and was popularized by the work of Binet, who frankly acknowledged his debt to Galton's investigations. Both were keen to rectify the misleading implications of the old faculty psychology, which still dominated the writings of the psychologists of their day. The evidence on which they relied was partly introspective, partly biological, and partly the fruit of observational or experimental studies of individual cases.[7]

Galton's twofold hypothesis was subjected to a long series of attacks on a double front. Thorndike and Thurstone in America and Brown and Thomson in this country denied the existence of any 'general factor', and recognized nothing but a miscellaneous set of 'primary abilities'. Spearman, on the other hand, denied the existence of special aptitudes; these, he maintained, were merely the product of special interest or special experience and training. There were thus three rival theories, each with distinctive corollaries of its own, which could readily be tested by the correlational technique known as factor analysis. A vast number of factorial researches have now been carried out; and it is, I think, fair to say the result of every investigation which has been adequately planned conclusively rebuts the two simpler hypotheses of a general factor alone or of special factors alone, but is entirely consistent with the Galtonian hypothesis, which postulates both.[8]

To my mind, however, the neurological evidence is by far the most convincing. Recent work has shown that the localization of functions in the brain is much less sharply defined than was formerly supposed. In practically every activity the whole brain participates. Moreover, the latest microscopical research with unusually refined techniques has demonstrated that the differences between one individual's brain and another's are quite as conspicuous as those between different areas in the brain of the same individual. Under the microscope sections of the brain-cortex from low-grade defectives reveal marked architectural differences as compared with sections from persons of normal ability; in the normal cortex the nerve-cells are larger and more numerous; the connecting fibres growing out of them exhibit far more delicate ramifications; and the general texture formed by cells and fibres has a neat, regular, systematic appearance, quite distinct from the irregular and higgledy-piggledy arrangement displayed by the cortical tissue of the imbecile brain. These distinctive features are discernible in all parts of the brain of the same individual: his nervous tissue, like every other tissue—skin, hair, muscle, bone, and fat—thus shows much the same general structure throughout, with minor local variations. And, so far as they go, microscopical studies *post mortem* of young children at different ages fully support Spencer's theory of a progressive maturation and differentiation, stage by stage, of the growing brain.

3. *Innate versus Acquired.* During recent years the direction of the main attack has shifted. Today the object of the fiercest criticism is not the assumption of general ability, but the claim that individual differences in this ability are largely innate. Now if, as we have seen, such differences are the reflection of differences in the nerve-structure, then surely, even were there no factual evidence to guide us, we should nevertheless be compelled to infer that, as with every other trait depending on physical differences, variations in ability would be largely determined by the individual's genetic constitution, and we should expect their transmission to obey the same laws of inheritance as other bodily characteristics. Unfortunately, however, the whole controversy has been conducted on very misleading lines because both the champions of mental heredity and its opponents have based their arguments on completely obsolete assumptions. First, they assume that what is inherited are the characteristics actually measured or observed; secondly, they both still cling to the old Aristotelian doctrine of 'blended inheritance', expressed by the traditional definition that heredity means 'the tendency of like to beget like'. The modern biologist, on the other hand, maintains that, with rare exceptions such as the differences between blood-groups and possibly in eye-colour, every observable characteristic is in fact the composite resultant of a prolonged interaction between the genes which the child receives from his parents and the environmental conditions into which he is born and under which he grows up. There are in fact no such things as inheritable traits; there are only inheritable tendencies.

The hypothesis of blended inheritance, it is true, had the powerful support of both Darwin and Karl Pearson. Galton, however, who, by an odd coincidence, was born in the same year as Mendel, put forward, quite independently, an alternative theory of 'particulate inheritance'. And, as developed by Mendel and his followers, that theory is now accepted by every biologist. As the modern geneticist sees it, the crucial problem is to explain, not so much why like begets like, but why in so many instances like begets unlike. For those who adopt the principle of blended inheritance, and still more for those who insist on the overwhelming influence of environment, one of the most puzzling phenomena is the occasional occurrence of exceptionally bright youngsters in poverty-stricken families where the personal, cultural, and economic conditions of the parents would, one might suppose, have foredoomed them to inevitable failure. On the Mendelian hypothesis these anomalies are just what we should expect.

It is a popular fallacy that Mendelian principles hold good only of characteristics that exhibit sharp qualitative differences, like the white and purple flowers of the peas which Mendel studied. The transmission of qualitative characteristics of course can readily be accounted for by a unifactorial hypothesis, that is, in terms of single genes. But Mendel himself went on to demonstrate how, by assuming a large number of genes (or 'factors' as he called them)—each having a similar, small, but cumulative effect—the inheritance of quantitative or graded characteristics could also be explained. In the case of intellectual ability all the available evidence seems to prove that both types of transmission are at work—the majority of the individual deviations being due to multifactorial transmission, while the rare and larger deviations are due to unifactorial transmission. A simple mathematical deduction shows that this twofold method of transmission would explain the peculiar way in which different degrees of intellectual ability are distributed among the general population. Their frequencies conform, roughly but not precisely, to the so-called 'normal curve', with tails straggling out widely in either direction, and the lower tail predominating, so that the whole distribution is slightly skewed.

In work on plants and animals a number of experimental techniques have been devised to estimate the extent to which variations in any given character are affected by environment and heredity respectively. We can, for example, take a strain that has been inbred for years and regularly selected according to its agreement with some particular type; and, after about a dozen generations, it can be shown that all the offspring must have virtually the same genetic constitution. If they are then subjected to different environmental conditions, any dissimilarity they exhibit must be due to these post-natal differences. With human beings such experiments are hardly feasible. But a similar situation is produced when 'identical twins' have for various reasons been separated in early infancy and brought up in homes of widely different types. We have now traced as many as 42 pairs of this kind; sometimes one twin has been brought up by foster-parents in the slums, while the other has been reared in a relatively well-to-do and highly cultured home. The relevant results can be most simply stated in terms of the correlations found: with tests intended to measure inborn ability the correlation for the twins was 0–88—a coefficient not far short of the figure for twins brought up in the same home, and much higher than that for ordinary brothers and sisters brought up together (0–54). With tests of educational attainments the contrast was reversed: the correlations were 0–68 and 0–81 respectively. I may add that for other degrees of kinship—parents and children, grandparents and grandchildren, uncles (or aunts) and nephews (or nieces), and first or second cousins—the correlations corresponded almost exactly with the values we should expect on the multifactorial hypothesis. From these and many other lines of evidence we may confidently infer that the degree of general ability possessed by each individual is determined mainly by his genetic constitution in accordance with the almost universal laws of Mendelian inheritance.

In view of all this evidence there can, I think, be no doubt whatever about the existence of an important characteristic which may be described as 'innate, general, intellectual ability', provided we ascribe to the three defining adjectives the interpretations I have proposed. For purposes of reference it is convenient to have one short familiar word to designate the characteristic so defined: the old Latin name, revived by Herbert Spencer and popularized by Binet—'intelligence'—has been almost universally adopted; and, at the risk of oversimplification, we might perhaps compress the whole underlying theory into three brief formulae: (i) intelligence *plus* native aptitude equals inborn capacity; (ii) inborn capacity *plus* acquired knowledge and skill equals resultant intellectual ability; (iii) resultant intellectual ability *plus* resultant emotional drive equals total personal efficiency.

IV. The Examination

Standardized Tests. The idea of assessing the abilities of children by means of experimental tests is due to the versatile genius of Galton. His original object was to use them as a kind of mental tape-measure in the course of a 'nation-wide survey of mind-power', which he was planning with the cooperation of the British Association for the Advancement of Science. Partly by way of preliminary trial and partly to demonstrate the value of these new techniques, he and Professor Sully regularly employed such tests as part of their scheme of scientific 'child guidance'. Teachers and parents were invited to bring children—normal, subnormal, and supernormal—to the laboratory at University College for a systematic examination; and on the basis of the results recommendations were made as to the best method of instruction or the most appropriate type of vocation in each individual case. As it turned out, the majority of the cases brought for special study were dull, backward, or difficult pupils on the borderline of mental deficiency. In France a similar problem had arisen; and Binet, who was a member of an official committee appointed to report on the whole question, developed a set of standardized scales for measuring both inborn intelligence and elementary school attainments with the 'mental year' as the unit. A few years later, with his generous help, the final version of his 'intelligence scale' was translated and adapted for use with English children.[9] It was suggested that for practical purposes the results should be converted to terms of the 'mental ratio' or 'intelligence quotient', and that for purposes of scientific research a more precise unit based on the 'standard deviation' should be substituted.[10]

All these earlier tests were 'individual' tests, suitable only for examining children singly in a personal interview; and, being intended primarily for younger and duller children, covered nothing but the most elementary mental processes—sensory discrimination, quickness of reaction, simple memorization, and the like. To examine larger groups at higher ages and higher levels of ability a different method was required; and in 1911 Dr. R. C. Moore and I were able to show that 'group tests', carried out with paper and pencil and involving what Galton had called 'higher mental processes', could be quite as effective as the tests already proposed for diagnosing defectives. The types of problem included in our battery were intended to assess sheer efficient thinking, regardless of acquired skill, knowledge, or experience. The tests then developed—'Opposites', 'Synonyms and Antonyms', 'Analogies', 'Matrices', 'Syllogisms', 'Completion Tests', in both verbal and non-verbal form—still furnish the bulk of the so-called 'intelligence' tests used in the 11+ examinations of the present day. And it was in the course of these earlier studies that we were led to the definition of 'intelligence', already quoted, as epitomizing in a single phrase that particular mental quality which Galton, Binet, and their followers were endeavouring to measure.[11] Group tests of this nature, it was argued, would prove serviceable for three main purposes: first, for surveys and for general screening, where, owing to the need to economize time and expense, large numbers of children were to be examined in the mass; secondly, for equating and standardizing assessments sent in by different teachers at different schools; and thirdly, for the use of teachers themselves when assessing the abilities of their own pupils in the classroom.

Preliminary Surveys. In 1913, when the London County Council decided to appoint a psychologist to assist in the work of its Education Department, the first step was to make surveys of the entire school population by methods such as I have described. Broadly speaking, we found that the intelligence of pupils in the elementary schools ranged from about 50 to 150 I.Q., that is to say, for children aged 10 to 11 by the calendar, from a mental age of 5 to 15 years; and between these two extremes every grade was discovered. The distribution proved to be almost exactly normal[12] with a standard deviation of about 15 I.Q. Approximately 50 per cent had I.Q.'s between 85 and 115 and 3 per cent I.Q.'s over 130. It was the object of the junior county scholarship scheme to discover these exceptionally able pupils, and transfer them, with maintenance grants where necessary, to the secondary (grammar) schools.

The scholarship examination at that date consisted of papers in English and Arithmetic; and, as our surveys showed, bright youngsters from poverty-stricken or semi-illiterate homes were badly handicapped. In the poorest boroughs, such as Shoreditch, Bethnal Green, or Southwark, the proportion of scholarship winners was well under 1 per cent; in the well-to-do, such as Wandsworth or Lewisham, over 8 per cent. Accordingly in 1915, with the help of the Chief Examiner, we began a series of experiments in which so-called 'intelligence tests' were introduced both into the written papers and into the oral interviews for borderline candidates. As a result, when the war was over, several authorities outside London—particularly, in areas where the level of the teaching varied widely from school to school— embarked on experiments of a similar kind—Bradford in 1919, Northumberland in 1921, and a number of others shortly afterwards.[13]

The conclusions drawn from these early experiments have, I fancy, been the subject of some misunderstanding. The time for testing *innate* ability is not 11 plus but 11 minus: indeed it should be undertaken by teachers themselves as soon as each pupil enters the junior school, and repeated at annual intervals. To be fit to enter a grammar school a child at 11 plus needs to be equipped, not merely with the requisite intelligence, but also with an aptitude for academic work and with a certain minimum of educational attainments, well above those of the ordinary pupil at that age. To acquire this minimum the bright child must be spotted at an early age, and promoted rather more rapidly than his fellows. For the same reason tests of English and Arithmetic must be included in the examination. At the same time, owing to the wide variations both in educational standards and in teaching efficiency from one school to another, a third test, which does not depend on attainment, is nearly always desirable. These are the real grounds for introducing a so-called 'intelligence' test of a 'predominantly verbal and intellectual type'.[14] But, since the object is no longer to test innate ability as such, much confusion would be avoided if such a test was called 'general classification test'.

Selection Procedures. In allocating pupils to different types of secondary school education authorities are free under the existing regulations to devise their own procedure. It is therefore hardly accurate to talk of '*the* 11+ examination'. At present less than half the authorities maintain a definite tripartite or bipartite organization, i.e., 'modern' and 'grammar' schools with or without 'technical' schools. The remainder are for the most part experimenting with various alternatives, usually intended to postpone, or at least to modify, the sharp differentiation between curricula. Yet, even in areas in which the 'comprehensive' type of school prevails, the pupils are still usually separated, almost from the outset, into two or three distinct 'streams' within the school.

In 1956 (the last year for which figures are available) 88 per cent of the authorities were using a standardized 'intelligence' test (a proportion which has been steadily increasing), and 73 per cent standardized papers in English and Arithmetic. Many of the others employ analogous tests, but describe them as un-standardized. During recent years too there has been a growing tendency to re-introduce an English essay.[15] In addition about 85 per cent use teachers' estimates, especially for borderline cases.

Predictive Value. The value of a selection procedure is to be judged primarily by the accuracy with which it forecasts the future educational progress of the children selected. A variety of criteria may be employed. The simplest and most obvious is the application of further tests of educational attainment towards the end of the school leaving period; but other considerations should also be taken into account. As the result of follow-up inquiries by a number of investigators, it is now generally agreed that at the age of 11+ a combination of (i) standardized tests of attainments in Arithmetic and English, (ii) a standardized test of 'intelligence' (so-called), and (iii) the teachers' assessments of their pupils, suitably rescaled, yields far better predictions than any one or any pair of these taken by themselves. That even this triple scheme is not entirely satisfactory is shown by the marked disparity occasionally discovered between the teachers' assessments and the results of the tests. Its predictive accuracy appears, on an average, to be equal to a correlation of about 0–75. The most obvious causes of inaccuracy are the transitory ailments and emotional disturbances which nearly always overtake a few of the candidates on the day of the tests. But a more important factor is the need for certain qualities of character—industry, ambition, and a readiness to set educational achievement above the immediate temptations of a good wage and an early independence— qualities that cannot very easily be assessed in advance.

Thus the practical outcome of the examination is to classify the candidates not into two groups, but into three: (i) those who are almost certainly suitable for a grammar school; (ii) those who are almost certainly unsuitable; and (iii) a number of intermediate and more doubtful cases on the verge between the other two groups. For these borderline cases therefore a further and more intensive study is essential; and a number of authorities do in fact call them up for a special interview or for additional tests usually of an 'individual' type. With these supplementary inquiries the predictive accuracy of the whole procedure is raised to about 0–80. It is highly unlikely that any more elaborate method would appreciably improve the limited amount of accuracy thus secured. After all, at every age of school life, and particularly during the prepubertal period, the mental development of certain individuals is apt to fluctuate in a way that is quite incalculable, since it is partly dependent on external circumstances and unforeseen events. That, of course, is one of the many reasons for a freer use of cross-transference at a larger stage, and for the inclusion in the modern school of courses not unlike those provided for weaker pupils at the grammar school.[16]

What do these figures mean in actual practice? Suppose, as was actually the case 40 years ago, the number of free places in the grammar schools is sufficient for only 3 per cent of each age group, and that we transfer the top 3 per cent as assessed by the results of the 11 plus examination. Less than half of these (viz., 1–3 per cent of the entire group) will be among the highest 3 per cent, as judged by their after-histories. This is not so bad as it sounds, since nearly all the 1–7 per cent who might be called as 'wrong' allocations will be well above the general average: if they are mistakes, they are not bad mistakes. Suppose, however, we want to be quite sure of including all the brightest 3 per cent as judged by the after-histories; then we must transfer the top 25 per cent: by that means we shall miss less than 1 in 500. As it happens, 25 per cent is the average proportion who are now actually transferred. But, of course, with the correlation given above, another 8 per cent of those who are allocated to a modern school will prove to be just as bright as some of the 25 per cent who have been lucky enough to scrape through into the grammar school. Consequently the disappointed parents may be tempted to complain. Yet in many ways, I suggest, they ought rather to rejoice: in all probability the child thus rejected would have had an anxious struggle to come up to the standard demanded had he in fact been transferred, and in the end would have joined the crowd of weaker pupils who fail to stay the course and leave the grammar school at the earliest possible moment.[17]

V. The Need For Selection

The Subnormal, the Normal, and the Supernormal. Although it is the 11+ examination that forms the stock and ostensible object of the critics' attacks, the real ground for their opposition is not so much the method of the selection, but selection itself. The fact that many are called but few chosen is always an unwelcome thought to those who are rejected. But, apart from all personal feelings, there are many who hold that the idea of segregating children according to their abilities is contrary to the very notion of a democratic state: it emphasizes the minor differences between individuals, and overlooks the major fact of our common human nature which binds us all together. Why then do so many educationists regard selection essential?

The real answer is that such a policy has been gradually forced upon them by the actual facts. During the earlier years of the present century educational psychologists and administrators concentrated their efforts chiefly on the subnormal—the dull, the backward, and the mentally defective: with them at any rate, as the teachers were the first to point out, some kind of classification is indispensable in the interests of the children themselves. The present age, we are told, is to be the 'golden age of the common man'; and consequently attention has now been diverted more and more towards the ideal of a common school. What then of the common child—the mean or average pupil, the father of *l'homme moyen sensuel*?

Those who believe that the improvement of environmental conditions should bring with it an improvement in the average ability of ordinary pupils have already accomplished a notable experiment in this direction; and it is instructive to study the results. Our rapid progress towards the Welfare State has all but stamped out the poverty, the destitution, and the crass ignorance that were once held responsible for the lower level of intelligence found among children from the humbler classes. And indeed, a comparison of tests applied before the first world war and after the second show that, in educational attainments and in general knowledge, there has been a striking rise during the past fifty years; on the other hand, there is not a shred of evidence for any similar rise in the level of innate ability either in the population as a whole or in what were once called the 'handicapped and underprivileged groups'.[18]

Assuredly it is a national duty to do our utmost, not only for the subnormal and the handicapped, but also for the normal and average child. Yet from the standpoint of future progress and of international competition there is no escaping the fact that it is the creative few who confer the greatest benefits on the uncreative many—the man who can make ten bushels grow where one grew before, the woman who discovers radium and suggests its use as a cure for cancer, the black-smith's son whose electrical discoveries today provide light, heat, transport, and television programmes for millions, the statesman who can save his country from armies of the dictator. The influence of great men on the course of history and civilization is a well-worn platitude. But too often, I fancy, both historian and biographer have allowed us to forget the many occasions on which disaster has befallen both nations and empires just because the 'great man' was lacking at the critical moment. What catastrophes might have been averted had Athens found another Miltiades in 413 B.C., Jerusalem another Judas Maccabaeus in A.D. 70, Rome another Julius Caesar in the fifth century. Or—to pick but a single instance from science—suppose that Ptolemy, the author of *The Great Syntaxis* (the *Almagest*), had possessed the brain of a Newton or an Archimedes: already in A.D. 150 practically all the essential data and methods were available for constructing the Newtonian system of dynamics and cosmology.[19] What a world of difference that one exchange would have made to the development of astronomy, technology, and even religion during the next fourteen hundred years.

But an age of technology and automation[20] demands far more than a few out-standing men of genius. 'Success depends on team-work.' But what kind of people make up the team? As the records show, Zeta, the Black Knight, and the Comet were all designed and built by men who got to a grammar school as a result of a scholarship examination or some similar test; the key-men got to the university by yet another selective ladder. And the same holds true of the majority of doctors, civil servants, engineers, secondary school teachers, and the technologists of modernized industries. The real bottleneck is the shortage of personnel with the requisite ability. By the end of the next decade, we are told that at least 55,000 young people (about 7½ per cent of each age group) should be proceeding annually to the Universities, the Technical College, and the Teachers' Training Colleges; and presumably just as many should be passing direct into industry, commerce, and the administrative services from the sixth form of the grammar schools or their equivalent. It is plainly essential that these 15 per cent should, so far as practicable, be recruited from the highest available levels of intelligence. If, however, near the borderline a small proportion should slip through the meshes, that should not, in my view, be deplored as 'sheer wastage': an admixture of men and women of high intelligence and character is desirable in every social grade, and a hierarchy of castes based on a complete re-sorting according to genetic quality would carry with it latent risks and drawbacks of its own.[21]

Nevertheless, a division of labour is and must be the basis of every organized society; and for the immediate future our paramount aim must be to make far better use of the best human material than we have done up to the present, and to do this we must first discover it.

Hitherto, I venture to think, our discussions about the desirability and the methods of selection have been based more on Utopian wishes and ideals than on a realistic study of the actual facts. Let me therefore end by summarizing the main conclusions that emerge from the factual evidence I have tried to outline in my thumbnail sketch. They are at bottom biological. Man as a species owes his amazing success in the evolutionary battle chiefly to the circumstance that he carries within him a richer store of genetic variability than any other creature; and this holds true of his mental qualities as well as his physical. Of his mental qualities the most decisive is what is technically called 'intelligence', that is (in the semi-popular terms used in the current literature) 'innate, general, intellectual ability'—a phrase which we have found it necessary to re-define with greater precision. Since individuals differ so widely in this and other inborn capacities, it is essential, in the interests alike of the children themselves and of the nation as a whole, that those who possess the highest ability—the cleverest of the clever—should be identified as accurately as possible. Of the methods hitherto tried out the so-called 11+ examination has proved to be by far the most trustworthy. That does not mean that further experiments with alternative or supplementary procedures can now be abandoned; but it would be the height of folly to substitute some other method without first demonstrating, objectively and empirically, that the projected method is really more efficient than the old. Yet intelligence by itself will not guarantee success. Hence in allocating children to different types of educational career other qualities should be considered, though, in theory at any rate, it is intelligence that sets the upper ceiling. Nor should the process of discovering the ablest children be

confined to a single age or date, much less to a single examination. It should start
at the earliest possible age, and should be continued throughout school life. In
this way, and this way alone, can we be sure of exploiting to the full our untapped
sources of human ability and of warding off the ultimate decline and fall that has
overtaken each of the great civilizations of the past.

Notes

1 *The Education of the Adolescent*, pp. 72f.
2 A subsequent report of the Consultative Committee recommended the establishment
   of 'a new type of higher school', to be known as 'Technical High Schools', which
   should be accorded 'equality of status' with schools of the grammar type and
   should recruit their pupils at the age of 17 + by the means of the same general
   selective examination (*Secondary Education*, 1938, p. 372).
3 This argument appears to have been strongly pressed by those headmasters whose
   schools prepare pupils for entrance to the universities, and is evidently one of the
   main reasons why the committee determined that the secondary stage should start
   as early as 11 +, and favoured separate schools (rather than a separate stream in a
   comprehensive school) for those who might eventually prove to be 'of the most
   gifted type'.
4 The following arguments are set out more fully in a paper on 'General Abilities
   and Special Aptitudes' (*Educational Research*, II, ii, pp. 81f.). The terminology
   adopted by the consultative committee as intelligible to ordinary teachers is largely
   that employed by Nunn in his well-known text book *Education: Its Data and First
   Principles* (1920; 2nd ed. 1945).
5 Cf. D. A. Sholl, *The Organization of the Cerebral Cortex* (1956) and K. S. Lashley,
   Brain Mechanisms and Intelligence (1929). It may be noted that Piaget, in
   discussing *The Psychology of Intelligence* (1950), adopts a similar interpretation: he
   too starts with the distinction between 'the *energetic* or affective aspect and the
   structural or cognitive aspect involved in every human action' (pp. 4–5).
6 It is not easy to suggest a more appropriate term. Plato, it will be remembered,
   compared the organized guidance of the individual to the organized guidance
   needed in an efficient state; and the ship of state, as he so often reminds us,
   requires a *cybernetes*, i.e., a steersman or pilot (whence our word *governor* in both
   the engineering and the political sense). Today 'cybernetics' is the fashionable
   name for that branch of science which is concerned with the study of self-regulating
   mechanisms. Sherrington speaks of the '*integrative* action of the nervous system';
   but, as Nunn points out (*op. cit.*, p. 216), its action is always *analytico-synthetic*. Von
   Neumann and Morgenstern (*Theory of Games and Economic Behaviour*) describe
   the function of the intelligent mind as 'the forming and carrying out of adaptive
   strategies'. I myself would favour another illuminating term that is frequently used
   by Plato, *syntaxis*—the Greek technical word for the organization of the tactical
   manoeuvres of an army or fleet (cf. esp. Plato, *Republic* 462 D); it may be regarded as
   the opposite of *ataxia* (the word used by the modern neurologist to describe the
   absence or loss of coordination in the activities of the neuro-muscular system).
7 The doctrine of faculties was adopted as a basis for individual psychology by the
   phrenologists of the early 19th century; and their views seemed at first to be confirmed by apparent localization of brain-functions revealed by the effects of local
   haemorrhage on such processes as speech and by the results of the electrical
   stimulation of the brains of animals. Galton's conclusions were based primarily on
   his study of the family-trees of British men of genius (*Hereditary Genius*, 1869,
   pp. 23f.). Spencer, who was at first an ardent phrenologist, eventually accepted a

similar view. As a result of his neurological and biological theories he put forward the notion of a kind of superfaculty for adaptation or adjustment, which he christened 'intelligence', and which progressively differentiated, during the evolution of the animal kingdom and during the evolution of each individual, into a 'hierarchy' of increasingly specialized capacities (*Principles of Psychology*, 1870, I, esp. pt. iv).

8 With minor differences of phraseology and emphasis, Thorndike, Brown, Thomson, and even Spearman himself eventually came round to this conclusion. And Thurstone subsequently put forward the notion of 'second order factors', which he believed would effect a reconciliation between his earlier theory and that which envisaged a general factor as well as primary abilities. Professor Vernon also accepts what he describes as 'the theory of general *plus* group factors' (*The Structure of Human Abilities*, 1950, pp. 11f.).

9 Cf. C. Burt, *Mental and Scholastic Tests: Three Memoranda by the Psychologist to the London County Council* (1921).

10 No one ever suggested that the I.Q. would remain constant for each individual: nothing but an *approximate* constancy was claimed, and the occurrence of exceptions was explicitly emphasized (*op. cit.*, 1921, pp. 152f.).

11 C. Burt, 'Experimental Tests of Higher Mental Processes and their Relation to General Intelligence', *J.Exp.Pedag.*, I, 1911, pp. 93–112.

12 In institutions for mental defectives there were children with I.Q.'s well below 50, running in fact down to zero, and in certain preparatory and public schools (Rugby, for example) children with I.Q,'s running up to nearly 200. It was mainly, though perhaps not wholly, these further cases that accounted for the larger 'tails' exhibited by the frequency-distribution, as described above.

13 A brief account of these earlier trials will be found in the Consultative Committee's report on *Psychological Tests of Educable Capacity* (1923, pp. 37, 115, 149f.). The reader who is interested in the details will find them fully set out in the booklet of tests which I prepared for the Northumberland Committee and the accompanying manual of instructions (both afterwards published by the University of London Press, 1925). The tests prepared for use in London and Bradford are given in *Mental and Scholastic Tests* (1921, pp. 223–56). Professor Godfrey Thomson and his staff prepared similar booklets year after year; and today the majority of tests used by education authorities are supplied either by Moray House or by the National Foundation for Educational Research.

14 In this context the term intellectual is used in the narrower sense in which it is contrasted with practical or technical ability. How far it is really possible at this early age to distinguish pupils whose aptitudes fit them for the academic education of the grammar school and those fitted rather for the more concrete type of instruction given in technical schools is a question discussed more fully in *Studies in Education: Problems of Secondary Education Today* (University of London Institute of Education, 1954, pp. 14f.). It may be noted that Moray House has now renamed the 'intelligence' tests supplied to local authorities 'tests of verbal reasoning'.

15 Cf. A. Yates and D. A. Pidgeon, *Admission to Grammar Schools* (1957). The original reason for excluding the essay was the unreliability of the usual subjective methods of marking. Experiments carried out in London schools, however, showed that it was quite possible to devise an objective scheme which would give reasonably trustworthy scores (cf. M. D. Cast, 'The Efficiency of Different Methods of Marking English Compositions', *Brit. J. Educ. Psychol.* IX, pp. 257–69 and X, pp. 49–60).

16 The figures I have given seem somewhat higher than those quoted in the report of the working party appointed by the British Psychological Society (*Secondary School Selection*, 1957), but less optimistic than that suggested by the investigators for the National Foundation, which was based on results obtained in an area where the

procedure was unusually efficient. They estimate that in 1955, out of 640,000 pupils eligible for transfer, about 78,000 were 'wrongly' allocated as judged by a later follow up. 'Wrongly' is placed between inverted commas; but the phrase, torn from its context, has been pounced on by certain critics as avowing the inadequacy of the existing procedure. However, as the investigators themselves remark, most of the 'wrong' allocations could not have been put right at the time, since they were largely the effect of subsequent changes which no selection procedure could have possibly foretold.

17   I attach little importance to two further criticisms commonly made, namely, that the aim of the examination can be frustrated by special coaching given to the pupils and that the whole ordeal imposes a cruel nervous strain upon the candidates. Any undue advantages that special coaching might conceivably confer can always be detected or avoided by a properly conducted procedure. And the actual evidence shows that both the amount and the frequency of nervous strain have been greatly magnified; when present, it is nearly always communicated to the child by the over-anxious parent or the over-eager teacher, and a better understanding of the purpose of the examination should forestall any undue pressure. After all every one of us, however successful, has sooner or later to acknowledge that there are others who are better than we are. And it should be an essential part of the child's education to teach him how to face a possible beating in the 11+ (or any other) examination, just as he should learn to take a beating in a half-mile race, or in a bout with boxing gloves or a football match with a rival school.

18   Whether or not there has been an actual decline in national intelligence is a question too intricate to be answered with any confidence in the light of the data so far available. My own conclusion would be that what little information we possess confirms the verdict uttered by Professor J. B. S. Haldane 20 years ago that, so long as the existing class-differences in fertility continue, we must 'expect a slow decline of 1 or 2 per cent per generation in the mean intelligent quotient' (*Heredity and Politics*, 1938, p. 117).

19   From Apollonius' work on conic sections he might have deduced the possibility of elliptical orbits for the planets, and so corrected Aristarchus's anticipation of the heliocentric hypothesis, although without Tycho's observation to supplement the records of Hipparchus he might have found it hard to distinguish ellipses from approximate circles.

I may add that it is always difficult to apportion the contributions made towards any particular achievement between the innovator with whose name it is popularly linked, the band of workers who happened to precede, surround, or follow him, and finally what Goethe has taught us to call the *Zeitgeist*. Nevertheless, the members of such co-operative groups are always themselves exceptional individuals; and the *Zeitgeist* is only effective so far as it is embodied in other individuals who are also exceptional, though in a lowlier degree. Economic, social, and political conditions may throw up new and crucial problems, and even pave the way for the solution furnished by the genius; but they cannot themselves ensure that a solution will be discovered.

20   The opponents of selection are fond of pointing to the non-selective systems of education in the U.S.S.R. and the U.S.A., and the results those systems have achieved. 'The whole concept of inherited ability as determining a child's achievement' (we are told) 'has been rejected in the U.S.S.R.; and almost the whole adolescent population of the Iron Curtain countries successfully attains *full* secondary education'. 'In the U.S.A., the home of the common man, the principle of the common school for all prevails; and even if the American system does to some extent retard the top 10 per cent, it does more for the average pupil and the late developer, who fail to get the chance they deserve under English conditions' (*Secondary School Selection*, 1957, pp. 48, 84, 92f.). The events of the last

18 months have gravely shaken these familiar arguments. The advertised picture the Soviet educational system may have represented an ideal, but it certainly does not represent the facts; and the new Russian scheme frankly envisages 'special schools for the specially gifted'. In America the news of the first sputnik was followed by a spate of books and articles urging the need for a more rigorous selection of able individuals, and expressing the same admiration for the British educational system that so many British writers had shown for the American.

21 See Michael Young's imaginative analysis of this problem in *The Rise of the Meritocracy* (1958).

4   The 1870 Education Act

W. H. G. Armytage

Author

Walter Harry Green Armytage (1915–98) first published in the *Journal* in 1956, alongside other historians and comparative educationists. His paper, *Some sources for the history of technical education in England – Part 1* (5, 1: 72–79), reflected not only his considerable ability as an historian but also his interest in engineering, as befitted a Professor of Education in Sheffield. And the history of engineering education was an area he wrote much about. But, amongst his many historical studies, his greatest achievement was, in 1970, his *Four Hundred Years of English Education* (Cambridge University Press).

Introduction

The *Journal* has over the years produced scholarly papers on the significant events that have shaped British educational systems, and continues to do so. Armytage's paper, *The 1870 Education Act* (18, 2: 121–33), is within that excellent tradition, written on the centenary of one of the most significant Acts of Parliament. Furthermore, the debates and disputes which accompanied the passage of the legislation and its subsequent adaptations presage the contentions which remain with us today – as no doubt Armytage, were he still alive, would acknowledge as proof of the value of history.

The 1870 Act introduced School Boards with a view to ensuring elementary education for all, supplementing the education which depended on the provisions of Church schools. The pressure for a secular alternative is here described – from the National Education League (a group of business men fearing the competition from American and German better educated workforces), from representatives of workers (who did not want 'to have the gospel and geography mixed together'), and from the Factory Inspectorate (who recorded the failure of previous Factory Acts to ensure children were not deprived of elementary education). Why pay for education when they could be paid to go to work? Issues debated concerned, as now, the relation of education to economic needs, the extent to which Church schools should be supported on rates as would be the Board schools, the non-denominational character of religious instruction, the appropriate school-leaving age and the broader connections between school provision and a healthier childhood. There was inevitable resistance by the Church as they saw their power over education being diminished by locally elected councils, for, in the words of Prime Minister Forster, the defining principle was

> the education of the people's children, by the people's officers, chosen in their local assemblies, controlled by the people's representatives in Parliament.

But religion was maintained so long as the School Boards would, in the words of the Cowper-Temple amendment, teach 'no catechism or religious formulary distinctive of any particular denomination'. And that survived the 1944 Education Act and remains with us today.

Connected articles from the *Journal* are: *Lord Butler and the Education Act of 1944* (20, 2: 178–91); *Planning the Education Bill of 1902* (9, 1: 153–75, 1960); *Board of Education Act 1899* (11, 1: 44–60, 1962); *Church and Children – a Study in the Controversy over the 1902 Education Act* (8, 1: 1959); *50 Years On* [Spens Report] (38, 1: 1989).

The 1870 Education Act

by W. H. G. Armytage, Professor of Education, University of Sheffield

(i)

'England must come to our open national system sooner or later, and I trust will avail itself of our experience at the outset and not wait to be taught her error.' So, the superintendent of schools in Philadelphia reinforced the case made by Follett Osier, F.R.S. on 13 October 1869 for a comprehensive Education Act by the British government. As one of a steady flow of such transatlantic homilectics, it was, over the ensuing year, to be reinforced by many others whom Osier was addressing at Birmingham. For Osier was Birmingham made flesh. As the inventor of an anemometer he was professionally concerned with registering the winds of change; as a glass manufacturer he was concerned with their strength; and as a technologist he was concerned with what we call a systems approach. So he asked for an act which would embrace 'all classes' in a 'whole system ... worked on one broad plan ... embracing even the higher departments of knowledge, so that while all go on together, each pupil may be able, as he advances, to study such special subjects as his abilities or the circumstances of his case may render desirable'.[1] After all that is the way he had himself been educated at that remarkable experimental school, Hazelwood, the one institutional collateral of the Lunar Society:[2] the 'general staff' of Britain's first industrial revolution.

He was speaking to a remarkable assembly from industry, the trade unions and the House of Commons, gathered together at Birmingham to press for national legislation to provide every child in the country with a school place. These schools were to be provided by local rates, supplemented by government grants, managed by the local authorities, subject to government inspection, unsectarian and free. Moreover local authorities or the state were to have the power to compel children to attend them. The need for more schools was generally admitted: indeed the government had supplemented numerous private surveys.[3] But why Birmingham? The occasion was the first meeting of the National Education League, a group of business men of that city to whom intimations of American and German industrial hegemony were vouchsafed earlier than to any others.[4] As its largest manufacturer of hardware, Alfred Field remarked, 'With almost as much personal knowledge of America as I have of England, I have often pointed out to my fellow merchants that the United States are now manufacturing and exporting to the English Colonies and the common markets of the world many articles to a large amount, that were formerly made in this district.' 'What is the explanation?' he asked, and replied, 'There is none other than that of the greater intelligence of the American workmen. And the foundation of this high intelligence and ductility of mind is the American public free schools.' Field was also aware of the German merchants who 'have been for years, and rapidly too, supplanting English goods the world over, with the products of the educated workmen'. To make England more competitive he suggested the immediate establishment of 'efficient primary schools', followed by 'a complete and connected system of secondary and high schools—all free' which might 'readily be connected with the long-endowed schools of the county, and perhaps, by a system of scholarships to the University'.[5]

The need for transcending the suspicions of church and chapel[6] had of course been visible ever since Cobden's time, and was indeed responsible for the formulation of the Revised Code (an early 'efficiency' measure), and for the institution of a 'conscience-clause' whereby voluntary schools had to take church and chapel children if they received grants. For the parents of such children—working men and women—did not want, as they said, 'to have the gospel and geography mixed together'. That is why trade unionists came to Birmingham to support the League, 'not because its 'principles reach exactly and altogether the wants of the working classes but because it goes a step in the right direction'.[7] And, voicing the newly founded corporate strength of the T.U.C., its leaders, Applegarth, Cremer and Lloyd Jones, spoke out for unsectarian schools.

Lined up behind the battering ram was also the corporate strength (then very considerable) of the Royal Society for the Encouragement of Arts, Manufacturers and Commerce. Representing it came the Rev. William ('Hang Theology') Rogers, who ten years earlier had been a member of the Newcastle Commission; Edwin Chadwick, who nearly thirty years earlier had served on the Royal Commission investigating the condition of factory children,[8] and E. Carleton Tufnell, who with Kay Shuttleworth had founded the first teachers' college in the country.

(ii)

Tufnell's silent presence indicates the powerful internal impetus for change represented by the Factory Inspectorate, of which he had original and almost unrivalled experience,[9] as a reviewer of the hours of labour of children in factories and workshops other than textile and calico print works. The results of his (and his fellow Royal Commissioners') labours were regulatory Acts of Parliament in 1864 and 1867, obligating employers to send such children to school. But schools, as the factory inspectors then pointed out, posed a problem, even if the acts were to be gradually enforced. Thus Tufnell's fellow commissioner, Alexander Redgrave, found that though the number of works under his inspection had been more than doubled by the Factory Act of 1867, from 7,000 to 15,000, only 733 extra children were going to school.[10] The reason was, of course, that they would have to pay to go to school, whereas they had been paid to go to the factory. Redgrave, an authoritative and influential figure whose name is forever associated with the standard treatise on factory legislation, wrote:

'I consider the time has arrived when two material alterations may be made in existing conditions. … First, that the age at which young persons may be employed full time be raised by one year, i.e. that children should work half time and attend school until they are fourteen years of age instead of thirteen at present. Second, that no young persons under the age of 16 should be employed for full time unless a certificate be produced, given in a prescribed form by a certified schoolmaster, minister, inspector of schools or justice of the peace, certifying that the young person can read and write well and work sums in the first four rules of arithmetic.'[11]

That Redgrave's observations should be cited by a Manchester delegate to the League[12] was yet another portent. For his presence, together with that of W. B. Hodgson (a former member of the Newcastle Commission) and of William Harris and H. B. S. Thompson, showed that the League had now inherited the agitant role discharged over the previous twenty years by the Lancashire industrialists and their satellites. After twenty years of bill drafting and pressure they were quite content to hand over to George Dixon, Joseph Chamberlain and Jesse Collings to get steam up for rate/state aided schools managed by locally elected authorities armed with powers to compel attendance. And get up steam Birmingham did. To generate heat for a ten year agitation, a substantial fund of some £60,000 was raised. Full page advertisements were taken in *The Times*. Over a hundred public meetings were held in various parts of the country. So fast and far did the Birmingham express look like going, that to impede its progress two defensive 'unions', one based on Birmingham and the other on Manchester, were formed. The reactive nature of these defensive unions was acknowledged by the Bishop of Manchester, James Fraser, at a meeting of the latter, when he said that 'if it had not been for the Education League, and the programme they put forth, this Education Union, which has assembled us here tonight, would have had no existence.'[13]

On such swirling currents Forster launched the government bill on 17 February 1870.

(iii)

Read a second time from 14–18 March, committed on 16 June, emerging on 21 July, and then, after its third reading on 22 July, going to the Lords, it emerged to receive Royal Assent as 33 and 34 Vict. C. 75 on 9 August 1870. It could truly be said to have been hammered out. The hammering was not so much by the hundred-and-seventy-four M.P.s who spoke on it in the Commons, the 8 bishops and 26 temporal peers who spoke on it in the Lords, as by the specialist groups that worked it over outside the House of Commons. One has only to read the press, editorials or reports of public meetings and assemblies to realize that this act was a classic example of the political mediation of specialist interests.[14]

For specialist interests, from the civil service to industry and organized labour, buoyed this bill (as no other Education Bill had been supported) through the

House of Commons. The only opposition it encountered was from those who thought it did not go far enough. Even more remarkable, instead of encountering opposition from dissenters, the organizational strength of that body was used to strengthen it. By doing so, they inadvertently turned themselves not so much into the Liberal Party at prayer, as the Nonconformists at politics,[15] with disastrous consequences—as was to be seen forty years later. By undertaking the political task of amending the bill to conform to the League's prescriptions, organized dissent became the liberal 'caucus' organization.

In its original form the government bill proposed that the Committee of Council be given powers to ascertain existing deficiencies in schooling by dividing the country up into school districts based on boroughs and parishes. Existing denominations were to have a year's grace to make up these deficiencies. They were also to lose their own inspectors. If they failed, School Boards were to be elected by Town Council or select vestries. These boards were to be themselves endowed with powers to rate, remit fees, assist existing schools and, if they wished, frame byelaws compelling children between the ages of five and twelve to attend schools and offer religious instruction subject to a conscience clause.

Such concessions to the Anglicans as 'the year's grace', 'permissive compulsion', the 'conscience clause' and 'the election of boards by vestries', inflamed the League, which reacted swiftly by demanding universal School Boards, elected immediately on passage of the act by ballot of the ratepayers, providing free schools at which attendance was to be compulsory and in which 'no creed, catechism or tenet peculiar to any sect was to be taught'. These points they made in a deputation of 46 M.P.s and 400 members representing 96 branches, described by its secretary and historian as 'probably the most numerous and representative which had ever visited Downing Street',[16] to the Prime Minister on 9 March 1870.

The battle for alterations continued. The League's chairman during the second reading of the bill threatened that, unless concessions were made, a movement for exclusively secular education would arise. After a three-night debate, he secured a promise from the Prime Minister that alterations would be made. Here the Central Nonconformist Committee went critical, and secured the signatures of two-thirds of all the nonconformist ministers in England and Wales to a petition to the House of Commons against allowing local boards to determine religious teaching in schools. The petition was followed by a deputation to the Prime Minister. Even Forster's advisers changed their minds, and against such pressure the government withdrew, conceding ballot elections for the School Boards, with a time-table conscience clause for their schools. Elections were to be based on a cumulative vote, and the 'year of grace' was reduced to five months.

(iv)

If such needs involved harnessing the Central Nonconformist Committee into the shafts of the Radical bandwagon by Chamberlain's political stable-boy, Francis Schnadhorst, it also accelerated the emergence of what one could call a liberal 'intelligentsia'. Its spokesman, W. V. Harcourt, was particularly active at this very time, pressing the full implementation of the American type school system of locally elected School Boards empowered to levy a rate for secular education. It was, as Forster himself acknowledged in introducing his bill on 17 February, 'the ultimate force which rests behind every clause'. Forster defined this principle as 'the education of the people's children, by the people's officers, chosen in their local assemblies, controlled by the people's representatives in Parliament'.

Harcourt pressed this concept to its logical conclusion. Like Cobden before him, he was an admirer of the Massachusetts system and told the House on 7 July:

'that little state (Massachusetts), out of its state funds, expended upon education an amount larger by several thousand pounds than the whole expenditure of the British Empire in the same direction'.

In saying so he was speaking not only for the League, then assiduously circulating 20,000 copies of Jesse Collings' study of American Common Schools, but for the liberal generation which preceded his, a generation led by Cobden, and brigaded into the Lancashire (later the National) Public Schools Association.

There is indeed some justice in the claim that 'no one more' than W. V. Harcourt enlarged the scope of the original bill introduced by Forster in the House of Commons.[17] As Professor of International Law at Cambridge and M.P. for Oxford he represented the new establishment of liberal intelligentsia that was in time to supersede the Anglican parson and the ranting dissenter. He was the archetypal 'consensus man' to whom 'education, reflection and religion' would keep men within the bounds of moderation, and free from alien pressures. 'As a politician,' he told a friend, 'I am quite satisfied that neither in the House of Commons nor in the country can we beat denominationalism by secularism.' Moving in this comfortable haze of compromise and brokerage he supported the free compulsory national programme of the League, but moderated their demand for rate aid from a third of the total cost of the board schools to one-sixth. It was Harcourt's amendment that board schools should offer undenominational and unsectarian religious teaching in their schools, and that the School Boards should be established in every district to enforce attendance of all children of school age, which prompted Cowper-Temple's more famous counteramendment that board schools should teach 'no catechism or religious formulary distinctive of any particular denomination'.

Utterly modern was Harcourt's conviction that education was a legitimate charge on the national exchequer. Rightly he argued that the mainspring of the act was finance. For, whatever machinery was constructed, without the steady tensile force of exchequer finance, local boards would only tax the house of the poor man as the squirearchy had taxed his bread. And since such taxes would fall most heavily on the districts where there was the least school provision, like Liverpool, the whole system of the bill would 'stink'. Education for Harcourt was as national a need as the army or the navy:

'Millions are being spent to protect the country from an invasion which had never occurred and which I do not think is likely to occur. But here at home, and in every town and hamlet of the country, a hostile force of ignorance and vice was encamped against which we are striving to make head.'[18]

(v)

An equally difficult case to argue was that for over-riding working people's hostility to losing the fruits of their children's labour. Here the case for compulsion rested on current German practice, and was voiced by a manufacturer with interests in Saxony as well as Nottingham, A. J. Mundella.[19] He considered that America was 'fast sinking into ignorance', because only 42.6% of New York children actually attended school, only 58.9 per cent in Chicago and 70.1 per cent in Cincinatti.[20] Like America, he continued, we should look to Prussia, whose Labour Act of 1868 set high standards. There, no child was allowed to begin working till 12, every child between the ages of 12 and 14 had to go to school for three hours a day, and every child from 14 to 16 for six hours a week. Unlike Harcourt (who argued for universal School Boards) Mundella pressed for better integration with the Factory Acts.

In this he was supported by other manufacturers like Edmund Potter and Bernhard Samuelson, and Thomas Bazley. Potter described the Factory Acts as having 'completely failed in sending large numbers of children to school, except in those cases in which masters have taken a Christian interest in their workpeople and have provided education for their children.'[21] Bernhard Samuelson (the ironmaster to whose select committee on Technical Education in 1867 much information on continental competition had been routed) argued that the permissive compulsion envisaged by the original 66th clause could be replaced by compulsory compulsion (i.e. that boards should be obliged to make byelaws enforcing attendance at school instead of being merely enabled to) since only such a compulsion would put teeth into the Factory Acts of 1867.[22] So too Sir Thomas Bazley argued for the compulsion alongside Lyon Playfair.

(vi)

But the spectre of a bureaucratic police state on the Berlin model was too strong for the House. For holding the view that the parent should be as accountable to the state for depriving his child of schooling as he would be if he deprived him of food, Mundella was described as 'for ever casting a longing glance at the ways and institutions of the continent, continental notions of government, and continental notions of liberty'. Britain, he was reminded, 'was not a drilled nation, not registered and inspected and certified from the cradle to the grave, that every Englishman's house is still his castle'. Germany was 'one of the least self-reliant, the least energetic, the most reverent for authority', Britain 'one of the most self-reliant and the least tolerant of either ecclesiastical or police interference in the world'.[23]

So, whilst providing schools for children to attend, section 74 of the 1870 Act did not in fact limit the employment of children during school hours. That was done by the Education Act of 1876 which, in addition to enabling school attendance committees to legislate for attendance at school, prohibited the employment of children under 10, of children above the age of 10 who had not obtained a certificate of educational proficiency or of attendance.

This fight over compulsion is another illustration of the metamorphosis of opinion between 1870 to 1880. For in the latter year Mundella, as Vice-President of the Council, in a brief, almost peremptory act, imposed on boards and school attendance committees alike, the duty of enforcing attendance at school.

It was through compulsion that the real results of the 1870 Act were seen, because once children were roped into the schools the extent of underfeeding and undernourishment was discovered, and another chain of movement began. From helping with 'penny dinners' it developed into a health service, and into yet more curtailment of factory labour, with the pace, as might be expected, set by Germany.[24]

(vii)

The immediate impact of the 1870 Act was to stimulate the voluntary schools. For in the period of grace the application for grants increased by over four hundred per cent—from 150 a year to over 3,000. And though only some 1,600 of these were granted, even this represented an increase of over two hundred per cent. These enabled the churches to supply twice as many new school places (a million) as the new board schools (half a million).

But this was only a short-term effect. The long-range effect of the act on the voluntary schools had been shrewdly forecast by Dr. Lyon Playfair, F.R.S., then the national spokesman for science and technology. This technical Isaiah was the real prophet. Just as his disturbing diagnosis of Britain's educational handicaps in the industrial race, having done so much to bring about the debate, he argued that the Bible was the only cheap available classic in the schools, and as such, was a necessary antidote to the mechanical drudgery of the three R's. So for economic reasons alone it could not be dispensed with.[25]

In the then relevant metaphor of the race track he prophesied that the new denominational schools would be prevented from even keeping up with the board schools. They would have to be built by subscription, whereas board schools would be built by rates. Further subscriptions would be needed to provide a sixth of their income. They would have no compulsory powers (this was, it is true, remedied by Lord Sandon's Act in 1876) and they would of course be short on what he called 'educational appliances of the best kind'.[26]

Voluntary schools appealed to others on sound economic grounds, not so much because they saved money on the rates as because they stimulated competition. Thus in 1876 the journal and organization which existed to defend the interests of industrial inventors (formed in 1861 as a defence group to prevent 'property' in invention being destroyed) was lamenting 'the strong feeling existing among board school members that their schools, or such as may be upon their model, ought to be the only means of education'. 'Far from it,' it concluded, 'competition, where not excessive, is good in education as in everything else.' Moreover it argued that 'such children as may show themselves to be worthy of higher instruction should be enabled to receive it not perhaps by means of public rates and taxes, but by the use of those magnificent endowments left by the philanthropy and piety of our ancestors'.

And such an education, it continued, should be in sound information—not in 'classics and literature'. Even 'education in science' should be only 'as far as it is useful in the arts, and not in regard to its higher and abstract forms'.[27]

When one considers that this journal, by its own admission, was intended for inventors, manufacturers, intelligent artisans and young persons preparing for trades and professions, one can see that Arnold did not write in vain.

But by 1882 such competition was seen, even by faithful churchmen schoolmasters, to be at best idealistic. In that very year the Church Congress was told by T. E. Heller, a foundation *member* of the London Church Teachers' Association and the first full-time, paid secretary of the N.U.E.T., that it should let the School Boards take over their schools if they could not afford to maintain them adequately.[28]

(viii)

Heller's stance illustrates the momentum destined to be generated in the educational system itself. When the elementary school teachers were convened as a body on 9 April 1870 by John Whitwell M.P. for Kendal to give their opinions, one important principle emerged: consultation.

Later in the year Whitwell was to press for 'some prudential plan of mutual assurance, assisted by the Privy Council'. A month and a half later, on 25 June, their various unions came together to form a National Union of Elementary School Teachers, later (1889) to be known as the N.U.T. Further association of board and church school teachers strengthened mutual self-respect *vis à vis* School Boards and clerical employers alike, whilst the abolition of clerical inspectors and the trend (accelerated by Mundella) to look for promising teachers as H.M.I.s, opened up a career pattern.

Their enhanced status was presciently anticipated by Disraeli when he warned the government:

'You will not entrust the priest or the presbyter with the privilege of expounding the Holy Scriptures to the scholars; but for that purpose you are inventing and establishing a new sacerdotal class. The schoolmaster who will exercise these functions, and who will occupy this position, will be a member of a class which will, in the future, exercise an extraordinary influence upon the history of England and upon the conduct of Englishmen.'[29]

The displacement of the old clerisy was to be accelerated by the behaviour of the clergy and managers of church schools. For just as they resisted the introduction of a conscience clause before 1870, so after 1870, by denouncing School Boards as godless institutions, they threw away what J.G. Fitch called 'the best chance—possibly the last chance that will be given them in English history—of exercising a salutary influence over primary education, and identifying themselves heartily with popular institutions.'[30]

(ix)

In assessing the results of 1870 we must beware of taking inspectors' reports at their face value. As a writer of many of them, Fitch warned his contemporaries (and by implication posterity) against taking their reports too seriously, since inspectors have to

'expose faults in a frank and inspiring manner, in the hope of elevating the aims of all parties from year to year'. But, he added 'all this criticism is perfectly consistent with the belief that in the large majority of aided schools the work for which they exist is honestly and efficiently done; and that neither the schools nor the teachers can, as a class, be correctly described in the language which is officially applied to a portion of them.'[31]

Secondly, we must also re-examine the statistical evidence of deprivation. The pre-1870 estimate of from one to two million children growing up without education was described by Horace Mann[32] as 'an obvious arithmetical fallacy', which he hoped would not stampede the government into 'premature, imperfect compromising measures' whereby 'any real settlement would be hindered'. Mann thought the future of the country might be affected less by the quantity of education as by the nature of the system which provided it. So he argued (1) for education to be paid for out of general taxation (and not the rates), and (2) for it to apply equally to all classes of the community and not to workmen alone. He put forward another argument, that the working classes should be consulted as to whether they wanted charity schools or common schools—'stereotyped distinctions' or the 'fusion of classes'. 'Surely,' he wrote, 'we are not yet morally competent to decide upon the form of an extensive change which, one way or another, must exert an incalculable influence on the future history of England.' He argued, and I think conclusively, that

'we should advance to the only logical resting place, and regard the whole education of the community, upper, middle and lower sections all together, as a task to be accomplished jointly instead of severally—by the co-operation of the whole body rather than by the individual efforts, aided and unaided of each member. ... The time has surely arrived for perceiving there is no stopping short of this.'[33]

(x)

Are we as ready in 1970 to do this as in 1870? The strength of our assent is a measure of what Forster's Act set in motion. And what it did set in motion were more sophisticated attempts to measure what the educational process was trying to do. For within fifteen years of the Act coming on to the Statute Book the School Board visitors of Birmingham had been able to supply such useful information to the Royal Commission on the Housing of the Working Classes that Joseph Chamberlain suggested to Beatrice Potter (later to marry Sidney Webb) that they might be useful to her uncle Charles Booth who was attracted by the terrible Darwinian struggle for mastery that went on in the mean streets of London's East End.[34] As a natural conservative he challenged the emotive socialist statistic that one in four lived in abject poverty and that this might incubate a real revolution. Indeed he told F. D. Hyndman, of the Social Democratic Federation, that he would refute this case. This led him to go beyond Horace Mann's reliance on the census reports and, with the help of his niece Beatrice and numerous other workers, he supplemented his findings by those of the 250 London School Board visitors. By 1891 Mary Tabot was able to report of the board schools in his second of his seventeen volume study:

> 'The health and convenience of both children and teachers have been carefully considered, and in the later ones especially have been increasingly secured. They accommodate a little over 443,000 children, and have been erected at a cost of about four and a half millions sterling. Taken as a whole they may be said fairly to represent the high-water-mark of the public conscience in this country in its relation to the children of the people.'[35]

When Booth himself came to sum up in the seventeenth and final volume of his study, the School Boards had just been supplanted by the County and County Borough authorities. His words provide a conservative estimate of their achievement:

> 'A whole generation has been through the schools, but in scholarship there is not much to show for it. Almost all can, indeed, read, though with some effort; and write, after a fashion; but those who can do either the one or the other with the facility that comes of constant practice are comparatively few. Nevertheless, popular education has been far from wasted even in the case of those who may seem to have learnt but very little. Obedience to discipline and rules of proper behaviour have been inculcated; habits of order and cleanliness have been acquired; and from these habits of self-respect arises. Thus the boys who have experienced school life, however rudimentary their knowledge of the most elementary subjects, and although they may remember nothing else that has been taught, may yet be better fitted to take up the duties of adult life. The same is true of girls, whose teaching moreover seems to be more directly useful as well as more successful than that of boys; while with regard to the parents, the fathers and mothers who have experienced school life, are no longer unfriendly to education. They do, indeed, nearly always take their children away from school at the earliest possible age, but are nevertheless far more anxious that they should benefit by the advantages offered than were their own parents. The old attitude of suspicion, often amounting to hostility, has almost passed away.'

Though generally sceptical of large-scale measures of socialist panaceas, Booth nevertheless concluded:

> 'Brighter light breaks through when we pass from the general to the particular. If we think of the overwhelming mass of ignorance that still persists, we must not forget the case of boys and girls who eagerly grasp every opportunity, and, even if by units, justify the perfecting of the ladder of learning now reaching from elementary school to university. Once more two tasks lie before us: To lift the whole level by recognizing the part which elementary education can really play, and then adapting it for that part; and also to increase the number and the opportunities of those who are capable of profiting more fully by the training they receive.'[36]

Notes

1 *Report of the First General Meeting of Members of the National Education League held at Birmingham on Tuesday and Wednesday, October 12 and 13 1869*, Birmingham, The Journal Printing Offices, New Street, 1869, p. 185. Hereafter cited as *Report*.

2 For the connection between Hill Top and the late eighteenth-century scientific group in Birmingham known as the Lunar Society, see *University of Birmingham Historical Journal*, XI, No. 1, 1967, pp. 65–67.

3 E.g. the findings of those made by the Manchester Education Aid Society in 1864 and those made by a similar society in Birmingham had led on 12 March 1869 to a debate in the House of Commons which resulted in the appointment of J. G. Fitch to report on the shortage in Birmingham and Leeds, and of D. R. Feason to report on Liverpool and Manchester.

4 In his article 'The Genesis of American Engineering Competition 1850–70', *Economic History*, ii, 1930, pp. 292, 311, D. L. Burn argues (pp. 302–3) that it 'had developed most in regard to certain Birmingham industries and it was described in 1867 to a Parliamentary Committee by A. Field, President of the Birmingham Chamber of Commerce, who was concerned in the hardware export trade'.

5 N. 1 supra, p. 152 ff.

6 For their change of heart at this time see W. O. Lester Smith, *To Whom Do the Schools Belong*, Oxford, Basil Blackwell, 1942.

7 *Report*, p. 88.

8 A. W. Humphrey, *A History of Labour Representation*, London, Constable & Co., 1912; Robert Applegarth, *Trade Unionist, educationist, reformer*, London, National Labour Press, 1913.

9 Chadwick's suggestion that the Factory, School and Prison Inspectorate should be integrated in each district, and thrown open to teachers, or to those who had passed an examination in teaching method. See *Transaction of the National Association for the Promotion of Social Science*.

10 *Reports of Inspectors of Factories*, Parliamentary Papers, 1868–69, XIV, p. 479.

11 *Ibid.*, p. 501.

12 Report, *op. cit.*, p. 114.

13 Francis Adams, *The Elementary School Contest*, London, Chapman & Hall, 1882, pp. 200, 208. It is worth noting that Jesse Collings' *An Outline of the American School System with Remarks on the Establishment of Common Schools in England*, Birmingham, Journal Office, 1868, was avowedly 'extracted almost literally' from the report by the Bishop of Manchester, James Fraser.

14 The secretary of the National Education Union, the League's opponent, the R William Stanyer, published *A verbatim report, with indexes, of the debate in Parliament during the progress of the Elementary Education Bill 1870 together with a reprint of the Act* (Manchester and London n.d.) which is most useful. Hereafter cited as *Verbatim Report.*

15 Its secretary, Francis Schnadhorst (1840–1900), graduated to secretaryship of the Birmingham Liberal Association. He later founded the National Liberal Federation on 31 May 1877, which was mainly responsible for the Liberal election victories of 1880, 1885 and 1892.

16 Francis Adams, *op. cit.*, p. 215.

17 A. G. Gardiner, *Life of Harcourt*, 1923, Vol. I, p. 2.

18 *Verbatim Report*, p. 168.

19 *Ibid.*, p. 392.

20 *Report*, p. 132.

21 *Ibid.*, p. 40.

22 *Verbatim Report*, p. 74.

23 *Ibid.*, pp. 420–22.

24 S. and V. Leff, *The School Health Service*, London, H. K. Lewis, 1959, p. 29.

25 *Verbatim Report*, p. 192.

26 *Ibid.*, p. 194.

27 *Scientific Review and Scientific and Literary Review. A Record of Progress in Arts, Industry and Manufacture incorporating the Journal of the Inventors' Institute,* December, Vol. XI (1875), pp. 175–76.

28 A. Tropp, *The School Teachers: The Growth of the Teaching Profession in England and Wales from 1800 to the Present Day*, London, Heinemann, 1957, p. 173.

29 *Verbatim Report*, pp. 158–59.

30 J. G. Fitch, 'Statistical Fallacies Respecting Public Instruction', *Fortnightly Review,* XIV, p. 627.

31 *Ibid.*, pp. 623–24.

32 Horace Mann, 'National Education', *Transactions of the National Association for the Promotion of Social Science,* Bristol Meeting 1869, London, Longmans, Green, Reader and Dyer, 1870, pp. 364–72. Mann is one of the neglected figures *in* English education. We should not, as Frank Smith did, confuse him with his American namesake for he deserves attention in his own right. He is perhaps best known for his analysis of the 1851 census in educational terms, though this was often quoted later by Cobden in the Commons and Brougham in the Lords to pressurize their demand for national legislation. See Frank Smith, *A History of English Elementary Education 1760–1902*, London, University of London Press, 1931, p. 200.

33 *Ibid.*

34 T. S. and M. B. Simey, *Charles Booth, Social Scientist*, Oxford, University Press, 1960, pp. 80–81.

35 Charles Booth (ed.), *Labour and Life of the People. Vol ii London,* London, Williams & Norgate, 1891, p. 49.

36 Charles Booth, *Labour and Life of the People in London.* Final Volume: *Notes on Social Influences and Conclusion,* 1903, pp. 203–4. In view of the influence of America on the school boards it is interesting to note that two Americans, Albert Fried and Richard M. Elman who edited and selected Booth's writings under the title *of Charles Booth's London,* London, Hutchinson, 1969, remark p. xiii on the 'relevance' of that era to their own time, the anticipatory nature of many of his recommendations, and the model nature of his enquiry into urban poverty.

5 Christian Theology and Educational Theory: Can there be Connections?

J. Hull

1976

Author

John Hull is Emeritus Professor of Religious Education in the University of Birmingham and the only Australian and blind man in this collection of articles. In 1989 he was awarded a personal chair at Birmingham as the first Professor of Religious Education in a United Kingdom university. He became Dean of the then Faculty of Education and Continuing Studies in 1990, and held this post for three and a half years. Hull has been a leading figure in the transformation of religious education in English and Welsh schools, and he is a co-founder of the International Seminar on Religious Education and Values. In recent years he has been particularly concerned to understand the problems of the education of adults in relation to the Church and Christian faith. From 1971 to 1996 Hull was Editor of the *British Journal of Religious Education*. In January 2006 the University of Cambridge conferred the degree of Litt.D. on him.

Introduction

John Hull's article *Christian Theology and Educational Theory: Can there be Connections?* (2, 2: 127–43) is unique in the sense that it is the first article to appear in the *Journal* to directly address Christianity and the theory of education. A. V. Beales, the editor at the time, had included previous articles on Christianity and education in the pages of the *Journal*, such as *Neo-Thomism and Education* (7, 1: 27–35), and *The Christian fathers and the moral training of the young* (3, 1: 24–32), but Hull's was the first to make a serious theoretical attempt at using the Christian theology as a discipline within education in order to suggest a theology of education. The article is concerned with the nature of the relation between theology and educational theory and attempts to criticise, clarify and give new directions to education in the light of contemporary religious ideas. Hull effectively challenges Paul Hirst's claims that there can be no useful and coherent relations between theology and educational theory. He attempts in this article to expand thinking in this relatively under-developed interdisciplinary field of theology of education, but on the question of what is theology of education Hull answers that there are almost as many theologies of education as there are theologies.

Consequently, he argues that there are Jewish, Christian, Islamic and Hindu theologies of education and recognises that there are further complications because they are mediated by the word 'education'. The article was reprinted twice in his *Studies in Religion and Education* (1984) and in Jeff Astley and Leslie J. Francis (eds) *Critical Perspectives on Christian Education: a Reader on the Aims, Principles and Philosophy of Christian Education* (1994).

Hull's work was also celebrated by the publication of *Education, Religion and Society – Essays in Honour of John M. Hull* (2005), which was edited by Dennis Bates, Gloria Durka and Friedrich Schweitzer. The book contains his writings up to the beginning of 2005 and provides both an excellent introduction to contemporary issues of religious education together with the most complete critical account of his work, including his article on theology of education.

Christian Theology and Educational Theory: Can there be Connections?

by John M. Hull, School of Education, University of Birmingham

A. Introduction

This paper is not concerned with religious education in the curriculum but with the nature of the relation between theology and educational theory. All sophisticated religious belief systems have histories of such relations, the literature of Christianity, Judaism and Islam being particularly rich. Theology of education at the present time is an active field of interdisciplinary study. Recent dissertation abstracts indicate the sort of work taking place[1] in an effort to criticize, clarify and give new directions to education in the light of contemporary religious ideas.

It has now been denied that this activity is a legitimate one.

B. Exposition

In his book *Moral Education in a Secular Society* (University of London Press, 1974) Professor Paul Hirst claims that there can be no useful and coherent relations between theology and educational theory. Hirst argues that 'there has now emerged in our society a concept of education which makes the whole idea of Christian education a kind of nonsense' (p. 77). Just as mathematics, engineering and farming are characterized by intrinsic and autonomous norms, so is education. There can no more be a 'characteristically or distinctively Christian form of education' than there can be a 'distinctively Christian form of mathematics' (p. 77). The process of secularization, which has already brought about autonomy in these fields, is now according 'an exactly similar status' to education (p. 68).

Hirst describes two ways in which one might attempt to create a Christian philosophy of education. First, one might start with 'very general moral principles' and seek to draw educational conclusions. But, Hirst remarks, even although these moral principles might be supported from Christian sources, they are 'usually not in any sense significantly Christian' (p. 78). Second, one might begin with what is said in the Bible about education and try to apply this to teaching today. Problems such as the cultural remoteness of the Bible and the controversies surrounding its interpretation vitiate this enterprise, so that 'a distinctive Biblical or Christian view of education simply is not discoverable' (p. 79).

Hirst then distinguishes two concepts of education. The first is 'primitive' education, which is the view a 'primitive tribe' might have of education as the uncritical passing on of customs and beliefs.[2] There may be distinctively Christian, Humanist or Buddhist concepts of this sort of education 'according to which Christians seek that the next generation shall think likewise' (p. 80). The second concept of education is marked by a concern for objective knowledge, for truth and for reasons, and it will set out for pupils the methods and procedures of the various disciplines according to public criteria. But religious and Humanist beliefs, continues the argument, must themselves be assessed by such criteria and so the principles of education are 'logically more fundamental' than those of the particular religious communities. Consequently, 'the character of education is not settled by any appeal to Christian, Humanist or Buddhist beliefs' (p. 81).

The autonomy of education is then compared with various other pursuits, such as morality and history; it is concluded that although education may certainly promote an understanding of a faith it may not seek to develop 'a disposition to worship in that faith' (p. 84).

I have no quarrel with this account of the sort of religious education proper to an educational curriculum. It may be worth pointing out that from his 1965 article on religious education[3] through his 1973 article in *Learning for Living*[4] right up to the present book, Hirst has consistently defended the existence of a critical, open study of religion in the schools. Reviewers of *Moral Education in a Secular Society*, confusing a denial that theology of education is proper with a denial that teaching religion is proper, are mistakenly claiming that Hirst is now against any teaching of religion in schools.[5] But Hirst is wrong, in my view, in thinking that in order to protect the independence of secular education against proselytizing groups such as Christians it is necessary to deny the possibility of constructing a useful relation between Christian faith and this concept of critical, open education.

Before we consider his discussion in detail, it may be helpful to distinguish five kinds of possible relations between Christian theology and education.

1 Christian theology might be both necessary and sufficient for an understanding of education.
2 Christian theology might provide a necessary but not a sufficient understanding of education. Theology might, in this case, need assistance from philosophy or psychology.
3 Christian theology might provide a sufficient but not a necessary understanding of education. Other belief systems, including nonreligious ones, might also be able to offer sufficient accounts of education.
4 Christian theology might provide a possible and legitimate understanding of education, but one which is neither sufficient nor necessary.
5 Christian theology might be impossible and illegitimate as a way of understanding education. It would have no contribution to offer.

It is the last of these positions which Hirst adopts. ' ... the search for a Christian approach to, or philosophy of, education [is] a huge mistake'.[6] ' ... judging what is good or bad in education is nothing to do with whether one is a Christian, a Humanist or a Buddhist'.[7] This, for Hirst, is a matter of principle. 'But if I once thought ... the pursuit of a distinctively Christian form of education in principle satisfactory, I have now come to the conclusion that even that is not so.'[8] Moreover, having relentlessly pressed the attack by showing the insufficiency of the Bible for an understanding of education, he will not allow the poor Christian to make a last stand in a tiny corner of the field. 'If one cannot get everything necessary for educational practice from Christian teaching, surely one can get something distinctive' (p. 79). Hirst's reply is that any relation between Christian theology and education will be only with the primitive notion of education. With this area, in which the 'tribe ... seeks to pass on to the next generation its rituals' (p. 80), Christians must be content, and here 'there will be as many concepts of education as there are systems of beliefs and values' (p. 80). This is small comfort indeed, since Hirst goes on to ask whether in this tribal sense the word 'education' should be used at all. 'Indeed I suggest that this pursuit is in fact now increasingly considered immoral.'[9] When it comes to rational, sophisticated education 'dominated by a concern for knowledge, for truth, for reasons' (p. 80) then 'there can be no such thing as Christian education'.[10]

Hirst seems to be reacting against the sort of relations I have set out above as numbers one, two and three. He sometimes uses forensic terminology to describe the improper relations between theology and education. Nothing in education can be 'decided properly by appeal' to Christian sources; 'the issues must be settled independently of any questions of religious belief' (pp. 77f.). He not only undertakes to attack the first three positions and to defend the final one but he seeks to commend this fifth relation to the Christian. He agrees that not all Christians will find his approach acceptable, especially those 'who are convinced of the total sufficiency of biblical revelation for the conduct of all human affairs',[11] but there is no 'necessary contradiction between Christian beliefs and education in this [sophisticated] sense, provided Christian beliefs form a rationally coherent system'.[12] Considerable attention is given to the 'secular Christian', to whom Hirst thinks the fifth position should be acceptable.

Hirst does not appear to envisage the modest modus vivendi between theology and education suggested in my fourth kind of relation. Hirst and I are in agreement in rejecting the first three models. In what follows the various arguments used to support the 'impossible and illegitimate' relation will be examined. We will then estimate Hirst's success in commending this position to the 'secular Christian'.

C. Criticism

1. *The Sociological Arguments*

The central concept in this opening group of arguments is 'secularization'. This is described in the opening chapter, applied to morals in following chapters and to the relation between theology and education in chapter five. Secularization is regarded as 'a decay in the use of religious concepts and beliefs' (p. i). This means that 'supernatural interpretations of experience have been progressively replaced by others' (p. 2). The status of science, morals, aesthetics and other modes of thought is now such that 'religious considerations can be ignored'. This does not mean that 'all religious beliefs can be shown to be unintelligible or false. It is rather that [they] come to be seen as of no consequence, having nothing to contribute in our efforts to understand ourselves and our world and to determine how we are to live' (p. 2).

It is difficult to ascertain whether Hirst is merely offering a description of certain historical and social processes, or whether he thinks the processes are significant for the logical relations between religion and other modes of thought. Frequently, the former is the impression given, although conclusions tend to be drawn as if the latter had been established. Thus the decay is in the 'use' of religious concepts. 'There was a time when more people were … involved' in religion, and religious views are now but 'rarely voiced'. So 'religious understanding has … come to look more and more redundant' and religious beliefs 'come to be seen as of no consequence'. This is the language of mere description. No doubt such a situation exists, and is quite properly bringing about important changes in the relations between the churches and the schools and the way religion is now taught as a subject in schools.[13] But this has little to do with the logical possibility or the intellectual legitimacy of attempting to formulate conceptual links between theology and theories of education.

Basic distinctions about the secularization processes are ignored. One can usefully distinguish between 'secularization' as the historical process whereby social and intellectual life has been freed from dominance by theological concepts, and 'secularism', the stronger claim that this has the (logical or psychological) consequence of rendering religious belief (actually or apparently) meaningless and irrelevant. One can also distinguish between ecclesiastical secularization, which has to do with the relations between institutionalized religion and the rest of society, and theological or conceptual secularization, which has to do with the coherence and vitality of theology in relations with the secular world. These distinctions between the sociology of religion and the logical relations which theology has with other fields are blurred in general descriptions of 'religion' or 'religious belief'. It could be pointed out, for example, that ecclesiastical secularization has been followed by the secularization of theology itself which now exists in a state of secular autonomy similar to that enjoyed by the other intellectual disciplines. Hirst concludes that the autonomy of the secular spheres (he does not reckon theology to be one of them) means that religious considerations 'can be ignored'. Of course they can. Theology is no longer, as it was in the world of the Thomistic *Summa*, both necessary and sufficient for all systematic thought. But must it be ignored? Is the alleged irrelevancy of religious thought a possibility or a necessity? No evidence is offered for believing that the latter is the case, and so Hirst jumps from the first of the five relations between theology and the world of thought to the fourth (or something like it) when considering theology and morals and straight on to the fifth when considering theology and education, without pausing to offer reasons for being required to adopt these later forms of relation.

The second part of Hirst's discussion of secularization has to do with the 'privatization' of religion. In interpreting this discussion, it may be helpful to consider an earlier account of privatization, in which Hirst had suggested that the values upon which the common school must be based should be 'acceptable to all irrespective of any particular religious or non-religious claims'.[14] 'Public values' must be distinguished from these latter 'private values'. The domain of scientific knowledge seems part of the public world but religious beliefs 'which have no generally acceptable public tests of validity'[15] are probably in the private area. Values which 'necessarily rest on particular religious beliefs' are also private, although a citizen may have an education consistent with his private religion. In order not to create the impression that the public school is non-religious or anti-religious, it should be understood that the education it offers can be but partial.

Hirst seems to have held that what the private communities of faith do in their schools is genuinely educational, in that it deals with areas of private values with which the public school cannot deal, and in this way such private education is a necessary or at least a legitimate complement to public education. In the later writings we are considering, the distinction between 'primitive' and 'sophisticated' education seems to take the place of the earlier distinction between 'private' and 'public' value education, and the idea of the religious community offering a legitimate complement to public education, a complement arising directly from its own values yet still being educational, becomes less important, if not immoral.

In the public schools, Hirst continues, methods of teaching must also be in terms of public values. 'Are there Christian methods of teaching Boyle's law which differ from atheistic methods?'[16] Hirst however does not deny that a teacher's private values may affect his teaching, only that it can never be claimed that his private values must affect his teaching. Hirst seems then at this stage to have had in mind something rather like the fourth of our relations between theology and education, in which religious beliefs could provide a possible but not a necessary or sufficient contribution.

The criteria of knowledge, Hirst continues, are public, and the public school can offer education in at least 'established areas of knowledge'.[17] The idea of the 'autonomy' of a 'domain of knowledge' is now introduced in this 1967 essay. Some agreement, Hirst remarks, is mere consensus but some is 'rationally compelled' on the basis of public criteria.[18] At present, we only have consensus agreement in the moral area. But if moral agreement could be won on the basis of public, rational criteria, then we would have an autonomous basis for the common school. In his 1965 article 'Liberal education and the nature of knowledge' the idea of the 'autonomy' of the various forms of knowledge does not appear, but in another article from the same year, 'Morals, religion and the maintained school',[19] the idea of 'autonomy' does emerge when discussing the extent to which morals may be regarded as independent of theology. 'Autonomy' and 'privatization' both become key concepts in the 1974 book under discussion. The germs of the 1967 article on 'privatization' are now mature. Morals may at last be justified on independent, rational grounds. Religion however is now severely privatized and the conclusion is drawn that 'When the domain of religious beliefs is so manifestly one in which there are at present no clearly recognizable objective grounds for judging claims, to base education on any such claims would be to forsake the pursuit of objectivity' (p. 81).

So, in a society in which religion has become privatized, 'the widest range of attitudes to religious beliefs is acceptable, provided they are never allowed to determine public issues', and 'it is a mark of the secular society that it is religiously plural, tolerating all forms of religious belief and practice that do not contravene agreed public principles' (p. 3).

One notices the strangely conservative social attitude implied by this approach. Nothing must contravene the public order. We also observe that in discussing society in this way, Hirst is not speaking of the logic or the epistemology of the forms of knowledge, but of convention. The significant 1967 distinction between consensus agreement and rational agreement does not appear. No logical conclusions can be drawn therefore one way or the other about the possibility of relating the conceptual worlds of theology and education on the basis of such an undifferentiated concept of 'privatization'. We observe finally the stringency of Hirst's conditions. Religion must not be allowed to 'determine' public issues. It must not 'contravene' public principles. But may it not even influence them? (Cf. p. 55.) May it not be allowed to have some legitimate effect? Why, on this argument, must it be thought of as having nothing to contribute? How can a claim (of whatever strength) that religion must not be allowed to determine public issues such as education lead to the conclusion that there can be no legitimate attempt to construct a Christian philosophy of education in which Christian theology would be but one (influencing but not determining) factor amongst others? What has happened to the private religious values of 1967? A citizen could express these through education provided they did not contravene public values. Must theology now necessarily contravene them? Can Christian faith then never be an ally of the open society?

2. The Logical Arguments

Hirst claims that the emerging, secular concept of education makes the possibility of a relation between Christianity and education 'a kind of nonsense' (p. 77).

First Argument

Education, like mathematics, engineering and farming, is governed by its own intrinsic principles. What is good of its kind in each of these areas is determined by those inner principles and not by reference to theological factors. Bridges stay or fall down for Christians and atheists alike. God, we may add, sends his rain upon the just and the unjust.

But is there really a parallel of this sort between education and mathematics? Does what appertains in the latter, abstract, self-sufficient form of knowledge in which inescapable conclusions are drawn also apply to a value-laden, practical enterprise like education? Education, it must be remembered, is not one of the forms of knowledge. It does not have a unique and distinctive mode of thought nor a characteristic epistemology, but is, like medicine, an applied field in which various other disciplines, some of which are true forms of knowledge, impinge in order to enable the activity to take place. In the cases of medicine and education, these other disciplines are things like anatomy, chemistry, immunology, philosophy and psychology. Medicine and education do not however lack coherence.

They derive it not from the structure of their epistemology but from their concentration upon healing or educating people. Their coherence is such as is demanded by a practical enterprise; it is not the coherence of internally self-sufficient principles and it should not therefore be compared to the logical 'autonomy' of mathematics.

In his 1965 article on 'Liberal education' Hirst described political, legal and educational theory as 'fields where moral knowledge of a developed kind is to be found'.[20] Engineering, in the same article, is described as a 'field' and no doubt this would be true of farming as well. We are thus comparing

(a)   an indisputable form of knowledge in which moral knowledge of a developed kind is not found (mathematics);
(b)   two fields in which moral knowledge is similarly not well developed (engineering and farming);
(c)   a field in which moral knowledge is well developed (education); and
(d)   a disputable form of knowledge in which moral knowledge is well developed (religion).

It is obvious that (a), (b) and (c) do not exhibit 'exactly similar status' (p. 78) in the kinds and degrees of the autonomy they possess. Their relations both with the moral sphere and the religious sphere will be different in each case. Farming, for example, does not have the self-sufficient logic of mathematics. What is good farming may quite properly be determined by political principles in China, by religious principles in India, and by environmentalist considerations in Western Europe. There will be no clash between the principles of good farming and any of these contexts, because the context has a significant part to play in determining what the principles of good farming actually are. There is, of course, a level of unchangeable circumstances, usually based upon cause and effect sequence in the natural world, at which the techniques of farming and education will be autonomous. Even the devil, if he wants tares, has to sow tares. Wheat produces wheat for angels and devils alike. But whether you pluck the tares up or leave them both to grow together until the harvest is a matter of value judgments and long-term considerations involving questions of religion and philosophy which goes far beyond the simple technical level. The objective psychological test will yield the same result for both the Christian and the atheist educational psychologist, and the techniques for the early diagnosis of speech defects are just whatever they are, since speech is just what it is, and defects are defined accordingly. Christians and atheists sharing the same speech conventions will not differ at this level. But to whom the objective test is to be administered, and what use is to be made of the results and why—these problems introduce evaluative questions as well as a wider factual context and at this point the techniques themselves are no longer autonomous. They need the help of sociology, ethics and so on. Secularization has had considerable effect even at this technical level, since the sensible Christian and the sensible atheist agree in using terms like 'emotional disorder' rather than ones like 'demonic possession', and they agree to use the techniques of medical therapy not those of exorcism. There are other Christians who resist this sort of secularization, but neither Hirst nor I are concerned with them.

The impact of the secularization process must not be denied, but it must be carefully qualified. Technical autonomy does not bring self-sufficiency to education.

Pedagogy may be described as a conglomerate of technical skills applied in the education of children. Education offers the ideals, the purposes and the values which guide this application. Pedagogy is thus applied education, education is applied philosophical anthropology, and it certainly cannot be claimed that philosophical anthropology is determined by principles which are 'neither for nor against' theological anthropology. Even although philosophical anthropology cannot perhaps be 'settled' by 'appeal' to theological anthropology, or to anything else, theology has a legitimate and perhaps a significant contribution to make to its elucidation. When it comes to the question, what is man?, theologians are also men, and if, like philosophers, they are sensible and rational men, their theological reflections need not be silenced.

Second Argument

On this second view (the sophisticated one), the character of education is not settled by any appeal to Christian, Humanist or Buddhist beliefs. Such an appeal is illegitimate, for the basis is logically more fundamental, being found in the canons of objectivity and reasons, canons against which Christian, Humanist and Buddhist beliefs must, in their turn and in the appropriate way, be assessed (p. 81). This may be paraphrased as follows. The sophisticated concept of education is governed by rational, objective principles. But these very principles must be used to assess the religious and non-religious belief systems. No such belief system can therefore generate an understanding of such a critical concept of education, because the principles upon which the latter rests are more fundamental than the belief systems themselves.

But

(a) if this is so, education cannot be appraised by anything, since psychology, sociology, and all the rest of the scrutinizing disciplines are also, in their turn and in the appropriate way, to be assessed by rational criteria more fundamental than their particular and distinctive techniques of assessment. Even particular moral criticism is subject to more basic rational moral principles which are used to assess the status of the moral claims being made. This is transcendental autonomy for education with a vengeance.

(b) It may be that Hirst is influenced by the thought that theology is in some way a supernatural activity, pretending immunity from rational criticism. If this is in his mind, then it is rather a restricted and perhaps an old-fashioned view of theology. Theology is concerned with the concepts of religion, with their adequacy as expressive of religious experience and with the problems of constructing them into coherent belief systems. It claims validity according to distinctive but not supernatural norms.[21]

(c)   It may be objected that Hirst does not say 'cannot generate an understanding of' but 'is not settled by any appeal to'. But (i) Hirst does not distinguish between the adjudicating function of a discipline and its illuminating function. This is a major criticism of his approach. The paraphrase, expressing the milder, illuminatory function, does no injustice to his discernible intentions, (ii) If however the stronger interpretation is insisted upon, then point (a) above not only still holds good but is strengthened. Disciplines which cannot even illuminate certainly cannot adjudicate.

Third Argument

'When the domain of religious belief is so manifestly one in which there are at present no clearly recognizable objective grounds for judging claims, to base education on any such claims would be to forsake the pursuit of objectivity' (p. 81).

(a)   Such a strongly worded, negative conclusion about the possibility of recognizing objective tests of truth in religion appears to be new in Hirst's writings. As recently as 1973, discussing whether religion is a unique form of knowledge in his important article, 'The forms of knowledge revisited', Hirst concluded, 'On the answer to that question few would dare to pronounce categorically. My own view, as in the case of the arts, is that in the present state of affairs we must at least take the claim to knowledge seriously. ... Equally, it seems to me unclear that one can coherently claim that there is a logically unique domain of religious beliefs [Hirst's emphasis] such that none of them can be known to be true, all being matters of faith.'[22] It would be interesting to know, since we are not told, what further reflections have enabled Hirst to move from the earlier position where the claim to religious knowledge had at least to be taken seriously to the position in the present book where it is 'so manifest' that religion lacks this status. It is difficult to avoid the impression that in order to break the links between theology and education Hirst is slightly exaggerating the clarity and the unanimity of the alleged negative verdict upon the logical status of religious claims.

(b)   But even if we move with Hirst, although he gives us no reason to do so, to the new, severe position, would it follow that there could be no proper or useful relation between theology and education? Although in the 1973 article just mentioned, religion was still being seriously considered for 'form of knowledge' status, history and the social sciences had already been abandoned. 'I now think it best not to refer to history or the social sciences in any statement of the forms of knowledge as such. These pursuits ... may well be concerned with truths of several different logical kinds.'[23] (There is, by the way, a parallel here with religion, since 'Christian theology' is regarded by Hirst as a discipline within religion, and religious studies is cross-disciplinary in several senses.[24]) Indeed, the result of Hirst's 1973 revision of the forms of knowledge argument, which is now cast in more strictly propositional shape, is, as Hirst emphasizes, to reduce the forms of the categories of true propositions to only two: 'truths of the physical world' and 'truths of a mental or personal kind'.[25]

It would appear then that either not being a domain of knowledge does not vitiate the capacity of an area of enquiry to relate itself meaningfully to the practical field of education or if only domains of knowledge may appraise education, then not only can there be no theology of education, but no historical appraisal of education, only a dubious aesthetic scrutiny and no psychology or sociology of education.

(c) Hirst remarks that the application of the whole theory of the domains of knowledge to education is strictly limited. It may be then that one contribution of theology (if it were to fail to secure 'domain of knowledge' status) might lie in those areas with which the formal epistemological categories do not so easily deal. Hirst mentions several of these.[26]

(d) In this argument Hirst again employs the device we find so frequently in the pages we are considering. He sets the most severe conditions, and then allows no place at all in education to a discipline which cannot meet them. So we are required to contemplate the possibility of basing education on theology. What does this mean? Does Hirst really anticipate a situation in which Christians would argue that only theists could be educators? This is certainly not what contemporary theology of education seeks to show. Far from insisting that all educators must be theologians, it is only asked that some theologians be allowed to remain educators. Hirst's argument appears then as an unconvincing attempt to establish an excluded middle.

Fourth Argument

' ... an education based on a concern for objectivity and reason, far from allying itself with any specific religious claims, must involve teaching the radically controversial character of all such claims. An understanding of religious claims it can perfectly well aim at, but commitment to any one set, in the interests of objectivity, it cannot either assume or pursue' (p. 81).

This claim about the relationship between the 'basis' of education and the need for a critical curriculum raises two questions, (a) By what characteristic can a theology generate an understanding of the critical, sophisticated concept of education? (b) What is the relation between the aims of theology of education and the aims of teaching religion as a school subject?

On (a), not all theological systems can avoid the difficulty Hirst mentions. There certainly are forms of theology which can lead only to the 'primitive' concept of education in which, for example, the task would be to ensure that subsequent generations of Christians all thought alike. But just as not all theologies avoid the danger, so also not all of them succumb to it. There are forms of Christian theology in which critical enquiry and controversial examination flow directly and necessarily from the values and beliefs to which the theology is committed. It then exhibits these intellectual characteristics not in spite of its commitment but because of it. An alliance (which does not mean an exclusive, unique or necessary derivation of education from this theology) between such theology and such education, far from hindering the critical freedom of education, might do a little to enhance and support it. It is apparent therefore that Hirst does not sufficiently discriminate between the degrees to which different religious belief systems have built into their structures necessary elements of on-going self-criticism.

On (b), Hirst and I do not disagree about the aims and limits of religious education as a classroom subject. But whereas he thinks the commitment of the theologian in education inhibits him in the carrying out of this critical task, I think it may help him. I agree too that public educational institutions in a pluralist, secular society ought not to be committed to one religion, and consequently that compulsory, unanimous or official school worship is wrong in principle. Again, the question is whether a Christian philosophy or theology of education precludes or advances that view of religious education and of the stance to be adopted by such institutions.

3. The Methodological Arguments

Hirst claims that even if it were a legitimate enterprise, the methodological difficulties are such that no worthwhile work can be done in this area. His discussion has been summarized above.

Naturally, there are difficulties of method in any interdisciplinary study, and the various fields of practical or applied theology are not exempt. Theology receives no special supernatural aid. There is an extensive modern literature dealing with the relations between Christian theology and, for example, culture, the arts, politics, science and medicine. Many of these studies include detailed consideration of problems of method.[27] In theology of education, the two methods discussed by Hirst are by no means the only ones; indeed, they are, as he points out, rather naïve and inadequate. This is not the place to enter into a discussion of how it might be undertaken, it being sufficient for our present purposes to remark that it is not appropriate to contrast sophisticated educational thinking with a sample of simple and even crude theological methods.

4. The 'Secular Christian'

Hirst suggests that the position he outlines between Christian faith and education is one which ought to commend itself to certain Christians. ' … it seems to me it is precisely the concept of education an intelligent Christian must accept' (p. 85).

But this Christian presumably accepts this view of education in so far as he is intelligent and not in so far as he is a Christian per se. For if the latter were the case, the secular Christian would have been able to understand the critical concept of education from within the resources of his faith and we would then have a Christian theology of secular education which is what Hirst says we cannot have. Nevertheless, Hirst takes some pains to show that the general position in the book is not hostile to Christian faith, and at several points there are quite extended discussions of this matter. It seems to me that in this respect he has failed, and if he had not failed, then the position he advocates regarding the impossibility of a Christian understanding of education would have had to undergo revision. In other words, chapters one to four are inconsistent with chapter five, since if Hirst is right in presenting a satisfactory relation between the secular Christian and the secular society with its secularized morals, there remains no reason why he could not also assert a positive relationship between the secularized Christian and secularized education. As it is, he affirms the one and denies the other.

The problems begin in the opening pages. Secular Christians are those 'who seek to go along with the total secularist to the full in all nonreligious areas' but continue to maintain that religious beliefs are meaningful. These beliefs 'combine with' or 'complement these other forms of belief in some way' (pp. 2f.). But, we observe, before he can go along with the total secularist to the full, the Christian must come to see that his faith has 'nothing to contribute in our efforts to understand ourselves, and our world and to determine how we are to live'. Moreover, if religious beliefs are logically and existentially irrelevant, how can they be intelligibly combined with relevant and intelligible secular concepts? If religious beliefs, on the other hand, are not after all irrelevant, then total secularism is unnecessary. On Hirst's account therefore secular Christians are in an unintelligible position since in seeking to combine intelligible with unintelligible beliefs they are behaving irrationally, or, in insisting that religious belief does have something to contribute, they are refusing to go along with the total secularist.

The discussion of privatization has serious consequences for the Christian, unless, as argued above, it may be thought of as simply a sociological phenomenon. If it is thought to be significant in determining the logical relations between religious beliefs and secular ones, then the privatization of religion separates the Christian, no matter how secular he may be, from rationality, from the secular reality in and around him, from science and (to use the theological word) from creation. No Christian seeking wholeness and truth can accept this account of privatization. But if only the sociological sense is intended, then there is no logical reason why we should not try to construct relations between theology and secular education. Hirst hopes that his argument will be of interest to those who remain convinced 'even perhaps of the truth of certain central tenets of Christianity' (p. 6). How can one be rationally convinced of the truth of private claims? For 'truth is correspondence with reality' (p. 22).

Hirst outlines two traditional Christian approaches towards morals. The first (pp. 18–21) takes the will of God as ultimate in morals. The second (pp. 21–23) sees morality as based on natural law and therefore supposes a degree of natural autonomy for the moral life. This natural, rational morality is based on God's creation of man as free, rational and moral. On this second view the autonomy of science and morals is 'seen as built into Christianity rightly understood' (p. 23). The reader is bound to ask why this argument is not applied to education as well. And then if the autonomy, rationality and secularity of education are similarly built into the structure of Christian faith and can be so elucidated, then the Christian faith does produce a view of education, namely, that it is secular and (in important respects) autonomous. I am not concerned with whether this is a good or bad way to approach the problem; I am merely pointing out a failure in consistency in the argument. Hirst does not seem to see that just as secular Christians like Harvey Cox, whom he quotes, can become advocates of the secular city (an advocacy of which Hirst approves), so they can become advocates of secular education within the secular city,[28] which advocacy Hirst disallows in principle, although it could flow from the very arguments used by him to justify secular morals to the Christian. Whatever secularization may mean to the secular Christian, it cannot mean that the secular and the autonomous fall outside the scope of Christian appraisal.

This inconsistency can be seen clearly when it is understood that what Hirst proposes in his discussion of the Christian and secular morality is in fact a Christian theological rationale for secular morality. ' ... a coherent Christian view of morality positively requires it' (p. 52). The teaching of the Bible supports this view of natural, rational morals. So the relation between Christian faith and secular morals is that the former leads to the latter, although it is not the only path to it, and the secular morals would still be there even if that particular path to it did not happen to exist. Nevertheless, it remains the case that this is the special kind of morality to which Christian faith actually does lead, and it can be called both the Christian form of ethics and the secular form of ethics. Why then can there not be a Christian form of education which will also be the secular form of education? Hirst thinks that some of 'the most powerful intellectual seeds of secularization' (p. 23) lie within Christian theology, and are so integral to it that the forging of a theology of the secular is necessary to preserve the rational integrity of Christian theology itself. 'Christian teaching can never hope to be coherent if it denies the legitimacy of living in secular terms' (p. 27). Why not admit then that some of the seeds of the secularization of education lie within Christian faith and that the elaboration and further justification of these may constitute a Christian theology of education for today? 'If this emphasizes yet again that certain roots of secularization are to be found in Christianity, let that be recognized' (pp. 26f.).

But even in his justification of secular morals to the Christian, Hirst is less ready to grant the full impact of theological ethics than he should be on his own argument. Moral principles have an 'ultimate status' (pp. 46, 50) and morals have to be 'argued back to the most fundamental principles of all' (p. 27). Religion is often described by Hirst as depending upon appeal to authority (e.g. pp. 5, 18f., 53). But Christianity sees morality as having 'its place in some ultimate transcendent scheme of things' (p. 55) and as dealing with 'the ultimate principles of human existence' (p. 55). 'It is in the additional emphasis that religion brings to the development of appropriate moral aspects of the personal life, by seeing them within beliefs, dispositions, and emotions of a wider and metaphysically more ulti-mate nature, that the religious impact upon morality is centred' (p. 75). Religion thus appears to offer a wider and more coherent pattern of justification for morals. Surely one is morally obliged to accept the most coherent frame of reference provided that frame is not irrational?

Although he writes as if privatization has the effect of isolating religion and depriving theology of applicability, Hirst also speaks of theology as coherent, rational, a systematic whole from which conclusions can be drawn and impetus discovered for other forms of life. Religious morality is concerned with life's 'ultimate metaphysical understanding, its ultimate source and character' (p. 73). Enquiry into theological ethics would appear then to be morally obligatory since it must be a principle of rational morals to seek the widest possible framework and the most ultimate basis. The insistence that what theology contributes to morals is its metaphysical belief system (i.e. its religious doctrines) and the repeated denial that religion has anything other than the purely rational (i.e. not religious doctrines) to offer cannot be easily reconciled in Hirst's discussion. His thought about the relation between theology and secular ethics is ambivalent rather than ambiguous.

D. Conclusions

I have tried to show that the arguments which Hirst uses to disallow the possibility of connections between Christian theology and educational theory are unconvincing in themselves and inconsistent with his arguments elsewhere in the book about the relation between Christian theology and other spheres such as ethics. I have also tried to show that he does not succeed in commending this approach to the secular Christian, let alone the more traditional Christian, because the notion of a secular Christian is, in his account, not intelligible, and because the consequences from that part of his argument which is intelligible would be unacceptable to any Christian in pursuit of rational wholeness. It remains to ask why Hirst should make such genuine efforts to commend his view of ethics to the Christian but remain so adamant about the impossibility of a relation between Christianity and education. I can only assume that an educational philosopher in Britain today, being well aware of the rather unhappy history of some attempts by some churches and of some aspects of theology to control education and to retain it at a 'primitive' level, is particularly sensitive in this area. This is an understandable attitude, but not a philosophical one.

Notes

1 J. W. Daines, 'A review of unpublished theses in religious education 1968–72', *Learning for Living*, 12, No. 4 (1973), 16–21; Derek Webster, 'American research in religious education: A review of selected doctoral theses', *Learning for Living*, 14, No. 5 (1975), 187–93; David S. Steward, 'Abstracts of doctoral dissertations in religious education 1971–72', *Religious Education*, LXIX, No. 4 (1974), 475ff.
2 Cf. ' … the older and undifferentiated concept which refers just to any process of bringing up or rearing'. Paul H. Hirst and R. S. Peters, *The Logic of Education* (Routledge & Kegan Paul, 1970), 25.

3 Hirst speaks of 'thoroughly open instruction about religious beliefs' and adds a note to the 1974 reprint which reads, 'My view then is that maintained schools should teach "about" religion, provided that it is interpreted to include a direct study of religions, which means entering as fully as possible into an understanding of what they claim to be true.' Paul H. Hirst, 'Morals, religion and the maintained school', *British Journal of Educational Studies*, XIV, No. 1; now in Paul H. Hirst, *Knowledge and the Curriculum* (Routledge & Kegan Paul, 1974), 186f.

4 ' ... there is a proper place in the maintained school for religious studies'. 'Religion, a form of knowledge? A reply', *Learning for Living*, 12, No. 4 (1973), 10.

5 See the review in *Education for Teaching*, Summer 1975, No. 97, 88–90.

6 Paul H. Hirst, 'Christian education: a contradiction in terms', *Learning for Living*, 11, No. 4 (1972), 6.

7 *Ibid.*

8 *Ibid.*, 7.

9 *Ibid.*, 10.

10 *Ibid.*, 11.

11 *Ibid.*, 7.

12 *Ibid.*, 11.

13 I have discussed such matters in 'Worship and the secularization of religious education', chapter four of my *School Worship, an Obituary,* SCM Press, 1975, and in 'Religious education in a pluralistic society', in *Progress and Problems in Moral Education,* ed. Monica Taylor (NFER Publishing Co., 1975), 195–205.

14 Paul H. Hirst, 'Public and private values and religious educational content', in *Religion and Public Education,* ed. T. R. Sizer, Boston, 1967, 330.

15 *Ibid.*, 331.

16 *Ibid.*, 332.

17 *Ibid.*, 333.

18 *Ibid.*, 335.

19 Both articles are now available in *Knowledge and the Curriculum*, cf. note 3.

20 Paul H. Hirst, 'Liberal education and the nature of knowledge', in *Philosophical Analysis and Education,* ed. R. D. Archambault (Routledge & Kegan Paul, 1965), 131.

21 See for example Bernard Lonergan, *Method in Theology* (Darton, Longman & Todd, 1972), Ray L. Hart, *Unfinished Man and the Imagination* (Herder & Herder, 1968), and Paul Tillich, *Systematic Theology* (Nisbet, 1968), for characteristically modern approaches to theology, and F. Schleiermacher, *The Christian Faith* (T. & T. Clark, 1928) for a now classical example of theological method from the early nineteenth century in Germany.

22 *Knowledge and the Curriculum*, 88.

23 *Ibid.*, 87.

24 *Ibid.*, 97.

25 *Ibid.*, 86.

26 *Ibid.*, 96.

27 Illustrations, from theology of culture, of method in modern applied theology are Paul Tillich, *Theology of Culture* (OUP, 1964), Walter J. Ong, *The Presence of the Word* (Yale University Press, 1967), and G. Spiegler, *The Eternal Covenant* (Harper & Row, 1967).

28 See the symposium 'Religious education in the secular city' by Harvey Cox *et al.* in *Religious Education*, LXI, no. 2 (1966), 83–113.

6 The Impact of Research on Educational Studies

P. Broadfoot and J. Nisbet   1981

Authors

Patricia Broadfoot's first academic post was as a lecturer (and later a senior lecturer) at Westhill College, Birmingham (1977–81). She moved to the University of Bristol in 1981 and was appointed Professor of Education in 1991. In 2006, she became Vice Chancellor of the University of Gloucestershire and was appointed CBE for her services to social science. She has published widely in the areas of assessment and comparative education.

John Nisbet was Professor of Education at the University of Aberdeen from 1963 to 1988. He was Chair of Educational Research Board of Social Science Research Council from 1972 to 1975, when he became the first President of the British Educational Research Association. He also chaired the Scottish Council for Research in Education from 1975 to 1978. His initial research interests and publications were in educational psychology and research policy, but later primarily in the history of educational research.

Article

As the then editor of the *BJES*, Professor Margaret Sutherland, notes in the editorial 'Patricia Broadfoot and John Nisbet illuminate the dangers of unperceived controls of areas of research and subtle constraints by funding agencies and others on the freedom and scope of researchers' thinking' (29, 2: 101). *The Impact of Research on Educational Studies* (29, 2: 115–22) had been presented at the previous year's conference of the Standing Conference on Studies in Education held in King's College, London, on 12 December 1980. The title of the conference was 'The Impact of Research on Educational Studies'.

In the same volume of the *Journal* is another paper from the conference by Lawrence Stenhouse, *What counts as research?* (pp. 103–14). Other related articles in other volumes of the *Journal* include: *Research in educational theory* (1, 1: 52–55); *Educational theory, practical philosophy and action research* (35, 2: 149–69); *Editorial: Educational Research* (48, 1: 1–9); '*Disciplines Contributing to Education?*' *Educational Studies and the Disciplines* (50, 1: 100–119); *Educational Studies in* the United Kingdom, 1940–2002 (50, 1: 3–56) and *Political Control: A Way For-ward for Educational Research?* (50, 3: 378–89).

   In *The Impact of Research on Educational Studies* Broadfoot and Nisbet explore the nature of educational studies and educational research. They warn:

> 'Research is commonly regarded as a force for change; but in education, research which is concerned primarily with process in the existing educational system and problems as defined by current policy, results only in marginal change. ... The current utilitarian climate makes it more likely that some issues will be organized out of debate, questions on educational values being taken as agreed.' (p.119)

A report of the December 1980 conference elsewhere in the same volume of the *Journal* recounts:

> 'Many observations were directed to questions of researcher motivation, research funding and the utilization—if any—of research findings. Much, it was said, is expected of the researcher: but two main threats to research were emphasized. One was the difficulty of obtaining access to data in the UK. ... The second, major, threat was the preference of funding agencies for topics of a 'non-challenging' or utilitarian nature. Young researchers might be well, if cynically, advised to keep clear of 'threat' areas—or secure funding by keeping on the edge of threat ... Then too, while research is ultimately political, the amount of money devoted to it by government is so small as to be negligible from the government point of view.' (p. 168)

Somewhat familiarly, the conference report also notes, 'A proposal for change in the conceptualization of teacher education indicated how necessary such a change is' but 'some research, while studied by academics, had had no effect at all on policy decision-making' (p. 169), thereby providing a salutary lens through which to observe the nature and manner of the 2011 review of Initial Teacher Education instituted by Secretary of State for Education, Mr Michael Gove MP.

   Another observation in the same report also provides an example of the truth of C. P. Snow's observation about the politics of university life:

> 'But one gloomy comment noted the sniping by academics at other aca-demics' research, which goes on not only in the conclaves of research councils but on occasion in public—an occurrence which is unhelpful to research workers' general credibility.' (29, 2: 169)

Plus ça change. ...

The Impact of Research on Educational Studies

by *Patricia Broadfoot*, Westhill College,
and John Nisbet, Department of Education,
University of Aberdeen

Synopsis

The impact of research on educational studies is essentially in determining what kinds of questions and evidence are seen as important, and how they are seen— how practitioners and researchers (and administrators and policy makers) structure their perceptions of their work. In this way, research creates an agenda of concern. Research is commonly considered to be a force for change; but when emphasis is placed on 'relevant' research—that is, research which is concerned primarily with processes in the existing educational system—its influence is often reactionary. Research of this kind focuses attention on existing theories and practices, legitimating their priority in the agenda of concern and discouraging alternative perspectives. The pressure for 'utilization' in current government funding policy both in Britain and USA is likely to accentuate this narrowing effect, emphasizing an instrumental function for research and limiting it within the constraints of existing policy and practice.

The new 'collaborative movement' in educational research (working with teachers, even allowing teachers to define the problems to be researched) emphasizes mildly reformist rather than radical research. Yet it need not do so, for the very act of teachers addressing their own classroom problems from a research perspective may be the most fertile soil for educational research to grow in.

If research is to have a radical influence on educational studies, it must do more than produce information on the processes of education. It should be concerned with the parameters used for thinking about education, and strive to redefine issues. Only then can research be a progressive rather than a reactionary force.

Educational studies and educational research

What are educational studies? The term is commonly taken to include a range of specialist disciplines which are thought to have some bearing on the practice of education: sociology, psychology, curriculum, philosophy, history, administration and so on. Some of these involve empirical study, while others such as philosophy are predominantly theoretical, but in so far as they are educational studies they all have something to contribute to the understanding of education. What is their rationale, what is the nature of their contribution? If we reject the trend for educational studies to degenerate into 'tips for teachers', we can distinguish two reasons for including educational studies in professional training:

(a)   that it is valuable for teachers to understand something of the context in which they work in terms of its structural features and prevailing values;
(b)   that the study of these disciplines makes clear that 'being educated' is a problematic concept, and consequently that how and what to teach is problematic too.

The impact of research on educational studies is not limited to building up a substantive content to the disciplines, but also and more importantly, research influences the style of thinking within these disciplines. Research is not so much concerned with finding answers, but rather with identifying questions. To quote Einstein:[1]

> 'The formulation of a problem is often more essential than its solution, which may be merely a matter of mathematical or experimental skill. To raise new questions, new possibilities, to regard old questions from a new angle, requires imagination and marks real advance in science.'

More precisely, the impact of research on educational studies is essentially in determining what kinds of questions and evidence are seen as important. It also determines how they are seen: how practitioners and researchers (and administrators and policy makers too) structure their perceptions of their work. In this way, research creates an agenda of concern.

Two levels of educational research may be distinguished: one concerned with practical and 'useful' studies, the other concerned with theoretical and 'enlightening' studies. The first of these was what Sir William Pile (Permanent Secretary of DES, 1976) was looking for when he complained:[2]

> 'Part of it (research) is rubbish, and another part leads nowhere and is really rather indifferent; it is, I am afraid, exceptional to find a piece of research that really hits the nail on the head and tells you pretty clearly what is wrong or what is happening or what should be done ... People say they have done some research when they really mean they have stopped to think for three minutes.'

The assumption at this level of research is that decisions on aims have been taken, and the researcher's task is to pursue generalizations about the most effective means of achieving desired educational goals. Examples of areas when research of this kind has had a substantial impact include:

vocabulary studies—reading materials, the design of textbooks, language in the classroom;

stages in development—age-placement and the sequencing of subject matter to fit
the pupil's stage of thinking;
testing—remedial education, screening and diagnostic work, academic and vocational guidance;
attitudes—classroom climate, moral education, attitudes and values;

and many others, such as the education of handicapped children (especially the
deaf), learning a second language, and so on. These are all areas where research
has influenced what is done. What they have in common is that they are all relatively
non-controversial areas. In topics where there is a general consensus on values,
research findings seem to be particularly effective: they are readily incorporated
into policy or action. But when basic assumptions are challenged, then research
seems to lose its relevance, or at least is not readily accepted. If there is no consensus on values, research is treated merely as one more pressure group with
vested interests. The example of testing and selection, the n-plus examination and
the selective secondary school, illustrates this point: research was widely used to
improve the selection procedure, and it did it extremely well; but with the introduction of comprehensive schools this research was discarded (although it still
had much to contribute), because it was based on a model which no longer
commanded a consensus of support.

The second level of research has a quite different kind of impact. To quote Travers:[3]

'One important influence of research has been to develop a philosophy of
education which embodies a conception of human nature—a philosophy
appropriate for research but not easy to fit into an administrative context ... '

Or Rousseau (1762):[4]

'People are always telling me to make practical suggestions. You might as well
tell me to suggest improvements which can be incorporated with the wrong
methods at present in use.'

This level of research is not directly concerned with process; but rather takes the
educational system as its focus. Although some of this research may be directly
addressed to policy issues (such as comprehensive schools, 16–19 provision,
examination reform, the role of inspectors, and so on), much of it is strongly
theoretical and has the academic community as its principal audience. While it can
be argued that nearly all research has implications for practice in the long term (for
example, studies of teachers' careers, comparative child-rearing practices, or historical studies), the link between the knowledge produced by such studies and any
specific action a classroom teacher or policy maker could take in the light of them
is tenuous indeed. Equally, conclusions are unlikely to be unambiguous and defi-
nitive, qualifications and hypotheses being more often the product.

Thus, educational studies may be said to span a continuum between the specific
practical problems of teachers at one end and general enlightenment at the other.

Research has a potential impact at every point. At present, however, there is strong pressure for more 'useful' research. There are many reasons for this: the growth of public expenditure on research and development in education, leading to a need to demonstrate a return for this outlay; the creation of R & D organizations (like the NFER and the Schools Council) and the present vulnerability of quangos (illustrated by the recent review of the Central Committee on the Curriculum in Scotland); and a change of attitude in central government, which can be illustrated from Mrs. Thatcher (1970), who, as Secretary of State for Education and Science, declared[5] that the Department's research policy should be

'the active initiation of work by the Department on problems of its own choosing, within a procedure and timetable which were relevant to its needs'.

Or Rothschild:[6]

'The customer says what he wants; the contractor does it (if he can); and the customer pays.'

This trend is not limited to this country. Gideonse declares[7]

'The single most powerful organizing principle for explaining the developments in educational research policy in USA over the past twenty years is the almost over-riding concern for maximizing impact.'

The prevailing utilitarian ethos is increasingly squeezing out the 'enlightenment' function of research. This development can be related to a more general trend in this country and abroad towards a technocratic, corporate-management approach to decision-making. To the extent that this approach prevails, policy decisions are seen not as normative, but rather as the search for the optimum mode of implementation, on the assumption that there is some sort of 'right answer'. This development is partly attributable to the feeling that we can no longer afford the luxury of open-ended debate, and partly to the general proliferation of government function and bureaucracy.

A restrictive or reactionary influence of research is not however to be explained merely as the result of a recent political change. As Kuhn[8] has argued, there is a sense in which the whole course of scientific research is directed towards supporting established theories—until some new scientific revolution overthrows accepted beliefs and establishes a new orthodoxy which then dominates the pattern of research. Elton[9] expresses the point concisely:

'Even as researchers, academics are not basically innovative, for most of them for most of the time practise what Kuhn (1970) calls "normal science". Popper (1970)[10] somewhat unkindly but not inaccurately describes this activity as 'content to solve ... routine problems, that is, problems in which a dominant theory (a "paradigm") is applied'.'

Research is commonly regarded as a force for change; but in education, research which is concerned primarily with process in the existing educational system and problems as defined by current policy, results only in marginal change. By reinforcing the importance of the framework of thought which has produced certain aspects as 'problems', legitimating their priority in the agenda of concern, it has a deeper, stabilizing effect which discourages alternative perspectives. Challenging interpretations are seen as less relevant, or less important; are less likely to be funded, and less likely to be accepted by editors for publication, and if published, less likely to be read or quoted.

The current utilitarian climate makes it more likely that some issues will be organized out of debate, questions on educational values being taken as agreed. Indeed, some would argue that educational research has always treated what it is to be educated as unproblematic. The 'scientific movement' of the 1920s and 1930s aimed to build a science of education, by which was implied a structure of knowledge and methodology which could be used instrumentally to resolve educational issues. This positivist attitude survives in the cruder forms of educational technology, but it has been challenged in the 'two cultures' debate, 'grounded theory' and 'illuminative evaluation'.

> 'The crucial distinction ... is that between a positivist and a relativist view of the educational enterprise. A positivist perspective makes two assumptions. First, that there is a fixed and unchanging reality based on constant relationships which is amenable to scientifically-modelled, objective research. Second, that the formulation of the research question itself is part of an objective process. The relativist rejection of this position for social and, in particular, educational research, involves not so much the rejection of pseudo-scientific modes of enquiry (although it frequently has involved this in educational research in recent years) but fundamentally it emphasises the problematic nature of education itself. The distinction is essentially that between regarding the concept of what it is to be "educated" as a fixed and immutable absolute—a philosophical concept of the Hirst and Peters variety—and regarding "education" as a social process with important political, economic and socializing functions which therefore varies from time to time and from society to society.'[11]

In its search for scientific status and credibility, educational research has chosen through most of its history to ignore the normative in favour of the technocratic. Perhaps one of the reasons why it has not been more influential is its inability to maintain such a stance, given the problematic nature of what is to be counted as education. Educational research cannot be a 'neutral handmaiden', but is bound to reify existing assumptions: delineation of problems, choice of methodology and extrapolation from conclusions are all influenced by a particular ideology.

Research in alliance with authority can be a powerful force for maintaining the status quo, for identifying stress points through evaluation and trimming a policy accordingly, or for reinforcing a case for change. For example, the recent Scottish

Inspectorate survey of primary schools[12] used a research design of classroom observation in a random sample of schools: this basis of evidence gives more credibility to the inspectors' recommendations, even where these recommendations are value judgments. The growth of evaluation studies commissioned by both central and local authorities is another example of the use of research as an instrument of management and control.

The new 'collaborative movement' in educational research, set in the current climate, may aggravate the situation. Researchers are urged to work in collaboration with teachers, to delegate responsibility to them, to allow teachers to define the problems to be researched, and to think in terms of 'clients'' perceptions. Walker,[13] for example, writes of

> 'a form of educational research ... (which) would start with, and remain close to, the common-sense knowledge of the practitioner, and the constraints within which he works. It would aim to systematize and build on practitioner lore rather than to supplant it.'

A somewhat similar position, on a different topic, is argued persuasively in the Scottish Munn report.[14]

> 'No major curricular reform can hope to succeed unless it wins the support of the profession which will have to put it into practice.'

Collaborative action favours mildly reformist rather than radical research, and thus removes much of the implicit threat of innovative studies. At the same time, by exposing more of the reality of classroom life, it may lead to a tightening of the reflexive bond between policy makers, researchers and practitioners. Since 'trouble shooting' studies are likely to have more impact than more discursive studies whose relevance is at the 'enlightenment' end of the continuum, we can anticipate a growing acceptability of this new mode of research activity, and a narrowing, restrictive effect on what is seen as appropriate to educational studies.

However, there is a place for all kinds of research, and the purpose of this paper is not to attack the collaborative movement (though it does stake a claim for maintaining a balance among the different kinds of research). Since ideas have a habit of ebbing and flowing in an uncontrollable way, it may be that the very act of teachers' addressing their own classroom problems from a research perspective will be the most fertile soil for educational research to grow in. Fundamental research can grow from modest questioning. Collaborative research can be developed in quite a different way, retaining its democratic devolvement of responsibility so as to prevent the emergence of an élite group of researchers in alliance with those responsible for management and control. If it can be developed so as to provide teachers (and administrators and parents and all those concerned with education) with the means of improving their own understanding, then its effect will be to put educational studies into a questioning framework. To do this, it must go beyond 'routine problems', and be concerned instead with the parameters used for thinking about education, redefining issues and restructuring perceptions. This no small task, but one well worth attempting. We should then be nearer to the ideal expressed by Whitehead[15] some fifty years ago:

'Education should begin in research and end in research ... An education which does not begin by evoking initiative and end by encouraging it is wrong. For its whole aim is the production of active wisdom.'

Notes

1 A. Einstein. Quoted in P. Suppes (ed.), *Impact of Research on Education: some case studies* (National Academy of Education, Washington, 1978).

2 W. Pile. Quoted in Tenth Report of the Expenditure Committee: *Decision-making in DES* (HMSO, 1976).

3 Travers: see J. Nisbet and P. Broadfoot: *The Impact of Research on Policy and Practice in Education* (Aberdeen University Press, 1980).

4 J. J. Rousseau: *Emile*.

5 M. Thatcher: DES Circular, 1970.

6 Rothschild Committee: *A Framework for Government Research and Development* (HMSO, 1971).

7 Gideonse: see J. Nisbet and P. Broadfoot, *op. cit.*

8 T. S. Kuhn: *The Structure of Scientific Revolutions* (revised edition) (Chicago University Press, 1970).

9 L. R. B. Elton: Can universities change? *Studies in Higher Education* pp. 23–33, Vol. 6, Issue 1, 1981.

10 K. R. Popper: 'Normal science and its dangers' in I. Lakatos and A. Musgrove (eds.), *Criticism and the Growth of Knowledge* (Cambridge University Press, 1970).

11 P. Broadfoot: 'Educational research through the looking glass' (*Scottish Educational Review,* 11, 1979), pp. 133–42.

12 Scottish Education Department: *Learning and Teaching in Primary 4 and Primary 7* (HMSO, 1980).

13 R. Walker: 'Innovation, evaluation, research and the problem of control', *Workshop Curriculum No. 1* (Care, University of East Anglia, 1974).

14 Scottish Education Department: *The Structure of the Curriculum in the Third and Fourth Years of the Scottish Secondary School* (HMSO, 1977).

15 A. Whitehead: *The Aims of Education and Other Essays* (Williams and Norgate, 1932).

7 Philosophy of Education, 1952–82

R. F. Dearden

Author

Robert Dearden (1934–2005) left school at 16, but later, realising his intellectual potential, studied to become a primary school teacher (which he remained for eight years) and studied part-time for his BA in philosophy. His philosophical ability was recognised by Richard Peters, who, shortly after his appointment as Professor of Philosophy of Education at the Institute of Education, University of London, persuaded him to join his team at the Institute – a team which transformed the philosophy of education in Britain and more widely. Amongst his many publications, *The Philosophy of Primary Education* in 1968 was most influential in its critique of child-centred education. In 1978 he was appointed Professor of Education at the University of Birmingham.

Introduction

In *Philosophy of Education, 1952–82* (30, 1: 57–72), Dearden charts the development of the philosophy of education in the 30 years from the inception of the *Journal*. At the beginning, the *Journal* focused mainly on history and philosophy, psychology having its own journal and sociology still to emerge. Indeed, the opening article in the first issue of the *BJES* was by the first Professor of Philosophy of Education in Britain, Louis Arnaud Reid. There were indeed, as Dearden points out, mainstream philosophers who had something to say about education, but it was with the establishment of the B.Ed degree in the 1960s that a distinctive philosophy of education began to flourish under the leadership of Professor Richard Peters and his team of Paul Hirst, John and Pat White, Robert Dearden, and then Ray Elliott.

This team, taking the lead from Peters' detailed analysis of what it means to be educated (outlined in his inaugural lecture in 1963 entitled 'Education as Initiation' and in his subsequent book in 1965, *Ethics and Education*), introduced the discipline of linguistic philosophy, then dominant in British universities, to the examination of educational thinking and its contested concepts such as indoctrination, child-centred education, and children's interests and needs. Hirst was particularly influential with his 'Liberal Education and the Nature of Knowledge' and Hirst and Peters together with their book in 1970, *The Logic of Education*. The Institute team, now with satellites around the Colleges of Education and University Departments, and with partners in Australia and North America, were responsible for a range of books and papers that dominated educational theory, reflected for instance in *Education and the Development of Reason* and in the publications in Routledge's Students' Library of Education series. The establishment of Philosophy of Education Society of Great Britain in 1965 and the publication of its Proceedings in 1966 (later to develop into the *Journal of the Philosophy of Education*) provided an alternative outlet to the *BJES* and remained an active and flourishing mouthpiece of the discipline.

However, success bred its critics as Dearden outlines – the sociologists of knowledge in particular (who questioned, first, the value neutrality of linguistic analysis, and, second, the failure to relate knowledge as 'constructed' with the source of power), but also those, like Ray Elliott from within a phenomenological tradition. Hence, this paper tells the tale of the growth of an influential discipline in educational studies, its expansion and the basis of its present flourishing.

Connected articles from the *Journal* are: *Education and the Map of Knowledge* (1, 1952: 3–42); *Is education a good thing?* (50, 3: 327–38); *R.S. Peters' Philosophy of Education: Review Article* (34, 3: 268–74); *Philosophy and Educational Theory* (7, 1: 51–64); *Commonsense thought, Knowledge and Judgement, and their importance for education* (13, 2: 125–38); *In defence of Bingo: a rejoinder to R.S. Peters* (15, 1: 5–27).

Philosophy of Education, 1952–82

by R. F. Dearden, Faculty of Education, University of Birmingham

I

When the first volume of the *British Journal of Educational Studies* appeared in 1952, the opening article in the first issue was by a philosopher. Its title was 'Education and the Map of Knowledge' and its author was Louis Arnaud Reid, who had earlier moved from a chair in general philosophy to occupy the new chair of philosophy of education at the University of London Institute of Education. Shortly before his retirement a more comprehensive statement of Reid's views on education appeared in his book *Philosophy and Education* (1962).

Other early examples from the period could be found of people trained in general philosophy turning their attention to philosophy of education. Such might include C. D. Hardie's *Truth and Fallacy in Educational Theory* (1942), D. J. O'Connor's *An Introduction to the Philosophy of Education* (1957), R. S. Peters' *Authority, Responsibility and Education* (1959) and Israel Scheffler's *Language and Education* (1960). And there were, of course, the works of the 'great educators', some of them also great philosophers, such as Plato, Aristotle, Locke, Kant and John Dewey, whose obituary also appeared in the first issue of the *BJES*.

Throughout the 1950s, and in direct response to developments in general philosophy, a new conception of philosophy of education was slowly forming and finding sporadic expression. But all of this was very far from a state of affairs in which it would become natural to think of educational studies as divided into various disciplines, of which philosophy of education would be one. Yet by 1977, Mary Warnock could uncontroversially open her book *Schools of Thought* by saying that 'it cannot any longer be seriously doubted that there is such a thing as the philosophy of education'. How did this transition come about?

The opportunity came in the early 1960s. The teacher training colleges were extending their certificate courses from two or three years, while the Robbins Report was recommending that the colleges themselves be redesignated 'colleges of education' and that, for some students, there should be a new education degree, the B.Ed. These changes combined to require more and academically better qualified lecturers and new courses which would be of a rigour deserving the award of a degree.

A comparable change was taking place in the U.S.A. where such bitter critics of the 'Mickey Mouse' education courses offered to teachers as J. B. Conant and

J. D. Koerner were urging a much stronger grounding in the disciplines relevant to education. Yet a further factor in the creation of an opportunity for new academic initiatives was the state of the schools, in which many controversial changes were taking place, such as the 'revolution' in the primary schools, re-organisation at the secondary level and the trial runs of various curriculum development projects. There was never a time more ripe for someone to mark out the claims of any newly emerging discipline of education.

So far as philosophy of education was concerned, the opportunity was taken, and with maximum impact, by Reid's successor at London, Professor R. S. Peters. Peters' background in general philosophy, coupled with a longstanding interest in education, fired him with a missionary zeal to raise the standards of educational theorizing. His inaugural lecture, given in 1963 with the title 'Education as Initiation', was published in the following year as a booklet of 42 pages.[1] It intimated an agenda of topics for discussion and gave a paradigm of method which were formative for the decade to follow. Topics woven into his theme included the debate between traditionalists and progressives, the education of the emotions, the nature of creativity and of critical thinking, the role of the economist's and the sociologist's views of education and the relation of means to ends in education. Various points were linked with the historical views of Plato, Quintilian, Froebel, Dewey and Whitehead.

But the centrepiece, and it was this that was taken as the paradigm of method, was the analysis of the concept of education. Peters argued, as has by now become very familiar, that 'education' is a family of morally legitimate procedures which aim to develop intrinsically worthwhile states of mind with wide-ranging cognitive content. The process as a whole was conceived by Peters as a development of mind through initiation into public traditions which incorporate impersonal standards and which, if mastered, give a distinctive quality to life. Peters' fuller statement of his views, which also brought in his strong interest in ethics and social philosophy to add to his already apparent interest in philosophy of mind, appeared in his book *Ethics and Education* (1966).

In his inaugural, Peters had characterised philosophical concerns as being to do with the demarcation of concepts and the grounds of knowledge. In fact this second, epistemological aspect was developed in Britain more by Paul Hirst, who was also in the London department at that time, though from America Israel Scheffler's *Conditions of Knowledge* (1965) came to be widely used. Peters did probe the grounds of certain knowledge claims, especially in ethics in terms of the 'transcendental deduction', but it was Hirst who was to make the greater impact in terms of general epistemology.

Hirst's article 'Liberal Education and the Nature of Knowledge' soon became a classic.[2] Not just fellow philosophers of education but also members of the Inspectorate, writers of Schools Council working papers as well as students and teachers became aware of the 'forms of knowledge' and pondered their implications for curriculum and method. This thesis readily combined with Peters' more formal account of education to provide a powerful synthesis, expressed in Hirst and Peters' jointly authored book *The Logic of Education* (1970). This synthesis found no equally well articulated rival, though some might have seen Phenix's *Realms of Meaning* (1964) as such.

Hirst had already in 1963 written another article which also rapidly gained the status of a classic. This was his 'Philosophy and Educational Theory'.[3] Here he argued that there was no single discipline of education and that philosophy was itself but one of several disciplines each having their distinctive bearing on educational principles and practice. A revised version of this article stated the argument for an approach through the disciplines in J. W. Tibbie's *The Study of Education* (1966), which also served as the lead publication for a whole new publishing venture of Routledge and Kegan Paul's: the Student's Library of Education series. Whilst Hirst was thus locating the contribution of philosophy, Peters was providing a manifesto on its nature and content for the colleges, in his paper 'The Place of Philosophy in the Training of Teachers'.[4]

There followed a burst of activity which scarcely seems credible in the sober, not to say sombre, 1980s. Courses in philosophy of education at all levels and in all teacher education institutions (save the Open University) were offered and were even mandatory. Many new specialist appointments had to be made to cope with the demand. Philosophers began to occupy chairs in education in addition to Peters' own at the London Institute, first Perry and Hirst, and rather later Elliott, Dearden, Sockett, Pring and Aspin. Pure philosophers, such as Professors Hamlyn, Hare, Oakeshott, O'Connor, Passmore, D. Z. Phillips, A. Phillips Griffiths and Ryle also took an interest, which was greatly facilitated by Peters' established reputation amongst general philosophers. In 1973, the Royal Institute of Philosophy combined with the by then existing Philosophy of Education Society to hold a major conference at the University of Exeter, the proceedings of which eventually appeared in book form as *Philosophers Discuss Education* (1975), edited by Stuart Brown.

There was also a publications explosion. Peters himself added the International Library of the Philosophy of Education to the philosophical branch of Routledge's Student's Library of Education series. Influential collections appeared, such as T.H. Hollins' *Aims of Education* (1964), R. D. Archambault's *Philosophical Analysis and Education* (1965), Peters' *The Concept of Education* (1967) and Dearden, Hirst and Peters' *Education and the Development of Reason* (1972). Peters also edited a collection for the Oxford Readings in Philosophy series under the title *Philosophy of Education* (1973), while Hirst collected together many of his articles in his *Knowledge and the Curriculum* (1974). My own *Philosophy of Primary Education* (1968) gave a more specific focus to some general themes and was widely used in the colleges. John Wilson and Robin Barrow both wrote extensively. Nor did all publishing originate in the universities. Particularly strong philosophy of education departments at Stockwell and Homerton Colleges produced such collections as D. I. Lloyd's *Philosophy and the Teacher* (1976) and Bridges and Scrimshaw's *Values and Authority in Schools* (1976).

Since 1941 there had been a Philosophy of Education Society in the U.S.A. but towards the end of 1965 Peters set about founding a Philosophy of Education Society of Great Britain. Its first annual general meeting and the publication of its first set of proceedings took place in 1966. Peters was himself chairman, while Louis Arnaud Reid was asked to be the first president and Hirst brought formative influence to bear as the first secretary. Since 1978 the proceedings have been retitled *the Journal of Philosophy of Education* to make clear that the publication is not confined to the proceedings of the annual conference. The journal now appears in two issues a year and by the end of 1980 altogether 169 articles had appeared by 113 different authors, and the journal was being taken in 44 different countries. Membership of the society was between four and five hundred and as well as the regular national meetings in London, meetings were also being held in some fourteen branches round the country.

II

The 'revolution' in philosophy of education which took place in the 1960s, not only in Britain but also in North America and Australasia, involved greater consciousness of and involvement with the methods and results of philosophy as an academic discipline. These methods and results were directly applied to educational questions (which presupposed rather more of an acquaintance with the parent discipline than some lecturers possessed or could readily acquire in the rapid expansion of opportunities). Most importantly of all, this influence by the parent discipline carried with it the then fashionable paradigm, which was that of linguistic philosophy.

Linguistic philosophy looked to 'ordinary use' as its guide. Different senses of some ordinary term, or neighbouring terms, would be distinguished. Points would be substantiated by reference to 'what we would say', 'what we would call' and 'what would count as'. Linguistic intuitions would be explored to see what some term 'suggested' or what it 'sounds odd to say'. Strictly, the object of the enquiry was not the English word but the concept which it marked out. Such concepts might be the same across different languages, or might not be handily marked out by a single word at all. Concepts also needed to be distinguished from the more or less personal psychological associations which a word might have for some individual. If things went well, then criteria for the application of the concept would hopefully be laid out, amounting in especially favourable cases to a set of necessary and sufficient conditions. If the going was less easy, then one might have to identify the 'central' uses, setting aside as secondary those cases that could not so easily be fitted under the concept.

The origins of this style of philosophising were found as far back as Socrates and Aristotle, though the more immediate stimulus to it came, in different ways, from Wittgenstein and J. L. Austin. Philosophy was conceived as a fight against bewitchment by language, best waged by looking at 'language games' and their associated 'forms of life'. Ordinary language was regarded by Austin as a repository of subtle distinctions which had been forged, tried and tested in everyday life and which were likely to be more sound than any rationalistic prescriptions of disengaged philosophers.

This relation to 'life' was important because, without it, references to linguistic habits and intuitions would have seemed so incredibly flimsy as a basis for anything as not to deserve taking seriously. Nevertheless, there was a paradox in the whole approach, namely that in ordinary language 'philosophy' is *not* some kind of study of ordinary language. Disconcerting also was the practice of making 'conceptual points' by means of deliberately trivial examples. This was done for the understandable reason of not wishing to get bogged down in controversy over a fairly arbitrary choice of example, so losing sight of the main point. But it was disconcerting to find grand themes of ethics apparently degenerating into criteria for the grading of apples, or even for assessing sewage effluent.

Peters' paradigmatic example of the analysis of education was in a linguistic style, with appropriate references to what we would say, what the term suggests, what the dictionary records, and so on. In reality, Peters always did very much more than this programme would require. He brought in his considerable knowledge of psychology, his experience of a variety of educational institutions and his extensive knowledge of the history of philosophy. Far from just recording 'uses', he articulated a comprehensive ethical and social philosophical position and extensively worked out its educational implications. But the stated paradigm stuck, later reinforced by a further paradigmatic analysis of 'punishment'. An early sign that all might not be well with this approach was a persistent tendency for students to decline to recognise 'ordinary use' in what was put to them, but to refer instead to 'the philosophical sense', while disputes over the correct analysis of 'education' were endless.

Serious doubts about linguistic analysis were already spreading in the parent discipline, while thoughtful and constructive critics like Abraham Edel,[5] and hostile sociological ones like David Adelstein,[6] were raising fundamental difficulties specifically related to Peters' own work. The broadly Marxist mood of the period of student unrest in the late 1960s, and the horrors of the Vietnam War, were making value-neutrality, which was a supposed virtue of linguistic analysis, seem irresponsible.

If philosophers could find nothing better to do than, so to speak, cock an ear for linguistic nuances, then they were likely to be ignored, or alternatively to be pilloried by Ernest Gellner.[7] Linguistic philosophy created the impression that philosophy was a trivial squabble over words, or a perverse focusing of attention just on the finger of someone intent on pointing at a reality.

Was philosophy really just a linguistic technique? Did its subject matter have no history, or at least require no knowledge of that history for an understanding of it? Might not 'ordinary use' be confused or inconsistent? What would be the 'ordinary use' for some quite new term? When was an analysis 'correct'? If philosophers are really describing ordinary use, ought they not to be out doing some sort of empirical survey work? If analysis 'leaves everything as it is', what is the point of it? And if it is said that the point of analysis is to clear our heads so as to reveal 'further questions', whose job is it to answer those, especially as they may well seem to be the really important questions? Again, could use and meaning really be equated, for one might very well know the use of a word such as 'amen' but not know its meaning.

To my mind, however, two major criticisms stand out. The first arises from taking much more seriously the already acknowledged connections between concepts and 'life'. Concepts reflect interests, frequently competing interests, especially in a practical field such as education. It is not that the Latin 'educare' is struggling with the Latin 'educere' in some ethereal medium but that people and groups are contending for different things. As Marxist critics were quick to point out, the linguistic philosopher's 'we' may therefore be a disguised sectional interest bidding for universal validity.

Again, when teachers say they 'teach children and not subjects', is it really just that they have failed to grasp a point of grammar? To offer the prospect of major benefit, linguistic analysis must assume that conflicts are due to the conceptual confusion which it unravels, and that its concepts actually apply to reality. Neither of these two assumptions may be justified. Edel supplied an interesting example of how a wider perspective might be taken when he related the distinction between 'knowing that' and 'knowing how' to the division of mental and manual labour in society and the differing traditions of liberal and vocational education.[8]

The second criticism follows on from the first, and concerns the supposed value-neutrality of linguistic analysis. Why has *this* concept been chosen for analysis? Is there not some version of the naturalistic fallacy committed in passing from a description of use to a judgment that it is correct use? Will the historic act of analysing not itself be a help, a hindrance or a distraction to some cause? May not analysis very well embody a species of conservatism, serving to give ideological reassurance to those resisting change? Is analysis confined *to* picking old bones when the battle is over, like Hegel's Owl of Minerva?

It remains true that philosophers nevertheless do well to be sensitive to language. It is not pedantry accurately to determine the meaning of what is said, or the sense in which it is meant, for that is a necessary preliminary to the appraisal of its truth. Without clear propositions and dependency relations, validity and truth cannot be assessed. And many useful preliminary distinctions were marked out and remain from the linguistic period: between education and training, between being in and being an authority, between being interested in and being in one's interests, between being neutral in intention and neutral in effect, between teaching that, how to and to, between needs and wants, and so on.

The strongest recent reaffirmation of a linguistic approach to conceptual analysis has come from John Wilson, from whose prolific pen one might choose as a major example his book *Preface to the Philosophy of Education* (1979) or his article 'Concepts, Contestability and the Philosophy of Education'.[9] But even he places this analysis in a wider context by seeking to show certain concepts not to be optional, and by construing analysis as being at the same time a kind of psychotherapy.

III

Concerning possible alternatives, one might have expected a distinctive Catholic school of philosophy *of* education to have developed, but this has not happened. Many philosophers of education are Catholics but they generally follow the mainstream in their choice of topics and methods. The nearest to a distinctive

Catholic perspective is probably Jacques Maritain's book *Education at the Crossroads* (1954), though this has had very little influence.

Pure philosophers continue to take a lively and invigorating interest in philosophy of education and a steady stream of books appears from that direction. For example, Downie, Loudfoot and Telfer have written on *Education and Personal Relationships* (1974), and Anthony Flew criticised the 'new sociology of education' in *Sociology, Equality and Education* (1976). Mary Warnock presented a new view of aims in her *Schools of Thought* (1977), while David Hamlyn ranged over the work of Piaget and Chomsky in his *Knowledge and the Growth of Understanding* (1978). Most recently, David Cooper has examined egalitarianism in his *Illusions of Equality* (1980), R. F. Holland has written *Against Empiricism* (1980), John Passmore has discussed *The Philosophy of Teaching* (1980) and Anthony O'Hear has written a new introduction to philosophy of education called *Education, Society and Human Nature* (1981).

Phenomenology represents another possible approach, but Curtis and Mays' *Phenomenology and Education* (1978), which was an edited collection of conference papers, appears to have convinced no one that here was a fruitful new approach. In a review article on the book, one of the most scholarly contemporary phenomenologists in education, Francis Dunlop, argued that many of the contributors are not even very clear what phenomenology is. Dunlop himself takes the work of Husserl as the essential point of origin for the movement. Phenomenological arguments, however, are apt to have much the same character as ethical intuitionism in containing more assertion than argument.

Much of R. K. Elliott's work might be regarded as phenomenological, yet by contrast it explores what introspection and subjective experience might have to yield in a way that is of very much more than private interest. Elliott's major articles on 'Education and Human Being'[10] and 'Education and Justification'[11] were a powerful critique of certain theses in Hirst and Peters, though they did not amount to a fully developed alternative conception. Elliott's articles on aesthetics and the imagination have also been greatly valued.[12]

Marxist criticisms of philosophy of education have stemmed largely from writers in the social sciences, such as Michael Young, Madan Sarup and Bowles and Gintis, but in *Education and Knowledge* (1979) Kevin Harris proposed a materialist paradigm for future philosophical work and clearly saw his book as a new start in the philosophy of education. Marxist analyses seem generally to turn on two major claims. The first claim is that the ways in which we conceive of reality are socially constructed, and in a qualified sense this is probably true. The second claim is that a ruling class exploits the rest, especially through the medium of educational institutions, by a 'structured misrepresentation of reality'.

The method of analysis is then to 'lay bare' where this exploitation is occurring. Educational arrangements are 'de-mystified' in a way which exhibits pupils and teachers alike as being conned into serving not their own interests but those of the ruling class. The learner, like the factory worker, is seen as alienated and indeed the alienation of the first is seen as being preparation for the alienation of the second. Some writers, such as Esland, are massively and depressingly cynical.

Nothing is what it seems for them: if you try to say something true, you are really bolstering your power by defining reality; if you try to discover the truth, you are really negotiating it; if you try to justify anything, you are engaging in the rhetoric of legitimation. An air of scandalous revelation pervades it all, though like much scandal it is rarely substantiated, the arguments of Bowles and Gintis being exceptional in this respect.

It would appear that Marxist analyses may so bewitch their authors and their audiences with the sense of being privy to a final unveiling of the real truth that they lose a robust sense of reality. 'Truth and objectivity are human products' Gorbutt asserts, characteristically not noticing what this would imply for the status of his own assertions.[13] But whether we are discovering a pre-existing reality or creating a new one, there are limits to the concepts that will be found *to* have, or that can be given, application, not to mention requirements of consistency. In the vogue for finding fraudulent ideology everywhere, more attention could profitably be given to the severe conditions that any such ideology must meet if it is to be remotely plausible. The revelation of ideology and alienation (and there surely is some to reveal) is itself of presumptive interest only because there are universal values, such as truth, justice, liberty and self-realisation. These values are evident in more constructive, less cynical work such as Harold Entwistle's *Class, Culture and Education* (1978) or in his commentary *Antonio Gramsci* (1979).

There are, however, two broad redirections of attention for which Marxist criticism has been at least partly responsible and with some benefit. The first of these is towards the connections between education and work, or the backwash from the division of labour in society. The ways in which schooling is functional or non-functional in this respect, and whether it is so intentionally or unintentionally, certainly deserve attention, both empirical and philosophical. The second is towards a much livelier sense of what seems natural, or is taken for granted, as really being chosen, whether deliberately or by default. This is, of course, also a strong theme in the Existentialism of such philosophers as Heidegger and Sartre, the common root being the Idealist element of meaning-bestowal and spontaneity. The excesses to which these insights have nevertheless led are well exposed in the later chapters of David Cooper's *Illusions of Equality* (1980), though Richard Pring's aptly titled article 'Knowledge out of Control'[14] and his book *Knowledge and Schooling* (1976) were an earlier much needed exposure of some serious epistemological shortcomings in the genre.

IV

If linguistic, phenomenological and Marxist modes of argument are each limited in their usefulness, as I claim that they are, what paradigm might better serve? Should philosophers of education perhaps return to their historical predecessors? Although the 'history of educational ideas' tended to be swept aside in the self-confident optimism of the sixties, earlier philosophers have never been quite lost from view. Robin Barrow in his *Plato, Utilitarianism and Education* (1975) re-examined the writings of Plato. John White, in an interesting joint authorship with a historian, has looked at the Idealist tradition of educational reformers in *Philosophers as Educational Reformers* (1979). F. W. Garforth at Hull has produced several books on different historical philosophers and Peters' book *Essays on Educators* (1981) similarly looks back. Much benefit can still be gained from Dewey's classic *Democracy and Education* (1916) for its comprehensiveness, its historical sense and its awareness of other disciplines. But Dewey's arguments lack sharpness, he was elusive on fundamental questions of value and he overdid the role of science as a model for all problem-solving. Dewey was reassessed in Peters' collection *John Dewey Re-considered* (1977).

I do not myself think that philosophy of education stands in any need of a single paradigm. Its patterns and strategies of argument should be tailored to the subject matter under discussion, which is normally certain general concepts, principles, positions or practices. It should make any necessary distinctions to clarify meaning, explore conceptual possibilities and try to identify what is necessary and what is contingent. It should expose question-begging, misleading claims and inconsistency.

It should draw implications, show the full extent of someone's commitments, reveal absurd consequences, highlight by parallel arguments, draw attention to unnoticed alternatives and test assumptions. It should probe the validity of justifications, draw attention to areas of undeserved neglect, redress serious imbalances and assemble pertinent reminders.

Further, philosophy of education should expose narrow conceptions, probe presuppositions and reveal hidden connections, or expose spurious unity. It should clarify ideals and articulate imaginative new conceptions. It should re-describe to bring into different focus, show how certain notions will or will not do the work expected of them, show how one thing prevents the recognition of another, identify misplaced emphases or misdirected attention and set things in a wider illuminating context.

All of this and more carries us far beyond the narrowness of a linguistic technique, indifferent even as to its subject matter. It is a mode of critical thinking related to an evolving tradition of inquiry which it would be doctrinal to try to render more precise.

Amongst the many values implicit in these activities should be consistency, truth and adequacy. By 'adequacy' I mean doing justice to the question and the issues which it raises. This will typically imply an awareness of the range of interests with which the question is tangled, something of the historical context and the possible further implications. In fact even in the linguistic period much work of this broader kind was done. When Peters, in his inaugural lecture, used a linguistic paradigm *to* examine education, and contrasted his own approach with the more synthetic approach of his predecessor, he did less than justice to the contributions which he then himself proceeded to make. For his work on the education of the emotions, motivation, moral education, behaviourism, the transcendental deduction and various social principles itself amounted to an ambitious synthesis. The wide range of Peters' output can be seen in his collections of his own papers *Psychology and Ethical Development* (1974) and *Education and the Education of Teachers* (1977).

To illustrate the generality of theme and the variety of critical tactics which are characteristic of philosophy of education, I will very briefly outline some issues which have been of continuing interest. As a first example, I take Hirst's still very influential 'forms of knowledge' thesis. This was to the effect that propositional knowledge is of some seven or so irreducibly different kinds, each having their own distinctive categorial concepts and truth-tests. The thesis had the widest of educational implications as is evident from the echoes of it that are to be found in many working papers, official reports and articles. It was a bold conception, providing a coherent modern version of what a liberal education might be. It had implications for the possibility of curricular integration, balance, mental abilities and development, and the nature of the teacher's authority.

The thesis has, however, not been short *of* critics, quite apart from certain sociologists whose philosophical naivety promptly led them into a crude misunderstanding of it. The very notion of a 'form' has been declared unclear. The list of the forms has been challenged in its completeness and indeed its correctness. Is religion really a form of *knowledge*? Does history have distinctive concepts? Is not geometry a very different 'form' from algebra? The conception of a distinctive truth-test has been argued to be much too simple and the analytic strategy has been seen as scientistic. The exhaustiveness of the division has been challenged on the grounds that much commonsense knowledge appears to fall into none of the forms, so that it must be a set of specialised disciplines which are being described. In that case, the forms will not be the conditions of any possible experience or of all mental development. If that is true, will the forms not then lack universality and be historically relative? And what of justification? Why attach importance to an initiation into forms of knowledge? Surely their importance cannot lie just in their formal distinctiveness? And can they really be regarded as being of equal weight?

This cannot be the place to assess the validity of each of these criticisms, or such alternative conceptions as Elliott's. At least two important elements of the original thesis seem to come through as of lasting interest: that knowledge is not all of a piece and that this diversity could well have a bearing on ideas of balance in the curriculum. And since Hirst's thesis will not be in every way totally different from any other, then many of the insights generated in this debate will have much wider applications.

A second continuing theme with wide implications is that of behaviourism. By this I mean the Skinnerian thesis that 'mental life and the world in which it is lived are inventions',[15] the preferred alternative conception being that of an organism emitting incipient movements which can be shaped into desired topographies by controlling the environmental contingencies of reinforcement. Philosophers of education have, for a change, been at one with Marxists in attacking this doctrine, though on somewhat different grounds.

A first difficulty has been to understand the unit of 'behaviour', since physical movements are highly ambiguous in their meaning. It has been argued that human behaviour is not to be understood without reference to the person's beliefs, desires, intentions and self-images, which link more widely still with a social world of customs, practices, rules and institutions. Apart from this web of shared understanding, we have no criterion for what the unit of behaviour is supposed to be. There are still further problems of how, apart from such an understanding, appropriate reinforcers can be chosen and how they are to be connected with what they are supposed to reinforce. And how does the Skinnerian propose to get the 'first instance' of a line of behaviour he wishes to shape in, say, learning physics or French, or appreciating poetry?

Whereas the arguments surrounding Hirst's thesis are concerned to test the validity of a positive conception, those surrounding Skinnerian behaviourism are designed more to avert an educational disaster. For behaviourism is likely, as Hugh Sockett argued in his book *Designing the Curriculum* (1976), to narrow educational objectives, to confine what is taught to what can be measured and to produce 'teaching for the test'. So far is it from being an ethically neutral technology that it typically presupposes that experimental 'subjects' must be adapted to unchanged institutions, and it incorporates a very limited version of utilitarianism as its ethic. It may even take on a note of messianism. In so far as the practices of 'behaviour modification' escape these dangers, it is probably because the practitioners are more human than their doctrine and are really only making more systematic and intelligent use of ordinary encouragement and discouragement.

As a final example of a philosophical topic that has been of continuing interest, we might take personal autonomy considered as an educational aim. Whereas at first this was discussed chiefly in the context of moral education, it was soon realised that this was a value relevant to the whole curriculum. I traced its connections with progressivism in my book *The Philosophy of Primary Education* (1964) and with discovery methods in *Problems in Primary Education* (1976), while J. P. White, in his book *Towards a Compulsory Curriculum* (1973), even went so far as to argue for the justifiability of a uniform compulsory curriculum on the grounds that it would equip pupils precisely for the exercise of autonomy.

A threefold analysis of the nature of autonomy has been fairly widely accepted, embracing the making of independent judgments (or authenticity), a degree of reflectiveness on the criteria of judgment and integrity in acting according to one's judgments. But the value of this educational aim has been less easy to explicate, some stressing the paradox of questioning it, some relating it to prudence, while others point to the establishment of a definite identity or to the personal dignity that goes with accepting final responsibility for one's life and actions. The connections with the conditions which might best foster its development, and its economic and political implications, are very much open questions. There is also a problem of reconciling autonomy with the necessity for authority, both in early learning and at the level of political action. A varied collection of perspectives on autonomy is contained in Doyle's *Educational Judgements* (1973).

Philosophical understanding develops organically and not aggregatively. What one later comes to see modifies what earlier one had thought to have been settled. In philosophy, everything connects with everything else. For example, if behaviourism was valid as a conception of human beings, then Hirst's distinctive 'form' of 'understanding other people' would disappear and become a part of natural science. Again, if Skinner was right, then we should have to agree that autonomous man 'has been constructed from our ignorance, and as our understanding increases, the very stuff of which he is composed vanishes'.[16] To complete the third side of this triangle of relations, if the Hirstian forms were really the irreducible bases of all our knowledge, then would they not be the necessary foundation on which autonomy should be built?

There will surely be a place from time to time in philosophy of education for some limited Lockean underlabouring, clearing the ground a little of weeds and obstacles. But by contrast with the narrow discussions typical of the linguistic period, there is now much more of a sense of the wholeness of problems. A survey of all and everything would be too much to ask of anyone, but at least a critical widening of perspective is to be expected as one of the gains from a study of philosophy. And in so far as the transformation of our understanding affects our conception of the situation, then this will have its pervasive effects on our action too. For as we think, so we act, in schools and out of them.

V

As to the future, that can hardly be regarded as encouraging. Any discipline benefits from new emphases and new approaches as fresh minds tackle both new and perennial problems, whereas new appointments are now likely to be a rarity or even non-existent. The schools are likely to be pre-occupied with the management of contraction and coping with cuts of one sort or another. In the absence of any major curricular or institutional innovations to loosen the deeper structures of practice, the perceived needs of practitioners are likely to be increasingly of a narrow and immediate kind, which will create a climate of expectation inimical to the kinds of insight offered by the liberalising disciplines.

It is therefore most unlikely that a major alternative to the present broadly analytic style of doing philosophy of education will emerge in the immediate future, though the linguistic paradigm is likely to have increasingly restricted use. Fresh attacks will doubtless be made on the perennial problems of aims, curriculum, learning, authority, equality and the relation of theory to practice. New or newly prominent topics may well become the centre of attention, such as the political control of education, political education,[17] the curriculum and work[18] and the nature of further education.

In such a situation, one benefit that may accrue is that the great dust raised by the activity of the late sixties and early seventies will settle and it will be possible to distinguish more clearly the solid shapes from insubstantial phantoms and passing fancies. Perhaps on a larger timescale it is good that there should be such a rhythm of rapid advance followed by a period of stocktaking and consolidation.

Notes

1 R. S. Peters: *Education as Initiation* (Evans, London, 1964).
2 In R. D. Archambault (ed.): *Philosophical Analysis and Education* (RKP, London, 1965), pp. 113–38.

3 P. H. Hirst: 'Philosophy and Educational Theory', *British Journal of Educational Studies* (12, 1, 1963).
4 P. H. Hirst: '*Philosophy and Educational Theory*', *British Journal of Educational Studies* (12, 1, 1963).
5 In J. Doyle (ed.): *Educational Judgements* (RKP, London, 1973), Ch. 14.
6 In T. Pateman (ed.): *Counter Course* (Penguin, Harmondsworth, 1972), pp. 115–39.
7 E. Gellner: *Words and Things* (Gollancz, London, 1959).
8 See reference 5.
9 J. Wilson: 'Concepts, Contestability and the Philosophy of Education', *Journal of Philosophy of Education* (15, 1, 198).
10 In S. C. Brown (ed.): *Philosophers Discuss Education* (Macmillan, London, 1975), Ch. 4.
11 R. K. Elliott: 'Education and Justification', *Proceedings of the Philosophy of Education Society* (11, 1977).
12 For example, R. K. Elliott: 'Aestheticism, Imagination and Schooling', *Journal of Philosophy of Education* (15, 1, 198).
13 D. Gorbutt: 'The New Sociology of Education', *Education for Teaching* (No. 89, 1972).
14 R. Pring: 'Knowledge out of Control', *Education for Teaching*, (No. 89, 1972).
15 B. F. Skinner: *About Behaviourism* (Cape, London, 1974), p. 104.
16 B. F. Skinner: *Beyond Freedom and Dignity* (Cape, London, 1972), p. 200.
17 For example, see P. A. White: 'Work-place Democracy and Political Education', *Journal of Philosophy of Education* (13, 1979).
18 For example, see C. Wringe: 'Education, Schooling and the World of Work', *British Journal of Educational Studies* (29, 2, 1981).

Note on Journal Articles

It has been possible to refer to only a very few journal articles in this paper, though some philosophers of education have made important contributions primarily or entirely through journal articles. The principal British outlet was and remains the *Proceedings of the Philosophy of Education Society*, since 1978 retitled the *Journal of Philosophy of Education*. Philosophical articles have also regularly appeared in such British journals as *British Journal of Educational Studies, Cambridge Journal of Education, Journal of Curriculum Studies, Journal of Further and Higher Education* (formerly *Education for Teaching*), *Journal of Moral Education*, and the *Oxford Review of Education*.

Abroad, the principal outlets have been *Educational Philosophy and Theory* (Australia), *Educational Theory* (USA), *Studies in Philosophy and Education* (USA) and the proceedings entitled *Philosophy of Education of the American Philosophy of Education Society.*

8 The Sociology of Education, 1952–82

O. Banks

Author

Olive Banks (1923–2006) published her classic sociological work *Parity and Prestige in English Secondary Education* in 1955: a rigorous critique of the social divisiveness inherent in the tripartite secondary education system. In 1968 she published the first textbook in the field of the Sociology of Education. She was Professor of Sociology at the University of Leicester from 1973 to 1982. During the 1980s and 1990s she published key works on feminism including: *Faces of Feminism* (1981), *Becoming a Feminist: the Social Origins of 'First Wave' Feminism* (1987) and *The Politics of British Feminism 1918–1970* (1993). Her own accomplishments in the male-dominated academy were also achieved in the face of prejudice: when she retired in 1982, she was the only female professor at the University of Leicester.

Article

The Sociology of Education, 1952–82 (30, 1: 18–31) was published in the 30th Anniversary volume of the *BJES*, within which, according to the editorial, colleagues 'engaged in a kind of stock-taking of thinking and writing about education in the past and present'. (Other articles from the volume may be found on pages 94 and 123 in this book.) The article is a thoroughly scholarly, detailed and passionate account of the development of the field in the decades following the Second World War. It critically examines the role of the London School of Economics, the work of Glass, Floud and Halsey relating to social stratification and social mobility in the 1950s. The article considers the expansion in sociology and the sociology of education, in the 1960s and 1970s when there 'was the increasing involvement of those engaged in some form or other of teacher education both as researchers and as consumers whether of research reports or, even more importantly, of teaching material such as readers and textbooks'.

It perhaps comes as no surprise that the article is imbued with Banks' optimism: an optimism that is easy to understand when one considers the following extract:

> Looking back, therefore, over thirty years of the sociology of education in Britain, the most immediate impression is one of tremendous expansion.

Moreover this was not simply an expansion in numbers, whether of teachers or students, although this was certainly important. Even more significant was the expansion in the scope of the subject, and the inclusion, throughout the 1970s, of new theoretical perspectives, new methods, and new subject areas.

The influences in the 1970s and 1980s of the role of the Institute of Education, University of London; the works of Bernstein, Hargreaves, Lacey and Young; the feminist writings of Byrne, Deem and Delamont, are also considered, as is the part played by the Open University.

Written thirty years ago, the article ends on a note of 'cautious optimism':

The future, it is true, is uncertain but at least for the present the subject is still very much alive. In the present educational climate perhaps we cannot ask for more.

If one scans the lists of current journals, explores the wealth of new, high-quality publications related to research into race, gender and class issues, it is perhaps easy to agree with Olive Banks. What she could not have foreseen, perhaps, has been the stripping out of the sociological, historical, philosophical and psychological theoretical bases underpinning teacher education in England and Wales and its replacement by a competence-, latterly standards-, based model of teacher training. In the present educational climate, should we ask for more?

Other related articles include: *Karl Mannheim and the Sociology of Education* (1, 2: 99–113) on page 1 in this book; *Sociology of education and the education of teachers* (20, 2: 137–47); *Post mortem or post modern? Some reflections on British sociology of education* (44, 4: 395–408); *Education and the middle classes: Against reductionism in educational theory and research* (55, 1: 37–55).

The Sociology of Education, 1952–82

by Olive Banks, Department of Sociology, University of Leicester

Thirty years ago, when the *British Journal of Educational Studies* was founded, sociology itself was still only in an early stage of its development so far as this country was concerned. Although well established at the London School of Economics, it was not until the late 1940s that it began to attract more than very small numbers of students, and the boom which was to carry it, not only into every university, but into every branch of higher education and eventually into the schools, was still quite undreamed of by teachers and students alike. The thirty years of publication which the *British Journal of Educational Studies* is now celebrating were therefore years in which both sociology itself and the sociology of education as one of its branches established themselves firmly in the British educational scene.

In 1952 sociology was still largely dominated by the London School of Economics and the newly emerging sociology of education may be said to have its origins there in the years after the end of the Second World War. The School's enquiry into social mobility in Britain,[1] directed by David Glass, looked closely at the educational system as an aspect of social stratification and may be said to have focused attention upon education as a subject matter of *sociological* enquiry. At the same time, a pre-occupation with social mobility was to shape the developing subject for almost all of the next twenty years. Jean Floud, who had been deeply involved in the social mobility survey, was later to collaborate with A. H. Halsey in one of the first post-war studies of educational inequality;[2] but even more significant was the bibliography and trend report they prepared for *Current Sociology*[3] and the Reader they edited with C. A. Anderson in 1961.[4]

The subject during these years was characterized by a concern for the ways in which the educational system related to both the division of labour and social stratification. This concern was set moreover in a theoretical perspective, largely American in origin, which saw education in terms of its function in the provision of a literate and adaptable work-force to meet the needs of an advanced technological society. In the British context, however, this functionalist perspective was combined with a critical attitude towards a wastage of working-class ability, which was seen as both unjust *and* inefficient.[5] Moreover because it was both descriptive *and* prescriptive the analysis of social-class inequality, which was its most distinctive feature, was combined with a search for what Floud and Halsey in 1958 called the 'social determinants of educability', a search indeed which was to be very characteristic of the sociology of education throughout the 1960s. It is interesting to notice for example that Bernstein, also a product of the London School of Economics, was concerned during these years with similar problems,[6] although his own individual theoretical approach differentiated him from most other British sociologists.

During these years the explanation for working-class wastage was seen partly within the educational system itself, partly with a disjunction between school and home which was usually expressed in terms of a failure on the part of working-class parents to prepare their children to succeed in school. It is not fair, therefore, to accuse sociologists of failing to examine the school system as a cause of the lower levels of working-class achievement. These were years in which both the system of selection for secondary education and the system of organizing schools into streams came under attack, and although most of those who became involved in the debate were not sociologists, it is probably fair to say that the general con-sensus amongst sociologists working in the field of education was in favour of comprehensive schools and against streaming. Nevertheless a great deal of attention was also paid by sociologists to the influence of home background on educability. This involved a very wide range of perspectives, including amongst others Bernstein's socio-linguistic codes, family size, parental aspirations and values, and the influence of such material standards as income and housing.[7]

The belief that there was a great deal of wastage of working-class ability led sociologists to consider not only the causes of such wastage but also its remedies and this created a natural alliance between sociologists and policy-makers, and especially, although not entirely,[8] between sociologists and the Labour Party. This involved them not only in a critical evaluation of particular educational policies but also in a search for new strategies, of which Halsey's own involvement in action research into Educational Priority Areas is perhaps the best example.[9] It also drew policy-makers into research on educational wastage and educability.[10] The result was a large body of material, making use of a wide variety of perspectives, which demonstrated the intractability of the problems rather than contributing very much towards a solution. The extent of inequalities in education was certainly documented, and this in itself was a useful antidote to the optimism of the 1950s, but the causes of these inequalities still remained largely unexplained.

The 1960s, as we have seen, were years of expansion in sociology, and the sociology of education shared in this boom, particularly in the colleges of education which now, for the first time, began to accept sociology as an important element in teacher training. By 1970, indeed, the ascendancy not simply of the London School of Economics and its ex-students but of university departments of sociology was over, and university departments of education and colleges of education began to take their place. Of these, by far the most important was the London Institute of Education, which already housed the influential Basil Bernstein. Later the Open University was to become equally important. Under their joint influence a new approach to the subject was propagated which was to look more closely at the actual process of schooling. Both Hargreaves in 1967[11] and Lacey in 1970[12] had attempted to look much more closely at what went on in schools but the 'new' sociology, as it came to be called, went much further in its rejection of what had gone before. Anti-functionalist, and anti-deterministic, it preached an interactionist perspective in which man creates and defines his own social reality. The central task of the sociology of education, therefore, was seen as an examination of the participants in the educational process through an exploration of their perceptions and assumptions as well as their interaction with each other. There was a change in method, most significantly, in the exchange of observation for the social survey, and a change in what were seen as problem areas. The questions which interested the new generation of researchers were no longer which children fail, or even why these children fail, but what was the nature or, perhaps more accurately, the status of school knowledge. In fact what were now being asked were much more fundamental questions on the nature of failure itself. The causes of failure moreover were no longer to be sought in concepts like educability. Indeed, attention was to be focused on the assumptions held within the school, and especially by the teachers, on the meaning of success and failure, on definitions of good and bad pupils and on differences between what teachers say and what they do. The content of education became a new focus of concern, and so did the day-to-day interaction within the classroom.

The new approach spread very rapidly, propagated both by M. Young's Reader *Knowledge and Control*[13] and by the Open University Course No 282 *School and Society*.[14] It appealed particularly to those in teacher training institutions,[15] partly because of its apparently more practical implications. Perhaps most important of all, however, was the message in much of the new writing that by raising the consciousness of teachers schools would be revitalised and the promise made in 1944 of education for all would be met.[16]

The 'new' sociology of education was not, however, to hold its dominance for very long. It was soon superseded in its turn by what, for want of a better term, we may call the neo-Marxist perspective. Nevertheless it has left its mark on the subject, not least in the impetus it has given to work set within the framework of the school, and particularly of the classroom. Although some of this work owes its inspiration to an older ethnographic tradition within social anthropology there is no doubt that the new sociology has had a very significant part to play. Actual research programmes were indeed slow to develop but more recently a number of collections of papers, many based on actual work in schools, have been published, several under the editorship of Peter Woods at the Open University.[17] Other sociologists at work in this field include Sara Delamont,[18] John Eggleston[19] and Ronald King.[20]

The claim of the 'new' sociology of education that it represented a totally new direction for the subject has not therefore been fulfilled. Although it continues to attract supporters it no longer dominates the field. Moreover many, even of its founders, have become disenchanted with its approach and have turned, in part at least, back, not certainly to the 'old' sociology of education as it existed in the 1960s, but to a version of Marxism which once more brings macro-sociology back to the centre of the stage. Part of the reason for this move is a recognition of theoretical weaknesses within the approach itself, which have become increasingly obvious even to its own adherents. The most important of these is a failure to concern itself with the constraints imposed by the wider social structure. Sharp and Green, for example, criticize it for losing sight of the 'sociological phenomenon of externality and constraint'[21] and Young and Whitty accuse it of presenting education as if it were 'being carried on in a social vacuum'.[22] Critics have also pointed to the romanticism which lies at the heart of the new approach[23] and the naivety which envisages that inviting teachers to examine their own practices will in itself be sufficient to transform their behaviour.[24] Indeed, in spite of the relativism implicit at least theoretically in the new approach, most of its supporters were as anxious to reform the educational system as their predecessors had been, and if they pinned their faith on teacher consciousness rather than such structural changes as comprehensive schools, mixed ability groupings or pre-school education, the optimism as to the possibility of reform was shared by practitioners of both the 'new' and the 'old' sociology.

The neo-Marxist approach was a move back to macro-sociology in which political and economic forces replaced the classroom and even the school itself as the central focus of analysis, and to this extent the issues which had concerned Floud and Halsey in the late 1950s were now reinstated. Indeed, Halsey himself has pointed to the extent to which sociologists during this period were concerned to point out the ways in which the educational system reproduces the class structure of Western industrial societies,[25] an aspect of the educational system which is also absolutely central to neo-Marxist analysis. The difference, and it is an important one, lies not so much in the level of analysis itself, as in the implications for social change as between the two perspectives. Whereas the 'old' sociology of education was optimistic about reform, much of the neo-Marxist sociology is pessimistic. Both sociologies, it is true, want to break out of the present situation, but the neo-Marxists have little, if any, faith in purely educational remedies. As Marxists, even if only in a loosely interpreted sense, they see the only hope for the future in a total transformation of class relationships in society, and this is not to be achieved by the kind of structural alterations advocated during the 1950s and 1960s. If the educational system itself is to play a part in this transformation it will be through a radicalization of pupils and teachers to play their part in the class struggle.

It is impossible to understand the significance of this particular perspective simply in terms of the theoretical imperfections of earlier sociologists. The appeal of one or other versions of Marxism is very widespread at the present time, and is largely a consequence of changes in the economic climate which seem to demonstrate the weaknesses of capitalism, and so enhance the apparent validity of some kind of Marxist solution to the problems of our time. As the buoyancy of the affluent 1960s was replaced by the pessimism of the 1970s, in the face of world recession and runaway inflation, the faith in the social and economic solutions of the 1950s and 1960s became more difficult to sustain. Moreover the early 1970s saw an end to the belief in education as a panacea which had been so marked a feature of the postwar years in all industrial societies. Whether as a form of human capital, a means of individual advancement, an enhancement of intellectual life, or a way to achieve a more equal society, there was a general consensus that education was both an individual and a social good. This consensus was shattered by a series of attacks which not only denied the economic and social benefits of educational advance, but even, in some instances, went so far as to advocate the actual de-schooling of society.[26]

Although many of these attacks originated in the United States they were widely read and discussed in Britain. At the same time, the failure of many educational reforms actually to achieve their ends strengthened the mood of pessimism and contributed to the persuasiveness of a Marxist or neo-Marxist analysis.[27]

A number of collections of papers in the mid-70s heralded the move from an interactionist to a neo-Marxist perspective. One of the earliest was *Educability, Schools and Ideology* edited by Michael Flude and John Ahier and published in 1974.[28] This was chiefly important, however, as a vehicle for a largely Marxist critique of the 'new' sociology of education. More significant, because it attracted a lot of publicity and reached a wider audience, was the Open University Reader, *Schooling and Capitalism*, issued in 1976.[29] It was associated with a new course E202, *Schooling and Society*, in which, while some contributors remained loyal to an interactionist approach, others had moved towards a Marxist sociology strongly influenced by the American attempt by Bowles and Gintis to apply a Marxist analysis to the American educational system.[30]

At this time, too, Bernstein's work was entering a new phase, largely influenced by the French sociologist Bourdieu. Although Durkheim still remained the strongest influence on Bernstein, as indeed, it may be argued, on Bourdieu himself, there are also Marxist elements in the relationship between the educational system and the class structure.

The general effect of both Bowles and Gintis and Bourdieu was to re-affirm some of the functionalist elements in the sociology of education. That is to say, educational systems were once more the unit of analysis, rather than schools, or classrooms, and these systems were analysed in terms of their *function*, although the nature of that function had now changed. I have argued elsewhere, for example, that 'whereas the structural functionalist sees the educational system functioning in the interest of society as a whole the Marxists see it functioning in the interests of a dominant class'.[31] Both Bowles and Gintis and Bourdieu, moreover, stress above all else the way in which the educational system *reproduces* the class structure in which it is embedded.

A somewhat different influence, although still within a generally Marxist frame of reference, has impinged upon the sociology of education from the Centre for Contemporary Cultural Studies. Specifically historical in its emphasis, one of its main themes, illustrated, for example, in an early paper by Richard Johnson, is the way in which nineteenth-century education was used to control the 'patterns of thought, sentiments and behaviour of the working class'.[32] Working-class culture, and the extent to which it has been dominated by an educational system designed to serve the needs of a capitalist society, has since become a predominant theme of the Centre, illustrated both by the collection of historical papers edited by McCann[33] and Willis's[34] ethnographic account of working-class boys today in

Learning to Labour. There are differences, particularly of methodology, between
the work of the Centre and that of Bowles and Gintis and Bourdieu, but it is
important to note that both, quite unlike the functionalists of the 1950s and
1960s, see the role of education in terms of authority and social control, rather
than as a matter simply of the acquisition of skills and knowledge.

It is too early, as yet, to assess the full impact of neo-Marxism on the sociology
of education. Initially at least it has had the same divisive effect as the eruption of
the new directions in sociology in the early 1970s, since the neo-Marxists tend to
work within their own intellectual tradition. It has seemed therefore in recent
years that there are not two sociologies of education but three. Possibly, and this
will be discussed later in the article, this phase is now coming to an end.

In the meantime there is no doubt that neo-Marxism has had several desirable
consequences, not least of which has been the return of the macro dimension to
the subject and a renewed concern with structural aspects of society. More important
still, since after all macro-sociology had been dominant right through the 1950s
and 1960s, was a quite new emphasis on history. This is not to argue that no
sociologists working in education have been interested in history. Warwick and
Williams have discussed several historical studies in their recent article 'History and
the Sociology of Education'[35] and to these might be added my own early *Parity
and Prestige in English Secondary Education*[36] which actually started life as a PhD
thesis under the joint supervision of David Glass and Jean Floud in the early
1950s, when all three of us were at the London School of Economics. Moreover
some of the contributions to *Knowledge and Control,* which pioneered the 'new'
sociology of education in 1971, were making a strong plea for more comparative
and historical studies in the sociology of education. This was particularly true of the
editor, M. Young, in his own contribution to the volume[37] and, indeed, later
on he was to be highly critical of the way in which the 'new' approach had
ignored macro-sociology and devoted itself to the 'minutiae of classroom
interaction'.[38]

Nevertheless, neither the structural functionalism of the 1950s and 1960s nor
the interactionism of the 1970s allowed much scope for history, dominated as they
were by methodologies that stressed the collection of new material, whether by
interview and questionnaire or by observation and tape-recorder. It was left to the
neo-Marxists, therefore, with their preoccupation with problems of historical
change and historical process to bring history back to the centre of the stage.

It may also be argued that neo-Marxism found a way out of the relativism that
was a feature of much of the 'new' sociology. As we have seen already, this relativism
was by no means carried through consistently and many were led into a 'romantic
possibilitarianism' in which changes in teachers' perceptions seemed to offer a means
to transform the schools and even society itself. In practice, indeed, the relativism
involved was often no more than a desire to affirm the validity of alternative cultures,
especially those of the 'underdog', as against those of authority figures, including
sociologists themselves. The attraction of neo-Marxism was that it appeared to
offer a way of demonstrating that the 'underdog' was not only exploited but destined, under socialism, to triumph. Undoubtedly this is an over-simplified way of

looking at Marxism but there is little doubt that it goes a long way to explain the ease with which so many converts *to* the 'new' sociology of education soon found one or other variety of neo-Marxism an even more congenial home.

Neo-Marxism has, of course, its own dangers to avoid, not least a tendency to dogmatism which springs from an attitude to Marx which has in it more of religious faith than scientific scepticism, and which can lead Marxist writings out of the realm of sociology altogether.[39] Fortunately for the sociology of education, much recent work, if inspired by Marx, is also alive to the need for both argument and evidence. A more immediate danger is the tendency to move into a kind of Marxist functionalism which is as deterministic as anything in structural functionalism itself. The educational system indeed is pictured as so effective in its role that it is difficult to conceive any way forward, so that the general effect is as pessimistic as anything to be found in functionalism. Indeed, because British sociology of education in the 1950s and 1960s believed in gradualism it was always optimistic about future reform.

Pessimistic determinism has not, however, remained a dominant mood in the sociology of education in this country. Perhaps because of the strongly antideterministic stance of the 'new' sociology, and its insistence that man was essentially an active not a passive being, there has been a deliberate search for ways to break out of the apparently closed circle in which the educational system reproduces the class structure. Although perhaps less consistently worked out than theories like those of Bourdieu, which attempt to explain why the system succeeds, there have been several attempts to examine working-class resistance, and particularly the interpretation of such resistance as aspects of the class struggle. Such attempts may sometimes indeed be records of failure, and this is perhaps particularly well exemplified in the study by Willis, already mentioned.[40] He demonstrates how resistance to school succeeds only in locking working-class boys even further into the world of manual labour. Another approach to resistance is found in Richard Johnson's study of radical education as it existed in Britain in the early nineteenth century.[41] Again the emphasis is on failure rather than success, but it does point the way beyond a simple correspondence theory of the relationship between education and social class.

The attention paid here to neo-Marxism is not intended to imply that this particular school of thought has totally dominated the subject in recent years. The 'old' sociology of education has never been completely eclipsed by new approaches[42] and, as we have already noticed, studies of classroom interaction continue to flourish. Durkheim, too, remains an important alternative influence, especially through his influence on both Bernstein and Bourdieu. Moreover a recently translated study by Durkheim *The Evolution of Educational Thought* has received quite a lot of favourable attention.[43] The work of Margaret Scotford Archer is also influenced by Durkheim, but perhaps even more strongly by Max Weber. Determinedly historical and comparative in its methodology her work is nevertheless outside the Marxist tradition.[44]

One major development in the subject still remains to be described, although in this case, its novelty lies in its subject matter, rather than either its methodology or its theoretical antecedents. The driving force behind this new development has been feminism, and, more specifically, Women's Studies, and it takes the form of an attempt to bring the education of girls out of its somewhat peripheral position on the fringes of the subject and to make it a central concern. Within this objective the approach may be interactionist or neo-Marxist or, in some cases, an attempt to combine the two so that it may be said to cut across the distinctions that have been made in this paper. Its enemy is the traditional sociology of education which has shown such marked neglect of sexual inequality as either a theoretical or (and perhaps this is more important) a moral problem.

Sandra Acker[45] has recently documented the extent of this neglect, although it should perhaps be mentioned in passing that this was by no means peculiar to the study of education and was very general in sociology.[46] More recently an emergence of feminist scholarship is beginning to devote increasing attention to the education of girls, and particularly the way in which the school plays its part in the reproduction of gender relationship. In these studies, which are at the level of both the school and the classroom, gender appears as a powerful differentiating device both for teachers and pupils.[47] Moreover content analysis of school texts shows not only much neglect of women, but considerable stereotyping. Women for example are regularly shown in a much narrower range of roles than is the case in real life.[48] By 1978 there was sufficient interest in the topic to allow the almost simultaneous publication of two textbooks in the field, Eileen M. Byrne's *Women and Education*[49] and Rosemary Deem's *Women and Schooling.*[50] Although written from different points of view[51] their contents, taken together, give a good idea of the range of material already becoming available.

The concentration on studies of schools and classrooms, however valuable their findings, does however give rise to precisely those problems which were discussed earlier in a more general context. There is an absence in short of both a historical and a structural perspective and it is encouraging to see that attention is turning increasingly in this direction. One such approach is through the relationship between school and work, since it is clear that gender differentiation in school cannot be understood apart from gender differentiation in the world of work. The recent publication of *Schooling for Women's Work*, edited by Rosemary Deem,[52] is a good indication of recent work which is being carried out in this particular area and which demonstrates not only that discrimination against women in education militates against their achievement in employment, but that their role in the labour market also works to their detriment in the type and level of the schooling they receive.

On the other hand, it can be argued that it is woman's domestic role which is crucial to an understanding of both women's schooling and women's work. There is a need therefore for the sociology of education to explore the sexual division of labour in the home as well as in the work place. It is for this reason that Miriam David's *The State, the Family and Education*[53] is particularly relevant as a possible pointer to demonstrating as it does the way in which social and educational policy maintains existing relationships within both the family and the economy.

The extent to which women's studies of this kind will influence the sociology of education as a subject has yet to be determined. Although they hold out the hope that gender will no longer be a neglected category, Sandra Acker has pointed to the extent to which this material has been published *outside* the regular educational journals, with the danger that it will pass unnoticed outside the field of women's studies itself. To some extent of course there is a preference on the part of some women academics to address themselves to other women, but the earlier neglect by a profession dominated by male sociologists suggests that this is not the complete answer. It is indeed surely significant that the subject of women's schooling even today is still largely the province of *women* academics, and the future of this aspect of the sociology of education may depend on the continuing and active presence of *women* researchers.[54]

Looking back, therefore, over thirty years of the sociology of education in Britain, the most immediate impression is one of tremendous expansion. Moreover this was not simply an expansion in numbers, whether of teachers or students, although this was certainly important. Even more significant was the expansion in the scope of the subject, and the inclusion, throughout the 1970s, of new theoretical perspectives, new methods, and new subject areas. Another feature of the late 1960s and 1970s was the increasing involvement of those engaged in some form or other of teacher education both as researchers and as consumers whether of research reports or, even more importantly, of teaching material such as Readers and textbooks. The part played by the Open University Courses and Readers throughout the 1970s has also been noted, for example in connection with the 'new' sociology of education and the neo-Marxist approach.

Although, therefore, the subject continued to display great vitality throughout the 1970s, in spite of shrinking numbers involved in teacher education towards the end of the period, the existence of what amounted to rival factions, and the controversy between them seemed at times to threaten the future of the subject. Indeed to some extent there was a split, with different schools of sociology pursuing their own interpretation of the subject and denying the usefulness, if not the actual validity, of other schools of thought.

The 1980s, on the other hand, seem to have opened on a more optimistic note. There has been less rancour in the debate, and calls for some kind of synthesis, which had begun in the late 1970s, increased in number. The first issue, in March 1980, of the *British Journal of the Sociology of Education* also declared its intention of trying to reflect different points of view. There is no doubt therefore of a growing will to cooperate. What is more in question is whether such a move has any chance of success.

At one level, certainly, the extreme divisions of the early 1970s are no more. Interactionists confess the need for understanding structures and neo-Marxists and other macro-sociologists are increasingly aware that they must avoid deterministic theories of social processes which leave out of account human wills and human purposes. There is, therefore, not only a desire for greater unity but a move away from positions which in their extreme form, at least, are certainly quite irreconcilable. There still remains the actual task of synthesis, and, as Andy Hargreaves has pointed out, progress in this direction has been slow and those attempts that have been made are far from satisfactory.[55] The difficulties in achieving a real synthesis are indeed very great and it should, perhaps, cause no surprise that early attempts in that direction offer no more than suggestions to follow.[56] What is encouraging, perhaps, is the fact that more and more attempts are being made.[57]

It is also possible to take comfort from the general buoyancy of the subject as a whole. This is illustrated, for example, by the continuing success of the Sociology of Education Conferences held annually at West Hill College, Birmingham and by the launching in 1980 of the first British journal of the sociology of education. If teacher education is now diminished in quantity, the appeal of the subject does not seem to have fallen for those who remain. On this ground, too, therefore, there are reasons for cautious optimism. The future, it is true, is uncertain but at least for the present the subject is still very much alive. In the present educational climate perhaps we cannot ask for more.

Notes

1 D. V. Glass: *Social Mobility in Britain* (Routledge & Kegan Paul, London, 1954).
2 J. Floud, A. H. Halsey, F. M. Martin: *Social Class and Educational Opportunity* (Heinemann, London, 1957).
3 J. Floud, A. H. Halsey: 'The Sociology of Education', *Current Sociology* (Vol. 7, 1958).
4 J. Floud, A. H. Halsey, C. A. Anderson: *Education, Economy and Society: A Reader in the Sociology of Education* (Collier-Macmillan, London, 1961).
5 G. Bernbaum: *Knowledge and Ideology in the Sociology of Education* (Macmillan, London, 1977).
6 Especially B. Bernstein: *Class Codes and Control—Theoretical Studies towards a Sociology of Education* (Routledge & Kegan Paul, London, 1971).
7 For a summary of research in this area during the 1950s and 1960s see: O. Banks: *The Sociology of Education* (Batsford, London, 1968, 1971, 1976), chapters 3, 4, 5.
8 See for example the remarks of Edward Boyle quoted in: M. Kogan (ed.): *The Politics of Education* (Penguin, Harmondsworth, 1971), pp. 91–92.
9 A. H. Halsey *et al.*: *Educational Priority* (Department of Education & Science, HMSO, London, 1972).
10 Sometimes successfully, as in the case of the Robbins Report, but sometimes less so. The Plowden Report was severely criticized for its clumsy attempt to use sociological categories.
11 D. H. Hargreaves: *Social Relations in a Secondary School* (Routledge & Kegan Paul, London, 1967).
12 C. Lacey: *Hightown Grammar* (Manchester University Press, 1970).
13 M. Young: *Knowledge and Control* (Collier-Macmillan, London, 1971).
14 Open University: *E282 School and Society Units 1–17* (Open University, 1972).
15 L. Barton and S. Walker: 'Sociology of Education at the Cross-roads', *Educational Review* (1978, Vol. 30).
16 See especially the enthusiasm of D. Gorbutt: 'The New Sociology of Education' in *Education for Teaching* (Vol. 89, 1972).
17 See for example: P. Woods and M. Hammersley (eds): *School Experience* (Croom Helm, London, 1977), P. Woods (ed.): *Teacher Strategies* (Croom Helm, London, 1980), P. Woods (ed.): *Pupil Strategies* (Croom Helm, London, 1980).
18 S. Delamont: *Interaction in the Classroom* (Methuen, London, 1976).

19 J. Eggleston (ed.): *Teacher Decision-making in the Classroom* (Routledge & Kegan Paul, London, 1979).
20 R. King: *All Things Bright and Beautiful?* (Wiley, Chichester, 1979).
21 R. Sharp and A. Green: *Education and Social Control* (Routledge & Kegan Paul, London, 1975).
22 M. Young and G. Whitty (eds): *Society, State and Schooling* (Falmer Press, Brighton, 1977).
23 G. Whitty: 'Sociology and the Problem of Radical Educational Change' in M. Flude and J. Ahier, *Educability, Schools and Ideology* (Croom Helm, London, 1974).
24 M. Young and G. Whitty, *op. cit.* (1977).
25 A. H. Halsey: 'Theoretical advance and empirical challenge', in E. Hopper (ed.) *Readings in the Theory of Educational Systems* (Hutchinson, London, 1971).
26 See for example: I. Illich: *Deschooling Society* (Harper & Row, New York, 1971).
27 For a good account of changing attitudes to education during this period see G. Bernbaum (ed.): *Schooling in Decline* (Macmillan, London, 1979).
28 M. Flude and J. Ahier: *Educability, Schools and Ideology* (Croom Helm, London, 1974).
29 R. Dale *et al.* (eds): *Schooling and Capitalism* (Routledge & Kegan Paul, London, 1977).
30 S. Bowles and H. Gintis: *Schooling in Capitalist America* (Routledge & Kegan Paul, London, 1976).
31 O. Banks: 'School and Society' in L. Barton and R. Meighan, *Sociological Interpretations of Schooling and Classrooms: a Reappraisal* (Nafferton, 1978).
32 R. Johnson: 'Educational policy and social control in early Victorian England', *Past and Present* (Vol. 49, 1970).
33 P. McCann (ed.): *Popular Education and Socialization in the Nineteenth Century* (Macmillan, London, 1977).
34 P. Willis: *Learning to Labour* (Saxon House, London, 1977).
35 D. Warwick and J. Williams: 'History and the Sociology of Education', *British Journal of Sociology of Education* (Vol. 1, 1980).
36 O. Banks: *Parity and Prestige in English Secondary Education* (Routledge & Kegan Paul, London, 1955).
37 M. Young: *Knowledge and Control, op. cit.* (1971), pp. 1–46.
38 M. Young and G. Whitty, *op. cit.* (1977).
39 At least in the view of the present writer.
40 P. Willis, *op. cit.*
41 R. Johnson: 'Really Useful Knowledge' in J. Clarke, C. Critcher and R. Johnson (eds): *Working Class Culture* (Hutchinson, London, 1979).
42 See for example: A. H. Halsey, A. F. Heath and J. M. Ridge: *Origins and Destinations: Family Class and Education in Modern Britain* (Clarendon Press, Oxford, 1980).
43 See for example the comments in D. Warwick and J. Williams, *op. cit.*
44 See for example: M. C. Vaughan and M. S. Archer: *Social Conflict and Educational Change in England and France 1789–1848* (Cambridge University Press, London, 1971). Also M. S. Archer: *The Social Origins of Educational Systems* (Sage, London, 1979).
45 S. L. Acker: 'No Woman's Land. British Sociology of Education 1960–79', *The Sociological Review* (Vol. 29, 1981).
46 It is very obvious in industrial sociology, for example.
47 See for example: À. M. Wolpe: *Some Processes in Sexist Education* (Women's Research and Resources Centre, London, 1977). Also L. Davies and R. Meighan: 'A review of schooling and sex roles with particular reference to the experience of girls in secondary schools', *Educational Review* (Vol. 27, 1975).

48 See for example: G. Lobban: 'Sex roles in reading schemes', *Educational Review* (Vol. 27, 1975).
49 E. M. Byrne: *Women and Education* (Tavistock, London, 1978).
50 R. Deem: *Women and Schooling* (Routledge & Kegan Paul, London, 1978).
51 See my comparison and critique in O. Banks: 'Women and Education' in *British Journal of Sociology of Education* (Vol. 1, 1980).
52 R. Deem (ed.): *Schooling for Women's Work* (Routledge & Kegan Paul, London, 1980).
53 M. E. David: *The State, the Family and Education* (Routledge & Kegan Paul, London, 1980).
54 On the other hand, it is perhaps not without significance that the new Open University Course *E353: Society, Education and the State*, which started in 1981, has a strong emphasis on gender throughout. This may reflect a growing interest on the part of men.
55 A. Hargreaves: 'Synthesis and the study of strategies: a project for the sociological imagination' in P. Woods (ed.): *Pupil Strategies, op. cit.* (1980). The same point has been made more recently by S. A. Walker: see his extended review of 'The Language of Teaching' in *British Journal of Sociology of Education* (Vol. 1, 1980).
56 This is true of both Bernstein and Bourdieu, for example, whose theories involve both micro and macro elements.
57 See A. Hargreaves, *op. cit.*, for a review of some of these attempts (1980).

9 The History of Education in the 1980s

B. Simon

Author

Brian Simon (1915–2002) remains the most distinguished historian of education in Britain. His 'Four Studies in the History of Education' (*The Two Nations and the Educational Structure 1780–1870, Education and the Labour Movement 1870–1920, The Politics of Educational Reform 1920–1940*, and *Education and the Social Order 1940–1990*) shaped historical studies in education. As a student in Cambridge, he joined the Communist Party, trained as a teacher, taught in elementary, modern and grammar schools and finally at Leicester University, where he became Professor of Education in 1966 – alongside Geoffrey Bantock, also a major contributor to this *Journal*.

Introduction

History of Education was established in the early 1900s, along with psychology, as one of the two subjects in the theoretical aspects of teacher training. Such a theoretical base for teaching was indeed limited (there was no philosophy or sociology of education) even more so because of the narrow interest of the history. Indeed, the inter-war years 'were not a stimulating period and untouched by significant research or revision': hence, the importance of the launch of the *BJES* in 1952 under the editorship of the distinguished historian, A. C. F. Beales. Psychology of Education had its own journal, and so, as Simon points out, the *BJES* provided the opportunity for historical studies to develop (with, initially, a series of papers on 'Sources in History of Education'). This opportunity was shared by the philosophy of education, as that too began to flourish but had not yet established its own journal (see Robert Dearden's article on page 94 in this volume).

This history of 'the history of education' shows the growth from the interests of relatively few individuals (see Armytage on page 54 in this volume) and from a focus on specific schools and Victorian concerns to giving historical depth and context to matters of current concern. The history of education needed to adapt to the pressures of the other disciplines as they came to prominence in the growth of educational theory, especially after the beginning of the Bachelor of Education

(B. Ed.) degree in the 1970s. There was a 'conscious move to write social history', to bring historical discipline to views about socialisation and social class, to engage with psychological assumptions about fixed intelligence (see the paper by Burt in this volume) and to contribute to the emerging discipline of cultural studies. In 1982, when *The History of Education in the 1980s* (30, 1: 85–96) was published, Simon was able to say that

> the history of education ... during the past decade or more has been in anything but a stagnant situation, ... [therefore] no longer the kind of isolation that in a more conservative age led mainstream historians to look on this area as a kind of backwood under cultivation by mere educationists whose partisanship for their own professional subject precluded historical treatment.

Related papers in the *Journal* are: *The 1870 Education Act* (20, 1: 121–35); *Philosophy of Education, 1952–82* (30, 1: 57–72).

The History of Education in the 1980s

by Brian Simon, University of Leicester

It is a commonplace that every generation writes history anew, although there are historians who dispute this. It is difficult to gainsay in the case of education, given the clear relation between periods of change and questioning on the ground and renewal of interest in historical investigation. Undoubtedly the lively and extending interest today among historians of different periods, gathering way since the 1950s, has accompanied wideranging change on the ground; not least, of course, an extension of higher education which has provided new scope for research. Nor is it surprising that, in the educational field, the threads taken up derive from the earlier decades of the century when departments of education were first established in modern universities—for education has not been a subject honoured by the two ancient universities, except in so far as their own history is concerned. In this connection the work of Hastings Rashdall and John Venn might well be counted first in the field from the 1880s and in some ways it has yet to be superseded, although a major new history of the university of Oxford has been in the pipeline for some years. Meanwhile Venn's hard graft on such matters as student numbers and the social origin of entrants to Cambridge colleges at different periods has come in for considerable attention with the current turn to quantification, although sometimes accorded less than due acknowledgement. As for schooling, there was the work of the former charity commissioner, A. F. Leach, whose primary interest was ancient school foundations and who, until his death in 1915, acted as chief contributor to the volumes of the Victoria County History whose standard coverage of institutions treated as separate entities constituted the accepted form of local history. Moreover the key interests of leading students and teachers of the subject—W. H. Woodward, Foster Watson, J. W. Adamson—lay in the sixteenth and seventeenth centuries although the latter's major publication eventually covered the period 1789 to 1902. But for the most part histories of elementary and secondary schools, or of particular institutions or practitioners, did duty for analysis of a Victorian age in the immediate past.[1]

It was during the early years of this century that history was established alongside psychology as a main subject of study for teachers in training, so directly linking interest in the educational past with operation in the present. Whatever its advantages this also brings the subject into the area of examinable matter with the consequent danger of a multiplication of textbook treatments, crystallising complex issues into convenient responses. This was the greater in that historians of different periods, with the exception of mediaevalists who have always shown a close interest in universities, paid little or no attention to educational developments except in terms of a formal outline of legislation or the kind of discussion of 'state intervention' which coincided with a predominant interest in constitutional or political history. One exception deserves mention to whom the present writer owes a considerable debt, a historian of modern England who treated education as of key importance to social and political development—Elie Halévy, himself from France, who not only covered the century up to 1914 in a series of volumes but also analysed the views of the philosophic radicals in terms of their educational implications. It may be added that another who pioneered a departure from the traditional treatment of formal schooling to consider social relations and outcomes was A. E. Dobbs whose Education and Social Movements appeared back in 1919.

The interwar years were not a stimulating period and, untouched by significant research or revision, the earlier history of English education became bedded down into something approaching a reverent commentary on the findings of predecessors, notably the interpretations of Leach which were as commonly recited by historians at large as by those in departments of education. Consequently, it was generally affirmed, or inferred, that the Reformation had swept away a flourishing system of mediaeval schools and nothing had been the same since. Setting up as interpreter with *The English Tradition of Education* (1929), Cyril Norwood—then Head-master of Harrow (whose final contribution to that tradition was to act as chairman of the committee which produced the 1943 Norwood Report)—characterised both the Renaissance and the Reformation as 'disintegrating influences'; particularly the latter since 'it broke up the unity of the nation' and, old ideals lost to sight, 'the seventeenth and eighteenth centuries are a dark period in the history of education'. By 1950 the point was sufficiently well established to be disposed of in a sentence: 'Between the end of the Middle Ages and the Industrial Revolution there was a period of little change in education.'[2] It was an easy relegation of decades now recognised as covering a vast expansion of facilities not to mention reorientation of content, indeed as marking the origin of the modern system of schooling, while it also consigned to oblivion the eighteenth century which has yet to be rescued from neglect.

Such was the climate as work resumed after the war and the *British Journal of Educational Studies* entered on the scene under the editorship of a dedicated and enthusiastic historian of education, A. C. F. Beales of King's College, London, whose own specialist subject was the Roman Catholic educational outlook and tradition, notably from the Reformation in England but also in Spain and elsewhere. Launched, so it was announced, to make better known the results of research in education, the first number included surveys of three areas, comparative education, theory, history—an indication of the awkward division between theory and practice which operated to reduce historical study to organisational aspects while 'ideas' or 'great educators' were allotted to another department.

The two pages allotted to history drew on a modest list of theses produced during the previous thirty years and lacked any system of references, even dates of publication. On the other hand, a decision not to trespass on the territory of journals of the British Psychological Society left the more space for historical articles in this one—for a time at least; that is, until new concerns came to the forefront, notably philosophy in its new guise which replaced the traditional mode of theorising. By comparison this had little or no impact on the history of education except perhaps in terms of encouraging a certain precision of utterance; though its advent released educational ideas from the former corral in which they were preserved to enable the development of an historical approach in the round. There are, of course, still disputes about theory and theoretical approaches but nowadays of a very different order and within the history of education.

A brief glance at some of the early numbers of the *Journal* may help to bring home the atmosphere of the 1950s. From the first issue a series of articles was introduced in line with stated aims, 'Sources in the History of Education'. It opened with one on primary schools by the editor of the Victoria History of the Counties of England followed by a series on 'History of the English Grammar Schools' by that doyen of local history, and warm admirer of the work of Leach, W. E. Täte, of Leeds University. These eventually spread through three issues, to be succeeded by an article on sources for 'Spanish Educational History'—never a matter in the forefront of attention—by the editor which also spread to two issues. Alongside the second of these, however, appeared the first serious piece of iconoclasm, reacting against the orthodoxy upheld by Täte—a strongly critical piece headed 'A. F. Leach on the Reformation' by Joan Simon. The publication of this contribution, which apparently caused some heart-searchings on the part of the editor, marked a new phase in that received interpretations were now more generally challenged. Its immediate effect was to halt, once and for all, plans in hand to re-issue all Leach's books, so clearing the road for a fresh cultivation of the field which is still actively in train.

This episode indicates, as examination of the early years of the *Journal* confirms, how small and relatively self-contained was the world of the history of education at the time; more or less ruled by a handful of elder statesmen until a younger generation, returned from the war, became active in what were soon expanding departments in both colleges and universities. But time was necessary before a body of new work was built up and it was not until 1968 that a History of Education society was launched, marking a new confidence and providing a focal point for discussion and interchange. In the intervening years individual contributions are to be noted rather than a developing trend. There were varied publications from that polymath, W. H. G. Armytage, from 1951, ranging from studies of A. J. Mundella and civic universities to the social history of engineering and an analysis of Utopian writings. By contrast there was the concentrated attention devoted by Eric Eaglesham to a key period when the upward thrust of the national school system, consolidated after 1870, was abruptly cut off and the scene thus set for the twentieth century. And one might continue with such juxtapositions.

In 1960 new light was thrown on the perennial 'religious problem in English education' by James Murphy, in a concentrated analysis of a single instance and in 1962 a tightly reasoned article (presaging a lengthy book) on the pivotal issue of examinations policy, at a key period, came from John Roach.[3] Of another order were a first volume of studies in the history of English education by the present writer (1960) and J. F. C. Harrison's *Learning and Living, 1790–1960* (1961). These bring to mind the establishment in 1960 of the Society for the Study of Labour History which co-ordinated and fostered work since dubbed 'history from below'; work which, combined with a move to accumulate oral evidence, has since attained a wide, if sometimes diffuse, development in the journal *History Workshop* and associated conferences which often raise interesting educational issues. In 1963 the traditionally central problem was again tackled in the first contribution to come from Marjorie Cruickshank, *Church and State in English Education 1870 to the present* and there appeared a new model history of a single school by John Lawson, *A Town Grammar School through Six Centuries.* Unfortunately this has too seldom been followed but there has since been innovation in terms of surveys of the schools of a county since the Reformation or during a single century. Indeed there is now a bibliography of local studies, produced by the School of Education of the University of Leeds whose museum of education is well known, and from which a small journal focusing on administration and history has been published since 1968. The first of Peter Gosden's books, on the development of educational administration, was published in 1966.[4]

By 1965 a new collection of educational documents had supervened, edited by Stuart Maclure (now of the *Times Educational Supplement*) on traditional lines but covering the period 1816–1963—unlike Leach's version, going back to the landing of Augustine in Kent, which had occupied the field since 1910. Updated and reissued since (hardly a satisfactory arrangement if convenient to meet students' needs), this has since been supplemented by 'readers' of a new order, such as *Sociology, History and Education* (1971) edited by Peter Musgrave, author of one of the first frankly sociological treatments, *Society and Education in England since 1800* (1969), which has not been without its critics. But 1970, inevitably, saw centenary celebrations of the star piece of legislation in the history of nineteenth-century education. It may be added that about the only study relating directly to the twentieth century, in terms of treating the background to current attitudes or unrecognised assumptions, has been contributed from Australia, by R. J. W. Selleck. In *The New Education* (1968), the background to 'progressivism' is systematically teased out while in a later volume, specifically on primary education, the process by which a kind of watered down 'progressivism' became the orthodoxy by 1939 is traced.[5] Otherwise, as always, far too little has been done on the curriculum and methodology—on what is taught and how—by comparison with organisational aspects. Indeed there has been a new turn to the latter, if at another level, as an interest in administrative history among historians has spilled over into the educational field. Related, but nearer to the ground, have been moves to capture the life and work of local education officers which also recall a new interest in one of the key aspects of their work, and the work of schools—the changing nature of school buildings.[6]

It is also worth recalling that it was an American, back in 1941, who entered firmly on what had been (so far as objective treatment is concerned if not in terms of volume of publications) a 'no-go area', for it was then that the second volume of E. C. Mack's major study, *Public Schools and British Opinion from 1860 to date*, appeared. In the sequel, pride of place goes to T. W. Bamford's *Thomas Arnold* (1960) and his *The Rise of the Public Schools* (1967) and David Newsome's *Godliness and Good Learning* (1961), but the first of the new wave 'sociological' studies was Rupert Wilkinson's *The Prefects* (1964), subtitled 'British Leadership and the Public School Tradition, a comparative study in the making of rulers'.[7]

It would be true to say that it is also from America that the stimulus initially came to develop women's studies, including a new approach to the history of education for girls, but this is a more recent development well within the past decade during which the History of Education Society has been active. This has been responsible for issuing annual theses lists, besides a series of guides to sources and a bi-annual bulletin, supplemented since 1972 by the journal *History of Education*, now appearing quarterly. The Society has also taken the lead in establishing an international standing committee on the subject which has organised three conferences to date, at Leuven in 1979, Warsaw in 1980, and in Paris in 1981—in 1982 the annual conference will take place in Budapest. In the Spring of 1980 an international seminar was organised to enable intensive discussion of the history of literacy in the light, in particular, of research based on unique Swedish data preserved down the centuries since the Reformation. One of the most interesting contributors was the reader in mediaeval history at the University of Glasgow, Michael Clanchy, who has opened up a quite new area of enquiry in his *From Memory to Written Record* (1979). Much work on this subject has been done in France, but the subject of the Paris international conference last year (1981) was based around the centenary of the Jules Ferry law of 1881 imposing a popular system of universal, secular and free education. It may be hoped that events of this kind will further strengthen contacts and extend horizons in this country, in a way that can only benefit historical study. There has also, it may be added, been relatively close contact with those engaged in the history of education in the United States, where there has been a much more conscious, far-reaching and radical revision of the subject or change in modes of approach, a matter with which the society here has been kept in touch by various surveys. In the United States, it may be recalled, the U.S. Bureau of Education and American Historical Society have together commissioned a three-volume revision of the history of American education by a leading scholar, Lawrence Cremin.[8] By contrast, in this country there seems a marked official reluctance to give even that prominence to the historical approach which was earlier taken for granted. Compare the historical chapter of the Spens Report of 1938, which represented a welcome critique of traditional 'grammar school' values, with the amorphous and eclectic introductory chapter to the Plowden Report of 1967 (which evaded any attempt at a historical assessment of the role and nature of primary education).

To move back to domestic developments during the past decade, the advent of sociology has already been noted as a significant change but this has not necessarily been with revolutionary effect. Rather the existing tendency to confine mainstream history of education to consideration of the emergence of a national (or 'state') system, from the late eighteenth century, is reinforced by an approach which associates all significant events with 'modern industrialised society'. Nor is the situation improved when the latter is taken as given, from the standpoint of sociological theory, rather than considered in its formation. It may be more germane to recall that, no doubt in part under sociological influence but certainly under the influence of educational expansion on the ground and growing recognition of the links between education, the economy and society, historians of different periods are now increasingly taking account of the matter; in treatments veering away from the former concentration on the constitutional, political or diplomatic aspects and towards economic, social and cultural history. But the trend is most marked in relation to the conscious move to write social history, or follow up what figures now in most university prospectuses as 'economic and social history'. While there are wide variations, this may now cover a wide field. Indeed an economic historian has affirmed that, as a result of the extension of horizons, there is now not merely an interest in educational structure but also such matters as the family, kinship, and ways of bringing up children; even 'the knowledge and motivations imparted by particular styles of education have suddenly become relevant things for economic historians to discover'. There is not yet much to show for this in terms of new departures. On the contrary, the best known intervention from the area of economics, or more properly political economy, is still that of E. G. West which began as a highly polemical intervention relating to state education in the wake of the Black Papers, but has since settled into a more serious attempt to argue that private enterprise could well have educated the nation had not misguided politicians brought in grants from the state. Related to this area—and to other innovations issuing from the Centre for Advanced Studies of the University of Princeton where Lawrence Stone rules—has been the contention of an American historian that eighteenth- and early nineteenth-century Sunday Schools were, if one really looks into the matter, within the province of the working class, rather than imposed from above. Neither of these views has gone without challenge.[9]

Implicit in most treatments nowadays is the concept of 'socialisation' of the young, during life at large and within the home, not merely in the grip of formal schooling. On the one hand this has led on and outwards to interest in the history of the family and childhood, or peer groups more generally. On the other it has resulted in much use, or abuse, of the term 'social control'; one easily brought into play but less readily interpreted in a consistent and viable manner. As one example there are interesting studies in the volume edited by Philip McCann, *Popular Education and Socialisation in the Nineteenth Century* (1977), but this has nonetheless recently been taken as a text to preach against oversimplification; with some justice, perhaps, but considerable over-emphasis, in the pages of the *Economic History Review*. As for what Charles Webster, in a recent survey, called 'Marxist writing on education'—referring to dependence on interpretations of the state apparatus and its role by Gramsci and Althusser which allow a dynamic role to education—such interpretations have yet to enter into the history of education, his subsequent references being confined to sociological analyses.[10] Indeed it is one of the main problems that work directly relevant to, and influential on, current ideas and practice—Bowles and Gintis' *Schooling in Capitalist America* (1976), for example—usually lacks a sustained historical perspective. The nearest parallel in this country, it might be thought, is the work of Richard Johnson which, however, does have a historical perspective. The latest publication from the Birmingham University Centre for Contemporary Cultural Studies (first established under Richard Hoggart) is entitled *Unpopular Education*, sub-titled 'schooling and social democracy in England since 1944'—a joint (or collective) entry into important issues of contemporary education. Johnson's concern with cultural studies generally brings a wider approach than is usual to educational history. More in the mainstream is the textbook in which a mediaeval and modern historian collaborated, *A Social History of Education*, by John Lawson and Harold Silver. Silver's wide-ranging interests and research, particularly into 'neglected areas' of study, has opened new perspectives.[11]

With so much, of considerable variety, now in train it is hard to fit current developments at the outset of the eighties into a pattern. If subjects which have attracted the attention of conferences of the History of Education Society are taken as guide the first, perhaps predictably, discussed government and control but subsequent conferences covered local studies, comparative developments abroad and urban education in the nineteenth century. Of three recent conferences two have been on contemporary history—postwar curriculum developments and the course of development during the 1960s—while the third marked a move out of the region of formal education to consideration of influential 'informal agencies' at different periods. There should be interesting developments in this region in the near future, for various lines lead into this area. From history of the labour movement to 'history from below' in more general terms, taking in popular literature and religion, is one line of development. Another stems both from demography and from local history of the order pursued by Margaret Spufford whose fresh concern for aspects of the growth of literacy, including motivation to acquire it in the seventeenth century, does not preclude a perceptive approach to local schools. From local history to the history of the family, or households, of youth, or the nature of childhood at different periods of historical development, is a natural sequence, though it has not necessarily been the mode of approach. Another has been by way of anthropology, or drawing on anthropological findings to illuminate data deriving from historical study. Yet another, in more general terms, represents a premature attempt to devise a theoretical framework for writing the history of the family in England which, as things are, may well result in shaping the accumulation of evidence rather than illuminating the course of development. Somewhat similarly, moves to write the history of the development of literacy in dependence on demographic data involve a deployment of ideas which may often be open to question but are far less open to recognition and so critical examination.[12]

These are some of the questions now coming on to the agenda of the history of education which, during the past decade or more, has been in anything but a stagnant situation, although fruitful development is now endangered by economic stringencies. Weaknesses there still are, of course, but no longer the kind of isolation that in a more conservative age led mainstream historians to look on this area as a kind of backwood under cultivation by mere educationists whose partisanship for their own professional subject precluded historical treatment, even by those with the requisite qualifications. On the contrary, one now feels inclined to suggest that historians taking a new interest in educational developments and change would do well to find out more about the subject and its many ramifications before embarking on it. It is surprising how often, without overt acknowledgement, historians will introduce a character and his actions with a thumbnail sketch of upbringing and education. This may derive from a traditional respect for, or recognition of, the social pull of particular milieux or institutions, or from a dated adherence to the biologically oriented psychology from which 'intelligence testing' derived, or from the more fashionable dictates of psychohistory—although these, like all fashions, have now ceased to command the stage.

This raises a point worth making in this *Journal*, namely that there has been virtually no relationship between psychology and history in the educational field, but that the time has come when this would be well worth cultivating. Psychologists have been interested in the development of their own subject, and that now extends or finds practical application throughout the social spectrum, not least in and around the educational field, while quite new areas have opened up with recognition of the key importance of language—not merely in terms of psycholinguistics, sociolinguistics, neurolinguistics, but also the turn to cognitive psychology and learning theory. It may be that my own interests lead me to see matters in this guise for my work has of late lain in the area of research into primary education and this has led to activity within the British Educational Research Association among those whose approach has been within the paradigms associated with work in psychology. It has also been concerned, in historical terms, with posing the question 'Why no pedagogy in England?' by comparison with continental countries, and this is essentially one on the borders of education and psychology. But there are various pointers towards tackling this aspect, and not only by way of such studies as that of Goldstrom concerning the social content of education in early-mid-nineteenth century, which extracts the actual pedagogy from the teaching aids (school readers, etc.).[13] Once this aspect is given the attention it deserves, as at the very core of the educational enterprise of teaching and learning, there will be a new base for critical consideration of the place that enterprise holds in the history of human society in which, in sharp contrast to the mode of the animal world, the experiences of the species is preserved in exoteric form and acquired by active mastery. Considered in this context, education begins to appear as the mode of development proper to humanity in society, if at different levels of intensity and involvement, rather than something superimposed on creatures construed as a construct of heredity and environment. And this, it seems to me, enables the ditching of a great deal of dross—the opening of an exciting new perspective.

Notes

1   The titles of publications at this period are sufficiently well-known, but a chronological list figures as an appendix to my 'The History of Education' in J. W. Tibbie (ed.), *The Study of Education* (1966), pp. 91–131. See also *Research Perspectives in*

Education (ed. William Taylor, 1973), pp. 120–53, which makes a number of points to which I do not return here. There is an editorial survey by Charles Webster to two issues of the *Oxford Review of Education* devoted to the subject, 'Changing Perspectives in the History of Education', *loc. cit.*, Vol. 2, No. 3, 1976, pp. 201–13; and this refers to two others in the subsequent issue (Vol. 3, No. 1, 1977) by Harold Silver, 'Aspects of Neglect', pp. 57–69, and Joan Simon, 'The History of Education in *Past and Present*', pp. 71–86.

2 T. L. Jarman, in a chapter contributed to *Life Under the Stuarts* (1950), p. 69.

3 W. H. G. Armytage, *A. J. Mundella, 1825–1897* (1951), *Civic Universities: Aspects of a British Tradition* (1955), *A Social History of Engineering* (1961) and *Heavens Below: Utopian experiments in England, 1560–1960* (1961). Eric Eaglesham, *From School Board to Local Authority* (1956) and related articles in this journal. James Murphy, *The Religious Problem in English Education* (1959). John Roach, 'Middle-Class Education and Examinations: some early Victorian problems', *British Journal of Educational Studies* (May 1962), later expanded and extended in *Public Examinations in England, 1850–1900* (1971).

4 Peter Cunningham, *Local History of Education: a Bibliography* (1976). P. H. J. H. Gosden, *The Development of Educational Administration in England and Wales* (1966); see also his further cultivation of this field in *The Evolution of a Profession* (1972), *Education in the Second World War* (1976), and, with P. R. Sharp, *The Development of an Education Service, the West Riding, 1889–1974* (1978).

5 R. J. W. Selleck, *English Primary Education and the Progressives, 1914–1939* (1972).

6 G. Sutherland (ed.), *Growth in Nineteenth Century Government* (1972) and *Policymaking in Elementary Education, 1870–1895*. On local education officers, M. Seaborne, 'William Brockington, Director of Education for Leicestershire 1903–47', in B. Simon (ed.), *Education in Leicestershire, 1540–1940* (1968); H. Rée, *Educator Extraordinary: the life and achievement of Henry Morris, 1889–1961* (1973); D. W. Thorns, *Policy Making in Education: Robert Blair and the London County Council, 1904–1924* (Educational Administration and History Monographs, 1981); J. D. Browne, 'The Formation of an Educational Administrator' (*History of Education*, Vol. 10, No. 3, September, 1981) (on Bolton King of Warwickshire). On school buildings, M. Seaborne, *The English School, its Architecture and Organisation, 1370–1870* (1971) and the second volume, with R. Lowe, covering 1870 to 1970 (1977).

7 Other recent works on the public schools include T. J. H. Bishop and Rupert Wilkinson, *Winchester and the Public School Elite* (1967), A. Percival, *Very Superior Men* (1973), B. Simon and I. Bradley (eds), *The Victorian Public School* (1975), G. Gathorne Hardy, *The Public School Phenomenon* (1977), J. R. de S. Honey, *Tom Brown's Universe* (1977), and J. A. angan, *Athleticism in the Victorian and Edwardian Public School, the emergence and consolidation of an educational ideology* (1981).

8 On revisionism in the United States, see *History of Education*, Vol. 7, No. 3, October 1978 (special number in the history of American education), and Sol Cohen, 'The History of Urban Education in the United States: Historians of Education and their Discontents', in David Reeder (ed.), *Urban Education in the 19th Century* (1977). See also Lawrence Cremin, *American Education: the colonial experience, 1607–1783* (1970).

9 The quotation is from P. Mathias, '*Economic* history—direct and oblique', in M. Ballard (ed.), *New Movements in the Study and Teaching of History* (1970), p. 89. E. G. West's first book is entitled *Education and the State* (1965); his second, *Education and the Industrial Revolution* (1975), is concerned with the relationship between education and the process of industrialisation in the nineteenth century. On Sunday schools, T. W. Laqueur, *Religion and Respectability: Sunday Schools and Working Class Culture, 1780–1850*; for a critical analysis, M. Dick,

'The Myth of the Working Class Sunday School' (*History of Education,* Vol. 9, No. 1, March 1980). From the Princeton Center two volumes of essays on the history of education have appeared, *The University in Society* (1974) and *Schooling and Society* (1976), both edited by Lawrence Stone.

10 See F. M. W. Thompson, 'Social Control in Victorian Britain' (*Economic History Review,* 2nd series, Vol. XXXIV, No. 2); for the thesis generally, A. P. Donajgrodzski (ed.), *Social Control in Nineteenth Century Britain* (1977), which includes an article by Richard Johnson on education in the 1830s. Charles Webster, *loc. cit.* (note 1); but see Harold Entwistle, *Antonio Gramsci, conservative schooling for radical politics* for a balanced exposition of Gramsci's standpoint relating to education.

11 *Unpopular Education* is by Steve Baron, Dann Finn, Neil Grant, Michael Green and Richard Johnson. Earlier studies in the history of education by Johnson include 'Educational Policy and Social Control in Early Victorian England' (*Past and Present,* Vol. 49, 1970), pp. 96–119, *The Blue Books and Education, 1816–1896: the critical reading of educational sources* (Occasional Paper, 1976), and 'Notes on the schooling of the English working class, 1780–1850' in Roger Dale *et al.* (ed.), *Schooling and Capitalism* (1976). Harold Silver's studies include *The Concept of Popular Education* (1965), *Robert Owen on Education* (1969), *The Education of the Poor* (1974 with Pamela Silver), and *English Education and the Radicals* (1975).

12 Margaret Spufford, *Contrasting Communities: English villages in the sixteenth and seventeenth centuries* (1974) and 'First Steps in Literacy: the reading and writing experiences of the humblest seventeenth century spiritual autobiographies' (*Social History,* 4, 1979); see also *Small Books and Pleasant Histories* (1981). Alan Macfarlane, *The Family Life of Ralph Josselin. A Seventeenth century clergyman. An essay in historical anthropology* (1970). Lawrence Stone, *The Family, Sex and Marriage in England from 1500 to 1800* (1977). David Cressy, *Literacy and the Social Order. Reading and Writing in Tudor and Stuart England* (1980).

13 Brian Simon, 'Why no pedagogy in England?', in B. Simon and W. Taylor (eds), *Issues in the Eighties* (1981), pp. 124–45. J. M. Goldstrom, *The Social Content of Education, 1808–1870* (1972).

10 The Place of Theory of Education in Teacher Education

M. B. Sutherland

1985

Author

Margaret Sutherland, who died 13th April 2011 at the age of 90, edited the *British Journal of Educational Studies* from 1975 to 1985, when she also retired from the Chair of Education at the University of Leeds. Her distinguished career in education followed a First Class Honours degree from Glasgow University in 1942, her appointment as Chevalier in the Order of the Palm Académiques by the French government, teaching in several Glasgow schools, a lectureship and then readership in education at Queens University, Belfast – the head of department being Stanley Nisbet.

Introduction

The Place of Theory of Education in Teacher Education (33, 3: 222–34), the farewell paper of Professor Sutherland, as she relinquished editorship of the *Journal* after eleven years, appropriately addresses the place of theory of education in teacher education, for this was a period when such a place was under serious consideration, especially after the introduction of the B.Ed. degree. The same issue of the *Journal* had published a paper by Professor Paul Hirst entitled *Educational Studies and the PGCE Course* (33, 3: 211–21).

Why should the place of theory be a constant theme through the history of the *Journal?* Representatives of university education departments established the *BJES* for that very purpose. What other purpose could universities have in education other than the development of theory? That surely is the university's *raison d'être*. And yet educational theory will always be received with suspicion – by teachers who question its relevance to practice and by politicians who, whether to the right or to the left, see it as undermining their policy agendas. Those left-wing ideologues at the Institute! As Sutherland's opening remark declares

> we have to recognise that when it comes to teacher education, theory tends to have a bad name. It is often said to be divorced from what actually happens in schools, to waste the time of student-teachers and leave them longing for more practically oriented courses.

In response to such suspicions, she gives a robust defence of educational theory. 'For anyone who is to be a teacher systematic thought about the purpose and principles of education is essential.' Such thought constitutes the theory of education. Such 'systematic thought' about purposes and principles was essentially philosophical broadly conceived, to which psychology's contribution must be subordinate (and a specialist journal dealt with that). One needs to get beneath the superficial advocacy or condemnation of views on, for example, 'child-centred education' or 'indoctrination', to examine critically their presuppositions, to make distinctions where appropriate, and to perceive the underpinning values and assumptions.

> What is needed is a course explicitly in the principles of education taken by all students and taken seriously … to make students aware of the questions which have to be answered about providing education …

And these questions are then listed. To the 'systematic thought', the so-called disciplines of education make a contribution, but that thought must not be fragmented into the separate study of such disciplines.

Other related articles in the *Journal* are: *Educational studies and the PGCE course* (33, 3: 211–21); *Educational Studies in the United Kingdom 1940–2002* (50, 1: 3–56); *Disciplines contributing to education?: Educational studies and the disciplines* (50, 1: 100–119); *Teaching and Education: the teacher and the pupil* (4, 1: 24–31); *Teacher Education: Theory and Practice* (38, 4: 308–18); *Educational Theory, Practical Philosophy and Action Research* (35, 2: 149–69).

The Place of Theory of Education in Teacher Education

by Margaret B. Sutherland, School of Education, University of Leeds

We have to recognise that when it comes to teacher education, theory tends to have a bad name. It is often[1] said to be divorced from what actually happens in schools, to waste the time of student-teachers and leave them longing for more practically oriented courses: so the trend is to concentrate on the day-to-day activities of the classroom and give students more and more teaching practice, more contact with teachers, more discussion of control and class management. But the more insidious danger at present is that in so many cases teacher-educators are not quite sure what theory of education is. For some, 'theory' is perhaps thought to be consideration of the aims of teaching a specific subject in the curriculum: for others it may be any kind of reflection on what happens in the classroom – teachers thinking about their performance, as it were. For others, theory of education is assumed to be equivalent to bits of the 'disciplines of education'. For all too many, theory of education is certainly not something which they themselves have deliberately or explicitly studied. Special study of the theory of education may thus seem to them irrelevant since they are managing without it, they assume that 'everyone knows' what we are about in education, that there is a broad consensus – even if not explicit – about the aims of education and that student-teachers will 'pick up' theory via their method courses and practical teaching. What is not realised is that for anyone who is to be a teacher systematic thought about the purpose and principles of education is essential. Such thought constitutes the theory of education.

The present situation is the result of interesting pressures and developments in teacher education, of changes responsive to immediate circumstances rather than to thoughtful planning. We need now to reflect on the present state of affairs and decide what pressures and developments are to be accepted and encouraged and which assumptions and practices need to be challenged in the education of teachers.

Once upon a time there would have been no need to assert that theory of education should have a place in any course of teacher education. To those initiating such education it was self-evident that there are certain matters of which teachers cannot be permitted to be ignorant. The study of the principles on which education is founded, the *raison d'être* of the teaching profession had to be among these. Certainly various eminent authorities[2] also argued that psychology had an essential place in teacher education since it could provide understanding of the nature and development of children and thus afford guidance in devising methods of teaching. But it was clear that psychology's contribution must be subordinate to the study of Education itself, to philosophical consideration of the aims of the whole process, the definition of these aims and the principles to be observed in attempting to achieve them. In more recent times, some attention has been given – patchily – to contributions from the 'disciplines of education', including psychology, in PGCE courses, but the central focus, the study of Education itself, seems to have been lost. Why should it be restored? And what should be done to provide it?

Common ground

Let us consider first the effects of the absence of the study of Education. It is surely remarkable that at present we can send out as teachers people who may never have been required to reflect on the general purposes of education, that is, of the process in which they are to be engaged. They may of course have considered the purposes of teaching their particular part of the school curriculum, e.g., they may have discussed the aims of teaching mathematics. But such subject-bound discussions may have taken place in the absence of any explicit, systematic discussion of the over-riding aims of education. Similarly, new teachers may not have considered systematically the nature of the children and young people with whom they deal even if some have had a quick look at a selection of psychological – or even sociological – findings or speculations connected with cognitive development in their subject area. In general, in present conditions, many student-teachers' ideas about the aims of education owe rather more to the popular press – to be interpreted perhaps in this context as *The Guardian* or the *Observer*? – than to any study they engage in as part of their preparation for teaching. In the one-year PGCE course especially students' principles of education are often those current in literature and discussions *outside* the course. Students may differ as to the standards or type of achievement to be looked for even in their own subject areas. Beyond that, they may have varying notions as to forms of behaviour to be encouraged or discouraged. But they lack, in many cases, a clear understanding as to which behaviours and attitudes the schools *should* cultivate. Some at present may also be uncertain as to whether, indeed, the school system should take any part in seeking to influence the attitudes and standards of behaviour of pupils since, as students, they have been affected by relativist notions picked up from popularised sociology which lead them to consider as indecent any suggestion that one set of principles or standards is better than another. Others – a majority? – may have no considered view of the part schools should play in preparing pupils for employment or unemployment, for citizenship or world citizenship.

The consequences for the professionalism of teachers and for the unity of the teaching profession are obvious. Those entering the profession at present differ widely in the amount of time and thought given to principles underlying their activities. Yet if all teachers had some principles of education in common, coop-eration in the activities and discipline of schools could be expected to be better. Treatment of pupils is likely to have greater consistency if teachers are trying to achieve the same kind of end-product and have the same concepts of young people's course of development. While the circumstances of teaching and of life in school itself do induce some uniformity of outlook among teachers, yet in present conditions it is easily possible for members of the same staff to differ widely in their expectations of pupils and in their views as to appropriate standards – of behaviour as well as of work – in the school generally. The most marked differences in school staffs' beliefs about education and acceptance of educational principles become unhappily evident from time to time in media accounts of schools where overt dissension has broken out. But equally disastrous effects of the lack of common purpose and principles are probably passing without comment in many schools where teachers have no common ground; where they lack even the vocabulary for discussion of differences of principles and have no foundation of earlier thinking to put divergences of opinion on a more rational basis. Frustrations flourish.

Of course in schools where staff meetings give opportunities for working out the principles on which action is to be based the initial lack of common ground may be made good. But in rather few cases do staff meetings give this kind of opportunity. Admittedly, in their day-to-day work young teachers may not be frequently concerned with general policy decisions. Yet their interaction with pupils will be governed by their concepts of the teacher's role and purposes. And they will be involved in *some* policy decisions at departmental level or even at staff meetings. As members of teachers' unions they may also discuss policies based on principles. Yet as things are at present, policy discussions, at whatever level, for experienced and inexperienced teachers, must be among people who begin from a variety of standpoints, some having had no occasion earlier to reflect on such matters, some with unexamined prejudices. There are thus no common professional premises, no agreements as to the purpose and nature of education and of the role of the profession itself. Yet principles held in common would seem essential to a profession.[3]

It could be argued that lack of common definitions and aims results not from our kind of teacher education alone but from characteristics peculiar to the whole English educational system. In most countries the aims of education *are* defined in official publications. The standards of behaviour to be expected of pupils and the attitudes and personality traits to be cultivated are, in some systems, stated explicitly: the duties of the school with regard to developing good members of society are spelled out. It is not only in Soviet bloc countries that such explicit statements are made. Denmark, for example, has affirmed (in its Advisory Council Report *U 90*)[4] that there are in society common principles which the school system should try to inculcate in the young. West German states[5] producing 'guidelines' for schools indicate the need to develop respect for democratic principles. In Sweden[6] the Läroplan defines for teachers the aims of the schools and the qualities to be developed in pupils. So in many other systems all teachers have in common a definition of the aims and principles of their work.

(It is not of course argued here that such centralised definitions always have a uniform effect – or the desired effect. It is certainly true that in many countries teachers do not react to official guidance as the central authorities would wish. And where teacher education also has a centrally defined content and principles it is not always regarded as ideal by its recipients.[7] But at least in some other systems teachers have a common statement of purposes to be critical of.)

Teachers' common awareness of purposes in education can be important also at the in-service level, when the practice of education is to be reformed. When reforms in education prove unsuccessful – or only partly successful – it is often said that the failure is due to resistance to reform on the part of teachers. In such cases, it is often evident that the central authorities have failed to convince teachers of the value of the reform or have not explained the principles on which it is based sufficiently clearly in advance. Teachers then may not have accepted the aims and so failed to work with the reform measures; or they may have been unclear as to what the rationale of an apparently meaningless or unwise change has been and so have not properly implemented it. (Lack of necessary resources is of course another and sadly frequent reason for teacher failure to implement reforms.) Now if teachers have been so educated that they do not think about the general aims of education, or if they think general principles are irrelevant to their preoccupations in the classroom, it is not surprising that they remain apathetic or hostile when changes in their work are proposed or enforced. Thus a permanent resistance to reform can remain. Teachers educated to assess principles as well as practice might – occasionally – find reform proposals easier to accept and implement. (It is of course also possible that the judgment of educated teachers might discover fallacies in reform proposals or note that they were based on controversial principles. Which would be no bad thing.)

It must be acknowledged that occasionally there *are* central statements in England of aims for education. The Code for Elementary Schools at the beginning of the century stated general aims, not all concerning cognitive aspects: and these were repeated[8] in the 1937 *Handbook of Suggestions for Teachers* (but how widely read were these?). The UNESCO Recommendations[9] of 1974 concerning education for international understanding were ratified by this country and the DES sent a circular[10] to local authorities urging that schools try to achieve the stated aims. The results could have been quite astounding – and peace studies could surely have taken off to a flying start then? But how many teachers ever heard of the Recommendations? And how seriously did the DES, indicating that these aims were to be achieved without additional resources, expect them to be taken? Again, there was the recent document on *The School Curriculum*[11] produced after due process of consultation, offering a checklist of aims for the guidance of LEAs. Deducing the assumptions about the nature of education and the nature of children which underlie these statements is a fascinating ploy – which students can with advantage engage in. Is there, for instance, an accepted belief in innate abilities, a kind of child-centred approach, since the aims are 'to help the pupil to … ' – except of course when it comes to respect for the beliefs of others, where the respect is to be *instilled*? When there is proposed the development of lively, enquiring minds, does the proposal rest on a philosophical/religious/ psychological belief that all children naturally have such minds? And what are they to enquire about – really everything? Including the beliefs of others? Or nuclear disarmament?

And while there is a vague reference to preparing the young for participation in the adult world, there is no reference to citizenship – or patriotism. Are such omissions significant? So, while somewhat bland statements appear from time to time in official publications, there seems little impetus to serious consideration of central and general aims. One has rather the impression that, in the English educational system as in many other educational systems, fashions succeed each other and teachers – theirs not to reason why – are expected to change content and methods of their work in due conformity, following and climbing on to each successive band-wagon as it comes along.

The study of Education

In view of such considerations it seems evident that the study of Education needs to be restored. Without it the teaching profession lacks common ground and teachers in schools are uncertain as to the principles on which they are acting and divergent in the practices they derive from unexamined principles or prejudices.

It is true that some research studies in this country have suggested that professional training does affect the attitudes of future teachers.[12] In some instances apparently the effect of training was to induce more child-centred attitudes or beliefs: but it also appeared that this effect varied according to training institutions as well as according to the characteristics of students: and that the change, if any occurred, was unlikely to survive (frequently was reversed) after entry into the actual work of teaching.[13] The inculcation of child-centred views, if it did take place – possibly in times when tutors themselves were more enthusiastically child-centred (the results date from some years back) – would seem to have been less than efficient.

But is the proposal for a common study of Education a proposal for – horrendous thought! – indoctrination? Indoctrination is in fact one of the major concepts which should also be included in the study. For if one asks a group of PGGE students about it they will, almost without exception, assert that indoctrination is a Bad Thing: they are enthusiastic supporters of the view that each child must be encouraged to think for himself/herself. But for what reasons are they opposed to indoctrination? What precisely do they mean by it? Why do they believe children – or adults – to be capable of thinking out all sorts of things – ways of behaving, duties to others, scientific knowledge – for themselves? In what conditions? And are they really willing to accept any conclusions (however stupid or reactionary) thus arrived at by children or others? Further discussion may reveal that various students have simply made an acceptant response to the indoctrination of the media on this point. They have not considered thoughtfully what the word means, what the differences may be between teaching and indoctrination and setting a good example, whether indeed there is good indoctrination and bad indoctrination:

nor has there been systematic study of the ability of children at different ages to think about certain topics or to think upon certain events. (The uncertainty of the foundation on which students' opposition to indoctrination rests is all the more evident when one finds a group simultaneously agreeing that indoctrination is to be avoided and debating among themselves whether they should or should not ask permission of their teaching practice schools to wear CND badges (or other symbols of commitment) while in the school.)

Indoctrination is certainly an important issue for students to think about during their training year. But it cannot be said that – whether we accept that there is good and bad indoctrination or not – the teaching of theory of education is intended to develop unthinking acceptance of certain principles. What is urged is in fact that the future teacher should be encouraged to analyse and think about – for herself, for himself – the principles on which professional action is and should be based. It is a matter of making future teachers aware that theories exist, looking at examples of theories in action, leading them at least to preliminary formulations of their own theory.

In making such assertions one may admittedly feel pangs of regret that there is no one theory of education which can be offered – as has been possible in the past – as *the* theory for future teachers. Life would be so much simpler if we could contentedly accept that Herbart defined sufficiently and excellently the aims of education, the nature of the developing mind and – consequently – gave complete guidance as to the methods to be adopted and the choice of studies to be favoured. Or the educational theory of Froebel might have served – as at one stage in the colleges named after him – to provide the necessary framework of principles, understanding of child nature, and so of methods required. Even the educational views of John Dewey could have been used – if not so misinterpreted, misapplied and attacked in the past thirty years – to give future teachers a general and coherent view of the whole endeavour. Locke is perhaps a bit distant in time: yet Plato or Rousseau might have been candidates. Or Makarenko? (An advantage of the study of internationally known educationists like those just cited is that it gives common ground to teachers in different countries.) Certainly where an agreed theory has been present in the past, the views of the central theorist and those of the teaching tutors probably interacted to produce various modifications. (John Adams, it is said, put much of his own thought into his presentation of Herbart's.) But even so, if one central theory were available and taught we would have cohorts of teachers enjoying a common knowledge of accepted principles determining their professional work. Changing times and loss of faith in some theories of education seem to have ruled out this gloriously straightforward solution for us – though some teacher-educators still assert that they do know of one valid and unified theory of education worth teaching to all student-teachers. (All such tutors have to do is to convince their colleagues.) But in general a common study of educational theory can provide the necessary professional common ground even if some differences in choice of theory or principle remain among teachers: the absence of one agreed theory is no reason for dispensing with all theory of education.

Possible presentations

How is Theory of Education to be tackled if not by the presentation of one agreed theory?

In some departments of Education it is already happening to some extent by inclusion in the PGCE programme or in other programmes of presentations and discussions of general topics or contemporary problems. The weakness of some such provisions is that they may be regarded by students as optional – and indeed may be optional – and that they produce a 'bitty' effect with no awareness of common principles running through the various discussions. In other cases too an optional structure of courses means that students can opt for one or two of the so-called 'disciplines of education' and avoid the others. In this way, such general principles as may be invoked or discussed in the optional course will not relate to a central perspective and will not be common to all the students even within one department or institution. What is needed is a course explicitly on principles of education – given whatever title may seem appropriate – taken by all students and taken seriously. In this course the aim must be to make students aware of the questions which have to be answered about providing education – what are the aims; what are the rights of the children, parents, society, teachers; what are the influences of environment, class, caste, gender, religion; what should be the school's contribution to religious, moral, civic, as well as cognitive, education; is education a transmission process or a helping-growth process? What assumptions can be and should be made about the 'raw materials' of education, the children and young people (or, for that matter, adults) to whom education is directed, on whom it is to exercise influence? The answers to the questions may be incomplete or interim answers. It may be useful to look at answers already provided by various educationists so that, by consideration of these, future teachers realise to what extent they accept them or why they would reject them. Evidence on the large questions raised is by no means comprehensive. Current controversies may well be used to illuminate the questions and possible answers. But new teachers should at least have thought about the questions, considered seriously the answers suggested and arrived at least at temporary decisions as to their own positions as well as at awareness of the positions of others. This consideration of general principles determining responses in different educational activities is indeed the central core of the study of Education.

It is evident that the 'disciplines of education' (defined on various occasions as philosophy, sociology, psychology, history of education and comparative studies) have an important contribution to make to consideration of the questions listed. They can give greater understanding of the characteristics of human beings and of the social forces and circumstances which influence their behaviour as well as the traditions and habits of the past. Comparative studies can provide awareness of alternative ways of educating, of different structures of schooling and of results obtained in different systems as well as illustrations of common problems. In so far as philosophy contributes to clear thinking it too has a contribution to make – though whether students should study philosophy of education as such, at this preliminary stage, is highly doubtful. Sociology can illuminate the effects of family and social background on access to education and progress in it: it may also, one hopes, enable students to use such terms as 'social class' intelligently and critically. Some knowledge of the history of the educational system may improve under-standing of its present state; certainly the present structure and relevant recent legislation should be known by beginning teachers. The place of psychology in teacher education is now being critically reviewed[14] and its contribution to initial training recognised as more limited than was originally expected. But in all this, these disciplines are not to be studied as ends in themselves: rather a choice from their offerings is to be made and incorporated in the main study. For it must constantly be remembered that these disciplines of education are ancillary. Making considered value judgments, in the light of evidence provided by the disciplines and other sources, is a matter of the central theory of education. Such making of judgments should not be the result of unthinking acceptance of the values implicit or explicit in the contributory disciplines: these disciplines have, in themselves, no decisive guidance to give as to the appropriate choice of action. The choices are to be made by the educationist/teacher, having considered the values offered and the evidence available. Obviously, extensive consideration of methodology and specialist interests in the disciplines is inappropriate at the initial training stage. For those who are particularly attracted by one or other of the disciplines, in-service or higher degree work offers ample opportunity for systematic study at a level which cannot possibly be reached during the first training. Initial pre-paration of teachers can simply indicate the attractions and possibilities of these studies.

(In something of the same way, it is evident that any individual's theory of education is something which develops and matures with time and experience – and further study. It would be unwise to expect that students during their initial training should develop a complete and finished theory of education. Their theories will be modified as they gain further experience of the qualities and behaviour of those they teach as well as of colleagues and other people in society and as they perceive the responses of these others and the evolution of social trends. New research in one or other of the contributory disciplines may lead to modification of individual theories of education, though it seems improbable that the basic value judgments and principles will change radically for many people. In-service courses will also give individual teachers an opportunity to re-shape their theories by making them aware of current thinking and of new research results in the contributory disciplines or in 'educational research' itself, and by enabling them to express and discuss critically the ideas developed through their practical experience. Unhappily, however, we have to recognise that until now attendance at in-service courses has been mainly – almost exclusively – voluntary so that not all teachers benefit by such opportunities as those just indicated. At present, moreover, the increasing interest of employers in providing for teacher attendance at in-service courses is likely to direct teachers rather towards obviously 'relevant' – i.e. classroom-orientated – courses than to courses concerned with the disciplines of education or the theory of education.)

The question of depth and specialisation during the PGCE year is important. Many PGCE students, fresh from their final Honours work, rather expect to continue the same sort of activity, writing intensively researched essays or repeating the detailed and specialised exercises they carried out earlier. It must be made clear to them that they are now beginners in a new, and much more complex and difficult, field in which orthodox doctrine is not clearly defined: and while they are expected to work rather harder, perhaps, the initial approach is different. They are now to become acquainted with a wide range of ideas and topics before specialising: the one area of specialised focusing is in their teaching of their part of the curriculum.

This approach to the theory of education does have important implications for teaching and assessment procedures. Attendance at this part of the course should certainly not be optional: and as it is intended to give some kind of common ground to all future teachers its content can scarcely be left to choices by individual tutors – unless these tutors are very closely agreed in their approach and keep closely in touch as to the topics and principles studied. Some central input seems necessary, reinforced by participation in discussion where individuals can be effectively involved. Whether reliable and valid assessment of students' progress in this part of the programme can be made is doubtful. It is essentially a process rather than a product kind of study. Outcomes may vary. There are not necessarily 'right' answers nor an essential body of knowledge. But it is important that students take theory of education seriously and read round its topics, absorb at least some of the relevant evidence, get to know the major viewpoints and their consequences. Possibly the ideal criterion would be effective contribution to discussion. But there are problems about assessing such contributions. Most students have been conditioned to expect other kinds of assessment. Yet essay-writing, that compromise most readily accepted by many students as a less stress-laden and less challenging exercise than a written examination (an essay can be fairly comfortably done, with reasonable expectation of passing, if only the student can get at the recommended texts and sit quietly summarising them), does not seem a useful form of assessment in this instance: apart from the constant dangers of various kinds of plagiarism, the essay involves too much concentration on only one topic. Perhaps the tradition of oral examinations should be revived? (Granted, there is a problem of staff resources.)

And of course it all depends on how theory of education is taught. It needs to be presented in a knowledgeable and stimulating way, integrating colleagues' contributions from different disciplines and relating to 'real life'. There is the perennial danger that the theory-practice gap be alleged or be actually present. Students' practical needs for survival in the classroom should certainly not be neglected: but if their practical work is being well coped with, students will be all the more able to think about what they are doing and what the educational system generally is doing, with what justifications. Students should understand that they are not being presented with an abstract and unchallengeable set of ideas. The discussions of theory and education must be related to real situations (though students' lack of experience at times limits their knowledge of reality in the educational world). If theory is shown as thinking about what is real then lack of realism in students' theories can be corrected by experience. They can progress, as teachers, in realistic theorising.

The approach to theory of education which has been outlined here cannot be developed solely through discussions arising out of, or based upon, classroom situations encountered by students. There is a school outside the classroom; and an educational system outside (or encompassing) the school; and there is society and people generally. If we are to ensure that all students have the opportunity to consider basic questions and principles we cannot wait for these to trickle into individuals' experiences in different school settings: we must introduce them systematically in teacher education courses.

It would be highly valuable to know precisely which questions and principles are at present studied in theoretical parts of teacher-education courses. Are many common to many courses? Is there in fact some consensus as to the principles and problems to be considered? (The Leicester survey[15] of PGCE courses in universities in England and Wales seemed to indicate that there is in fact little consistency: but fuller information is needed.)

The view taken in this paper is in some ways characteristic of its time and place in its assertion that there is no one ideal theory. Teacher-educators at other times and in other countries would differ here. Yet even so, theorists of the past and in other countries would agree that a theory exists only as the result of thought on the part of individuals – critical and individual thought, even when an orthodox stand is taken. They would, one hopes, agree that such thought is essential if teachers are not to be simply highly skilled, classroom-based, classroom-orientated technicians, waiting upon directives from outside authorities.

Notes

1 Statements of this kind are too numerous to list here.
2 For example, James Sully: *The Teacher's Handbook of Psychology* (Longman, 1890).
3 See, *inter alia*, E. Hoyle: 'Professionalization and Deprofessionalization', in *World Yearbook of Education*, eds. J. Megarry, E. Hoyle (Kogan Page, 1980).
4 Central Council of Education: *U 90, Danish Educational Planning and Policy in a Social Context at the End of the 20th Century* (Schultz Forlag, Copenhagen, 1978).
5 For instance, Kultusminister des Landes Nordrhein-Westfalen: *Richtlinien für den Politik-Unterricht* (Düsseldorf, 1974).
6 See L. Boucher: *Tradition and Change in Swedish Education* (Pergamon, 1982).
7 M. Tournier: 'Theorie und Praxis in der Ausbildung der Lehrer an Primar- und Sekundarschulen in Frankreich' in *Lehrerbildung und Entprofessionalisierung* (Hrsg.) R. Süssmuth (Deutsches Institut für Internationale Pädagogische Forschung, Bohlau Verlag, 1984) gives an instance of such reactions.
8 Board of Education: *Handbook of Suggestions for Teachers* (HMSO, 1937).
9 UNESCO: 'Recommendations concerning education for international understanding, co-operation and peace' (Paris, 1974).
10 Department of Education and Science, Circular 9/76.
11 Department of Education and Science/Welsh Office: *The School Curriculum* (HMSO, 1981).

12 J. McLeish: *Students' Attitudes and College Environment* (Cambridge Institute Education, 1970).
13 A. Morrison, D.McIntyre: 'Opinions about Education during the First Year of Teaching' (*Br. J. Soc. Clin. Psych.* 6, 1967), pp. 161–63.
14 Notably in H. Francis (ed.): *Learning to Teach: The Place of Psychology in Teacher Education* (Falmer Press, 1985).
15 H. Patrick, G. Bernbaum, K. Reid: *The Structure and Process of Initial Teacher Education within Universities in England and Wales* (University of Leicester, School of Education, 1982).

11 The Importance of Traditional Learning

A. O'Hear

1987

Author

Anthony O'Hear is Professor of Philosophy at the University of Buckingham and former Head of the Department of Education. When he wrote this paper, he was the Professor responsible for the Undergraduate School of Interdisciplinary Human Studies at the University of Bradford. A distinguished philosopher, he has for many years edited *Philosophy*, the journal of the Royal Institute of Philosophy of which he is an Honorary Director. For ten years he was an adviser on education to Prime Ministers Margaret Thatcher and John Major.

Introduction

A quarter of a century does not diminish the force and the relevance of Anthony O'Hear's defence of what he refers to as 'traditional learning'. *The Importance of Traditional Learning* (35, 2: 102–14) was a powerful criticism of the educational forces to the left and to the right that sought to make education 'relevant'. And indeed examples are given of curriculum changes, promoted by Government, to ensure this relevance. It should be relevant, on the one hand (so the free marketers argued), to the needs of the economy and industry, or, on the other (so the critics of inequality and discrimination argued), to social issues and the betterment of society.

In this pursuit of utility and autonomy in matters of economic need and social improvement, traditional learning comes to be diminished. By traditional learning it is meant that immersion in 'the best that has been thought and known' embodied in literature, history and the humanities. As with Matthew Arnold, so does O'Hear rail against the 'barbarism' of an education without the wisdom and insights provided by the humanities. The humanities open up to the culture through which we have come to understand what it is to be a person, to appreciate what is worthwhile, and to engage critically with the present. They provide the standpoint from which the modern 'studies' curricula (women's studies, religious studies, film studies, etc.) or the pursuit of wealth for its own sake might be examined critically.

> Education, I would say, on the contrary is nothing, and its costs in terms of deprivation of liberty unjustified, unless it is a discipline enabling its initiates to

distance themselves from their present concerns and perceptions and achieving the proper distances of the feeling intellect. Through education we should enter into those human achievements that have endured and which have, through cultural forms, provided some distancing of the individual from his own greed and need and from the need and greed of others.

These same battles are still with us – witness the present conflict between the proposed EBacc and the threatened 'vocational' studies. And indeed that is to be expected for, as is reflected in several papers published by the *Journal* over 60 years, what counts as a general or liberal education is a perennial concern.

Other related articles from the *Journal* are: *Human nature, learning and ideology* (25, 3: 239–57); *The Anatomy of a Victorian Debate: an Essay in the History of Liberal Education* (34, 1: 38–65); *Towards a Theory of Learning* (44, 1: 9–26); *Reinventing the Past: the Case of the English Tradition of Education* (50, 2: 238–53).

The Importance of Traditional Learning

by *Anthony O'Hear*, University of Bradford

Perhaps I owe an explanation to anyone who has read my *Education, Society and Human Nature*,[1] which I now think had a rather uncritical stress on the type of autonomy one could be expected to attain by the exercise of pure reason, and put rather uncritically the thesis that it should be the job of education to enable students to make their own choices guided by pure reason. While still wishing to insist that education ought to be a liberating process for the learner, fully engaging the learner and his faculties, and enabling him to stand out against the narrow seductions and demands of the present fashion and cliché, consideration of work by writers such as A. MacIntyre, C. Taylor, B. Williams, M. Oakeshott has made me realise the extent to which the proper and effective exercise of reason must take place against the background of inherited forms of thought and experience, and that there is a sense in which all true education has a strongly conservative aspect, although I would not regard myself as a Conservative politically. The irony is that it is a self-styled Conservative administration which is pursuing, more vigorously than any previous government, policies in education which are the educational equivalent of the tower blocks and town centre 'developments' of the 1960's.

The pursuit of utility in education is likely to be as destructive of humane sensibility as the pursuit of function in architecture has been to the achievement of those senses of home and familiar ease in one's surroundings that people have hoped to find in domestic building since the earliest times. Just as modern architects have in effect told the general public that they may not have such a hope, and created wastelands and dereliction almost by intention, as it were, so utilitarian thinking and practice in education – which I take to be the education we are offered by the market-obsessed new Right – seek to produce a population ready only to fulfil technological functions in society, their minds being left to their own weightless and autonomous choices among the stimuli produced by that technology and the mass media. Equally, on the other side of the political spectrum, we have a proliferation of demands for courses allegedly designed in theory to enable pupils to assess for themselves the cultural and political values inherent in the culture and politics of present or past. But unless one has a secure basis within a culture from which to exercise such judgement, such studies are likely only to alienate the pupil from what he is studying, by setting up his judgement – or, more likely, the alienated judgement of his teachers – in opposition to what he is studying, by in effect emptying the forms he is examining of their content and seeing in them only their social context (encouraging him to see, for example, oil painting in general as simply an expression of a bourgeois desire for material self-advertisement, rather than teaching him to see in some oil paintings an expression of socially transcendent values and attitudes, some of which, as in the case of Turner, say, may be highly antithetical to material hopes and aspirations). An example of what I mean here is provided by a specimen syllabus for a GCE Integrated Humanities programme, whose aims include giving pupils

> an understanding of human societies which will enable informed and reasoned judgements to be made about significant contemporary issues

and

> an awareness of the meaning and diversity of human values and the range of possible personal futures.

My point is that such awareness and understandings will be quite empty, and the judgements simply reflect largely unthinking prejudice, in minds unformed in the values of one's culture and ignorant of them and their roots. I hope to show more of what I mean in the course of this paper, though a proposed list of topics for this course is more eloquent than I could be:

Community and Environment
People and Work
Urbanisation, The Family and Child Dev.
Industrialisation
Recreation and Conservation
Conflict
Beliefs and Values
Law and Order
Health and Welfare
Education
Political Movements
Environmental Management
Transport and Communications
The Impact of Technology
World Interdependence
The Mass Media
Prejudice
Race and Culture
Human Rights

There is no suggestion that this range of 'significant contemporary issues' is to be approached on the basis of any grasp at all of the real humanities – an immersion in the disciplines of history and literature – nor indeed on any understanding of our constitution or history that isn't geared immediately to what are felt to be significant contemporary issues, nothing, in other words, that could not be gleaned from a perusal of this year's newspapers. I am not in fact sure that education for utility and education for autonomy are necessarily antithetical. Although those who advocate autonomy as a value in education sometimes think that they are telling their pupils to exercise their own judgement, even on social and political matters, they may in practice be doing no more than instilling in their pupils a belief in the supremacy of individual choice not grounded in any real understanding of what they are choosing about or of the basis on what they are making their choices. In that, they are not so far from the market freedom advocated by industrialists and advertisers, who also insist on the cumulative merit of individual choice. If their pupils have no background against which to exercise these choices, the upshot is all too likely to be a race of Kierkegaardian 'aesthetic' men who act on immediate impulse, on the stimulations of the moment, a race very well suited to the consumer society. I am surprised that no one has made much of the fact that the political left and right are agreed in wanting to sweep traditional academic disciplines away in favour of instant 'studies': business studies, computer studies, management studies, on one side; women's studies, film studies, religious studies, world studies, on the other; all these studies are united in the fact that they do not involve any painstaking initiation into a traditional discipline and immersion in its achievements. As will become clear during this paper, an education which is not firmly based in traditional disciplines is easy game for any sort of political manipulation: this is not the least worrying feature of the present GCSE proposals.

Of course, the educational theorists and politicians who want to bring about a respect for 'wealth creation' and to make education 'relevant' to 'the needs of industry' would not see themselves as advocating the same sort of radicalism that swept university campuses in the 1960's and which has now become so much part of the educational scene particularly in inner city local authority areas. But in one significant respect, and educationally it is the most significant respect of all, campus radicalism of the freedom-now variety and a Josephite utilitarianism in education share a belief in the overweening importance of the present moment and the stimulations and demands of the present. Everything in education must be made relevant to the present, whether the outcome of the relevance is to reinforce or to replace. But even where one's ostensible aim is to replace, the means is always through studies designed to reinforce and concentrate on one's present sense of grievance with the present. Education, I would say, on the contrary is nothing, and its costs in terms of deprivation of liberty unjustified, unless it is a discipline enabling its initiates to distance themselves from their present concerns and perceptions and achieving the proper distances of the feeling intellect. Through education we should enter into those human achievements that have endured and which have, through cultural forms, provided some distancing of the individual from his own greed and need and from the need and greed of others. The hope of the true educator is that his pupils should resist the lure of the current fashions and ephemera, both in politics and in the marketplace, and also see their lure for what it is. By 'enter into human achievements' I do not mean 'study' in the sense of 'studies', as in Media Studies, Women's Studies, Film Studies, Religious Studies. What I do mean is something far more difficult to articulate, but it would be the sort of understanding that recognises that a particular gesture in a classical sculpture is full of grace, that a particular decision to turn and fight a god is the noblest thing a mortal can do. This sort of understanding can be achieved only by someone who has tried to gain some sort of understanding of the classical and Homeric worlds as if from within and in such a way as to bring out the continuities between these worlds and our own, which is their cultural successor.

The present government, though, is as we all know committed to centralising and directing education in the direction of industrial relevance. I don't believe any future government of whatever colour would go in for this any less, but the attempt to centralise and direct comes ill from a party which is ostensibly committed to the theory and practice of the invisible hand. On the invisible hand view, a large-scale human institution is so complex that it will never be actually surveyable or controllable by individual minds; individuals as individuals will inevitably be ignorant of its workings and of the effects of their interventions in it. However, to counterbalance the ignorance of individuals, knowledge is disseminated throughout the institution by the way the effects of the countless individual actions in the institution work their way through it, creating new demands and opportunities for individuals. The most famous example of this dialectic of ignorance and knowledge in a large-scale institution is, of course, the market economy; Adam Smith's talk of the invisible hand amounts to the claim that the most bénéficial way of operating it is to allow the signals sent out spontaneously by consumers and producers to resonate through the system unimpeded, so that labour and capital will be drawn to their most productive uses. What those uses might be is on this view something that no individual mind could know in advance of the actual working out of the countless demands and desires of the individuals in the system. The invisible hand argument against planning and in favour of the free development of institutions is a quite general epistemological claim, and must apply to an institution such as an education system, just as much as in economics. So there is, as I say, something contradictory about engaging in short-term planning for specific ends in education and advocating the unfettered play of market forces elsewhere. And in education and learning generally, there is something highly plausible and attractive about the invisible hand view, more so, perhaps, than in other fields of planning where it is doubtful that the conditions envisaged by Smith could be realised. But in the field of human thought, we cannot know in advance which discoveries might be made, which directions a tradition or discipline might take, or what the effects of educational policies might be on the minds of those yet to be introduced to them. In all these areas spontaneous mental developments is of the essence. So what I say here will apply in the educational field to other governments and administrations which are not committed to the invisible hand doctrine, but which attempt to centralise and determine educational policy by appeal to educationally extraneous goals, something that is already clearly rife in local authorities where the hard left determine educational policy by reference to what is called anti-racism and anti-sexism. Far better, then, to allow education and educational institutions to develop spontaneously, pluralistically and flexibly, guided both by their own traditions and values, whose virtues and defects we do have some experiential knowledge of, and by the creativity of scholars, teachers and learners, than to attempt in a rationalistic spirit globally to determine educational policies from without in the hope of attaining questionable and uncertain goals. For, as in all large-scale social engineering, reason here comes up against its limits; and the planners and the rest of us will inevitably be faced with the unforseeable and often unwanted consequences of their plans, as happened in architecture and town planning (which was also, incidentally, an educational failure, because the generation of architects and planners responsible for the devastations of the 1960's were the products of schools of architecture and planning, whose curricula were dominated by rationalistic principles rather than by immersion in traditional forms and orders).

That we are living in barbaric times hardly needs saying, but it is worth looking briefly at the form the barbarism takes in education, for in addition to the general objection to centralised planning in education just outlined, the actual proposals of the government for education are nothing if not barbaric. According to the DES document of 1981 on the school curriculum, the basic aim of education is 'to equip young people fully for adult and working life in a world which is changing very rapidly indeed in consequence of new technological developments'; for this it needs to give them 'a better understanding of the economic base of our society' and the importance to Britain of the wealth-creating process.[2] Some will no doubt jib at the possibly indoctrinatory tone of this last directive. I am far more concerned at the fact that the only reference to the humanities in the whole document is where, tacked on to a core curriculum to consist of English, mathematics, religious and physical education, and a modern language, there is to be 'some study of the humanities to yield lasting benefit'. The dismissiveness and empty-headedness of this reference shows clearly the degree of importance humanities has in the collective mind of the DES, quite consonant with Sir Keith Joseph's desire to rid the curriculum of 'clutter' (i.e. anything nonutilitarian) and Lord Young's claim, when head of the Manpower Services Commission, that the world of education should recognise that there is no difference between education and training and his further advice to young people not to bother with academic education, as represented (however feebly) by 'O' and 'A' levels, but to go out to get a job.

All this is quite in line, too, with the modern fashion cant of industrialists, politicians, and, regrettably, educationalists, according to whom education should aim at the acquisition of spurious and factitious 'skills' (such as telephone skills, communication skills, information skills and even, I believe, life skills), rather than initiation into these traditional channels of knowledge and experience which, over the centuries, have enabled people to soften and elevate the brutishness of immediate impulse, just because they take men into activities which respond directly neither to their narrow self-interest nor to extraneous utility. I suspect, further, that the aim of learning a modern foreign language, recommended by the DES, is not to gain entry into another aspect of our European culture, but rather to be able to do business in the EEC. A recently installed University Chancellor is on record as believing that the main point of the study of the humanities in the university is just to enable people to discover enough of the ways of foreigners to do this successfully, a remark deserving the equivalent in 1985 of Matthew Arnold's jibe in 1868 that when he studied Greek and Aristotle in Oxford, he had not thought of preparing himself by the study of modern languages to 'fight the battle of life with the waiters in foreign hotels'.[3] The Vice Chancellor of Surrey University, meanwhile, wantonly closed an excellent Philosophy Department at the same time as starting a degree in Dance Studies and increasing an already forty-strong department of 'Hotel Catering, and Tourism Management'.

Matthew Arnold's analysis of the England of his time can, with minor amendments, be applied to much that we see around us to-day: he saw a boorish aristocracy, intent mainly on their 'sports', and largely wedded to the conviction that the main thing about foreigners is that they don't wash (look at *The Tatler*); a working class 'more raw ... less enviable-looking, further removed from civilised and human life, than the common people almost anywhere' (one thinks of Heysel); and a middle-class mindlessly busy in the mechanical pursuit of wealth and personal liberty, though with little enough idea of what to do with either when they get them. This empty search for autonomy for its own sake, as Arnold says, militates against 'the erection of any very strict standard of excellence'.[4] For how can an autonomous individual on his own possibly add anything of value to the culture of a society, or even say anything of value about it, unless he has already submitted to the discipline involved in learning one or other of the forms of knowledge or expression valued in that society?

What is wrong both with the stress on an education that is aimed principally at being relevant to the needs of industry and with the notion which stems from Dewey (but which is also inherent in the politicised curricula of the new educational radicalism) that a genuine education can somehow arise from the current experience and expressive ability of the child, is very much the same thing. Both believe that there can be a satisfactory education rooted in and growing from the immediacies of the present, and responsive first and foremost to the stimulations and demands of the present, and that anyone with a hatfull of relevant 'skills' will be equipped to deal with whatever 'problems' come their way. Apart from anything else, questions of human relationships, of political aims, of death and of living one's life are not problems that can be solved, nor, except in the most corrupt and manipulative sense, are there skills to be exercised in these areas. A proper response to a death, or to a dilemma in politics, or to a work of art is not a thing that can be learned like a genuine skill, such as bowling an off-break; such things require the understanding and wisdom that come from seeing things in a wide human context, in their full complexity and interconnectedness. The rituals and forms of traditional ways of life no doubt gave people the means to live through the enigmas of life. Lacking such traditional forms, at least in any substantial, unreflective sense, it is plausible to suppose that an education focussing on history, literature and the arts will provide the best way of developing the sort of understanding and sensitivity to our lives and experience that will enable us to cherish what is higher, more complex, better-ordered and ultimately more fulfilling, and so to reject the seductions offered by the prospects of immediate satisfaction, either material or intellectual. I do not, of course, say that all art and all history represent what is higher or show man in a non-Hobbesian light. What I am saying is that from a study of history and the arts (in particular from a study of our history and our arts) and from the disciplines involved in these studies, the comparisons and discussions which bring to light what is humanly significant and valuable in a particular work of art or literature and the knowledge which history brings of the source of our present values and institutions, and the context of our artistic and literary heritage, one might hope to learn the sort of qualitative discrimination – the ability to reason on matters of value and human significance – needed to see possibilities and to make judgements and evaluations beyond the narrow exigencies of the present. One might, in other words, ascend to an understanding, from the inside, of civilization as harnessed passion, and culture as the recompense and the mode for sublimated desire (as Adrian Stokes put it).[5]

My insistence that a proper education here must centre on a study of our history and our artistic traditions is all of a piece with my rejection of utilitarian and studies-based curricula. The assumption underlying the latter forms of education is that in an education one can pick and choose what is needed or desirable without any firm grounding in a tradition imparting feelings and values. Utilitarian education neglects such matters altogether, treating man himself as utilitarian philosophy does, as simply a bundle of passing and disconnected desires and preferences manipulable and directable as industry requires and advertising stimulates; 'studies' – as in religious studies, political studies, world studies and the humanities proposals I have referred to – tend to present to the pupil the religious and cultural achievements of mankind as so many consumables from fully intelligible only when one has made oneself party to the form of life which sustains them and which is itself shaped by them. The historian Ranke spoke of all cultures being equal in the sight of God; no doubt they are equal from the point of view of the universe as a whole. But we are human beings and cannot adopt an abstract, inhuman perspective; things matter to us and affect us in unequal ways, and a culture is a means of expressing, reinforcing and teaching the ways things matter to one. What I mean here has been well expressed by Hans-Georg Gadamer: 'We stand always within tradition, and this is no objectifying process, i.e., we do not conceive of what tradition says as something other, something alien. It is always part of us, a model, an exemplar, a recognition of ourselves which our later historical judgement would hardly see as a kind of knowledge, but as the simplest preservation of tradition'.[6] The 'studies' approach to culture is flawed and dishonest because it pretends that one can adopt a divine or inhuman viewpoint (which comes to the same thing) and pick and choose weightlessly and in some way objectively from among value systems, whereas a human being in living and feeling at all will already have inherited certain outlooks, values and preferences simply by being part of a given culture, and his judgements will actually reflect that culture either by corroborating its insights and meanings or by reacting against them. In either case, there is a clear sense that he belongs to a given tradition, and in his reactions continues that tradition, for better or worse. It is my contention that the traditional academic disciplines in the humanities (by which I mean the study of history, literature and the arts, predominantly in the Graeco-Roman and European tradition) provide the best way for someone in our country to feel, understand, make his way in and even to criticize the values on which our institutions and civilization is and has been based. These values of course include – and perhaps this is a particular and peculiar feature of traditions stemming from classical Greece – the value of rational enquiry and scrutiny of beliefs and ideals. And this is no doubt a subsidiary reason why an education in this culture with its somewhat questioning, even sceptical spirit is particularly suited to an open and pluralistic society such as ours is. But more than this, what I am particularly concerned to stress in an education in the humanities is the training such an education can afford in what it is to see and feel the world in a particular way, and to learn to approach the world and one's fellows with a particular type of sensitivity.

Of course, in different works within our western tradition different types of approach and sensitivity will be manifested, and sometimes in the same work there will be differences of outlook and feeling: so the full appreciation of a work of art will necessarily involve what Leavis used to call a critical-creative conflict with the values which that work manifests. We might, for example, find repulsive the vision of man presented by the works of Francis Bacon, and it might be necessary to come to terms with this revulsion, and to understand what possibilities for our lives are ruled out by the Baconian vision. But that we can and must come to terms with Bacon, whereas a work expressing some crisis confronting someone from some other background will leave us largely untouched and remain an object of merely external curiosity, is due to the fact that Bacon's work not only expresses our predicament as the disinherited heirs of a certain religious and political tradition, but it does so by exploiting through distortion the characteristic images of that tradition with which we are all familiar as sacred objects. Bacon's work springs from the same soil as we do ourselves, and it is in that sense that we may deepen understanding and sensitivity to what we are by contemplating and evaluating his works. Of course, I am not saying that Bacon should feature large in any school curriculum. One learns far more about what one is, and what one might be and what one has lost, by study of one's roots and of these works which are classical in the sense of having formed and transformed the outlook of centuries down to our own and having at the same time borne witness to the possibilities of human creativity.

All the weight of present-day education militates against this, however, with calls for immediate and obvious relevance to the present moment. Our contemporary world is instant and full of conflicting babble, all for the present and militating against reflectiveness and any sense of time or history. The output of the mass media is characteristically loud, assertive, mechanical, repetitive, always promising and apparently requiring to promise immediate sensation and gratification. My thoughts here derive from those of Adorno on this subject, who would, I suppose, link the soul-lessness and mechanistic bombardment of the senses at the expense of coherent development in modern popular music with similar features in many other aspects of modern life and work. But it is just the mechanistic repetitiveness and assertiveness of the mass media which make it so internationally available, and which make television and pop music so destructive of traditional cultures, which, being particular in reference and articulating a specific local, historical vision of the world, require for their flourishing a way of life which by its nature cannot be international or instantly communicable to anyone. But the forms of education which I am criticizing also emphasize the universal present at the expense of the particular and the historically determined. The needs of industry as regards skilled manpower are presumably much the same in Japan or Nigeria or anywhere else, as in Britain, while the studies approach tends to see every particular value or culture or tradition in terms of its relevance to the needs of some supposedly detached rational observer who has escaped from the particular values and forms of expression of his or her historical circumstances, and is able to assess all from a world-historical (or world-revolutionary) point of view. The fact that the attainment of such a perspective is a chimera, and that what one calls one's reason is as much a produce of one's culture as it is a transcultural Archimedean point, does not make the myth that one might attain it and stand outside all local and historically conditioned viewpoints any the less pernicious; the myth serves to elevate one's own narrow-ness and ignorance and prejudices to a universal rationality supposedly applicable to all men and all times. (This, of course, was the substance of Nietzsche's criti-cism of the Kantian moral project.) But in pretending to achieve a universal per-spective, one also distances oneself from one's own culture, and its values, meanings and satisfactions. Against this, I would propose an education which begins by opening up to the pupil from the inside, as it were, the meanings which have been revealed to us through our history and literature and our art; and this requires, as I have already suggested, a study of these works which considers them as they are in themselves and not as someone takes them to bear on some imme-diately present need or concern. In this way, and only in this way, might we hope to reveal to ourselves meanings and significances which are part of our heritage and inherent in our institutions and language, but which have become hidden to present view. Equally only through some reflective sense of what it is to stand within a certain culture and tradition can one constructively understand the internalities of other traditions – and see their values as values, as part of a form of life rather than as 'strange' customs and forms to be looked on patronisingly or dismissively from without, as if we were tourists in some sort of Disneyland of world culture.

My ideas here are hardly original, but they need re-stating urgently and forcefully. We have witnessed, and continue to witness in education at the moment, an overwhelming stress on the educational relevance of the present. The government, industrialists and the DES appear to want – and in any case are getting – an edu-cation system designed to answer to the needs of 'industry'. Their mirror-image, the radical left, appear to want the focus of education to be current social pro-blems, viewed through narrow ideological spectacles. Neither party appears to care about transmitting a genuinely disinterested vision of the human world and the possibilities afforded to us by our cultural heritage, as a necessary prelude to any worthwhile life or action. I would follow Matthew Arnold in seeing the best hope for a democracy as lying not in the pursuit of self-government for its own sake, but in the imparting to its citizens ideals of high feeling and fine culture because it is high culture that we see a society, and particularly this culture, in a state of maximum alertness to the human in all its forms. There is nothing narrowing about this: to understand the high culture of Britain is to understand its links with the high cultures of France and Germany, Italy, Holland and Spain, and our roots in the dead cultures of Greece and Rome, and with somewhat more distant cultures of Arabia, Persia, India and even China, Japan and Africa.[7] The idea that education should centre in high culture was shared, incidentally, by the Marxist Antonio Gramsci who believed that a working class denied access to the humanistic rationality of the traditional academic approach was only too likely to remain satisfied with inferior cultural standards, and an easy prey to manipulation by ideology and advertising. I do not doubt that this is very much what is happening now, or that the process of cultural decay is accelerated by the present Government's emphasis on utilitarian values in education. Of course, some people will not get their education from the DES, and will continue to attend schools offering a humane education, engaging in that critical-creative conflict with our past and its best works which alone can inform our present with any significance beyond the mind-dulling clichés of the mass-media, with its tendency to destroy anything particular, anything rooted in a particular culture or place and the craving for the commodities of the industrial process. But those privileged educationally will tend also to be those privileged socially, and so the division of the country into two classes and two cultures will be perpetuated. And this is surely unacceptable, not only culturally, but also ethically.

Matthew Arnold wrote in *Culture and Anarchy* of what he called the social idea of culture, whereby education would not 'track down to the level of inferior classes', and the mass of the population would not be fobbed off with an 'intellectual food prepared and adapted in the way (others) think proper for the actual condition of the masses'.[8] The way of culture, by contrast, 'seeks to do away with classes' and to make the best that has been thought and known current and freely available to all, so that – I would add, in the spirit of the invisible hand – they might freely use the ideas thus made available. It seems to me that we are no nearer this social idea now than we were in 1868 when Arnold wrote, and in some ways we may be even further from it, given that the Government and the DES appear to be entirely ruled in educational matters by short-term market considerations. Architectural tower blocks may now be out of fashion, but an education system is now being fashioned to suit an intellectual horizon limited by the demands of industrialists and politicians of various shades, aided by plenty of educational theorists and administrators who have no standing in any traditional educational discipline. These demands are for centralised planning in education aimed at short-term utilitarian and political goals. Consideration of the effects of centralised planning of this sort suggests that the goals are not likely to be achieved in education any more than they were in modern architectural developments. But a generation of children will certainly be deprived of the cultural benefits of a traditional education according a central place to the humanities and this should be deeply worrying to true educators.

Notes

1 O'Hear, *Education, Society and Human Nature* (London, Routledge & Kegan Paul, 1981).
2 Department of Education and Science: *The School Curriculum* (London, HMSO, 1981).
3 M. Arnold: *Culture and Anarchy* in Arnold's *Complete Prose Works*, Vol. 5, ed. R. H. Super (Ann Arbor, 1965), p. 126.
4 Arnold, *op. cit.*, p. 146.
5 A. Stokes, *The Stones of Rimini* (London, Cape, 1934), p. 220.
6 H.-G. Gadamer: *Truth and Method* (London: Sheed & Ward, 1975), p. 259.
7 Cf. R. Scruton, 'The Myth of Cultural Relativism' in *Anti-Racism: An Assault on Education and Value*, ed. F. Palmer (London, 1986), pp. 127–35.
8 Arnold, *op. cit.*, p. 112.

12 City Technology Colleges: an Old Choice of School?

G. McCulloch

Author

As well as working in New Zealand, Gary McCulloch has held professorial posts in Lancaster University and the University of Sheffield. He was appointed to the Institute of Education, University of London, in 2003 as its inaugural Brian Simon professor of the history of education. Professor McCulloch is the former president of the History of Education Society and a former editor of the journal *History of Education*. He is also a member of the editorial boards of several journals, including *History of Education Quarterly, Journal of Educational Administration and History, History of Education Review, History of Education and Children's Literature*, and *Paedagogica Historica*. He has published widely in the field including *Documentary Research in Education, History and the Social Sciences, The Death of the Comprehensive High School? The Routledge International Encyclopædia of Education* and *The Struggle for the History of Education*. He is Academician of Academy of Social Sciences, Fellow of Royal Society of Arts and Fellow of Royal Historical Society. Professor McCulloch served on the HEFCE Research Assessment Exercise Education panel in 1996, 2001 and 2008.

Article

The 1980s were characterised by the reforming zeal of Margaret Thatcher's Conservative government. For education, the culmination of Secretary of State for Education Kenneth Baker's work may be found in the Education Reform Act (1988), which proposed, *inter alia*, the establishment of the National Curriculum for England, the Local Management of Schools, a national assessment and testing regime, the establishment of grant maintained schools, and what some have characterised as a vindictive act of educational vandalism, the abolition of the Inner London Education Authority. Published in the year following the Act, *City Technology Colleges: an Old Choice of School?* (37, 1: 30–43) questions optimistic Mr. Baker's intention to establish a network of about twenty such schools that had been described in the Department for Education's 1986 publication *A New Choice of School*. CTCs were to be government-funded, independent schools run by educational trusts, outside the control of Local Education Authorities. It was proposed that sponsors from the private sector would make a significant contribution towards the costs of such schools, offering a curriculum with a strong emphasis on technical, scientific and practical, business studies and design. In line with dominant Conservative educational thinking of the 1980s, CTCs would also seek to develop the qualities of enterprise, self-reliance, and responsibility, and secure the highest possible standards of achievement.

It is not unusual for politicians to propose educational initiatives with little or no reference to historical precursors. Therefore, the article proposes 'an analysis of the aims, problems and failures of the secondary technical schools, [so] we may be able to suggest their continuing significance in terms of the curriculum initiatives of the late 1980s'. The article draws on a wealth of historical evidence from the inter-war and post-war years to inform analysis. McCulloch's analysis is not a one-sided dismissal of technical education as it also suggests we may learn from some of the 'positive' lessons from the experience of the secondary technical schools. Nevertheless, drawing neatly upon the Spens Report, he reminds us that 'Educational policy surely should be "based on something more substantial than current opinion and popular views of the significance of what has occurred"': words as apposite in the second decade of the 21st Century as they were in 1989 and 1938.

The academic/technical and vocational divide in the British education system has been, and continues to be, discussed. With mixed success, several attempts have been made to address the issues of ability, aptitude, attainment, educational entitlement and the hierarchies of educational credibility that surround attitudes to the relative educational worth of academic and technical/vocational curricula. Latterly, what appeared to be a new dawn proposed by the Tomlinson Report (2004) now seems little more than a brief penumbral glimmer. The informed and scholarly analysis in *City Technology Colleges: an Old Choice of School?* would be useful reading for educational policy makers in the Coalition government and associated proponents of Academies and Free Schools.

Related articles in the *Journal* include: *The changing idea of technical education* (11, 2: 142–66); *Constant factors in the demand for technical education: 1860–1960* (14, 2: 173–87); *Technical education and the politicians (1870–1918)* (21, 1: 34–39); *City Technology Colleges: Schooling for the Thatcher generation?* (40, 3: 207–17).

City Technology Colleges: an Old Choice of School?

by *Gary McCulloch*, University of Auckland

In October 1986, the secretary of state for education and science, Mr Kenneth Baker, unveiled his new grand design for the inner cities of England and Wales. His speech to the Conservative Party's annual conference announced his decision 'to launch a pilot network of new schools in urban areas, including the disadvantaged inner cities'. These would provide free education for eleven-to eighteen-year-olds. They would be government-funded, independent schools run by educational trusts, and would not be part of the local education authority. Private sector sponsors would make a 'substantial contribution' towards the costs of the schools, which would offer 'a curriculum with a strong emphasis on technical, scientific and practical, business studies and design'. They would also 'seek to develop the qualities of enterprise, self-reliance, and responsibility, and secure the highest possible standards of achievement'. Baker hoped initially to establish a network of about twenty such schools, each with 750 to 1,000 pupils. The schools were to be known as city technology colleges (CTCs).[1]

Baker's message to the party faithful was reinforced the following week when the Department of Education and Science published a short, attractively illustrated booklet, *A New Choice of School*. Described by one observer as the 'Tory urban blueprint',[2] this set out to explain the idea of the city technology college, and also to appeal for financial support from industry and business interests. The purpose of CTCs would be, it suggested, 'to provide a broadly-based secondary education with a strong technological element thereby offering a wider choice of secondary school to parents in certain cities and a surer preparation for adult and working life to their children'.[3] Both Baker's speech and the subsequent booklet radiated optimism about the future prospects of this new policy and its likely effects on the education system, industry and society. Neither made any reference to the past, to what amounts to a century or more of experience in initiatives in secondary technical education. Nor was this forthcoming in the debate that followed. Much more was made of the contemporary and successful examples in other countries – the education systems of industrial competitors, the 'magnet schools' of the United States – than of the mixed record of endeavour, success and failure in Britain itself.

Least of all was there any serious discussion of the significance of a very similar innovation promoted at a national level in England only forty years ago: the secondary technical school. This was widely regarded as a vital aspect of 'secondary education for all' as it emerged in the 1940s. According to *The New Secondary Education*, published by the Ministry of Education in 1947, such schools were distinctive in 'selecting the sphere of industry or commerce' as their 'particular link with the adult world'. They were intended to cater for 'a minority of able children who are likely to make their best response when the curriculum is strongly coloured by these interests, both from the point of view of a career and because subject-matter of this kind appeals to them'.[4] To what extent should we see in these secondary technical schools the roots and exemplars of the initiatives of the 1980s – the Technical and Vocational Education Initiative (TVEI) and the CTCs?

Such a question, interesting in itself, assumes additional importance when one begins to consider the development and ultimate fate of the secondary technical schools. That they failed to live up to the hopes of their sponsors, despite determined efforts, cannot be doubted. By 1958 they were still catering for only 3.7 per cent of the total number of secondary school pupils. In the 1960s they were all but swept away along with the grammar schools as comprehensive reorganisation gathered momentum. Should we therefore regard the bitter experience of the secondary technical schools as a warning for our own generation? Do they demonstrate the futility of such exercises, or perhaps indicate potentially crippling problems that might be avoided? On such generally negative views of their significance, as P. J. Kemeny has argued, 'it would be as well to try to learn from the mistakes of this large and costly experiment aimed at alleviating some of the consequences of educational selection'.[5]

It may be on the other hand that secondary technical schools offer lessons of a more positive kind, that despite their general failure they were able to develop a curriculum and rationale that might still be of use today. Perhaps indeed they may suggest approaches to 'secondary technical education' that could assist the initiators of our contemporary developments, or that might prove more palatable to critics of these schemes. Such is the message of Geoffrey Taylor's unpublished account of the secondary technical schools, written over twenty years ago:

> Nomenclature matters not, but what is of fundamental importance is, that the way which has been illuminated by the technical schools of the past and those today ... should continue to influence secondary education and indeed offer a pointer to the wider adoption of the value of a carefully planned education, liberal in outlook, stimulating in content and producing men and women educated to meet the demanding scientific developments of the next decades, and be able to apply them through technology, to the benefit of man.[6]

This may be of particular use for the future of the CTCs, which, it has been suggested, look more 'like a throw-back to the technical schools of the 1950s' than the American city 'magnet' schools.[7] The historian Michael Sanderson sees the failure to develop junior technical and secondary technical schools as 'perhaps the greatest lost opportunity of twentieth century English education', and argues strongly that

Although we cannot turn the clock back to recreate this form [of school] as an alternative for non-academic teenagers, some of its characteristics are being resurrected by these new schemes. This is particularly so with the CTCs although their inevitably modest number cannot substitute for the lack of a national system.[8]

Through an analysis of the aims, problems and failures of the secondary technical schools, we may be able to suggest their continuing significance in terms of the curriculum initiatives of the late 1980s.

The experience of the secondary technical schools demonstrates the importance of creating a clear image and rationale for a 'new choice of school' of this kind, and the consequences of failing to do so. In the interwar years, local education authorities (LEAs) and technical institutions became anxious to raise the status of junior technical schools (JTSs) by broadening their curriculum and elevating them to comparable stature with that of the secondary (grammar) schools. The Association of Technical Institutions and Association of Principals of Technical Institutions complained of the 'social stigma' attached to JTSs, and the 'preference shown today for black-coated, sheltered occupations'. They argued strongly that the JTS, 'functioning under a new name and on modified lines', would have 'much of value to offer as an alternative New Secondary Education'.[9] The Spens committee on secondary education, dissatisfied with the academic character of existing secondary schools, accepted this. It concluded that JTSs based on the engineering and building industries should be encouraged to develop 'a form of secondary education which ought to be regarded as an alternative to that of a Grammar School'. It therefore recommended the 'conversion of a number of these schools into Technical High Schools in every respect equal in status to Grammar Schools'.[10] The Norwood report of 1943 rationalised this reform as catering for a particular 'type of mind', offering 'a general education, oriented no doubt from the age of 13+ towards the special technical courses which it offers, but broad in conception'.[11] But what this meant in practical terms remained far from clear.

Officials of the Board of Education had generally been opposed to such a reform. They preferred to retain the JTS, which had the virtue of possessing a clear function and purpose. As the Hadow report had affirmed in 1926, 'These Schools are definitely intended to prepare pupils either for artisan or other industrial occupations or for domestic employment'.[12] Officials feared that this definite intention would be lost and only an indeterminate identity gained through raising the status of the schools. A. Abbott, the Board's chief inspector for technical schools in the early 1930s, was strongly hostile to 'these what do you call them schools'.[13] He was emphatic that a broader JTS would lose its clear definition and its close link with industry, and would become simply an 'amorphous something'.[14] R. S. Wood, the Board's new principal assistant secretary for technical education, predicted in July 1937 that a new system of three distinct types of secondary school might well emerge following the Spens report,[15] and especially after the outbreak of war in 1939 Board officials began reluctantly to concede that secondary technical schools would be developed as one element of a 'tripartite' system. But H. B. Wallis, head of the technical branch, remained doubtful about their long-term prospects and identity.[16] Even after the war, another leading civil servant, A. A. Part, could still note that 'We are all feeling our way to some extent' over the conception of the secondary technical school 'because, with a very few possible exceptions, there are, I believe, no Secondary Technical Schools in the full sense of the word in existence to-day'. According to Part, some continued to see the new schools as 'a sort of hotted up JTS with what is in effect a preparatory department taking the pupils from the age of 11+ to 13+'. If this kind of view prevailed, Part added, 'it does not seem likely to me that the Secondary Technical School will easily win an esteem in the eyes of parents equal to that in which the average Grammar School is held at present'.[17] The Inspectorate's secondary education panel was unclear, as late as November 1945, on 'the content of the general education' and 'the place of vocational education' in the secondary technical school.[18] Its chairman, the chief inspector R. H. Charles, confessed in January 1946 that 'We don't know enough about these schools'.[19] The Ministry's 'principles of education' panel laboured under similar difficulties, which led it to question the need or rationale for independent technical schools.[20]

The ambivalence and lack of clarity that surrounded the secondary technical school from its inception are also illustrated in the unexpected growth of examination entries in such schools. It was noted at the end of 1954 that the 'least expected development' to have taken place in the secondary technical schools since the publication of *The New Secondary Education* was 'the trend towards the use of external examinations'. The schools tended to try to develop sixth forms, 'often mainly for prestige reasons'.[21] But this served also to highlight differences among the schools, and also to confirm earlier fears that an appropriate and distinctive form of assessment would be difficult to obtain. Initial recruitment to the secondary technical school, similarly, involved problems that failed to dissipate. Most Inspectors with experience of the JTS apparently believed that it was 'not practicable to select pupils for that type of school before the age of 13+'.[22] Some administrators pinned their hopes on further research finding an answer to this problem, or suggested that the schools might be able to resolve such difficulties themselves once they were established. But by the 1950s, hopes of finding a suitable test of practical ability at 11-plus equivalent to the 'intelligence test' had almost completely subsided. The result was to renew convictions that the secondary technical school was hedged with doubts and difficulties. Even more, it meant that grammar schools, already established with clear rationales and procedures, had a clear advantage in competing for admission of pupils at 11-plus. In practice, indeed, they tended to take the most successful candidates from the selection tests at 11-plus, leaving the technical schools to take a 'second creaming'. The principle that the secondary technical school should take the 'second best' pupils was bound to become a self-fulfilling prophecy about the schools themselves. Secondary technical schools for girls shared these problems of selection and assessment, but also had special problems of their own in attaining a distinct identity and approach. Again, such matters had never been fully worked out before 1945, and it was too late to do so once the schools were already running and exposed to public and political scrutiny.

These problems of image, function and procedures suggest in retrospect that the character of the secondary technical school needed to be thought out and defined much more clearly, before the policy was enacted, than was in fact the case. It was not enough to leave these considerations for the schools themselves to work out in practice, for they tended to follow different approaches to their problems which only added to the confusion and uncertainty about what such schools were really meant to do. This experience would appear to hold direct relevance for the proposed CTCs of the late 1980s. These too are apparently intended to be broadly-based rather than narrowly vocational, but their eventual image, identity, role and function remain unclear. We do not know whether the policy-makers of the 1980s have considered and sought to avoid the basic problems encountered in the 1940s; there is little outward indication that they have done so. Whether they have or not, there must be a risk involved in current policy of the CTCs sharing the fate of the secondary technical schools, and for much the same reasons.

A further 'lesson' of the secondary technical schools is surely that the Ministry of Education had only very limited power to ensure change along the lines that it favoured. It could certainly influence developments in many different ways, but such influence was not necessarily sufficient to ensure that the policies worked out in London would be translated into effective long-term reform in the localities. The fate of the Norwood report of 1943 – exploited, neglected, rigidified and abused – is a classic example of the gap between policy and practice, between the aspirations and ideals of the elite and the realities of everyday negotiations in the schools.[23] The secondary technical schools, likewise, did not turn out as the Ministry had expected. Interactions at the local level and within the schools themselves were crucial in determining the 'status' of the schools and the character of their curriculum. Flaws and lacunae that had always been potential features of the secondary technical school were cruelly exposed in these negotiations, and led all too often to incoherence, ineffectiveness, and failure.

It was left to the LEAs to interpret local needs, to define the character of secondary schools and to resolve the many unanswered questions and practical issues relating to the secondary technical school. Many responded by declining to develop such schools, often preferring 'bilateral' grammar-technical and technical-modern schools instead. The largely urbanised county boroughs were generally more sympathetic to the secondary technical school than rural county councils. Even here the successful development of such schools depended greatly on local circumstances, and on the good will and commitment of local education officers, head teachers, and parents. A common problem was a chronic lack of resources. Reese Edwards, chief education officer at Wigan and sympathetic to the secondary technical schools, felt that the 'biggest handicap' to their 'proper development' was 'the serious shortage of suitable school accommodation'.[24] As Anthony Part had feared, many of them were hampered by being situated within the premises of particular technical colleges and thus becoming 'a junior version of the technical college, both in atmosphere and in actual work', with a 'very limited corporate life of their own'.[25] They were expensive to establish and maintain as independent institutions, involving as they did expenditure on specialist staff, buildings and equipment. For this reason they were in most cases based in the same premises as the old JTSs, very often with the same staff, if not the same equipment. This inertia of resources that survived the change of status deepened the prevailing confusion about the identity and rationale of these schools. It tended to confirm what was already a deeply ingrained social prejudice against technical education and general preference for grammar school education.

Thus the success of the schools was heavily dependent on local support and resources for development. But local support was patchy and generally lukewarm. The Ministry had made little effort to involve the localities in its policy changes; the consequences were predictable. It is also fair to hold the Ministry ultimately responsible for the lack of resources which held back the schools, and for raising false expectations that resources would be provided. The policy was based upon the expectation of providing suitable buildings, equipment and staff; the practice fell well short of this. Again then we appear to have important lessons for the CTC initiative of the late 1980s: first, that it is important to develop the policy through a close relationship with local communities and interests, and second, that it is crucial to provide sufficient resources to develop and sustain the original purposes of the venture. In fact, the parallel between the 1940s and the 1980s is not quite as close as this assertion might imply. The CTCs, after all, are to be run by educational trusts, will not be part of the LEA, and will supposedly have much of their costs met by their private sponsors. Despite the differences, it is still reasonable to argue that the active support of LEAs and the secure provision of resources would greatly assist the future of the CTCs, and that the experience of the secondary technical schools underlines the likely consequences of not attaining these goals.

The fact that the CTCs will rely more upon local businesses and industry raises another feature of the secondary technical schools that is of direct relevance for today. Current Government policies, including the promotion of CTCs, imply a simple and unproblematic relationship between 'practical' education and the needs and demands of the 'world of work'.[26] Yet as the secondary technical schools learned to their cost, this is far from the truth. The secondary technical schools sought to promote themselves as being the 'prep schools of industry', appealing directly to industry and commerce to recruit their graduates.[27] But although many of their products did indeed go into industry, and a number of schools established strong ties with local industrial interests, in general organised industry showed little sympathy or support for their cause. The Federation of British Industries (FBI), for example, was much more concerned with attracting the products of the grammar schools and public schools to become the future 'captains of industry'.[28] According to A. G. Grant, the chairman of the FBI's education committee, in April 1956, 'It is clear that the Grammar Schools are now vividly aware of what the modern world needs and of the fact that science and industry largely *are* the modern world. The same, I feel, goes for the public Schools … and for the universities … ' Grant was content to leave these schools and universities, 'helped and stimulated now by the Minister of Education's re-built Advisory Committee', to 'get on with the job'.[29] It was by no means apparent to the FBI that the secondary technical schools had any special value or role to offer. G. Withers of the FBI's technical section reminded one colleague that 'Our problem is undoubtedly the grammar school leaver. There is a great deal of competition for his [sic] services from the banks and the Civil Service, and our job is to persuade the medium size and smaller concerns that, whilst they have not yet experienced the full force of this competition, sooner or later they will.'[30] Another industrialist noted in 1958 that 'The FBI has not given much special consideration to technical schools as such, but has concentrated more on the numerically much larger sphere of the grammar school and the secondary modern'.[31] The moral to be drawn from these attitudes is that industry and industrialists will not be automatically drawn to support a sector of education that styles itself as oriented towards industry and commerce. In industry, as in education, such decisions are related to complex interactions of cultural, political and social traditions and more pragmatic calculations. The failure of the secondary technical schools to attract the active interest of major industrial concerns should be a clear warning for the current CTC initiative.

It is possible also to suggest some more 'positive' lessons from the experience of the secondary technical schools. They were, for example, able to develop an interesting and useful rationale for their further development, especially through the work of their most representative pressure group, the Association of Heads of Secondary Technical Schools (AHSTS).[32] This Association succeeded in influencing the recommendations of the Crowther committee, established by the Ministry of Education in 1956 to investigate the education of boys and girls between fifteen and eighteen years of age. Chapter 35 of the Crowther report, which was published in 1959, attempted to outline the character of the 'Alternative Road' that the secondary technical schools embodied. Such schools, according to Crowther, should be encouraged to develop 'a practical education making progressively exacting intellectual demands'.[33] Such education, it added, would involve 'broad scientific curiosity' rather than 'narrow vocational interest'.[34] But Crowther conceded that this approach was only in its 'early stages of development', and therefore recommended that further inquiry should be made into the problems associated with the general notion of the 'alternative road'.[35] The AHSTS's leading ideologue, Edward Semper, was specially prominent in pursuing this aim. Semper had been seeking ways to end the confusion of purpose among the secondary technical schools ever since their inception.[36] He became headmaster of the Doncaster Technical High School for Boys in 1952, and spent the next few years trying to work out the practical implications of his approach. His staff were inexperienced and accommodation was restricted, but by 1959 his school had sixty sixth-formers and a new building in which craft work was practised as an 'instrument of general education'.[37] He led demands for the Ministry of Education to make further enquiry into the idea of the 'alternative road' and, when this failed to materialise, organised his own curriculum research project.[38]

The success of the Doncaster school in overcoming many of the characteristic problems of secondary technical schools may also indicate the possibility of at least some CTCs transcending the likely obstacles to their own progress. If so, one should take careful note of the factors that helped the few successful secondary technical schools to survive as they did. One of the most important requirements for success, as in the case of Doncaster, was a determined and resourceful head-teacher. Another advantage was a purpose-built school, such as Thomas Linacre School in Wigan, opened in 1953.[39] A further necessity was the active support of the local education authority, such as that enjoyed by the Wolverhampton Technical High School at least until the retirement of F. L. Mills as director of education in Wolverhampton in 1954. Mills had helped to establish the Wolverhampton school as the first designated secondary technical school in the country, and was, as the headmaster B. J. Edwards acknowledged, 'a great friend of technical education'.[40] His successor, G. W. R. Lines, proved less sympathetic, which helped to ensure an end to further development and a frustrating and ultimately unsuccessful struggle for survival. Another important ingredient for success was a strong local tradition in technical education, such as in Leicester where the Gateway School for Boys had been established as early as 1928. The ability of these schools to develop and prosper was heavily dependent upon such factors, which seem no less relevant today.[41]

On the other hand, we should also note that even the secondary technical schools in Doncaster, Wigan, Wolverhampton, and Leicester, with all their undoubted merits, failed to survive the general collapse of the policy at a national level in the 1960s. In local reorganisation plans they typically became comprehensive schools, although Gateway School in Leicester held on until the 1970s before becoming a sixth-form college.[42] The overall failure of the secondary technical schools to establish themselves, despite their initial optimism and isolated successes, must raise serious doubts as to the wisdom of creating separate schools as distinct from influencing the curriculum and practices of established schools. The proposals of the Spens report for an upgrading of technical schools provided a convenient excuse for grammar schools and Board officials to avoid having to contemplate radical reforms in the existing secondary schools. As Maurice Holmes of the Board of Education pointed out, 'Technical High Schools would in large measure be unnecessary if the curriculum of Secondary Schools were widened on the lines suggested in that Report'.[43] Arguably they proved counter-productive to this purpose. A strategy of 'absorption' by which established secondary schools were induced in some way to adopt novel approaches might also have been ineffective, given the resistance to change exhibited by most schools, teachers, parents and officials of that time. But in retrospect it might have been a more logical and realistic policy than that which was adopted.

Such reflections cast an interesting light upon the initiatives of the 1980s, especially the TVEI and the CTCs. The TVEI was launched in November 1982, originally as a pilot project, to incorporate a 'technical and vocational' element in the curriculum of pupils of fourteen to eighteen years of age. It was organised by the Manpower Services Commission, which was responsible to the Department of Employment, rather than by the Department of Education and Science. The political source of the scheme and its potential for establishing narrowly vocational curricula within secondary schools gave rise in the first instance to justifiable fears that it would create 'a divided curriculum perpetuating Victorian views of knowledge and social class'.[44] But its use of the established secondary schools and, eventually, of every LEA in the country meant that teachers and LEAs could interpret it in more appropriate ways in different contexts, often involving significant curriculum reform.[45] The CTC initiative, by contrast, bypassed both the LEAs and the already established secondary schools. It threatened to create local rivalries and conflict, and even to undermine the impact of the TVEI in comprehensive schools by diverting attention and resources.[46] Consideration of the earlier experience of the secondary technical schools might have indicated that the most viable policy was to strengthen the TVEI in comprehensive schools and encourage them to adapt it to a broader vision more characteristic, perhaps, of Spens and Crowther.[47] The CTCs appear to be a classic illustration of the view that those who ignore the past are condemned to repeat it.

This disregard for the historical dimension is typical of educational policy in England since the 1960s. An earlier historical tradition in education policy is clearly evident from a reading of major reports such as the Spens report on secondary education (1938), the Fleming report on the public schools (1944), and the Crowther report (1959). Spens, for example, devoted his first chapter to a 'Sketch of the development of the traditional curriculum in secondary schools of different types in England and Wales', arguing that

> As we see one view or theory of education subjected to criticism and in consequence modified or superseded by another, we may be able partially to understand and appraise the value and meaning of each successive phase, and to form opinions of our own which, though they cannot possibly claim to be final, may at any rate claim to be based on something more substantial than current opinion and popular views of the significance of what has occurred.[48]

Such perspectives seem potentially no less fruitful for our own day than for the policies developed in past decades. Educational policy surely should be 'based on something more substantial than current opinion and popular views of the significance of what has occurred'.

The consequences of neglecting history are manifest in the policy initiatives of the 1980s: policies that rise without trace, acquired in a fit of amnesia to be forgotten the next day. Critics of official policy, seeking to develop alternative policies of their own, should equally benefit from a stronger sense of historical understanding and experience. Of course such historical awareness should be grounded in a careful study of changing contexts, needs and demands. Crude parallels and unbalanced or inaccurate descriptions will hinder rather than assist policy analysis, and discredit the possible role of history in this process.[49] Yet to ignore or reject the potential role of historical leverage in education policy seems even more perilous an approach. This tendency, if unchecked, may well mar the prospects for success of the current initiative. It is on the whole fair to describe the CTCs as history masquerading as policy: not a 'new choice of school', as its publicity claims, but an *old* choice of school. If this simple truth is not acknowledged and acted upon, this is one policy that may itself be history.

Notes

I should like to thank participants at the ANZ History of Education Society Conference at Canberra, 26–28 August 1988, for their helpful comments on a draft of this paper.

1 *The Times Educational Supplement,* 10 October 1986, report, 'Baker's course to put governors at the helm'.
2 Ian Nash, report, 'Birth of the Tory urban blueprint', *TES,* 17 October 1986.
3 DES, *A New Choice of School: City Technology Colleges* (1986), p. 2.
4 Ministry of Education, *The New Secondary Education* (Pamphlet no.9, 1947), p. 48.
5 P.J. Kemeny, 'Dualism in secondary technical education', in *Br.Jnl. of Sociology,* 21 (1970), p. 93.
6 Geoffrey F. Taylor, 'Developments in secondary technical education, 1944–60' (Sheffield MA thesis, 1966), pp. 362–63.
7 *Education,* 17 October 1986, news in review, 'Colleges'.
8 Michael Sanderson, *Educational Opportunity and Social Change in England* (1987), pp. 60, 7.
9 ATT, APTI, memo to consultative committee of Board of Education, n.d. [c.1934] (Board of Education papers, P.R.O., ED.10/151).
10 Board of Education, *Report of the Consultative Committee on Secondary Education* (Spens report, 1938), xxvii.
11 Board of Education, *Report of the Committee on the Curriculum and Examinations in Secondary Schools* (Norwood report, 1943), p. 4.
12 Board of Education, *Report of the Consultative Committee on the Education of the Adolescent* (Hadow report, 1926), p. 33.
13 A. Abbott, note, 8 August 1930 (Bd. of Ed. papers, ED.12/419).
14 A. Abbott, note, 2 March 1932 (Bd. of Ed. papers, ED.12/419).
15 R. S. Wood, memo, 30 July 1937 (Bd. of Ed. papers, ED.10/273).
16 H. B. Wallis, memo, 'Technical education: post war policy and organisation', 15 October 1941 (Bd. of Ed. papers, ED.136/296).
17 A. A. Part, 'Draft pamphlet on the secondary technical school', n.d. [1946] (Ministry of Ed. papers, ED. 136/789).
18 Inspectorate: secondary education panel (A2), 1st meeting, 21 November 1945 (Ministry of Ed. papers, ED.158/18).
19 Secondary education panel, 2nd meeting, 17 January 1946 (Ministry of Ed. papers, ED.158/18).
20 Ministry of Education, principles of education panel, 5th meeting, 27 September 1946 (Ministry of Ed. papers, ED.158/14).
21 A. G. Gooch, 'Secondary technical education', 28 December 1954 (Ministry of Ed. papers, ED. 147/207).
22 A. A. Part, note, 'Draft pamphlet on the secondary technical school' (Ministry of Ed. papers, ED. 136/789).
23 See Gary McCulloch, 'The Norwood report and the secondary school curriculum', in *History of Education Review,* 17/2(1988), pp. 30–45, for a discussion of this factor.
24 Reese Edwards, *The Secondary Technical School* (1960), p. 35.
25 A. A. Part, note, 'The secondary technical school', 2 April 1946 (Ministry of Ed. papers, ED. 136/789).
26 See e.g. Cyril Taylor, 'Climbing towards a skilful revolution', *TES,* 22 January 1988. Also DES, Department of Employment, *Working Together: Education and Training* (1986).
27 *TES,* 16 March 1956, report, 'Industry's prep schools'.
28 See Gary McCulloch, 'A technocratic vision: the ideology of school science reform in the 1950s', *Social Studies of Science,* 18 (4) (1988).

29 A. G. Grant to F. J. C. Perry, 16 April 1956 (FBI papers, Warwick Universit Library, 200/F/3/T2/1/7).
30 G. Withers to James Wooding, 22 December 1952 (FBI papers, 200/F/3/T1/ 329).
31 Major-General A. J. H. Dove (FBI, London) to Captain E. C. L. Turner (FBI, Newcastle), 7 February 1958 (FBI papers, 200/F/3/T2/1/3).
32 See Gary McCulloch, 'Pioneers of an "Alternative Road"? The Association of Heads of Secondary Technical Schools, 1951–64', in Ivor Goodson (ed.), *Social Histories of the Secondary Curriculum: Subjects for Study* (1985), pp. 313–42, for further details on this Association.
33 Ministry of Education, *15 to 18: A Report of the Central Advisory Council for Education (England)* (Crowther report, 1959), p. 397.
34 *Ibid.*, p. 393.
35 *Ibid.*, p. 398. See also Gary McCulloch, 'Views of the Alternative Road: the Crowther concept', in David Layton (ed.), *The Alternative Road: The Rehabilitation of the Practical* (1984), pp. 57–73.
36 Edward Semper, 'The curriculum of the technical high school: with special reference to Bradford' (M.Ed. thesis, University of Leeds, 1946).
37 *Technical Education*, 1/4 (May 1959), 'Doncaster Technical High School – a pictorial survey', pp. 23–25.
38 Edward Semper, *Technology and the Sixth-Form Boy – the Teaching Aspect* (1964).
39 *The Wigan Examiner*, 27 November 1953, report, 'Thomas Linacre School officially opened: "blazing a pioneer trail of technical education"'.
40 Wolverhampton THS, headmaster's log book, 1 April 1954 (private).
41 For detailed case-studies of these schools and a fuller account of the secondary technical schools in general, see Gary McCulloch, *The Secondary Technical School: A Usable Past?* (Falmer Press, 1989).
42 Gerald T. Rimmington, *The Comprehensive School Issue in Leicester, 1945–1974, and Other Essays* (1984) is helpful on the context of the Gateway School.
43 Maurice Holmes, note to President of Board of Education, 5 July 1939 (Board of Education papers, ED.136/131).
44 Maurice Holt, 'The great education robbery', *TES*, 3 December 1982.
45 See e.g. Denis Gleeson (ed.), *TVEI and Secondary Education: A Critical Appraisal* (1987). Also Ian Nash, 'Taking the initiative to the most able students', *TES*, 4 September 1987; and *TES*, 30 October 1987, report, 'Extended TVEI set to broaden the curriculum'.
46 See John McLeod, 'City technology colleges – a study of the character and progress of an educational reform', in *Local Government Studies*, 14/1 (1988), pp.75–82.
47 A discussion of the contested character and historical significance of the TVEI is Gary McCulloch, 'History and policy: the politics of the TVEI', in Gleeson, *op. cit.*, pp. 13–37.
48 Spens report, p. 1.
49 See e.g. Ernest R. May, *'Lessons' of the Past: The Use and Misuse of History in American Foreign Policy* (1973); and Harvey J. Kaye, 'History hijacked', in *Times Higher Education Supplement*, 6 February 1987.

13 Education and Values

D. Carr

Author

David Carr is Emeritus Professor of Education in the University of Edinburgh where he was Professor of Philosophy of Education in the Moray House School of Education from 1999 to 2009. He is author of *Educating the Virtues* (1991), *Professionalism and Ethics in Teaching* (2000) and *Making Sense of Education* (2003), as well as of numerous articles in leading philosophical and educational journals. He is also editor of *Education, Knowledge and Truth* (1998), co-editor (with J. Steutel) of *Virtue Ethics and Moral Education* (1999), (with J. Haldane) of *Spirituality, Philosophy and Education* (2003), (with M. Halstead and R. Pring) of *Liberalism, Education and Schooling: Essays by T. H. McLaughlin* (2008), (with R. Bailey, R. Barrow and C. McCarthy) of the *Sage Handbook of Philosophy of Education* (2010), and (with L. Bondi, C. Clark and C. Clegg) of *Towards Professional Wisdom* (2011). He was secretary of the Scottish branch of the Philosophy of Education Society of Great Britain for thirty-five years.

Introduction

David Carr has had published more articles for the *British Journal of Educational Studies* than any other author in the last sixty years. Other articles of his, besides the one we publish in this book, have included: *Education and Values* (39, 3: 244–59), *Questions of Competence* (41, 3: 253–71), *The Uses of Literacy in Teacher Education* (45, 1: 53–68), *Education, Profession and Culture: Some Conceptual Questions* (48, 3: 248–68), *Personal and Interpersonal Relationships in Education and Teaching: A Virtue Ethics Perspective* (53, 3: 255–71), *Revisiting the Liberal and Vocational Dimension of University Education* (57, 1: 1–17) and *Education, Contestation and Confusions of Sense and Concept* (58, 1: 89–104). *Character in Teaching*, (55, 4: 369–89) was Professor Carr's seventh article for the *Journal* and it represents a significant further examination of the moral dimensions of teaching as a profession first extensively explored in his *Professionalism and Ethics in Teaching* (2000). In this important article, as in earlier books and papers, Carr applies a virtue ethical approach to education and teaching, arguing that good teaching is more than a matter of acquiring a given repertoire of technical skills or competences, since it requires the development of a range of virtues or qualities of moral character. Indeed, Carr argues that many of the forms of expertise that student teachers are encouraged to regard as skills or techniques – such as class discipline – only make coherent sense as involving moral qualities of character. At all events, Carr's argument supports a certain time-honoured intuition that good teachers need not only to possess a particular body of skills or techniques, but more fundamentally to be certain kinds of persons.

David Carr has produced an impressive body of work on the ethical aspects and dimensions of education and teaching. His *Professionalism and Ethics in Teaching* (2000) offers a pioneering conceptual analysis of both professionalism and teaching and has been rightly influential. Chapter 7 of that work addresses many of the same themes as the article published here. In the previous year, he co-edited (with Jan Steutel) a groundbreaking and well-reviewed collection of essays *Virtue Ethics and Moral Education* (1999) in which various distinguished contributors revisited various themes and issues of moral education in the light of Aristotelian virtue ethics. David Carr's book *Making Sense of Education* (2003) remains one of the best introductions to key ideas of educational philosophy and theory. He continues to write extensively on the issues of virtue, value and morality in education and – more recently – on the contribution of arts and literature to the development of moral virtue.

Education and Values

by David Carr, Moray House College

A fundamental question for Socrates in the course of his philosophical enquiries was: how should one live one's life?[1] Since education, as distinct from mere instruction or training, is at heart a matter of acquainting young people with what is good, of guiding them towards worthwhile rather than worthless lives, there is a strong case for saying that Socrates' question is *the* most important one for education.

But, it hardly needs saying, Socrates' question raises immense philosophical difficulties. First, it recalls explicitly for us what we are already aware of – that there are infinitely many ways in which a human life might be lived; but second, it implies the genuine possibility of some sort of ranking of different ways of life on the basis of rational evaluation – of deciding that some activities, pursuits and objects of pursuit are better, have more value, than others.

Whilst it is only fair to admit that the crucial matter of the relationship between education and values has been extensively acknowledged in most previous literature of educational philosophy and theory, it is also clear enough that a deep modern scepticism about the possibility of a genuinely rational response to Socrates' question concerning the evaluation of human life has pervaded many latter day discussions of this issue. There is much in the rhetoric of contemporary liberal education and in the philosophy of modernity that has informed it – to be found particularly in discussions of freedom, authority and indoctrination – which has served to obscure rather than clarify the nature of values and their relationship to education. The concern of this paper, then, is with the nature of values as such and with whether that nature raises any insuperable or intractable difficulties for their educational transmission.

First, what are values? The term is, of course, ambiguous between a number of different but related senses. In due course I shall consider the more rarified sense it has in such expressions as *values education*; for now I shall concentrate on the rather homelier or more ordinary use of the term to mean, quite generally, that which (whatever it is) we value.

In this sense, a value would certainly appear to be, amongst other things, a kind of belief; but it is equally surely not any kind of belief and it would seem to involve aspects of psychological life which go beyond the strictly cognitive. For a start, then, values are distinguished from more mundane factual beliefs by their metaphysical *objects*. The object at which the factual belief 'many hedgehogs die in road accidents' aims is the *truth*; but to believe truly that many hedgehogs so die is not (yet) to have acquired a value. Rather, the object at which a value aims is *goodness* – it is a belief that compassion, integrity, honesty, wealth, world peace, the protection of wildlife or whatever, is a good to be pursued (rather than just true).

But to value something is not merely to believe that it is good, for there would also appear to be an affective or motivational dimension to values. So although it is by no means unintelligible to speak of a person believing X to be good but not caring for it or wanting to pursue it, it would be rather odd to speak of such a person *valuing* X and these would not well represent the standard circumstances of valuation.

There is, of course, a familiar tradition of modern (ethical) thought which has been inclined to emphasise the affective aspects of value rather at the expense of the cognitive. An early expression of this perspective in modern times was David Hume's clear identification of values with the sentiments we feel at the contemplation of certain objects and events; he held that we project values onto the world subjectively in much the same way that the natural philosophy of his day maintained that we project the so-called secondary qualities of objects.[2]

Another equally well-known expression of much the same idea was the view of the ethical emotivists of the early part of this century that value judgements – statements of the form X is good/bad – though in principle meaningless (because not verifiable empirically) nevertheless serve to express our attitudes of approval or disapproval, like or dislike, for this or that state of affairs.[3] As the many critics of emotivism were quick to point out, however, this view serves only to muddy the waters by its crude assimilation of judgements of worth to judgements of approval. For since it is neither odd nor unintelligible for someone to say that he thinks X is good but he does not like it or that he likes X but does not believe it to be good, to hold that something is good or bad must be more than just to entertain some gut feeling for or against it.

But, as we have also previously indicated, neither of these cases in which a gap has opened up between approval and judgements of worth, should be regarded as valuing or disvaluing X, since to value something is not standardly *either* to believe it to be good *or* to approve of it, but some sort of coalition of these two states – a certain union of the cognitive and the affective. More conveniently, it may be best to think of a value as a kind of rational, informed or principled *preference*. But what, more precisely, is the rational nature of those preferences we call values and on what sorts of principles or other considerations are they based?

Whilst the prescriptivist heirs of emotivism certainly rejected their predecessors' identification of values with gut feelings, they nevertheless retained and reinforced the fundamental empiricist distinction between facts and values which placed values firmly on the personal and subjective rather than the impersonal and objective side of human affairs; for them, there are indeed rational grounds for believing that X is good and wanting to pursue it but there are still no objective or mind-independent grounds.[4] So, in the sphere of morality at least, those rational preferences we call values are based largely on a personal commitment to self-made rules of a basically

Kantian character; the individual undertakes to abide by a certain ethical code of his own making and moral preferences are grounded in autonomous acts of personal prescription and commendation.

There can be little doubt, of course, that there is some internal relationship between preference and prescription; the natural inclination is to commend or prescribe those and only those states of affairs which one prefers. But as others have previously pointed out, the prescriptivists seem to have taken a rather topsy-turvy view of this relationship. For surely it *is* precisely more usual for actions or events to be commended or prescribed on the grounds that one prefers them than for them to be preferred from an inclination to prescribe or commend them.[5] The prescriptivist project of having the cake of rational values but eating it subjectively seems incapable of implementation and it would appear that those preferences we call values, to be considered rational, require grounding in something rather more substantial than personal commitment; if there is to be much rhyme or reason behind commending or wanting to prescribe X, there must be something rather more solid beneath judgements that X is good or bad.

So with respect to any X, any action or state of affairs at all, is it possible to discover objective grounds for thinking it good which might light the way to a more general rational basis for judgements of value? First, a simple case: a friend informs me in her kitchen 'that's a good knife for slicing the vegetables'. I respond 'what about this one?' and she replies 'No, that other one is better'. What do 'good' and 'better' mean here? If my friend is merely commending the knife to me as her favourite, the one she feels subjectively best about, then what she says bears hardly at all on my problem about how best to slice the vegetables. Of course, I take her to mean rather that the knife she has recommended is more effective than the others for the task I have been assigned – it is keener, more manipulable and so on. In this fairly pedestrian case, then, 'this is a good knife' means roughly 'this knife is better (keener, more manipulable) than that one for slicing the vegetables' – it is of more value than the others here.

Quite generally, we may say that our preferences are rational if they are grounded objectively in considerations relating to what is more satisfactory, appropriate or effective in particular circumstances for a given purpose. Put more schematically: it is right or reasonable to prefer X to Y in some circumstances, if it is true that X is more satisfactory than Y in a given respect or for a given interest or purpose P. And if it *is* right to prefer X to Y on some such grounds then we can say that X has (objectively) greater value than Y for P.

This formula, by the way, makes clear the true nature of the much celebrated relativity of values; it is generally the straightforward and innocuous relativity (or better-relatedness) of goodness and value to particular specifiable human interests and purposes more than the vicious relativity of values to local custom or personal whim. This knife may be better than that only so long as I wish to slice the vegetables (I'll need another one to stab you with); but there is nothing here which fails any test of objective value. The knife is not better for the given purpose because I feel it is or because social convention has it that it is, but because, quite simply, it is sharper than the others.

But is all human preference, and thereby all that is valued, rationally anchored in the way I have just described – grounded, that is, in a sound evaluation of objective circumstances which bear on particular human interests and purposes? Clearly not – but this has no devastating implications for the subjectivity or otherwise of values.

Suppose, for example, that I say tinned tomatoes taste better than fresh tomatoes and you insist they do not. Whilst my preference is certainly based on the truth that I find X more congenial than Y in a certain respect – equally clearly it cannot be confirmed or disconfirmed by any objective comparison of the tastes in question; it is just my word against yours and I am engaged in little more than expressing what I like in the way of tomatoes. But though this makes my taste personal, what makes it subjective? A belief qualifies as subjective if it is held on the basis of bias or without due regard for evidence for or against; but what evidence do I require for my personal tastes and preferences?

In fact it is very likely, more generally, that *no* preferences of any kind, personal or otherwise, are aptly called subjective since they do not appear to enter into quite the right sort of relations with truth and falsity. To be sure, as we have seen, some preferences *are* related to truth and falsity – this knife has value for that if it is true that it is sharper – but that only makes my preference for this knife more reasonable or appropriate, it does not make it *true*. So there is hardly anything in the way of philosophical gain one way or the other to be had from describing personal preferences as subjective.

But, even if anyone is inclined to doubt this and to insist that personal tastes *are* a species of subjective preference, it would still be of small consequence for the subjectivity or otherwise of values; for since values require evaluation and evaluation depends on objective criteria, there is no good reason for referring to personal preferences as values. And, of course, it does sound more than a little strange to refer to my liking for tinned tomatoes or treacle as a *value,* or to speak of valuing one more than the other, when there are precisely no standards of objective comparison to which my judgement might be referred. So although there *are* preferences which are not rationally supported by objectively grounded considerations bearing on the satisfaction of particular human interests and purposes, it is hardly appropriate to regard these as *values.*

All this, however, may yet seem rather unhelpful. For clearly not all the judgements of value we base upon objective considerations are properly to be regarded as values; it may well be true that this knife has objectively more value than that for slicing vegetables, but it would be peculiar to count its value as one of *one's values* exactly. It is at this point, then, that we have to distinguish the humbler, more mundane sense of value as the object of everyday evaluation from the more rarified sense in which we speak of a person's *values* and of, for example, *values education.* (From here on this sense will be italicized.)

However, an important point about those preferences which are apt for inclusion among a person's *values* in this more exalted sense is that they are generally held to be of intrinsic rather than extrinsic significance to the valuer; they are the sort of preferences to which men are inclined unconditionally and we do not normally say of an individual that he *values* justice, power, pleasure or wealth unless he desires these for their own sake. But a problem which might appear to arise now is that if, in order to include justice among his values, a person must value it unconditionally, he cannot then also value it for an objectively grounded purpose. To be sure, we can determine on objective grounds that this knife will do nicely for what we want because it serves as a particular means to some further end; but in the case of *values* which require to be prized for their own sake how can there *be* a further end in relation to which their worth can be objectively determined? Isn't this, moreover, simply to concede that *values* are, after all, just personal (if not subjective) preferences akin to personal tastes?

This conclusion is, I think, a mistake. It has, for one thing, the paradoxical consequence that *values* cannot be regarded as objects of evaluation. If the idea of having intrinsic worth in the way just indicated is fundamentally at odds with that of having a purpose against which *value* can be measured then professing a *value* is more like my taste for tinned tomatoes than my choice of a good knife; in short, *values* are a subclass not of values but of personal affections. But in fact there is no fundamental incompatibility between having intrinsic value and having a purpose; the purpose of a *value* such as honesty or pacifism is not, to be sure, related to it as the value of a knife is related to the function of a knife, but this does not preclude an ideological perspective on whatever we might value intrinsically – ascribing, that is, purposes to *values*.

It has sometimes been said, for example, that we cannot talk both of aims of education and of education as having intrinsic worth, since to speak of the aims of education is precisely to justify it in instrumental terms. But this simply fails to recognise that the language of educational aims is ambiguous between talk of what we are trying to achieve through education and that of the uses to which education (or more usually schooling) is so often put in social and economic terms. There is indeed a tension between talk of intrinsic value and the latter but not so between such talk and the former. Thus, an activity or enterprise can have both intrinsic value and purpose (there is no value *at all* without purpose) if the purpose is related internally rather than merely externally to the activity in question; it is not just a means to some logically separable further end.

I shall try now to illustrate this point more fully in the course of discussing the educational implications of just *one* sort *of value* – moral *values* – which we are generally concerned to see taught in schools (though I believe that much of what I have to say here also has application, *mutatis mutandis*, to problems in other areas of *values* education).

As a place to start, it is important to distinguish, as best one can, moral *values* (e.g. tolerance, compassion) from other kinds of personal and socially implicated *values* (e.g. charm, amiability, security). There is no necessary conflict in a person's life, of course, between his moral values and the proper pursuit of personal goals and ambitions; but if it comes to the point at which a man seeks security by dishonest dealing, uses personal charm or position to seduce or declines to defend a cause in which he professes to believe for fear of personal loss or injury – this is evidence of moral failure more than moral conflict. A moral conflict is rather that in which a person is faced with the sort of dilemma in which he is uncertain what he should do for the best in terms of justice, honesty or decency; he recognises perhaps the equally weighty demands on him of honesty and loyalty or justice and compassion but he cannot simultaneously satisfy both.

Two principal sorts of candidate are usually held to qualify as objects of value from a moral point of view. The first of these constitutes the category of fairly high level abstract and formal principles – justice, equality, liberty and so on. There is a certain degree of vacuity, however, in speaking of a person valuing justice as a moral principle, largely because it amounts to little more than an empty affirmation of the value of morality; talk of valuing justice usually comes, more substantially, to asserting the claims of morality over other non-moral considerations – preferential treatment based perhaps on wealth or status. Much the same applies to freedom and equality which also tend to be affirmed as principles only when people feel that one is being promoted at the expense of the other; a proper commitment to what is just, it should go without saying, involves due weight being given to both these principles.

Rather better candidates for the role of substantial moral *values* are those particular dispositions towards right conduct which serve to instantiate the more formal and general constitutive and regulative principles of justice, equality and liberty. If it is somewhat empty to characterise justice and equality as moral *values*, it is clearly rather more material so to speak of tolerance, honesty, self control, compassion, courage and so on. These specific human qualities and attributes in which the more general constitutive principles of justice and so on should rightly inhere are, when sought unconditionally, what have traditionally been referred to as the *moral virtues*; it is precisely the virtues rather than the general principles which make up the stuff of moral *values*.

So is the unconditional pursuit of those moral dispositions called the virtues consistent with regarding them as value preferences grounded in objective considerations related to human interests and purposes? Is it possible, more briefly, to reconcile valuing the virtues for their own sake with recognising that they have an objective function in human affairs? By all means, for in fact it would seem that these two features of virtues, their intrinsic value and their objective function in human life, are logically inextricable.

In order to see this we first need to appreciate the precise role in human affairs of those moral evaluations which are grounded in reflection upon the virtues. Briefly, they serve to characterise what it is to *live well* as a person – not merely as an individual in any of the many and diverse sublunary roles which human beings may occupy from time to time – but as a person *per se*; the plain goal of the moral virtues is to promote human welfare and flourishing in personal and interpersonal terms.

It is crucial to grasp here that no argument should be needed or could be given to show that honesty, compassion, tolerance, courage, self-control and so on generally conduce to human benefit, and dishonesty, cruelty, intolerance, cowardice and spite conduce to harm in moral terms, because it is in terms of just this conceptual currency that moral benefit and harm are themselves understood – these *values,* attitudes and dispositions show us what benefit and harm *mean.* Some post-modern moral philosopher might enquire whether it might not perhaps be better morally to value cruelty over compassion – but unless he means here perhaps that it is sometimes necessary to be cruel to be kind – the question looks (using Wittgenstein's vivid metaphor) rather like the engine of language idling, like a cogwheel with which no other properly engages.[6]

To be sure, men are quite free to place the pursuit of other goals before moral considerations, to put avarice before honesty or ambition before loyalty; there are so many different ends for which men may live which carry costs in moral terms. But what is gained in the pursuit of temporal goals which have serious moral costs is generally bought at the high price of our personal and human diminution. In fact, the weight of such costs is estimated for us in scripture: what profit a man if he gain the whole world but lose his soul? Cases of such costs – in which the pursuit of some human career or ambition has entailed various moral failures – are by no means unfamiliar; here we speak tellingly of someone being a first-rate artist, brain surgeon or journalist, but not a very nice or good person.

To fail as a person, then, as distinct from failing as a king, a financier or an estate agent, is to fail precisely in respect of the honesty, integrity and decency we owe to ourselves and the duties and consideration we should rightly acknowledge in relation to others in the course of trying to live a worthwhile human life. For it is in terms of the common conceptual currency of the traditional virtues and vices that the quality of human personal life is evaluated for good or ill and personal failures are precisely failures of honesty, trust, compassion, courage, self-control and so on. Thus we can intelligibly ask whether it might not profit a man to live otherwise than by honesty, compassion and the rest, but there can be no coherent enquiry whether living otherwise would be to live as well as a *person* since such qualities just *are* those which promote that moral flourishing we call personal – whatever else might serve to promote a financier's flourishing.

But now, however, it cannot be difficult to see why those moral qualities and *values* called the virtues should be pursued for their own sake by all reasonable or right thinking persons. For although my endorsement of financial values – competition, acquisitiveness, parsimony or whatever – might depend entirely on whether I want to be a financier, something I can decide whether or not to be, it is not open in at all the same way for me to accept or reject the *values* inherent in living well as a person. Since, whether I like it or not, I *am* a person, I have every good reason to desire these qualities in terms of which personal worth and quality of life is measured. My prizing of the virtues for their own sake, then, is tied crucially to my recognition of the clear *purpose* of these moral qualities as conducive to the conduct of a worthwhile human life. The life in question is not, of course, one to which the virtues are related as so many means to a separately specifiable end; rather they are constitutive of that end, what precisely is *meant* by living well. But it *is* just because the virtues function in this way as constitutive of a good human life that I have every reason to value them for their own sake (hence, virtue is indeed its own reward).

But if all this is acceptable, it is now reasonably plain sailing to show that there is nothing in the least subjective or personal about those moral *values* we call the virtues. I do not decide, for example, merely by personal fiat or on the basis of subjective preference that some human quality of entirely my own choosing is rightly to be counted as courageous or charitable. My judgement that someone exhibits one or the other of these qualities is quite clearly answerable to objective criteria; no-one, in short, properly counts as courageous unless he can be seen doing his duty (whatever this is) or standing up for his beliefs (whatever these are) in the teeth of danger or difficulty and no-one qualifies as truly charitable unless his voluntary aid to others is bought at the cost of some inconvenience to himself.

Moreover, men may easily be compared in respect of their courage and charity; one man is (roughly) more courageous or resolute than another if he is prepared to pay the higher cost for sticking to his guns, and more charitable if, like the widow and her mite, he is prepared to make the greater sacrifice, relative to his means, for the benefit of others. To be sure, it may well be difficult in the rough and tumble of everyday life to tell whether we have got our moral assessments quite right or not – but that is entirely another matter. The basic logic of virtue ascriptions is that they are, in principle, quite susceptible of both objective application and objective comparison.

But even if the moral values known as virtues are objective in the sense just indicated – are they also of general or universal relevance, application and significance in all circumstances? Are we justified, for example, in commending all those values we have called moral virtues to all children in our schools when our schools exist to provide educational and other benefits for a culturally hetero-geneous society which exhibits considerable diversity in its subscription to moral codes and is somewhat unevenly committed *to* tolerance, charity, com-passion and the rest. In short, even if we have satisfactorily settled the problem of the objectivity or otherwise of moral *values*, we have not yet settled that of their possible relativity and diversity, also a matter of profound importance from the point of view of education. (And these two problems are quite distinct. My obedience to the Highway Code is rationally grounded in objective con-siderations and circumstances, but its importance is entirely local and relative; conversely a belief in Astrology could be quite universal without being objectively grounded.)

Generally, of course, the idea that moral *values* are relative rests largely on the joint observations, first, that people in different societies can be seen to live differently according to diverse, often cross-culturally incompatible, social assumptions, prin-ciples and beliefs, and second, that moral *values* and dispositions seem clearly to be phenomena of a socially-implicated nature. Whilst these observations can hardly be denied, however, they have a significant bearing on the question of the relativity or otherwise of moral values only if moral dispositions and other qualities *are* merely expressions of given patterns of social and cultural life – and I believe that there is some popular confusion over this.

To begin with, although it is clear enough that all human virtues, even such self regarding dispositions as fortitude and temperance, are socially implicated, it does not follow that they are socially determined in some more theoretically loaded sense. The fact that a mode of conduct has social origins and assumes definite social forms and expressions by no means entails that it is exclusively conditioned by social assumptions and expectations. Language, for example, is a form of socially generated behaviour which gives formal expression to the various locally constructed concepts and theories of specific human societies; the particular social and cultural circumstances in which we happen to find ourselves, then, certainly impose constraints of a conceptual kind on what we can express through our socially formed modes of discourse. But, of course, this does not at all mean that we can express through our language only those views which are largely accepted or endorsed by our society; we can and do use the very same language to be critical of the social perspectives and assumptions which it was partly formed to express.

But this socially critical function of a form of human behaviour is even more conspicuous in the case of moral virtues. Indeed, the precise purpose of those forms of moral deliberation which inform the virtues is to evaluate and where necessary to question the rightness of those individual inclinations and social assumptions which would otherwise motivate human practical conduct. In general, then, it could hardly be clearer that those moral responses called the virtues are honoured at least as often in the breach of social conventions as in strict conformity to them; we do not act well morally any more in regular obedience to social expectations than we do in servitude to our individual natural inclinations. If this were not so, then any attempts to criticise the *values* of a given society from either without or within would be entirely in vain; but it is clear that we are often quite justified in judging what is currently acceptable in our own or another society as unjust, self-serving, exploitative, cruel or dishonourable.

In fact, if any human conduct apt for evaluation in moral terms is rightly to be thought of as socially conditioned, it would appear to be the *vices* rather than the virtues. For just as men seek the truth in matters of theory and belief to free them from the error and illusion which we know to be inherent in many social perspectives, so the point of that practical reason which informs the moral virtues is to correct and to compensate for the unjust, hypocritical, self-deceptive, cruel and cowardly conduct to which men seem naturally enough prone as individuals and which social prejudices and biases have so frequently reinforced and endorsed. I believe that this is one of the actual reasons for the considerable variation in the incidence and prominence of virtues cross-culturally; in some societies certain vices are not so widespread that their compensating virtues require much emphasis and in others they are so widespread that the need for the compensating virtues is scarcely acknowledged.

But the neglect of tolerance and compassion in some places and the taken-for-grantedness of them in others hardly implies that they are moral qualities of only local significance and value – only that they have sometimes been so regarded. Virtues, then, are moral dispositions which stand primarily in the service, not of social prejudices and assumptions, but of what is right; they are, as St Paul said of the basic Christian virtue of love, happy only with the truth.[7] To be sure, St Paul also noted that human beings have considerable trouble recognising the truth – but that is another matter (and even to see through a glass darkly is not at all the same as failing to see at all).

The other common but potentially dangerous confusion about the socially implicated nature of moral *values* and dispositions concerns the fact that virtues may assume different forms at different times and places depending on social context; it appears that what *counts* as courage or compassion in society A is different from what so counts in society B. But despite the extraordinary heavy weather that has been made of this observation, it is really only to be expected that what counts as courageous or compassionate conduct will differ according to particular (social if you like) circumstances; it will clearly vary between different societies – but it will also vary within the same society and even on the part of the same individual at different times in different places. No consequences of any importance for the relativity or otherwise of moral *values*, however, follow from this point.

For since the circumstances which call for nerve, self-control and resolution are infinitely varied it is only reasonable to expect that what counts as a courageous response here may count as a foolhardy or even a cowardly one there. Courage may well be shown in a principled defence of one's country in what one has judged to be a just war, but if one is merely being swept along on a tide of vulgar and uncritical jingoistic euphoria then one's conduct could well be irresponsible or even cowardly rather than courageous. Long ago, Aristotle taught us that this is just how it is with moral life and with the dispositions called virtues; since, as he maintained, virtuous actions require to be done to the right person, to the right extent, at the right time, with the right motive and in the right way, it is hardly surprising that they take different forms in different contexts.[8] The trap which Aristotle skilfully avoided, then, was that of identifying moral dispositions with specific or set patterns of behaviour; he viewed them instead as forms of rational or principled response in which agents deliberately undertake to put what they judge to be right or good before their own personal safety, comfort, convenience or interest – but then, of course, circumstances *will* alter cases.

To date, then, I have argued that certain educationally important *values* – such moral virtues as tolerance, compassion, self-control, honesty and so on – are neither subjective nor relative; their worth is determined by reference neither to purely personal or private decision nor to the esteem in which they might or might not happen to be held in certain social contexts. What grounds the value of a moral virtue is precisely its role in establishing (objectively) what counts as a good or worthwhile human life and it is not conceptually possible to characterise such a life in terms other than the available moral vocabulary of tolerance, compassion, honesty, self-control and so forth. Since this is the case, we cannot seriously doubt the educational value of initiating children into the importance of these qualities; any 'alternative' moral educator who arrives with the radical aim of teaching children to be intolerant, indolent, shiftless, bullying and cowardly has got things very seriously wrong, not only about morality but about education as well.

To have argued that the values enshrined in the moral virtues are of objective and universal rather than subjective and relative status and significance in human affairs, however, is not at all to deny the problematic and controversial character of moral life and of our educational initiation of children into it. I should certainly not, for example, be construed as denying the possibility, indeed inevitability, or moral dispute and disagreement or the importance of assisting children to appreciate the complexities, uncertainties and the painful demands and costs of moral life. On the contrary, I believe that we require education in moral *values* in schools precisely because moral life is a far *more* complex matter and moral dilemmas more real and painful than the subjectivists and social relativists seem prone to suppose. It is precisely because we are all too frequently confronted in the real world (as distinct from some possible solipsistic or socially constructed world) with substantial objectively grounded moral dilemmas which are as often as not quite unsusceptible of any entirely satisfactory outcome that we need moral education and understanding to help us to respond with as much honesty, integrity, decency and compassion as we can possibly find within ourselves. My present concern, then, is partly to try to establish the precise logical contours which may assist us to define the true character of genuine moral dilemma and dispute and which I believe to have been wrongly drawn by subjectivist and social relativist theories of moral value.

For shallow moral theories based on suspect accounts of value have sometimes treated moral dilemmas as little more than theoretical problems to be solved, as though those very real and awful choices that not infrequently have to be made between telling the truth and loyalty to a friend or helping someone in need and keeping one's word can be happily resolved without painful reminder – perhaps by some simple rational calculation (worse still, an individual act of personal commitment or an appeal to social custom). The fact remains, however, that most, if not all, genuine moral dilemmas are liable to end in tears no matter what we do, and it is rarely in such circumstances that we require moral deliberation to inform us of what precisely we should do. What is more often required is the honesty and resolution to act with as much integrity and decency as we possibly can and the chief role of moral reason is to help dispel the clouds of self-deception, bad faith, hypocrisy, prejudice, weakness of will and general evasion which so often disincline us from doing what we know, however reluctantly, we ought to do.[9]

The basic purpose of moral education, then, is to try to develop those capacities for moral deliberation which may assist us to genuine self-knowledge and right conduct in precisely those testing circumstances in which hoping for the best is practically all we have. Thus, instruction in moral *values* and virtues, far from being indoctrinatory (as it surely would be if moral values were subjective or socially relative), precisely concerns the opening of children's hearts and minds to critical reflection on their own natural inclinations and social prejudices in the light of principled considerations about what a good human life (one, that is, characterised by aspiration to such objective qualities as honesty, tolerance, compassion and so forth) means in terms of practical human conduct.

I have tried to show, then, that general worries about the teaching of *values* based on the idea that all values must inevitably be either subjective or relative are by no means well grounded, because even in the hotly contested case of moral *values*, such values are neither subjective *nor* relative. Space has permitted a discussion of only one sort *of value* – the moral virtues – but I am confident that the kinds of objections I have mounted against the subjectivity and relativity of value preferences in general can be fairly well adapted to other cases of *values*. I believe that it is quite implausible to maintain, for example, that aesthetic and artistic judgements of value are grounded only in subjective or social responses. There are surely both individual and society independent grounds for valuing some works of art and artistic performances over others; to be more precise, we can explain by reference to the works themselves what is meant by 'better' or 'worse', 'more' or 'less', value. Even if, then, a thorough knowledge of the social and historical background of a work of art is required to *understand* it fully, the artistic significance of a Shakespeare play or a Beethoven symphony is something that nevertheless transcends its social character and origins.

By way of conclusion, however, one further point of some importance needs to be made concerning the general teaching of *values*. This relates to the vexed question of the relationship between *values* – especially those of a social and moral character – and human freedom. Plato (and almost certainly Socrates) believed firmly in the objectivity and universality of moral *values* and made out a case against subjectivism and relativism of the sort that I have tried to make here. Notoriously, however, Plato concluded that an unclouded vision of the absolute and objective value of certain fundamental moral principles and dispositions would entitle those to whom it had been vouchsafed the right to shape and determine the destinies of those to whom it had not.[10] His view was that once we are in a secure position to know what is best for all and sundry, we are thereby justified in constraining others to conduct themselves in the light of that knowledge. In sharp contrast, as we have seen, the modern liberal perspective on *values* and freedom, grounded as it is in a definite enlightenment scepticism about the objectivity of values, maintains that it is entirely up to the individual how he chooses to live his life so long as his conduct does not unduly curtail the freedom of others.

My own argument inclines me generally to the view that Socrates and Plato were far closer to the truth about the nature of *values* than the modern liberal tradition with its enlightenment roots. But equally clearly the liberal tradition is far closer than Plato to the truth about the relationship of human freedom to *values*. For, of course, it does not follow in the least that if I can see quite clearly, and certainly more clearly than you, what is in your best interest, I have any right to constrain you so to act. So *values* are ultimately a matter for free human choice – in *this* respect; that a man has the absolute right to go to the devil in his own way if he so pleases. What we must not and cannot obscure as educationalists is the important truth that practical human choices are nevertheless frequently *real* choices between objective goods and objective evils; between alternatives which our acts of choice do not in themselves make either good or bad.

Notes

1 This question is essentially a concern of Socrates in several Platonic dialogues but see especially: Plato: *The Republic*, translated by H. D. P. Lee (Harmondsworth: Penguin, 1987), 352 D.

2 D. Hume: *A Treatise of Human Nature*, edited by E. G. Mossner (Harmondsworth: Penguin, 1969), Part III, section I.

3 See, for example: A. J. Ayer: *Language, Truth and Logic* (London: Victor Gollancz, 1967), Chapter 6.

4 See, for example, R. M. Hare: *The Language of Morals* (Oxford University Press, 1952).

5 For criticisms along these lines see: P. T. Geach: *Logic Matters* (Oxford: Blackwell, 1972), Section 8 and several of the essays in P. Foot: *Virtues and Vices* (Oxford: Blackwell, 1978).

6 L. Wittgenstein: *Philosophical Investigations* (Oxford: Blackwell, 1953), Part I, section 132.

7 St Paul: First Letter to the Corinthians, chapter 13.

8 Aristotle: *The Nicomachean Ethics*, translated by Sir David Ross (Oxford University Press, 1925), Part II, section 9, p. 45.

9 I have argued more fully for this view in chapter 11 and elsewhere of my *Educating the Virtues* (London and New York: Routledge, 1991).

10 This is essentially the conclusion that is reached in, for example, Plato's *Republic*.

14 What is Evidence-Based Education?

P. Davies

1999

Author

Dr. Philip Davies was teaching in the Department for Continuing Education, University of Oxford, when he wrote this paper. He introduced the Master's Course in Evidence-Based Health Care. Subsequently, he was employed in the Cabinet Office, advising on evidence-based policy, in the Prime Minister's Strategy Unit and in H.M. Treasury. He advised governments in other countries on evidence-based policy as well as global agencies such as the United Nations, European Commission and African Union countries.

Introduction

Critical reflection on educational research has been a periodic concern of the *Journal* from its inception. But the 1990s saw a more hostile critique of such research, reflected in David Hargreaves' 1996 Teacher Training Agency Annual Lecture, 'Teaching as a Research Based Profession'; Tooley and Darby's 'Educational Research: an OFSTED Critique' (1998), and the Hillage Report (1998) 'Excellence in Research in Schools'. It was in this lively if not explosive context that the *Journal* published *What is Evidence-Based Education?* (47, 2: 108–121) in June 1999.

Davies drew on his considerable knowledge of evidence-based health care to provide recommendations for the future of educational research. As Hargreaves had argued, there was a need for the profession of teaching to subject professional judgment and decisions to carefully gathered, systematic analysis of evidence. In this same issue, Hargreaves argued for the 'knowledge creating school'. But Davies points to the lack of evidence to support such school as well as government interventions. There is a need, therefore, as in medical and health care, for creating a database (drawn from carefully designed and executed research) to provide that evidence. Such evidence would be subject to systematic reviews (not all published research would pass the test) and then 'meta-analysis' of those reviews to reach conclusions to perceived problems. Cochrane Collaboration of systematic reviews and meta-analyses in medicine were the models for research in education.

The significance of the paper lies, first, in its justification of Cochrane-style systematic reviews in education; second, in the impact of this advocacy in the establishment of the Evidence Based Centre at the Institute of Education, University of London and in the Cabinet Office itself.

Other related articles from the *Journal* are: *Evidence-based practice in education: the best medicine?* (49, 3: 316–136); *The need for randomised controlled trials in educational research* (49, 3: 316–328. See page 203 in this volume for a discussion of this article); *The place of systematic reviews in educational research* (53, 4: 399–416).

What is Evidence-Based Education?

by Philip Davies, Department for Continuing Education, University of Oxford

1. Introduction

In most societies education is constantly being asked to do more and more things, to higher and higher standards, with greater accountability and finite (if not diminishing) resources. Its agenda is often driven by political ideology, conventional wisdom, folklore, and wishful thinking as it strives to meet the needs and interests of the economy, business, employers, law and order, civil society, parental choice, and, at least rhetorically, the children, young people, and adults who make up the learning community (Apple, 1982; Apple and Weis, 1983; Ball, 1990, 1993; Bowles and Gintis, 1976; Giroux, 1983, 1992; Willis, 1977). Much of this impetus represents the triumph of hope over reason, sentiment over demonstrated effectiveness, intuition over evidence. Increasingly, the direction of change in educational thinking and practice is top-down from central governments, think tanks, opinion formers, educational regulators (such as OFSTED), the media, and academic departments whose research is often selective, unsystematic, and prone to political or scientific bias (or both). Some recent examples from the United Kingdom include: the form and content of the National Curriculum; the introduction of standardised tests and league tables as a means of 'raising standards' and supposedly increasing parental choice; the substitution of 'trendy' teaching methods based on activity-based, student-centred, self-directed learning and problem solving, with whole-class teaching based on 'rows and columns' classroom organisation, didactic instruction, and a more passive approach to learning, often by rote.

It is often unclear whether these developments in educational thinking and practice are better, or worse, than the regimes they replace. This is in part because educational activity is often inadequately evaluated by means of carefully designed and executed controlled trials, quasi-experiments, surveys, before-and-after studies, high-quality observational studies, ethnographic studies which look at outcomes as well as processes, or conversation and discourse analytic studies that link micro structures and actions to macro level issues. Moreover, the research and evaluation studies that do exist are seldom searched for systematically, retrieved and read, critically appraised for quality, validity and relevance, and organised and graded for power of evidence. This is the task of evidence-based education.

2. Using *Vs* Establishing Evidence

Evidence-based education operates at two levels. The first is to utilise existing evidence from worldwide research and literature on education and associated subjects. Educationalists at all levels need to be able to:

- pose an answerable question about education;
- know where and how to find evidence systematically and comprehensively using the electronic (computer-based) and non-electronic (print) media;
- retrieve and read such evidence competently and undertake critical appraisal and analysis of that evidence according to agreed professional and scientific standards;
- organise and grade the power of this evidence; and
- determine its relevance to *their* educational needs and environments.

The second level is to *establish* sound evidence where existing evidence is lacking or of a questionable, uncertain, or weak nature. Practitioners of evidence-based education working at this level need to be able to plan, carry out, and publish studies that meet the highest standards of scientific research and evaluation, incorporating the methods of the social sciences, the natural sciences, and the humanistic and interpretive disciplines. The objective of evidence-based education at this level is to ensure that future research on education meets the criteria of scientific validity, high-quality, and practical relevance that is sometimes lacking in existing evidence on educational activities, processes, and outcomes (Hargreaves, 1996, 1997; Hillage *et al.*, 1998; Tooley and Darby, 1998).

This view of evidence-based education is derived quite explicitly from the University of Oxford Master's programme in Evidence-Based Health Care. This programme offers health professionals of all types the opportunity to develop their professional skills whilst maintaining full-time professional practice. A central feature of the Oxford programme in Evidence-Based Health Care is that students learn by attempting to solve clinical and population-based problems that *they* bring to the course. This approach to learning, and teaching, is explicitly based on the problem-solving, self-directed model of adult education developed by Knowles (1990) and derived from the learning theory of Piaget, Bruner, Vygotsky, and the 'constructivist' school of learning (Davies, 1999).

The need for both levels of evidence-based practice in education seems clear. There have been a number of recent criticisms about the gap between the teaching and the research communities, the relevance, applicability and quality of educational research, the noncumulative nature of good educational research, and its effective dissemination (Hargreaves, 1996, 1997; Hillage *et al.*, 1998; Tooley and Darby, 1998). Hargreaves (1996:7), for instance, has called for an end to

> second-rate educational research which does not make a serious contribution to fundamental theory or knowledge; which is irrelevant to practice; which is uncoordinated with any preceding or follow-up research; and which clutters up academic journals that virtually nobody reads.

Such broad-brush characterisations of educational research have, not surprisingly, received a strong and critical response from the educational research community (Norris, 1996; Gray, 1996; Edwards, 1996; Hammersley, 1997), and a debate that has often shed more heat than light. There is a risk that observations such as those of Hargreaves may promote a narrowly utilitarian and philistine approach to research and intellectual life. What constitutes the relevance of research, for instance, depends to a large extent on what questions are being asked, in what context, and for what practical ends. The demands of practice in one context may make a seemingly narrow and esoteric piece of research highly relevant and very enlightening for those who use it. Similarly, research that is apparently more generalisable, cumulative, and based on highly representative samples for some purposes may be of little value to those with different practice needs and in quite different contexts from those in which the research took place. There is no such thing as context-free evidence.

Some of the criticisms of educational research, however, do have some validity. Hammersley, who has responded most critically to Hargreaves' 1996 lecture, acknowledges, with apparent sincerity, that educational research does lack a cumulative character and that it needs 'to move to a situation where new research builds more effectively on earlier work, and where greater attention is given to testing competing interpretations of data, whether descriptive or explanatory' (Hammersley, 1997: 144). Also, the claim that there is a gap between educational research and teachers (Hargreaves, 1996; Hillage *et al.*, 1998) is undoubtedly true, though perhaps in different ways to those suggested by these critics. The problem is not so much that teachers do not undertake research, or that they are often excluded from determining the research agenda (both of which may be true), but that there is often not a culture of teachers using research to inform their everyday school practice. Contrary to Hargreaves' claim about medicine, the same situation prevails in many areas of clinical practice. One of the ways in which evidence-based health care has had some influence in recent years is in getting clinicians to be clearer about the clinical problems for which they require solutions, and utilising existing evidence effectively and critically to help them solve these problems. There is no question of evidence replacing clinical judgement or experience, but of uniting these two dimensions of knowledge to provide a sound basis for action. Evidence-based practice can provide a similar basis for professional knowledge and action in education. It can also ensure that those who undertake educational research are properly trained in research methods, and understand its underlying theoretical and methodological principles, thereby enhancing its quality.

3. Some Objections

Some objections from the educational community to such a model of evidence-based education can be anticipated, and have been expressed by respondents to Hargreaves' (1996) call for teaching to be a research-based profession (Norris, 1996; Gray, 1996; Edwards, 1996; Hammersley, 1997). It is claimed that education is unlike health care, and medicine especially, because its activities, processes, and outcomes are complex and culturally, or contextually, specific. Consequently, it is argued, there are problems of measurement and causation in educational research that are not found in medicine and health care. Medicine and health care, however, face very similar, if not identical, problems of complexity, context-specificity, measurement, and causation that Hammersley (1997) has identified in education. The activities, processes, and outcomes of health care are also highly complex, often indeterminate, and context/culture specific, making their measurement both difficult and controversial (Le Grand and Illsley, 1986; Wilkinson, 1986; Samphier, Robertson and Bloor, 1988; MacBeth, 1996). The generalisability of evidence-based health care is one of its major concerns, as it is of all epidemiology and clinical practice. The uncertain relationship between how people behave in hospitals and in their own and other environments (i.e. ecological validity) is a well-documented problem in the medical and health care literature (Christmas *et al.*, 1974; Andrews and Stewart, 1979; Newcombe and Ratcliff, 1979; Davies and Mehan, 1988; Davies, 1996), with clear parallels with students' educational performances in schools and colleges on the one hand and in the 'real world' on the other. Greenhalgh and Worrall (1997) have recently argued that the concept of context-sensitive medicine is appropriate to describe the skill of applying the findings of research to the demands of everyday clinical practice.

So far as the measurement of outcomes is concerned, the only discrete and (usually) uncontroversial outcome of health care is death (or survival). Almost every other outcome of health care depends on whether one is concerned with objective or subjective dimensions of health and illness, the contexts within which health and illness occur, or the improvement, maintenance, or deterioration of people's health status. Central to these problems is the interaction of signs and symptoms on the one hand and variations in health and illness behaviour according to social class, gender, ethnicity, and cultural practices on the other. For Hammersley to claim that 'unlike in most areas of medicine, in education the "treatments", consist of symbolic interaction, with all the scope for multiple interpretations and responses which that implies', is to ignore his own detailed knowledge of both medical practice and the extensive sociological work on health and illness that has been inspired by symbolic interactionists such as Goffman (1959, 1963, 1964), Glaser and Strauss (1965, 1967), Davis (1963), Fagerhaugh and Strauss (1977), and Strong (1979).

The claim that medicine and health care are based on the natural sciences and their methodologies, whereas education is much more firmly embedded in social science and its approaches to research and evaluation, is also unsustainable. The rejection of natural science as the only basis of modern health care has come from such diverse sources as Balint (1957), Capra (1982), Laing (1965) and Sacks (1990), and the professional training and accreditation bodies of nursing and almost all allied professions, including medicine. Similarly, educational research draws upon the methodological principles and practices of the natural and the social sciences. Whilst it is undoubtedly the case that experimental and quasi-experimental research is harder to achieve in many aspects of education than it is in some aspects of health care, it is not unknown in educational research and other areas of social scientific inquiry (Oakley, 1998). Randomised controlled trials are difficult to undertake in valuations of teaching or learning effectiveness, though their potential has been recognised by some researchers (Boruch *et al.*, 1978; Oakley and Harris, 1996; Oakley, 1998). Consequently, researchers who evaluate educational methods or initiatives tend to rely more heavily on controlled comparisons of matched schools, classrooms, or communities, and to develop models of the effects of extraneous variables (Anderson, 1998).

An associated problem, often mentioned by people in the educational community, is that education is, and must be, concerned with *qualitative* research whereas health care is much more concerned with *quantitative* research and evaluation. This is also a false polemic, and one that is unsustainable when one examines research studies in education and health care. A recent review article on research methods in American educational research concluded that

> results are consistent with those of other studies in that the most commonly used methods were ANOVA and ANCOVA, multiple regression, bivariate correlation, descriptive statistics, multivariate analysis, non-parametric statistics and t-tests. The major difference in current methodology is the increase in the use of qualitative methods. (Elmore and Woehlke, 1996)

The journals reviewed by Elmore and Woehlke represent the more positivistic tradition of American educational research. Other journals, such as the *Harvard Educational Review, Anthropology and Education Quarterly, Qualitative Studies in Education, Social Psychology of Education*, and *Linguistics and Education*, have a tradition of publishing more qualitative research, and the proliferation of articles using qualitative methods and discourse analysis confirms the increase in these types of research in the educational field. This trend is also evident in the British educational research literature.

Another common feature of educational and health care research is the use of systematic reviews and meta-analyses. Indeed, meta-analysis and systematic reviews have their origins in educational research following the pioneering work of Glass (Glass, McGaw and Lee Smith, 1980). Glass's work on meta-analysis, like that of Kulik and Kulik (1989), has been described as 'a form of literature review (that) is not meant to test a hypothesis but to summarise features and outcomes of a body of research' (Bangert-Drowns, 1985). Others in the educational research field (Hunter and Schmidt, 1995; Hedges, 1992; Rosenthal, 1995) have used meta-analysis in a way that is more akin to that found in health care research, as a way of data-pooling and 'the use of statistical methods to combine the results of independent empirical research studies' (Hedges, 1992). Meta-analysis in educational research has the same problems as in health care research, such as ensuring the comparability of different samples, research designs, outcome and process measures, identifying confounding factors and bias, and determining the attributable effects of the intervention(s) being assessed. As Preiss (1988) points out 'the researcher will have several options when cumulating empirical studies and readers will have questions regarding judgment calls made during meta-analysis'.

4. What Is Evidence?

A key issue in developing evidence-based education, and evidence-based health care, is the uncertainty as to what counts as evidence. For those who ask questions such as 'does educational method (or health care intervention) *x* have a better outcome than educational method (or health care intervention) *y* in terms of achieving outcome *z*', evidence consists of the results of randomised controlled trials or other experimental and quasi-experimental studies. Other types of question, for which valid and reliable evidence is sought in both educational and health care research, require evidence about the strength and pattern of relationships between different variables that effect the processes and outcomes of education (and health care). These are best provided by survey and correlational research using methods such as simple and multiple correlation, regression analysis, and analysis of variance.

Yet other questions are more concerned about the *processes* by which educational and health care activities are undertaken and the *meanings* that education or health care have for different people (e.g. learners/patients, teachers/health care professionals, school governors, health care executives, purchasers, etc). The ways in which teachers and doctors typify students and patients, and use categories and practices that open up, and close down, opportunities for advancement in education (Cicourel and Kitsuse, 1963; Cicourel and Mehan, 1985; Mehan *et al.*, 1996) or health care (Strong, 1979; Davies, 1979), are important topics about which high-quality evidence is needed. Evidence is also required about the *consequences* of educational and health care activities on students' and parents' sense of self and their sense of social worth and identity. These types of question require more qualitative and 'naturalistic' research methods such as ethnography, detailed observations, and face-to-face interviews.

Other evidence may be sought about the patterns and structures of interaction, conversation, and discourse by means of which both educational and health care activities are accomplished. Such questions focus on naturally occurring activities between teachers and students, health professionals and patients, and between professionals. Studies such as those by Button and Lee (1987); Fisher and Todd (1983); Silverman (1987), in health care, and by Cazden (1988); Mehan (1977, 1996), and Spindler, D. (1982) in education represent types of research and evidence from within the conversation analysis and discourse analysis tradition.

Evidence is also required about ethical issues of educational or health care practice, such as whether or not it is right or warrantable to undertake a particular educational activity or health care intervention. Each of the methodological approaches mentioned above may inform these issues, but none will resolve them without additional considerations about the moral and ethical issues of universal versus selective action, informed choices, social inequalities and social justice, resource allocation and prioritisation, and the values underlying education and health care. There is a considerable literature on the ethics of research and professional practice in health care (Brazier, 1987; Fulford, 1990; Gillon, 1985; Veatch, 1989; Weiss, 1982) and education (Adair, Dushenko and Lindsay, 1985; Frankel, 1987;

Kimmel, 1988) which the competent practitioner needs to include in his or her considerations of appropriate evidence for best practice.

5. Bibliographic and Data-Base Problems

A third objection to evidence-based education is that the data-bases which serve educational research are less developed, and contain lower-quality filters, than those found in medical and health care research. It does seem that the ERIC Clearing House for educational research is less universal, comprehensive and systematically indexed than MEDLINE and other data-bases in health care (e.g. CINAHL), social science (SOCIOFILE, PSYCLIT, ECONLIT) and biological sciences (BIOLOGICAL ABSTRACTS), and that many studies in education fail to appear on it. This is an issue of improving the reporting and indexing of educational research and changing its reporting practices.

Educational research has also lacked a centralised data-base for the preparation, maintenance and dissemination of systemic reviews of education such as the Cochrane Collaboration, Best Evidence, and the Centre for NHS Reviews and Dissemination. The Cochrane Collaboration has already begun to assemble a data-base of reviews and meta-analysis of social and educational research. The Social, Psychological and Educational Controlled Trials Register (SPECTR) is an extension of the Cochrane Controlled Trials Register in health care (Milwain, 1998; Petrosino *et al.*, 1999). To date, hand-searching, electronic database searching and the searching of reference lists have identified over 5000 references to studies in education, criminology and psychosocial-learning research. These studies do not include research which uses methodologies other than experimental or quasi-experimental designs. Such studies also need systematic identification, review, and critical appraisal if the full range of educational research is to be used in the ways suggested in this paper.

This indicates an urgent need for the development of such infrastructural arrangements in education (see Hillage *et al.*, 1998: 53), and the financial support of central governments and the major research councils to develop and maintain them. The existence of many high-quality educational research centres throughout the world which can undertake systematic reviews and meta-analyses on different aspects of education suggests that a similar network of collaboration in educational research is feasible.

In short, the inadequacy of data-bases and bibliographic sources in education is a real problem, but one that is surmountable with appropriate effort and resources. The need for the continuing professional development of teachers, educational researchers, policy makers, and school governors, so that the principles and practices of evidence-based education can be nurtured and introduced into everyday educational life, is also clearly indicated.

6. Evidence and Professional Judgement

Establishing best practice, in both education and health care, is more than a matter of simply accessing, critically appraising, and implementing research findings. It also involves integrating such knowledge with professional judgement and experience. Much professional practice in education and health care is undertaken on the basis that things have always been done a certain way, or they carry the authority and legitimacy of some charismatic, highly valued practitioner. The role of 'common-sense' and 'back to basics' is also favoured by politicians and those charged with developing national educational policy.

Whilst tradition, charismatic authority, and experience can work against change and the development of best practice, they do have some merit. A teacher's experience and judgement can be much more sensitive to the important nuances of contextual and cultural factors than the findings of research alone, however thorough and valid that research may be. The question of the *relevance* of high-quality research to more local issues of teaching and learning (or treatment and change of health status) has already been noted, and is one which demands the highest levels of professional skill, judgement, and experience. Just as evidence-based health care means 'integrating individual clinical expertise with the best available external evidence from systematic research' (Sackett *et al.*, 1996), so evidence-based education means integrating individual teaching and learning expertise with the best available external evidence from systematic research. Indeed, a central feature of evidence-based education must be the two-way process of broadening the basis of individuals' experience and judgement by locating it within the available evidence, and generating research studies and evidence which explore and test the professional experience of teachers, students and other constituents of learning communities.

7. Conclusion

Education seems to be in a position remarkably similar to that of medicine and health care five or ten years ago. There are many research journals which contain a broad range of reports on research using different methodologies and addressing a diverse range of educational issues. Some of this research is of a high quality, some less so. The demands being made upon teachers and others who provide education call out for educational practice to be based on the best available evidence as well as the professional skills, experience, and competence of teachers. To do this, the educational research literature needs to be better registered, indexed, classified, appraised, and made accessible to researchers and teachers alike. Educators need access to this research and to be able to search and critically appraise it in order to determine its relevance (or lack of relevance) to *their* schools, students, and educational needs, Whether this is called evidence-based education, research-based education (Hargreaves, 1996), literature-based education (Hammersley, 1997), or context-sensitive practice (Greenhalgh and Worrall, 1997) is immaterial.

Evidence-based education, like evidence-based health care, is not a panacea, a quick fix, cookbook practice or the provider of readymade solutions to the demands of modern education. It is a set of principles and practices which can alter the way people think about education, the way they go about educational policy and practice, and the basis upon which they make professional judgements and deploy their expertise.

References

Adair, J. G., Dushenko, T.W. and Lindsay, R.C.L. (1985) Ethical regulations and their impact on research practices, *American Psychologist*, 40, 59–72.

Anderson, G. (1998) *Fundamentals of Educational Research* (London, The Falmer Press).

Andrews, K. and Stewart, J. (1979) Stroke recovery: he can but does he? *Rheumatology and Rehabilitation*, 18, 43–48.

Apple, M.W. (1982) *Education and Power* (Boston, Routledge and Kegan Paul).

Apple, M.W. and Weis, L. (1983) *Ideology and Practice in Education: A Political and Conceptual Introduction* (Philadelphia, Temple University Press).

Balint, M. (1957) *The Doctor, His Patient, and the Illness* (London, Tavistock).

Ball, S.J. (1990) *Politics and Policy Making in Education* (London, Routledge).

——(1993) Market Forces in Education, *Education Review*, 7 (1), 8–11.

Bangert-Drowns, R.L. (1985) The meta-analysis debate, *Paper presented at the Annual Meeting of the American Educational Research Association*, Chicago, April 4, 1985.

Boruch, R.F., Mcsweeney, A.J. and Sonderstrom, E.J. (1978) Randomised field experiments for program planning, development and evaluation, *Evaluation Quarterly*, 2, 655–695.

Bowles, S. and Gintis, H.I. (1976) *Schooling in Capitalist America* (New York, Basic Books).

Brazier, M. (1987) *Medicine, Patients and the Law* (Harmondsworth, Penguin Books).

Button, G. and Lee, J.R.E. (1987) *Talk and Social Organisation* (Clevedon and Philadelphia, Multilingual Matters).

Capra, F. (1982) *The Turning Point: Science, Society and the Rising Culture* (London, Wildwood House).

Cazden, C.B. (1988) *Classroom Discourse* (New York, Heinemann).

Christmas, E.M., Humphrey, M.E., Richardson, A.E. and Smith, E.M. (1974) The response of brain damage patients to a rehabilitation regime, *Rheumatology and Rehabilitation*, 13, 92–97.

Cicourel, A.V. and Kitsuse, J.I. (1963) *Educational Decision Makers* (Indianapolis, Bobbs-Merrill).

Cicourel, A.V. and Mehan, H., (1985) Universal development, stratifying practices, and status attainment, *Research in Social Stratification and Mobility*, 4, 3–27.

Davies, P.T. (1979) Motivation, sickness and responsibility in the psychiatric treatment of alcohol problems, *British Journal of Psychiatry*, 134 (1), 449–459.

——(1996) Sociological approaches to health outcomes. In H. Macbeth (ed.), *Health Outcomes Reviewed: Biological and Sociological Aspects* (Oxford University Press).

——(1999) Teaching evidence-based health care, in M.G. Dawes, P.T. Davies, A. Gray, J. mant, K. Seers and R. Snowball (1999) *Evidence-based Practice: A Primer for Health Professionals* (Edinburgh, Churchill Livingstone).

Davis, F. (1963) *Passage Through Crisis: Polio Victims and Their Families* (Indianapolis, Bobbs-Merrill).

Davies, P.T. and Mehan, H. (1988) Professional and family understanding of impaired communication, *British Journal of Disorders of Communication*, 23, 141–155.

Edwards, T. (1996) The research base of effective teacher education, *British Educational Research Association Newsletter*, Research Intelligence, Number 57, July, 7–12.

Elmore, P.B. and Woehlke, P.L. (1996) Research methods employed in *American Educational Research Journal, Educational Researcher* and *Review of Educational Research, 1978–1995. Paper presented at the Annual Meeting of the American Educational Research Association*, New York, April 8, 1996.

Fagerhaugh, S.Y. and Strauss, A.L. (1977) *Politics of Pain Management: Staff–Patient Interaction* (Menlo Park, Addison-Wesley Publishing Company).

Fisher, S. and Todd, A. (eds) (1983) *The Social Organisation of Doctor–Patient Communication* (Washington D.C., Center for Applied Linguistics).

Frankel, M.S. (ed.) (1987) *Values and Ethics in Organisation and Human Systems Development: An Annotated Bibliography* (Washington, D.C., American Association for the Advancement of Science).

Fulford, K.W.M. (1990) *Moral Theory and Medical Practice* (Cambridge, Cambridge University Press).

Gillon, R. (1985) *Philosophical Medical Ethics* (New York, John Wiley).

Giroux, H. (1983) *Theory and Resistance in Education* (London, Heinemann Education Books).

——(1992) *Border Crossing: Cultural Workers and the Politics of Education* (London, Routledge).

Glaser, B. and Strauss, A. (1965) *Awareness of Dying* (Chicago, Aldine Publishing Co.).

——(1967) *The Discovery of Grounded Theory: Strategies for Qualitative Research* (Chicago, Aldine Publishing Co.).

Glass, G., Mcgaw, B. and Lee Smith, M. (1980) *Meta-Analysis in Social Research* (Beverly Hills, Sage Publications).

Goffman, E. (1959) *The Presentation of Self in Everyday Life* (Harmondsworth, Penguin).

——(1963) *Stigma: Notes on the Management of Spoiled Identity* (Harmondsworth, Penguin).

——(1964) *Asylums: Essays on the Social Situation of Mental Patients and Other Inmates* (Harmondsworth, Penguin).

Gray, J. (1996) Track record of peer review: a reply to some remarks by David Hargreaves, *British Educational Research Association Newsletter*, Research Intelligence, Number 57, July, 5–6.

Greenhalgh, T. and Worrall, J.G. (1997) From EBM to CSM: the evolution of context-sensitive medicine, *Journal of Evaluation in Clinical Practice*, 3 (2), 105–108.

Hammersley, M. (1997) Educational research and a response to David Hargreaves, *British Educational Research Journal*, 23 (2), 141–161.

Hargreaves, D.H. (1996) *Teaching as a Research-Based Profession: Possibilities and Prospects* (Cambridge, Teacher Training Agency Annual Lecture).

——(1997) In defence of research for evidence-based teaching: a rejoinder to Martyn Hammersley, *British Educational Research Journal*, 23 (4), 405–419.

Hedges, L.V. (1992) Meta-analysis, *Journal of Educational Statistics*, 17 (4), 279–296.

Hillage, J., Pearson, R., Anderson, A. and Tamkin, P. (1998) *Excellence in Research on Schools, Research Report RR74*, Department for Education and Employment (Sudbury, DfEE Publications).

Hunter, J.E. and Schmidt, F.L. (1995) The impact of data-analysis methods on cumulative research knowledge: statistical significance testing, confidence intervals and meta-analysis, *Evaluation and the Health Professions*, 18 (4), 408–427.

Kimmel, A.J. (1988) *Ethics and Values in Applied Social Research* (Beverly Hills, Saga Publications).

Knowles, M. (1990) *The Adult Learner: A Neglected Species* (Houston, Gulf Publishing Company).

Kulik, J. and Kulik, C.C. (1989) Meta-analysis in education, *International Journal of Educational Research*, 13 (3), 220.

Laing, R.D. (1965) *The Divided Self* (Harmondsworth, Penguin).

Legrand, J. and Illsley, R. (1986) The measurement of inequality in health, *Paper presented to a meeting of the British Association for the Advancement of Science* (Bristol, 1–5 September 1986).

Macbeth, H. (ed.) (1996) *Health Outcomes Reviewed: Biological and Sociological Aspects* (Oxford, Oxford University Press).

Mehan, H. (1977) *Learning Lessons* (Cambridge, Mass., Harvard University Press).

Mehan, H., Villanueva, I., Hubbard, L. and Lintz, A. (1996) *Constructing School Success* (Cambridge, Cambridge University Press).

Milwain, C. (1998) *Assembling, Maintaining and Disseminating a Social and Educational Controlled Trials Register (SECTR): A Collaborative Endeavour* (Oxford, UK, Cochrane Centre).

Newcombe, F. and Ratcliff, G. (1979) Long term psychological consequences of cerebral lesions, in M. Gazzangia (ed.), *Handbook of Behavioural Neurobiology*, Vol 2, Chapter 16 (New York, Plenum Press).

Norris, N. (1996) Professor Hargreaves, the TTA and evidence-based practice, *British Educational Research Association Newsletter*, Research Intelligence, Number 57, July 2–4.

Oakley, A. (1998) Experimentation in social science: the case of health promotion, *Social Sciences in Health*, 4, (2), 73–88.

Oakley, A. and Roberts, H. (eds) (1996) *Evaluating Social Interventions*, Ilford, Essex, Barnados.

Petrosino, A.J., Rounding, C., Mcdonald, S. and Chalmers, I. (1999) *Improving Systematic Reviews of Evaluations: Preliminary Efforts to Assemble a Social, Psychological and Educational Controlled Trials Register (SPECTR)*, Paper prepared for the meeting on Research Synthesis and Public Policy, University College London, 15/16 July 1999.

PREISS, R.W. (1988) *Meta-Analysis: A Bibliography of Conceptual Issues and Statistical Methods*, Annandale, Virginia, Speech Communication Association.

Rosenthal, R. (1995) Interpreting and evaluating meta-analysis, *Evaluation and the Health Professions*, 18 (4), 393–407.

Sackett, D.L., Rosenberg, W., Gray, J.A.M., Haynes, R.B. and Richardson, W. (1996) Evidence-based medicine: what it is and what it isn't, *British Medical Journal*, 312, 71–72.

Sacks, O. (1990) Neurology and the soul, *New York Reviews of Books*, 37 (18), 44–50.

Samphier, M.L., Robertson, C. and Bloor, M.J. (1988) A possible artefactual component in specific cause mortality gradients. Social class variations in the clinical accuracy of death certificates, *Journal of Epidemiology and Community Health*, 42 (2) 138–43.

Silverman, D. (1987) *Communication and Medical Practice: Social Relations in the Clinic* (London and Newbury Park, Sage Publications).

Spindler, D. (ed.) (1982) *Doing the Ethnography of Schooling* (New York, Rinehart and Winston).

Strong, P.M. (1979) *The Ceremonial Order of the Clinic: Parents, Doctors and Medical Bureaucracies* (London, Routledge and Kegan Paul).

Tooley, J. and DARBY, D. (1998) *Educational Research: An Ofsted Critique* (London, OFSTED).

Veatch, R.M. (1989) *Medical Ethics* (London, Jones and Bartlett).

Weiss, B.D. (1982) Confidentiality expectations of patients, physicians and medical students, *Journal of the American Medical Association*, 247 (19), 2695–2697.

Wilkinson, R.G. (1986) Socio-economic differences in morality: interpreting the data on their size and trends. In R.G. Wilkinson (ed.) *Class and Health: Research and Longitudinal Data* (London, Tavistock).

Willis, P. (1977) *Learning to Labour: How Working Class Kids Get Working Class Jobs* (Westmead, Saxon House).

15 The Need for Randomised Controlled Trials in Educational Research

C. J. Torgerson and D. J. Torgerson

2 00

Authors

Carole J. Torgerson is Professor of Experimental Design in the School of Education at the University of Birmingham. She has focused most of her research on the design, conduct and reporting of randomised controlled trials (RCTs) and systematic reviews in general education, health education and medical education. She has co-authored a book, with David Torgerson on *The Design and Conduct of Randomised Controlled Trials in Health, Education and the Social Sciences* (Palgrave Macmillan, 2008). She is widely published in systematic reviews, trials and methodological research around experimental design.

Professor David J. Torgerson is Director of the York Trials Unit in the Department of Health Sciences at the University of York. He has worked extensively on randomised controlled trials in health, education, criminal justice and other social sciences. Professor Torgerson has published widely on the methodology and methods of randomised trials. He has a particular interest in the design and conduct of cluster trials of complex interventions.

Introduction

The first use of RCTs in education is uncertain. In the last century the use of the design pre-dated its use in medicine by at least a decade (although medical trials may have been undertaken in the 19th century). Forsetlund and colleagues (2007) identified two education trials conducted by Walters in 1931 and 1932, which predated the 1944 and 1948 medical trials run by the UK's Medical Research Council by more than a decade. The early interest in RCTs among some educational researchers was not sustained. Other, less robust, designs to demonstrate educational effectiveness were pursued. For example, quasi-experimental studies were often preferred, being relatively inexpensive, rapid to conduct and often able to generate politically attractive conclusions. However, their results are inherently less reliable than the results from RCTs as their internal validity is always potentially confounded by variables offering alternative explanations.

The Need for Randomised Controlled Trials in Educational Research (49, 3: 316–28) was published at the beginning of the resurgence of interest in the use of RCTs to evaluate educational interventions. The paper has been highly cited, including in the fields of: general education; educational psychology; special education; adult education; higher education; sociology of education; science education; linguistics; comparative education; economics of education; health education; medical education; education research design and methods. It was also cited in a subsequent issue of this *Journal* by Gorard (2003) to back up the assertion that sophisticated statistical techniques cannot compensate for poor design (51, 1: 46–63).

Torgerson and Torgerson have published a series of follow-up papers to this article on the need for more RCTs in educational research on issues relating to the design, conduct and reporting of RCTs in educational research, including a second paper published in the *BJES* in which they explore some common internal validity threats to RCTs and described some methods for dealing with them (51, 1: 46–45).

The need for randomised controlled trials in educational research has also been highly influential in terms of policy debates at the national level. On 19 December 2009 the Parliamentary Science and Technology Select Committee stated: 'It would have been particularly sensible [to do a RCT of Reading Recovery] in the light of calls from leading experts that RCTs were needed. In 2001, Carole Torgerson and David Torgerson [...] made a general call for more RCTs in educational research' and there followed a direct quotation from the paper. The Select Committee concluded: 'We recommend that the Government should draw up a set of criteria on which it decides whether a research project should be a randomised controlled trial'.

The Torgersons' book *The Design and Conduct of Randomised Controlled Trials in Health, Education and the Social Sciences* was published by Palgrave Macmillan in 2008.

For articles related to *The Need for Randomised Controlled Trials in Educational Research*, see *What is Evidence-Based Education?* on page 189 of this book and *Scholarship, Research and the Evidential Basis of Policy Development in Education* (49, 3: 329–52); *Educational Studies and Faith-Based Schooling: Moving from Prejudice to Evidence-Based Argument* (51, 2: 149–67); *Work-Based Knowledge, Evidence-Informed Practice and Education* (51, 4: 369–89).

The Need for Randomised Controlled Trials in Educational Research

by Carole J. Torgerson, The University of York,
and David J. Torgerson, The University of York

1. Introduction

The dominant paradigm in educational research is based on qualitative methodologies (interpretive paradigm). This is because there are complex interactive processes operating within the classroom situation requiring investigation and understanding. The written framework of a new educational intervention can be radically altered by the time it is delivered. Therefore, research into the quality of the complex processes involved is important to help us understand how and why things happen in the classroom. However, equally, if not more, important questions about outcomes in education also need to be asked. Currently, routine quantitative assessment of pupils is undertaken at the end of each Key Stage; SATs and GCSE results are routinely reported, and statistical analyses on such results are used to influence or justify educational policy. Quasi-experimental (quantitative) research is also undertaken in the field of education, but despite fairly widespread use of quantitative methods the most rigorous of these, the randomised controlled trial (RCT), is rarely used in British educational research. It is often assumed that the RCT is only appropriate in medical research. However, this is not the case. When the medical research community celebrated the 50th anniversary of the first RCT in health care – the seminal antibiotic trial for tuberculosis in 1946 (Medical Research Council, 1948) – it was pointed out that educational researchers have used the RCT methodology for a much longer period of time (Oakley, 1998). Indeed, some of the first recognisable RCTs were undertaken in the field of education early in the 20th century, predating the medical community's adoption of this method of research by nearly half a century (Oakley, 1998, 2000).

The medical research community has expanded and developed the use of RCTs and it has become the predominant research methodology in medicine. The educational research community has focused on the development of non-experimental research methods within the paradigm of qualitative methodologies, and relatively few randomised trials of educational innovations have been undertaken in recent years. Of the recent trials, many have tended to be linked to a health issue within education and these have attracted the attention of health care researchers rather than educationalists. The aims of this paper are to discuss the merits of the RCT and to call for educational researchers to rediscover this method and undertake more trials.

2. Why Use Randomisation?

In quantitative research there are a number of non-RCT methods (for example, the case control method) and these often seem to have been used in educational research where a randomised trial would have provided more reliable results. In a case control study schools that receive an intervention, such as a curriculum innovation, are matched with schools that do not receive the intervention. Data are then collected on both sets of schools and any differences in outcome, such as examination results, are ascribed to the innovation. However, a characteristic of this approach is that the two sets of schools may well be different in a number of aspects other than the intervention being tested, and this may affect the results.

Case Control Studies and Risk of Bias

A recent evaluation in Newcastle wanted to assess whether or not the National Literacy Strategy (NLS) could improve performance (Smith and Hardman, 2000). The researchers found no difference in examination results between the schools piloting the strategy and schools that had not yet started to implement the strategy. On the basis of this result, we could assume that the National Literacy Strategy had no effect on examination results. However, because the schools were not randomly allocated to receive the literacy strategy this conclusion cannot be reliably drawn. It is possible that the strategy had an educationally important effect on pupil performance but this change was masked due to selection bias. Furthermore, the schools chosen for the pilot were deliberately identified because they were schools with previously poor examination performance. The schools selected may have been on a downward trend in terms of their results and the NLS may have been successful in the sense that it had started to reverse this trend. However, because there was no control group for reliable comparison we cannot conclude exactly what was occurring. Clearly this example is of a particularly poorly controlled study. More robust non-randomised designs could have been used, such as matching schools with similar pupil intakes and past examination performance. Nevertheless even a well-designed quasi-experimental study is inferior to a well-designed randomised controlled trial.

Another example where a randomised trial approach would have been helpful is that of a recently published evaluation of Reading Recovery. This study used a case-control approach when a randomised design would have given a more precise and robust estimate of effect (Moore and Wade, 1998). Moore and Wade compared 121 children, whose reading scores were sufficiently low for them to be eligible for the Reading Recovery scheme, with 121 aged-matched children from the same classes, whose scores were not quite low enough for them to be eligible for the programme. Approximately four years later both groups of children were tested in terms of their reading ages. It was found that the Reading Recovery children had, on average, a reading age 12 months greater than the children who did not receive the programme. Whilst this result is suggestive of a beneficial effect of Reading Recovery, because the study was not a randomised controlled trial we cannot be completely sure that this apparent gain in reading ability was as a consequence of the novel intervention. There are a number of potential 'confounding' variables that could explain part or all of the apparent improvement in reading ability. The first problem is the statistical phenomenon of regression to the mean (Cook and Campbell, 1979; Torgerson, C.J., 2000). Because the children who were chosen for Reading Recovery had extremely poor scores, some of which would have occurred by chance, then re-testing the same children at a later date would show an improvement in test scores irrespective of the effectiveness or ineffectiveness of the intervention. As the comparison children had scores closer to the average, their test score change would have been affected far less by regression to the mean than the intervention children. Thus, some or all of the apparent difference between the groups of children could be due to differential regression to the mean effects. As well as this statistical problem one can envisage other potential confounding factors. For instance, parents of the intervention group children may have given more input to their children's reading: a factor that could not be controlled for in the analysis. Using a randomised design would have eliminated these problems. The two groups would then have had the same regression to the mean and the same educational influence of concerned parents.

Benefit of Randomisation

In contrast, a randomised controlled trial undertaken in the United States sought to examine whether allocating a small amount of extra funding to schools in deprived areas would have an impact on examination grades (Crain and York, 1976). Schools from deprived areas were asked to take part in the scheme and then randomly allocated into one of two groups. The experimental group received extra financial input, while the control group did not, and the examination performance of both groups of schools was monitored. The results showed that the reading scores of children from the most deprived backgrounds, who were in the intervention schools, improved from between six and nine months compared with similar children in the control school. This educational boost was achieved for relatively little cost but importantly it could not have been detected had the researchers not used the randomised methodology: crucially, randomisation ensured that the only difference between the two groups was the intervention (all other characteristics had been distributed evenly across both groups). In case control studies, this is not so.

Non-randomised quantitative methods are nearly always inferior to the randomised trial. The Newcastle evaluation cited above (Smith and Hardman, 2000) had obvious bias from the outset. However, even when control schools are more carefully selected, bias may still occur. For example, a common practice is for a new educational policy to be piloted among 'volunteer' schools. Schools can be carefully matched in terms of similar pupil catchment areas and past examination results in order to evaluate the new policy. It is possible to match schools on observable characteristics, but it is not possible to match them on variables which are unobserved but which may affect outcome. For example, volunteer schools are likely to possess head teachers and staff of different characteristics compared with staff from schools that do not volunteer, and these characteristics may compound any inaccuracy in the results. Any difference between the schools, therefore, may be an artifact of the different characteristics of the staff and not due to the new educational policy.

3. The Pragmatic Randomised Controlled Trial

Nearly 40 years ago Schwartz and Lellouch described two types of randomised trial: the 'explanatory trial' and the 'pragmatic trial' (Schwartz and Lellouch, 1967). The explanatory trial design is probably the one with which most people are familiar. This type of study is tightly controlled and, where possible, placebo interventions are used. Thus, one may take a large group of children all from a similar socio-economic background and attainment and randomly allocate them into two groups. One group receives the intervention under investigation whilst the other receives a dummy or sham intervention. For instance, Gall *et al.* (1978) took a group of 336 children and allocated them, at random, to different styles of teaching an ecological curriculum. The children allocated to the control group received a sham curriculum in the form of art lessons around ecology. The results of the different teaching methods were then assessed against this control group.

The Explanatory Trial

The advantages of the explanatory trial approach are as follows. Because children are selected so as to be as homogeneous a group as possible, the variation in outcome scores is minimised. This allows quite small differences in test scores to be ascribed to the intervention, which in turn leads to the need for a relatively small sample of children. In addition, because the children in the control group do not know that they are receiving a placebo curriculum, any extra motivation they derive from taking part in research is equally balanced across the different trial groups (i.e. the Hawthorne effect). On the other hand, there are a number of disadvantages of this approach. Teachers and educationalists often want to know whether teaching or curriculum innovations benefit children across the whole range of attainments, ages, socio-economic and ethnic groups. Therefore the results of a tightly controlled trial among, say, Year 7 girls who are native English speakers and are from a high socio-economic background are simply not generalisable to the average educational setting. Additionally, it is often not possible to use a placebo intervention or it may be unethical.

The Pragmatic Trial

An alternative to the explanatory trial approach is to use the pragmatic trial design (Schwartz and Lellouch, 1967). In this respect, the environment in which the trial is conducted is kept as close to normal educational practice as possible. Therefore, dummy or sham interventions are not used and all pupils to whom the intervention might eventually be used are included in the evaluation. The only thing that departs from normal practice is that the children, or schools, are allocated the new intervention at random. A disadvantage of the pragmatic approach is that the trials usually have to be much larger than the explanatory approach but the pragmatic trial approach is probably the most feasible and useful trial design for educational research. Because the trial mimics normal educational practice, there is a greater variation that can make it harder to detect a small effect. To cope with this the sample size needs to be increased accordingly.

Cluster or Individual Randomisation

Another important issue with respect to undertaking randomised trials is the choice between using a 'cluster' or 'individual' randomised design. In the latter, the children are randomised as individuals to the intervention. For many educational interventions this approach is simply not possible. For instance, studying a new way of teaching cannot be done with half a class and hidden from the other pupils, as 'leakage' to the control group would inevitably occur as children in the intervention group could talk with their friends about the different approach. To avoid these problems pragmatic educational trials can use a design whereby children are randomised by cluster or group (i.e. by schools or area). A cluster may be at the level of the class but more likely it will be at the level of the school. It could also be by region, LEA, county etc. Boruch, conjecturing about the future use of RCTs in social research, has suggested that randomisation will occur at the level of institution or organisation rather than at the level of the individual (Boruch, 1994). Typically, an educational trial will, therefore, recruit a number of schools to take part in the trial and then randomise the schools into the two trial groups.

4. Designing a Trial

The underlying idea of a randomised trial is exceedingly simple. Two or more groups of children, identical in all respects, are assembled. Clearly, the individual children are different but when groups of children are assembled by randomisation, and with a large enough sample size, they will be sufficiently similar at the group level in order to make meaningful comparisons. In other words, the differences are spread equally across both groups, making them essentially the same.

The only way to ensure that the groups are the same is by using random allocation. For instance, if we were going to run a study with 400 children we would use a random number table or a computer to assign 200 children to the intervention and 200 to act as controls. The intervention would then be delivered to one of the two groups and both groups would be given some kind of test to assess the outcome. Any differences in test results between the two groups could therefore be ascribed to the intervention. The analysis of a randomised trial is actually simpler than other forms of quantitative research because we know the two groups are similar at baseline. Complicated statistical methods using multivariate approaches are usually unnecessary, though pre-planned sub-group analyses can still be useful and incorporated from the outset.

One key consideration when designing a trial is to choose a sample size that is sufficiently large to demonstrate an educationally important difference. Because in educational interventions teachers and pupils tend to be very heterogeneous, large sample sizes will generally be required. For instance, Aveyard *et al.* wanted to detect a 4% reduction in smoking prevalence (i.e. the equivalent of one less child in an average-sized classroom taking up smoking) using a novel anti-smoking curriculum. They needed to randomise over 8,000 pupils (Aveyard *et al.*, 1999). Clearly, the research resource implications of mounting such a large study can be considerable. Nevertheless, in some respects, undertaking randomised trials in education could be simpler than in other research fields. Unlike virtually all other fields, teachers routinely measure the outcomes of their pupils either in the form of external examinations or by school tests and assessments. Therefore, one barrier to undertaking a trial (i.e. setting up data collection instruments) is largely avoided in education as existing measures can often be used, although some routine tests may not be ideal measurement tools (Torgerson, C.J., 2000) if there are issues of internal validity, for example.

Arguments Against Trials

Many arguments are deployed against the use of randomised trial methodology in education. However, these are often based on a misunderstanding of the methodology. It is argued that, because individual children are so different in factors that affect their educational outcome (such as social background), comparing groups will be meaningless. However, it is assumed that all these factors are present in equal proportions in the two or more groups when they are formed by randomisation. These differences cancel each other out over the groups. For example, randomisation creates groups with the same proportion of girls, with the same proportion of pupils from various socio-economic and ethnic groups, with the same distribution of ages, heights, weights etc. – this is the simple elegance of randomisation!

The RCT methodology has been criticised as being unethical because an intervention is withheld from some children. This would indeed be unethical if we knew that the intervention were effective; however, we do not. The health field is littered with examples of treatments which enthusiastic doctors believed would work and therefore did not require a randomised trial as proof. There are undoubtedly some educational innovations which are harmful to the educational prospects of children. Without testing them in robust trials we simply do not know what is helpful and what is downright detrimental. In healthcare it is widely recognised that the many disasters caused by doing non-randomised research make it unethical not to do a trial. Society insists that a new drug for, say, athlete's foot is required to undergo an evaluation by a RCT. However, a curriculum innovation such as the National Literacy Strategy, which will affect the lives of millions of children, is not exposed to the rigours of a randomised trial!

5. Recent Randomised Trials

Randomised trials can be, and are, undertaken in schools. Let us consider two recent curriculum evaluations: anti-smoking education and a violence-prevention curriculum. A large randomised trial was undertaken between 1988 and 1990 to assess the effectiveness of two types of anti-smoking curricula (Nutbeam *et al.*, 1993). Thirty-nine schools with over 4,500 pupils were randomised to receive the new anti-smoking health education curriculum or to be the control group, the latter receiving their usual health education. The results showed that the intervention had no effect. It is interesting to note that the health promotion programme evaluated in this study had been widely used within the UK since 1986, yet this ineffective method of smoking prevention was not subjected to a randomised trial for above five years (Nutbeam *et al.*, 1993). Therefore, resources were wasted in many schools training teachers in this ineffective teaching method. More recently another anti-smoking curriculum was developed using different psychological models and computer-aided learning programmes; but before this resource-intensive intervention was rolled out to schools it was evaluated in a rigorous trial. In that study, 52 schools with over 8,000 pupils were randomised to the new curriculum or to the control group. One year later pupils were followed up for smoking prevalence. The results showed that pupils in the intervention group had a slightly increased risk of smoking (although not statistically significant) compared with pupils in the control group (Aveyard *et al.*, 1999). Fortunately, the developers of this innovative curriculum were prepared to test it in a robust manner before this potentially hazardous, and expensive, form of anti-smoking education was given to the general school population.

On the other hand, a curriculum that was evaluated within a trial and showed a positive benefit was a novel curriculum aimed at primary school children in order to reduce pupil violence (Grossman *et al.*, 1997). In a randomised trial of nearly 800 pupils, the curriculum led to a significant reduction in physical violence among the 400 pupils in the intervention schools compared with pupils who were in the control schools. In contrast to the anti-smoking curricula this intervention was successful and demonstrated to be of benefit. The studies described above tested the usefulness of curriculum innovations that had an immediate health outcome. It would have been relatively simple to design an RCT to test the Literacy or Numeracy Strategies before these potentially damaging educational innovations were rolled out to the entire school population.

6. Quality Trials

Although the RCT is the most rigorous quantitative methodology care must be taken that any trial is of good quality as poor quality trials can be misleading. For instance, one key feature of a good RCT is blinded assessment of outcome. Thus, although it is not a necessary requirement to mask the intervention from teachers and pupils by using a dummy, placebo or sham educational intervention as a control, it is important that the researcher who assesses the outcome of the trial is blind to the allocated intervention. If blinded outcome assessment is not undertaken observer bias might occur. Furthermore, it is important that follow-up of randomised children should be as close to 100% as possible as the greater the loss to follow-up the greater the likelihood of 'attrition bias'. Nevertheless, it is perfectly possible to undertake high-quality randomised trials in the context of education, as recent trials demonstrate (Aveyard *et al.*, 1999; Grossman *et al.*, 1997; Nutbeam *et al.*, 1993).

7. Discussion

The invention of the RCT is one of the most important discoveries in research methodology in the last century. It is regrettable that the education research community has largely turned its back on this methodology, although it is not alone in this. MacDonald has argued that the social work profession largely abandoned trial methodology 20 to 30 years ago because the results of trials in that area often failed to show benefit (MacDonald, 1997). Long-term follow-up of a trial of a social work intervention among delinquent boys in the 1930s showed that the intervention group had poorer outcomes, such as being jailed more frequently, compared with those boys allocated to the control group. Rather than accepting the message from this study, among others, that seemingly helpful interventions can be harmful, the messenger – the RCT – was abandoned rather than the message (MacDonald, 1997).

In medicine, it took a series of disasters over many decades to convince the medical community and health policy makers that most, if not all, medical innovations should be subjected to evaluations by RCT. To list a few disasters may remind readers of the importance of trial evaluations. For example, about 10,000 premature babies were blinded between 1942 and 1954 because someone thought it was a good idea to give them extra oxygen and this damaged their sight (Silverman, 1997). The cause of this epidemic was only discovered after a trial had been conducted. Tens of thousands of patients died in the developed world because of the routine use of drugs, untested in RCTs, to suppress arhythmias of the heart, which later RCTs showed to be harmful (Silverman, 1997). It is of interest to note that many cardiologists thought these trials to be unethical at the time because, of course, they thought they knew that the drugs were effective (Silverman, 1997).

In education, like health, there are probably interventions that do more harm than good. Unfortunately, we have no way of knowing whether, for instance, the policy of introducing computers in schools was of benefit, or actually harmed our children's education. Had a large randomised trial been undertaken and confirmed the perceived benefits of introducing information technology in schools, introduction of an effective intervention could have been accelerated. Equally, a trial could have shown it to be of little or no benefit or even harmful, in which case the large sums of money could have been spent in other ways. Similarly, we cannot be sure whether the National Literacy and Numeracy Strategies improve or harm children's education as no RCT has been undertaken, and again there is a potential for benefit but also a potential possibility of harm. However, because of the absence of trials we cannot be sure what does and does not work. Whilst disasters in medicine can more readily be counted in mortality and morbidity, in education damaging interventions are not so obvious. Trying to monitor trends in examination results is a poor substitute given the temporal effects on these rates and the controversy as to whether or not the standard of external examinations remains constant.

Recently, Davies (1999) has called for educational policy to be 'Evidence-Based' and we support this view, particularly using RCT evidence. The Secretary of State for Education, David Blunkett, in a speech to a meeting convened by the Economic and Social Research Council, described the educational research that is needed by the present policy makers:

> We welcome studies which combine large scale, quantitative information on effect sizes which will allow us to generalise. (Blunkett, 2000)

We suggest that what in fact is required are large-scale randomised controlled trials. At present there is an absence of a reliable tool in educational policy; potentially, RCTs could meet that need. RCTs/quantitative research and qualitative research can be complementary; they need not be mutually exclusive. Qualitative methodologies are well suited to investigating what happens with individuals; RCTs are appropriate for looking at the larger units relevant to policy makers.

Whilst the presence of good quality randomised trials provides a stronger basis for decision making and policy development than when they are absent, they will not provide a complete solution. Government policy in all fields, whilst ideally informed by the evidence, is shaped by other political processes, which may override even the most robust trial data. However, because of the lack of randomised evidence, educational policy making is relatively 'evidence-free' at present.

Educational researchers helped to pioneer the randomised controlled trial. It is of immense regret that this methodology has largely been abandoned by many educational researchers. The potential benefits of trials are huge and the educational research community should replace quasi-experimental studies with a programme of RCTs urgently.

8. Acknowledgements

We thank the two anonymous referees for their helpful comments on an earlier draft of this paper.

9. Note

The opinions reflected in this paper are those of the authors, not those of the Department of Educational Studies or the Department of Health Studies, University of York.

References

Aveyard, P., Cheng, KK., Almond, J., Sherratt, E., Lancashire, R., Lawrence, T., Griffin, C. and Evens, O. (1999) Cluster randomised controlled trial of expert system based on the transtheoretical (stages of change) model for smoking prevention and cessation in schools. *British Medical Journal* 319, 948–53.

Blunkett, D. (2000). Influence or irrelevance: can social science improve government? *Research Intelligence*, 12–21.

Boruch, R.F. (1994) The Future of Controlled Randomized Experiments: A Briefing. *Evaluation Practice* 15, 265–74.

Cook, T.D. and Campbell, T.D. (1979) *Quasi-Experimentation: Design and Analysis Issues for Field Settings* (Boston, Houghton Mifflin).

Crain, R.L. and York, R.L. (1976) Evaluating a Successful Program: Experimental Method and Academic Bias. *School Review* 84, 233–54.

Davies, P. (1999) What is Evidence-Based Education? *British Journal of Educational Studies* 47, 108–21.

Gall, M.D., Ward, B.A., Berliner, D.C., Cahen, L.S., Winne, P.H., Elashoff, J.D. and Stanton, G.C. (1978) Effects of Questioning Techniques and Recitation on Student Learning. *American Educational Research Journal* 15, 175–99.

Grossman, D.C., Neckerman, H.J., Koepsall, T.D., Liu, P.Y., Asher, K.N., Frey, K., Beland, K. and Rivara, F.P. (1997) Effectiveness of a Violence Prevention Curriculum Among Children in Elementary School. *Journal of the American Medical Association* 277, 1605–11.

Macdonald, G. (ed.) (1997) Social Work: Beyond Control? in A. Maynard and I. Chalmers (eds) *Non-Random Reflections on Health Services Research* (London, BMJ Publications).

Medical Research Council (1948) Streptomycin treatment of pulmonary tuberculosis: a report of the streptomycin in tuberculosis trials committee. *British Medical Journal* 2, 769–82.

Moore, M. and WADE, B. (1998) Reading and Comprehension: a longitudinal study of ex-Reading Recovery students. *Educational Studies* 24, 195–203.

Nutbeam, D., Macaskill, P., Smith, C., Simpson, J.M. and Catford, J. (1993) Evaluation of two school smoking education programmes under normal classroom conditions. *British Medical Journal* 306, 102–7.

Oakley, A. (1998) Experimentation and social interventions: a forgotten but important history. *British Medical Journal* 317, 1239–42.

——(2000) *Experiments in Knowing: Gender and Method in the Social Sciences* (Cambridge, Polity Press).

Schwartz, D. and Lellouch, D. (1967) Explanatory and pragmatic attitudes in therapeutic trials. *Journal of Chronic Diseases* 20, 637–48.

Silverman, W. (Ed.) (1997) Risks and Benefits of Medical Innovations, in A. Maynard and I. Chalmers (eds) *Non-Random Reflections on Health Services Research* (London, BMJ Publications).

Smith, F. and Hardman, F. (2000) Evaluating the Effectiveness of the National Literacy Strategy: identifying indicators of success. *Educational Studies* 26, 365–78.

Torgerson, C.J. (2000) The Erroneous Use of Statistics to Monitor Performance of Schools and Teachers. *Curriculum* 21, 94–97.

16 The Educative Importance of Ethos

T. McLaughlin

2005

Author

Terence McLaughlin's (1949–2006) death at an early age came as a shock to all his many friends. He spent many years as a University Lecturer in Philosophy of Education and fellow at St. Edmund's College in the University of Cambridge before his appointment to the Chair in Philosophy of Education at the Institute of Education, University of London. He was also Chair of the Philosophy of Education Society of Great Britain and his list of achievements in the educational world is a long one. Professor McLaughlin was also a significant contributor and reviewer to the *British Journal of Educational Studies* as well as to the *Journal of Philosophy of Education, Studies in Philosophy of Education* and the *Journal of Moral Education*. He was a man of faith and his Catholic faith influenced many of the themes in the philosophy of education he wrote about.

Introduction

The Educative Importance of Ethos (53, 3: 306–25) was the last article that Professor McLaughlin published before his death. It addresses the educational importance of ethos in the context of classrooms and schools. It builds on the work of Caitlin Donnelly who had previously published *In Pursuit of School Ethos* (48, 2: 134–54) in the *British Journal of Educational Studies* five years earlier. McLaughlin proposes that much fuller critical attention is needed: to the meaning of ethos in the contexts of schools and education more broadly; to the kinds of educative achievement and influence which are characteristically associated with ethos; to the specific aspects of the educational aims and values of the classroom and school, with which ethos is particularly related, and to the exploration and justification of the evaluative aspects of ethos. He argues that an appropriate and sustained engagement with these questions at the level of the classroom and school by teachers and educational leaders should combat a tendency to deal with matters of ethos in an unduly superficial way.

In 1995 Terence McLaughlin had published *Return to the Crossroads: Maritain Fifty Years On* (43, 2: 162–78) in the *British Journal of Educational Studies*, with co-authors John Haldane and Richard Pring, which focused on this important

Catholic philosopher. While he made many distinguished and sophisticated contributions to the secular field of Philosophy of Education, he resisted the idea that a secular form of liberal education is the only defensible educational experience in modern society.

His life and work was celebrated in 2009 with the publication of *Faith in Education: A tribute to Terence McLaughlin* edited by Graham Haydon in which many of his academic colleagues contributed chapters commenting on Terence McLaughlin's life and philosophical works, particularly on his defence of Catholic schools. It was a recognition of the work of an important and much loved philosopher of education. He advocated the notion that Catholic schools should be characterized by celebration and festivity and he was fond of quoting Hilaire Belloc on this theme:

> Where'r the Catholic sun does shine
> There's music, laughter and good red wine
> At least I've always found it so
> Benedicamus Domino

A volume of Terence McLaughlin's writings appears as *Liberalism, Education and Schooling, Essays by T.H. McLaughlin* (St Andrews Studies in Philosophy and Public Affairs) (2008) edited by David Carr, Mark Halstead and Richard Pring. Related articles in the *British Journal of Educational Studies* are: *Revising the Comprehensive Ideal* (44, 4: 426–37); *In Pursuit of School Ethos* (48, 2: 134–54); *The Re-Emergence of Character Education in British Education Policy* (53, 3: 239–54).

The Educative Importance of Ethos

by Terence McLaughlin, Institute of Education, University of London

1. Introduction

The notion of 'ethos' is notoriously difficult to bring into clear focus in the context of teaching and schooling, as elsewhere. The educative importance of ethos is, however, widely acknowledged. One aspect of this acknowledgement involves specific claims about the relationship between ethos and particular educational 'outcomes' based on empirical research purporting to show a link of some kind between the two. Thus the Consultative Green Paper, *Schools: Building on Success,* claims that ' ... evidence suggests that schools with a strong sense of identity or ethos perform best' (DfEE, 2001, 4.11; compare, for example, Mortimore *et al.,* 1988; Rutter *et al.,* 1979). Another aspect of the acknowledgement of the educative importance of ethos arises from reflection upon the complex nature of educative influence itself. Philosophers, for example, are interested in ethos because of its close relationship with Aristotelian emphases on educational influence as involving the shaping of the dispositions, virtues, character and practical judgment of persons in a milieu in which tradition, habit and emulation play an important role.

Ethos is relatively underexplored as a form of educative influence by educational researchers, philosophers of education, educational policy makers and teachers and educational leaders at classroom and school level. The range of educational issues and questions which arise in relation to 'ethos' have not, of course, been totally neglected, not least because they are often dealt with in terms of related notions such as 'culture', 'climate' and the like, or by the invocation of 'ethos' in some unanalysed sense. What has been lacking, however, is the widely felt need for a more detailed and precise focus upon the notion of ethos itself and its educative importance. The educative importance of 'ethos' is worthy of detailed exploration for a number of reasons.

First, regardless of the specific perspective from which the matter is viewed, the 'ethos' of teaching and schooling is clearly a significant part of the overall educational experience of students, and, some have argued, the most important part (Williams, 2000, p. 76). As indicated above, an ethos of teaching and schooling not only facilitates (in a way which may be apt for appropriate empirical investigation) the kinds of educative influence which teachers and schools seek to exert, but also in an important sense constitutes and embodies (significant aspects of) that influence.

Any proper understanding of the processes of educative influence aimed at by teachers and schools is therefore incomplete in the absence of attention to ethos (on the general significance of ethos in the formation of children and young people see, for example, Bronfenbrenner, 1974).

Second, 'ethos' has featured prominently in recent developments in relation to educational policy in the UK and Ireland. For example, the Consultative Green Paper referred to above articulates proposals for the enhancement of the diversity of secondary schooling and for all secondary schools to be encouraged ' ... to develop a distinctive mission and ethos' (DfEE, 2001, 4.12) and to make a distinctive contribution to the educational system as a whole beyond the teaching of the National Curriculum, as faith schools, specialist schools, beacon schools and the like (*op. cit.*, 4.13–14.26). In addition, schools are encouraged to offer 'education with character', the most important feature of which is seen as the ethos of the school (*op. cit.*, 4.77). Further, proposals are made in the Green Paper to ensure that school ethos 'is given the attention it deserves' including discussions with OFSTED about how inspection can give greater recognition to ethos and with the National College for School Leadership about how heads and prospective heads can understand how a positive ethos can be established and sustained (*ibid.*). Many aspects of the proposals relating to school ethos were retained in the subsequent White Paper (DfES, 2001, ch. 5). Guidance recently published in relation both to citizenship education and to personal, social and health education has emphasised the importance of aspects of the life of schools which can be broadly described in terms of 'ethos' (Qualifications and Curriculum Authority, 2000a, pp. 10–18; Qualifications and Curriculum Authority, 2000b, pp. 6–8). The ethos of the school is one of the matters which is emphasised for attention by the Department for Education and Skills in Home–School agreements (www.standards.dfes.gov. uk/ parentalinvolvement). In the case of faith schools in the maintained sector, whether Foundation or Voluntary schools with a religious character, the Governors have a legal duty to secure an ethos statement from the school as part of the process of determining its specific aims and values (see, for example, www.natsoc. org.uk/schools/ curriculum/ethos). The ethos of faith schools is also an important focus of attention in the inspection of these schools (see, for example, Catholic Education Service, 1999). In Northern Ireland, school 'ethos' is seen as an important matter of concern (see, for example, Donnelly, 2000). The concept of school ethos has been particularly emphasised in Scotland in relation to 'ethos indicators' (Scottish Office Education Department and HM Inspectors of Schools, 1992a, 1992b) and in recent initiatives in Ireland associated with School Culture and Ethos Project based in the Marino Institute of Education in Dublin (Canavan and Monahan, 2000; Furlong and Monahan, 2000). A clear understanding of the educative importance of ethos is therefore important if current educational policy is to be fully understood and evaluated.

Third, a critical grasp of the educative importance of ethos enables a range of important questions relating to the role of ethos in classrooms and schools, including the recognition, assessment and improvement of ethos, to be identified and tackled by teachers and educational leaders in an appropriate way.

In this essay, I engage in a broadly philosophical exploration of the notion of ethos in the context of teaching and schooling with the aim of bringing the educative importance of ethos into clearer focus. Any full consideration of the educative importance of ethos necessarily involves a wide range of different forms of enquiry and research, including, for example, ethnographic studies of particular teachers and schools. The present discussion, therefore, in its focus on broadly philosophical considerations of a fundamental character, leaves many important issues and considerations to one side which require attention in a fuller account.

2. The Concept of Ethos

The concept of 'ethos' is notoriously difficult to analyse for at least two reasons. First, the concept of ethos is closely akin to, and often described in terms of, related notions such as 'ambience', 'atmosphere', 'climate', 'culture', 'ethical environment' and the like (see Allder, 1993, p. 60; Donnelly, 2000; Glover and Coleman, 2005; Haydon, 2006; Solvason, 2005). It is therefore difficult to focus attention on the specific meaning of ethos for the purposes of analysis and discussion. Second, the intangibility and elusiveness of the notion of ethos can be seen in the wide range of aspects of the life and work of the classroom and school through which it is manifested and in the wide range of modes of influence in which it is embodied. This wide range of aspects and modes can be illustrated by reference to the recent Scottish and Irish initiatives in relation to school ethos. The Scottish initiative identifies twelve 'ethos indicators': pupil morale, teacher morale, teachers' job satisfaction, the physical environment, the learning context, teacher–pupil relationships, equality and justice, extra-curricular activities, school leadership and discipline (Scottish Office Education Department and HM Inspectors of Schools, 1992a, 1992b, appendix one). The Irish initiative specifies 21 aspects of school life which determines ethos, including symbols/icons/emblems, rituals and ceremonies, communication systems and relationships with parents (Canavan and Monahan, 2000, Information sheet 13, cf. sheets 9 and 10. See also Furlong and Monahan, 2000). In relation to England and to faith schools, the Church of England identifies thirteen aspects of the ethos of a church school and offers 24 questions as guidance for ethos-related issues to be raised with headteachers and governors (www.natsoc.org.uk/schools/curriculum/ethos). Any aspect of the life and work of classrooms and schools and any mode of influence within classrooms and schools can be seen as apt for the manifestation of an ethos.

A good starting point for an exploration of the notion of ethos is Margaret Allder's claim that 'ethos' is a 'frontier word' in virtue of its closeness to the edges of linguistic expressibility. 'Ethos' is rendered intelligible in her view by 'connecting words' (such as 'ambience', 'spirit', 'atmosphere' and 'climate') which have clearer meanings and which, by lending some of their meaning to the notion of 'ethos', enable the meaning of 'ethos' itself to be illuminated and discerned (Allder, 1993).[1] From this approach via the consideration of 'connecting words', Allder draws out the following conclusions about the meaning of 'ethos': that it refers *inter alia* to human activities and behaviour, to the human environment within which these enterprises take place (especially the social system of an organisation), to behaviour and activity which has already occurred, to a mood or moods which are pervasive within this environment, to social interactions and their con-sequences, to something which is experienced, to norms rather than to exceptions, and to something that is unique (Allder, 1993, pp. 63–69). Whilst a number of Allder's points invite critical probing (for example, the meaning and justification of her claim that an ethos is 'unique')[2] her account covers a good deal of ground in relation to ethos in a useful way.

Whilst Allder takes ethos as the central point of reference in her enquiry, other related notions (such as culture – not considered by Allder) have been argued for various reasons to be preferable to 'ethos' in the discussion of educational influence. For Solvason, ethos is the *product* of the culture of the school (and we might add of the classroom), and 'culture' is seen as a preferred category of analysis because of its greater 'solidity' and accessibility: 'School culture is a tangible entity, whereas ethos is far more nebulous, always retaining a vagueness' (2005, p. 87). Glover and Coleman do not indicate any overall preference for any one of the terms 'climate', 'ethos' and 'culture' in the light of their review of the use of these terms in a range of educational research, although they argue that there is something to be gained from a consistent use of the terms by researchers (2005, p. 266). Haydon regards 'culture' as too broad a concept to capture his interest in the climate of values in which people live and in which young people grow up, but prefers the notion of an 'ethical environment' to that of an ethos as a category of analysis of his focus of interest (Haydon, 2006). The appropriateness or otherwise of the concept of 'ethos' for the analysis of educative influence cannot be settled in a final way, and depends in part on the specific interests of particular researchers. Researchers more interested in empirical research may favour concepts such as 'culture', whilst those with a focus of interest beyond the school, such as Haydon, may favour terms such as 'environment'.

There is some consistency among researchers in their use of the term 'ethos'. Glover and Coleman argue that the term tends to be used in relation to more general, 'subjective' and less measurable features of the atmosphere of schools, such as the relationship between people and the values and principles under-pinning policy and practice (2005, pp. 257–59). For Eisner, ethos refers to ' ... the underlying deep structure of a culture, the values that animate it, that collectively constitute its way of life' (1994, frontispiece). Eisner sees ethos as relating to the core values of the school and to that which is deep and fundamental in its life and work. Eisner makes the important point that there can be an important gap between what the school espouses with respect to ethos and what the ethos of the school actually is, and this potential gap is addressed in an interesting way by Donnelly (2000).

Donnelly makes a distinction between a 'positivist' and an 'antipositivist' viewpoint in relation to ethos. The 'positivist' viewpoint holds that ethos is ' ... an objective phenomenon, existing independently of the people and social events in an orga-nisation' (2000, p. 135). At first sight, this formulation brings to mind Ryle's illustration of the notion of a 'category mistake' via the case of a person who has been introduced to the functions of the various players and officials in the game of cricket (bowlers, batsmen, fielders, umpires, scorers and the like) and then proceeds to ask whose role it is to exercise *esprit de corps*. As Ryle points out, team spirit is not a determinate task to be undertaken, but ' ... roughly, the keenness with which each of the tasks is performed, and performing a task keenly is not performing two tasks' (1949, p. 17).[3] Similarly, we might wonder whether a 'category mistake' is involved in the identification of an ethos as an independently existing objective phenomenon. In fact, Donnelly is drawing attention to an important aspect of an ethos: its formal documentary expression by an authority as a set of prescriptive values for a school, as in the case of ecclesiastical authorities in the specification of a 'Catholic ethos' for Catholic schools in Northern Ireland. Donnelly is concerned to investigate the relationship between such formal expressions of ethos (an 'aspirational ethos') and an 'anti-positivist' perspective on ethos which focuses upon ethos in the lived reality of classrooms and schools emerging *inter alia* in social interaction. One of Donnelly's main concerns is to explore the relationship between formal and real expressions of ethos and the tensions and contradictions between the two in a Catholic and in a Grant-Maintained Integrated school in Northern Ireland.

Needless to say, in trying to achieve a greater clarity about the notion of an ethos, there is no question of searching for a single 'correct' meaning to which appeal can be made, but rather a task of attempting to embrace, in as full a way as possible, a range of meanings of the term which can yield a persuasive definition with practical uses and benefits in its application to educational influence. The following account is therefore offered in a preliminary way as a basis for further discussion, conscious of its potential limitations and difficulties.

At the most general level, an ethos can be regarded as the prevalent or char-acteristic tone, spirit or sentiment informing an identifiable entity involving human life and interaction (a 'human environment' in the broadest sense) such as a nation, a community, an age, a literature, an institution, an event and so forth. An ethos is evaluative in some sense and is manifested in many aspects of the entity in question and *via* many modes of pervasive influence. The influence of an ethos is seen in the shaping of human perceptions, attitudes, beliefs, dispositions and the like in a distinctive way which is implicated in that which is (in some sense) established. Although ethos most commonly refers to some-thing which is experienced, an 'intended' ethos as well as an 'experienced' ethos can be pointed to in the case of an ethos which is deliberately shaped or stipulated.

In relation to classrooms and schools, a number of aspects of 'ethos' can be usefully identified for specific attention. An important general preliminary point is that in the context of classrooms and schools, an ethos comes up for assessment in terms of the extent to which it embodies and facilitates educative influence. The potential tension between an 'intended' (or 'aspirational') ethos and an 'experienced' ethos is therefore an inescapable part of ethos in an educational context.

A number of related features of an ethos in relation to classrooms and schools are worthy of attention:

(i)   An ethos in both the 'intended' and 'experienced' sense is value-laden. Whilst it makes sense to speak of a 'toxic' *culture* (see, for example, Solvason, 2005, pp. 90–91) the notion of a 'toxic' *ethos* sounds odd. In the context of education, the values of an ethos are derived from the evaluative weight of education itself (see (ii) below). The evaluative ladenness of ethos in general is discernible in the Greek roots of the notion in 'character' and 'ethics'. For Aristotle, ethos was one of three main rhetorical styles, the others being logos and pathos. In ethos, an appeal is made to the audience from the character of the speaker revealed in certain specific qualities of character, such as good sense, good moral character and good will. An Aristotelian perspective on the evaluative basis of ethos in its application to classrooms and schools would similarly intimate the need for an ethos in these contexts to embody certain specific values. In present use, however, the term ethos tends to retain a general but unspecific evaluative force. This is not, however, a clear-cut matter, and forms of *de facto* influence which are negatively evaluated are sometimes referred to in terms of (a prevailing) ethos.

(ii)   An ethos in both the 'intended' or 'aspirational' sense, and in the 'experienced' sense, must, if it is to be explicitly justified educationally, relate the elements of the ethos to an articulated and defensible set of educational aims and values and to an overall vision of education. Recent work by John White and others has sought to align the various subjects of the national curriculum with the aims and values now stated for the curriculum as a whole (White, 2004). A similar process of alignment with educational aims and values needs to take place in relation to both the 'intended' and the 'experienced' senses of the ethos of classrooms and schools. A central matter for consideration here is the extent to which given ethos elements are genuinely expressive of defensible educational aims and values. There is no suggestion, here, of course, that this process can be conducted in a merely theoretical manner, much less that philosophical theorising can be applied to educational practice in a straightforward way (on the role of philosophy in relation to educational policy and practice see McLaughlin, 2000).

(iii)   An ethos in both the 'intended' and the 'experienced' sense must aspire to forms of coherence and congruence. Forms of inconsistency, conflict, fragmentation and disharmony within an ethos, in either sense of the term, can undermine it. This is not to claim, however, that forms of conflict and disharmony cannot be embodied within an ethos. An ethos, for example, can embody a coherent approach to the resolution of actual or potential conflict and disharmony. Conflict can, however, emerge between different 'experienced' ethoses in the same context (see (iv) below) and between 'intended' and 'experienced' ethos. Donnelly, for example, holds that processes relating to ethos are characterised by inherent contradictions and inconsistencies (2000, p. 150), such as those relating to gaps between the religious aspirations contained in the formal statement of the ethos of a Catholic school on the one hand and the actual reactions of teachers and students to these aspirations on the other. For Donnelly, ethos in the 'experienced' sense is ' ... a *negotiated* process whereby individuals come to some agreement about what should and should not be prioritised' (*op. cit.*, p. 150). Donnelly usefully draws attention to three dimensions of ethos relating to the extent to which members of a school embrace an ethos in a superficial or a deep way: 'aspirational ethos', 'ethos of outward attachment' and 'ethos of inward attachment' (*op. cit.*, p. 151). An ethos of 'inward attachment' is most expressive of the coherence and congruence to which ethos aspires. (For unease about the notion of an 'imposed ethos' see Hogan, 1984; Williams, 2000, pp. 81–82.)

(iv) An ethos in the 'experienced' sense must be potent and pervasive in the sense that it must exert a discernible influence within the 'atmosphere' and climate of classrooms and schools: it must have an 'impact' (on this see Dancy, 1979). In this matter, however, it is important to note there may be several ethoses competing for attention within a given school either at the level of the whole school or of sub-units within it, which are not all necessarily harmonious with each other (on conflicts of these kinds see, for example, Solvason, 2005, pp. 88–91). Tomlinson *et al.*, in their study *The School Effect*, concluded that it was the sub-units of schools, such as departments and classrooms, which had the greatest significance on whether the distinctive needs of students from ethnic minority backgrounds were being met: the school as a whole was less significant (Tomlinson *et al.*, 1989). An ethos in the 'experienced' sense aspires to pervasive influence, but this may not be straightforwardly achieved for the school as a whole.

(v) An ethos in the 'experienced' sense has a given, established or enduring feel to it in that it aspires to become 'taken for granted'. Aristotle in his *Ethics* (Aristotle, 1976, Bk 1.2) points out that what constitutes an ethos arises spontaneously from natural habits; from what has become second nature in one's dealings with one's associates (quoted in Hogan, 1984, p. 700). The force of this point is contained in Allder's observation that an 'ethos' is concerned with norms and not exceptions: isolated examples of rudeness and unkindness do not undermine an overall ethos of warm relationships within a school (Allder, 1993, p. 66). This is not, of course, to deny that a school ethos is constructed and reconstructed (even in radical ways). However, reconstructive efforts, if they are not to aim at the construction of a radically new replacement ethos, must be conducted in a way which is sensitive to the imperatives of givenness (on the difficulties of developing and changing a distinct ethos see, for example, Solvason, 2005, pp. 91–92). Haydon points out that while an 'ethical environment' may and should change, it should not be too fragile and needs to be sustained (Haydon, 2006, ch. 4).

(vi) It is characteristic of an ethos in the 'experienced' sense that it exerts (much of) its influence in an indirect and sometimes nontransparent and even unconscious way. This point is expressed rather roughly by Allder in her claim that an ethos is recognised in an experiential rather than a cognitive level (1993, p. 69). This general point can be accepted without subscribing to any overly simple distinction between the 'experiential' and the 'cognitive'. An ethos tends to 'speak for itself' and does not require constant and extensive articulation. There are clear resonances between the notion of an 'ethos' and Bourdieu's notion of a 'habitus': the deep-structured cultural dispositions within a community or an institution, which are part of primary socialisation and habit formation, perhaps in an unconscious way (Grace, 2002, p. 37). This is not to deny, however, that some ethoses embody an invitation to articulation as in, for example, an ethos related to a form of moral education which places a great emphasis on the clarification of matters of principle. Having drawn attention to some features of the concept of ethos in the context of classrooms and schools, I now turn to the educative influence of ethos and the difficulties and challenges to which it gives rise.

3. The Educative Influence of Ethos: Some Fundamental Questions

Many of the concerns of teachers and educational leaders about the ethos of classrooms and schools, in both the 'intended' and 'experienced' sense of ethos, focus upon what can be roughly described as the 'content' of an ethos. A common example of concern here relates to the potentially undue salience in ethos of values, imperatives and processes drawn from business and the market (on this matter see, for example, Pring, 2000). Processes of 'audit' and review with respect to the ethos of classrooms and schools are naturally concerned with particular matters relating to ethos which are apt for assessment, alteration, improvement or innovation. The leading questions in concerns of these kinds are of the form: What kind of 'intended' ethos do we want to have in our classrooms and schools, what is the nature of our existing 'experienced' ethos and in what respects does it match up to, or fail to match up to, our intentions? Posing and answering questions of these kinds is clearly vital, and apparently straightforward. However, such questions presuppose that the nature and importance of the educative influence exerted by an ethos is already clear. This more fundamental question should not be ignored, not least because attention to it can reap benefits in terms of the posing and answering of questions of a more directly practical kind.

Fundamental questions relating to the nature and importance of various forms of educational influence, and to the kinds of achievements with which education is concerned, are not the sole concern of philosophers. Many other forms of critical reflection (of, say, a sociological, psychological and anthropological kind) are highly relevant to such questions, as is the practical reflection and judgement of teachers and educational leaders themselves. The role of philosophy in relation to these questions is a contributory and collaborative one (see McLaughlin, 2000). Philosophy nevertheless has an important part to play in the achievement by teachers, educational leaders (and others) of appropriate forms of critical perspective and judgement with respect to their work, including forms of critical alertness with respect to forms of educational influence and educational achievement. The significance of philosophy in these matters can be briefly illustrated.

The kinds of educational influence which teachers and schools seek to exert upon students relate to many kinds of achievements (in the broad sense of the term) and take a wide range of forms. The kinds of achievement on the part of students which are aimed at include knowledge and understanding of various kinds and levels, dispositions, virtues, qualities of character, emotional responses, tendencies, skills, capacities and so forth. The forms of educational influence through which this range of achievements are aimed at by teachers and schools are similarly varied, including instruction, explanation, questioning, discussing, demonstrating and exemplifying. Two of the major concerns of philosophy with respect to these kinds of achievements and forms of influence is to draw attention to (a) the value-laden nature of the achievements and forms of influence, and need for justification of their pursuit by teachers and schools and (b) the need for a proper understanding of the character of the achievements and modes of influence and the logical and other kinds of relationship between them, as well as the need to avoid ill-conceived and possibly unjustifiable aims and practices at the level of the classroom and school based on conceptual confusions and potential misunderstandings.

With regard to (a), the inherently value-laden nature of educational achievements and forms of influence can be illustrated by reflection upon the notion of 'development' in an educational context. Development can be distinguished from mere *change*. To change is not necessarily to develop. For Hamlyn, what is essential to the notion of development is ' ... the interrelationship between pre-existing conditions, necessary sequence and end-states within a pattern which we see as natural to a given kind of thing ... ' (Hamlyn, 1983, p. 156). The change from an acorn into an oak tree can be regarded as a 'development' because it is characterised by these interrelated elements. Some aspects of change undergone by human beings correspond to this pattern. Certain physical changes (such as the acquisition of height and strength) lead us to speak of the 'physical development' of human beings in a relatively unproblematic way. As in the case of the acorns, the developmental character of the changes can be attributed in virtue of the presence of the interrelated elements of the sort specified by Hamlyn and assessed on largely empirical grounds. Other aspects of human 'development' are, of course, much more problematic because the changes in question are brought about by *learning*. Changes brought about by learning problematise each of the elements specified so far as characteristic of 'development': pre-existing conditions, necessary sequence, end-states and an overall pattern which is 'natural' to a kind of thing. All learning presupposes pre-existing conditions, but these are not necessarily seen in terms of 'potential' embodying a 'teleological blueprint' for an end-state realisable through propitious 'unfolding'. Nor can learning be seen unproblematically as involving or requiring a transition through a 'necessary sequence' of engagement, understanding and achievement, as controversies about developmental learning theories of the sort developed by Piaget amply demonstrate. Crucially, much learning cannot be seen as aimed at, or terminated in, a pre-specifiable and determinate end-point.

Learning is potentially open-ended. Nor is it possible to specify with any great degree of confidence what is 'natural' to 'the kind of thing' a human being is (on complexities in the notion of 'human nature' see, for example, Parekh, 2000, ch. 4). The attribution and assessment of 'development' in the case of human learning is therefore implicated in *normative* and not merely empirical considerations. Normative judgements in the attribution and assessment of human development are involved in such matters as the 'potential' which human beings are taken to have, the processes of learning which are seen as appropriate, the aims and direction of the learning (not an 'end-state' in any very precise sense) and in judgements about the kinds of 'things' that human beings are taken to be. The *value* of the kinds of learning in which human beings might engage (both *what* is being learnt and *how* it is being learnt) therefore enters into the picture. Education involves the wide-ranging shaping of persons in many ways and invites and requires attention to the justificatory issues involved in the development by teachers and schools of persons *of a certain sort* (on this see, for example, Pring, 1984, ch. 2).

With regard to (b), philosophers have long been active in trying to ease conceptual confusions and potential misunderstandings relating to the character of a wide range of educational achievements and modes of influence, including 'skills', 'competences', 'multiple intelligences', 'emotional literacy and emotional intelligence', 'selfesteem', 'active learning', 'negotiated learning', 'learning styles', and the like. In each case philosophers have drawn attention to conceptual confusions and potential misunderstandings about the achievements and modes of influence in question which have significant implications for defensible aims and practices at the level of the classroom and school. In some cases, philosophers have suggested that certain conceptualisations of achievements and modes of influence are incoherent and potentially damaging in terms of educational practice.

It is important to note that the philosophical concern with (a) and (b) should not be read as implying that the life and work of a classroom or school should or could be seen as wholly and solely based on theoretical considerations, let alone philosophical ones. The evaluative questions involved in (a), for example, can never be completely clarified and brought to bear on practice in a straightforward way, and in relation to (b) it is not only the case that there is no necessary connection between good theory and good practice (which is widely acknowledged) but also that there is no necessary connection between bad theory and bad practice: good practice can flourish despite bad theory.

How can the considerations relating to (a) and (b) be brought to bear on the specific question of ethos in the context of classrooms and schools? I will consider this matter in reverse order, beginning with (b).

4. Ethos in Classrooms and Schools: Educational Achievements and Modes of Influence

Several features of an ethos noted in section 2, for example, (v) its established and 'taken for granted' character and (vi) the nontransparent way in which it exerts its influence harmonises with certain concerns and emphases of Aristotle. As noted earlier, both the kinds of educational achievements apt for attention by an ethos and the modes of influence which an ethos exerts are consistent with broadly Aristotelian accounts of these matters. In these accounts the forms of educational achievement seen as particularly apt for development via an ethos are qualities of character and virtue, dispositions, sensitivities of perception and qualities of judgement, most notably practical wisdom or *phronesis*. The nature of the judgement involved in *phronesis* requires practical knowledge of the good, together with intelligent and personally engaged sensitivity to situations and individuals, including oneself, in making judgements about what constitutes an appropriate expression of the good in a given circumstance. Practical judgement of this kind is inherently supple, non-formulable and non-codifiable, although the extent to which principles of some kind are involved has been the subject of much debate. Aristotle's invocation of the 'mean' as illuminative of what should properly guide judgement is well known:

> Virtue is a character state concerned with choice, lying in the mean relative to us, being determined by reason and the way the person of practical wisdom would determine it. (Aristotle, 1976, 1107a1)

The particular kind of educative influence exerted by an ethos can best be seen in terms of the provision of a context in which a range of forms of educative influence and learning emphasised as significant by Aristotle can flourish, including imitation, habituation, training in feeling, attention and perception, induction into patterns of action and habit, forms of guidance and experience, and exemplification. For Aristotle, human development requires initiation into a culture in which qualities of personhood and character are recognised and practised. It is important to note that all these processes cannot be reduced to mere socialisation (on this matter see, for example, Carr, 1991, ch. 5).

Space precludes a fuller discussion at this point of these neglected forms of achievement and influence, both in their specifically Aristotelian form and more generally (on these matters see, for example, Carr, 1991; Carr and Steutel, 1999; Curren, 2000; Haydon, 2006; Lovibond, 2002; Lovlie, 1997; McLaughlin and Halstead, 1999).

Much greater reflection is needed on the kinds of educational achievement with which ethos is concerned, the specific aspects of the educational aims and values of the classroom and school with which it is particularly related and the modes via which its influence is exerted. Such reflection should lead to the realisation of the educational importance of ethos and its scope. The truth that the educative influence exerted by 'ethos' *cannot be confined to* the formally taught curriculum should not blind us to the role which 'ethos' does play across all aspects of the life and work of schools, including the formally taught curriculum. Three interesting aspects of educational influence exerted by ethos are worthy of brief emphasis here, each of which illuminates aspects of its educative importance.

First, ethos frequently exerts educative influence in relation to matters which cannot be explicitly articulated. For example, in his essay 'Learning and Teaching'

Michael Oakeshott points to the complex and living inheritance which teachers pass on to their pupils, the nature of which requires not merely the acquisition by students of information (which can be communicated by instruction) but also of judgement, involving the acquisition of the intellectual virtues and of 'style'(which can only be imparted unobtrusively in ways which are highly related to an ethos: tones of voice, gestures, asides, oblique utterances and by example) (Oakeshott, 1990). Second, and relatedly, an ethos gives rise to neglected questions about the broad range of kinds of example which we expect teachers to give in classrooms and schools (on these matters and the complexities which arise in relation to expectations concerning teacher example see McLaughlin, 2004, cf. Hansen, 1997). Third, an ethos is frequently a necessary counterpart to more explicit and systematic forms of teaching and learning. Kohlberg's acknowledgement of the necessity of a 'Just Community' within which to situate his programmes of moral education are an illustration of this point (see Reed, 1997, esp. chs 7, 8).[4] It should be noted, however, that an ethos is not a substitute for more systematic and explicit teaching and learning (on the need for such teaching and learning in personal, social and health education and in citizenship education in addition to attention to considerations which can be described broadly in terms of ethos see Office for Standards in Education, 2005a, 2005b).

Appropriate forms of reflection about the nature of the kinds of educational achievement with which ethos is concerned, the specific aspects of the educational aims and values of the classroom and school to which it is particularly related and the modes via which that influence is exerted should enable attention to be focused more precisely on a range of neglected matters of considerable educational significance.

5. Ethos in Classrooms and Schools: Values

Several features of an ethos noted in section 2, most notably (i) the general value-laden nature of an ethos and (ii) the need for an ethos to be justified with reference to an articulated and defensible set of educational aims and values, together with the discussion in (a) in section 3 of the fuller implications of the normative character of educative influence in general brings into clear focus the difficult question of clarifying and justifying the ethos of a given classroom and school in evaluative terms. Attention to evaluative influence in relation to ethos will enable *inter alia* matters of incoherence, incongruity and conflict in relation to ethos (see (iii) and (iv) in section 2) to be addressed. However, the difficulty and potentially controversial nature of evaluative judgement in relation to ethos is brought into focus when it is remembered that what is at stake is the formation of persons in a wide-ranging way. While Aristotle's analysis of the achievements and modes of influence involved in ethos may be found convincing, his own detailed account of the virtues which it should promote is unlikely to compel contemporary acceptance.

The task for teachers and educational leaders in getting to grips with the evaluative aspects of an ethos is complicated not only by the inherent complexities involved in getting to grips with an ethos itself, in both its 'intended' and 'experienced' senses, but also in complexities involved in getting to grips with educational values in a coherent and practical way at classroom and school level (on this matter, see, for example, McLaughlin, 1994).

One prominent difficulty which arises for the notion of an ethos from an evaluative point of view is that much recent educational debate has focused upon the need for schools to exert complex forms of evaluative influence on their students if that influence is to be justifiable in the face of the demands of legitimate plurality. In the common school, for example, I have argued that the school has a responsibility not to promote a secular view of life as a whole or an attitude of relativism towards differences, but to engage with matters of moral texture and complexity (McLaughlin, 2003a). However, this general perspective leaves the common school with dilemmas about the kind of ethos it is going to promote in relation to this educative task, given that an ethos must be in some sense substantive (and may not therefore be apt for the exercise of the subtle and nuanced educative influence which the demands of moral texture and complexity requires) and that it exerts its influence in an indirect and sometimes non-transparent and even unconscious way (see (v) and (vi) in section 2 above). Kenneth Strike addresses this problem in terms of raising critical questions about the kinds of school community which a common school can legitimately promote (Strike, 2000; cf. Gereluk, 2005). Although it might be considered that a faith school may have fewer problems in this regard, such schools need to face parallel, if different, complexities in the educational influence which they can exert (on this see McLaughlin, 1999). Concerns of these general kinds give rise to critical questions about the forms of character education in which schools of various kinds can legitimately engage (on this matter see, for example, Arthur, 2003; McLaughlin and Halstead, 1999; cf. DfEE, 2001, 4.76–4.79).

A further difficulty is that, even if educational values can be brought into adequate critical focus, the derivation of implications for ethos (or for other aspects of the life and work of the classroom and school) is not unproblematic: other mediating considerations come into play (see, however, Fielding, 1988).

A major conclusion which emerges from this part of the discussion is that consideration of the evaluative dimension of ethos at classroom and school level needs to be much broader and deeper than the rather superficial examination of necessarily schematic and abbreviated 'ethos statements' which prevail in many professional contexts today.

6. Conclusion

The educational importance of ethos in the context of classrooms and schools is manifest. Much fuller critical attention is needed to the meaning of ethos in these contexts, to the kinds of educative achievement and influence which are characteristically associated with ethos, to the specific aspects of the educational aims and values of the classroom and school with which ethos is particularly related and to the exploration and justification of the evaluative aspects of ethos. The present discussion has offered a preliminary consideration of these questions. Appropriate and sustained engagement with these questions at the level of the classroom and school by teachers and educational leaders should combat a tendency to deal with matters of ethos in an unduly superficial way. Any such engagement with such issues on the part of teachers and educational leaders must not merely be a form of theorising, but part of a process of the improvement of practice via forms of pedagogic wisdom, itself requiring a form of ethos for the practice of teaching and educational leadership which repays careful attention.[5]

References

Allder, M. (1993) The meaning of 'school ethos', *Westminster Studies in Education*, 16, 59–69.

Aristotle (1976) *The Ethics of Aristotle. The Nicomachean Ethics* (revised edition) (London, Penguin Books).

Arthur, J. (2003) *Education with Character. The Moral Economy of Schooling* (London, RoutledgeFalmer).

Bronfenbrenner, U. (1974) *Two Worlds of Childhood. US and USSR* (Harmondsworth, Penguin Education).

Canavan, N. and Monahan, L. (2000) *School Culture and Ethos. Releasing the Potential. A resource pack to enable schools to access, articulate and apply ethos values* (Dublin, Marino Institute of Education).

Carr, D. (1991) *Educating the Virtues. An Essay on the Philosophical Psychology of Moral Development and Education* (London, Routledge).

Carr, D. and Steutel, J. (Eds) (1999) *Virtue Ethics and Moral Education* (London, Routledge).

Catholic Education Service (1999) *Evaluating the Distinctive Nature of a Catholic School*, Revised Edition www.cesew.org.uk accessed 4 June 2005.

Curren, R.R. (2000) *Aristotle on the Necessity of Public Education* (Lanham, Maryland, Rowman and Littlefield).

Dancy, J. (1979) The concept of the ethos of a school, *Perspectives 1* (University of Exeter).

Department for Education and Employment (2001) *Schools: Building on Success*, Cm 5050 (London, The Stationery Office).

Department for Education and Skills (2001) *Schools Achieving Success* (London, The Stationery Office).

Donnelly, C. (2000) In pursuit of school ethos, *British Journal of Educational Studies*, 48 (2), 134–54.

Eisner, E. (1994) *Ethos and Education Perspectives. A Series of Papers on Values and Education* (Scottish Consultative Council on the Curriculum) www.ltscotland.org.uk accessed 4 June 2005.

Fielding, M. (1988) Democracy and fraternity: towards a new paradigm for the comprehensive school. In H. Lauder and S. Brown (Eds) *Education in Search of a Future* (London, Routledge).

Furlong, C. and Monahan, L. (Eds) (2000) *School Culture and Ethos. Cracking the Code* (Dublin, Marino Institute of Education).

Gereluk, D. (2005) Communities in a changing educational environment, *British Journal of Educational Studies*, 53 (1), 4–18.

Glover, D. and Coleman, M. (2005) School culture, climate and ethos: interchangeable or distinctive concepts? *Journal of In-Service Education* 31 (2), 251–71.

Grace, G. (2002) *Catholic Schools. Mission, Markets and Morality* (London, Routledge Falmer).

Hamlyn, D. (1983) The concept of development. In D. Hamlyn, *Perception, Learning and the Self. Essays in the Philosophy of Psychology* (London, Routledge and Kegan Paul).

Hansen, D.T. (1997) Being a good influence. In N.C. Burbules and D.T. Hansen (Eds) *Teaching and its Predicaments* (Boulder, Westview Press).

Haydon, G. (2006) *Education, Philosophy and the Ethical Environment* (London, RoutledgeFalmer).

Hogan, P. (1984) The question of ethos in schools, *The Furrow*, 35 (11), 693–704.

Lovibond, S. (2002) *Ethical Formation* (Cambridge MA, Harvard University Press).

Lovlie, L. (1997) The Use of Example in Moral Education, *Journal of Philosophy of Education*, 31 (1), 409–25.

Mclaughlin, T.H. (1994) Values, Coherence and the School, *Cambridge Journal of Education*, 24 (3), 453–450.

——(1999) Distinctiveness and the Catholic School. Balanced Judgement and the Temptations of Commonality. In J.C. Conroy (Ed.) *Catholic Education. Inside-Out, Outside-In* (Dublin, Veritas).

——(2000) Philosophy and Educational Policy: possibilities, tensions and tasks, *Journal of Educational Policy*, 15 (4), 441–57.

——(2003a) The burdens and dilemmas of common schooling. In K. McDONOUGH and W. Feinberg (Eds) *Citizenship Education in Liberal-Democratic Societies. Teaching for Cosmopolitan Values and Collective Identities* (Oxford, University Press).

——(2003b) Teaching as a practice and a community of practice. The limits of commonality and the demands of diversity, *Journal of Philosophy of Education*, 37 (2), 339–52.

——(2004) Philosophy, values and schooling: principles and predicaments of teacher example. In W. Aiken and J. Haldane (Eds) *Philosophy and its Public Role. Essays in Ethics, Politics, Society and Culture* (Charlottesville, VA and Exeter, Imprint Academic), 69–83.

Mclaughlin, T.H. and Halstead, J.M. (1999) Education in character and virtue. In J.M. Halstead and T.H. Mclaughlin (Eds) *Education in Morality* (London, Routledge).

Mortimore, P., Sammons, P., Stoll, L., Lewis, D. and ECOB, R. (1988) *School Matters. The Junior Years* (Wells, Open Books).

Oakeshott, M. (1990) Learning and teaching. In T. Fuller (Ed.) *The Voice of Liberal Learning. Michael Oakeshott on Education* (New Haven, Yale University Press).

Office for Standards in Education (2005a) *Personal, Social and Health Education in Secondary Schools*, HMI 2311 www.ofsted.gov.uk accessed 4 June 2005.

——(2005b) *Citizenship in Secondary Schools: evidence from OFSTED Inspections*, HMI 2335 www.ofsted.gov.uk accessed 4 June 2005.

Parekh, B. (2000) *Rethinking Multiculturalism. Cultural Diversity and Political Theory* (London, Macmillan).

Pring, R. (1984) *Personal and Social Education in the Curriculum. Concepts and Content* (London, Hodder and Stoughton).

——(2000) School culture and ethos: towards an understanding. In FURLONG, C. and MONAHAN, L. (Eds) (2000) *School Culture and Ethos. Cracking the Code* (Dublin, Marino Institute of Education).

Qualifications and Curriculum Authority (2000a) *Citizenship at Key Stages 3 and 4. Initial Guidance for Schools* (London, QCA).

232 The Educative Importance of Ethos

——(2000b) *Personal, Social and Health Education at Key Stages 3 and 4. Initial Guidance for Schools* (London, QCA).

Reed, D.R.C. (1997) *Following Kohlberg. Liberalism and the Practice of Democratic Community* (Notre Dame, University of Notre Dame Press).

Rutter, M., Maughan, B., Mortimore, P., Ouston, J. and Smith, A. (1979) *Fifteen Thousand Hours. Secondary Schools and their Effects on Children* (London, Open Books).

Ryle, G. (1949) *The Concept of Mind* (London, Hutchinson).

Scottish Office Education Department and HM Inspectors of Schools (1992a) *Using Ethos Indicators in Primary School Self-Evaluation. Taking Account of the Views of Pupils, Parents and Teachers. School Development Planning Support Materials* (Scottish Office Education Department).

——(1992b) *Using Ethos Indicators in Secondary School Self-Evaluation. Taking Account of the Views of Pupils, Parents and Teachers. School Development Planning Support Materials* (Scottish Office Education Department).

Solvason, C. (2005) Investigating specialist school ethos ... or do you mean culture? *Educational Studies*, 31 (1), 85–94.

Strike, K. (2000) Schools as communities: four metaphors, three models and a dilemma or two, *Journal of Philosophy of Education*, 34 (4), 617–42.

Tomlinson, S., Hogarth, T. and Thomas, H. (1989) *The School Effect. A Study of Multi-Racial Comprehensives* (London, Policy Studies Institute).

White, J. (Ed.) (2004) *Re-thinking the School Curriculum. Values, Aims and Purposes* (London, RoutledgeFalmer).

Williams, K. (2000) Understanding ethos – a philosophical and literary exploration in Furlong, C. and Monahan, L. (Eds) (2000) *School Culture and Ethos. Cracking the Code* (Dublin, Marino Institute of Education).

Notes

1 Allder's use of the terms 'frontier' and 'connecting' words is drawn from the work of the philosopher of religion Paul van Buren. For complexities in the relationship between 'frontier' and 'connecting' words see Allder, 1993, pp. 62–63.

2 Graham Haydon is surely right to point out, for example, that no school ethos could be wholly separate from the school system of which it is part (Haydon, 2006).

3 I owe this example to Jeremy Hayward.

4 Reed argues that Kohlberg's work on the construction and practice of democratic community ('the just community') is in fact the most important and enduring element in Kohlberg's theory of moral development as a whole (see 1997, esp. chs 7, 8).

5 On this notion of 'communities of practice' in relation to this matter see, for example, McLaughlin, 2003b.

17 The Very Idea of a University: Aristotle, Newman and Us

A. MacIntyre

2009

Author

Alasdair MacIntyre is one of the most distinguished philosophers of our time. He is a British philosopher and although he has written influential works on theology, Marxism, rationality, metaphysics, ethics, and the history of philosophy, he has also directly addressed questions of education. He gave the R. S. Peters Lecture on 'Education and Values' in 1985 at the Institute of Education, University of London and in 2002 published in the *Journal of Philosophy of Education*. MacIntyre is a key figure in the recent surge of interest in virtue ethics, which identifies the central question of morality as having to do with the habits and knowledge concerning how to live a good life. His approach seeks to demonstrate that good judgment emanates from good character. He has been a powerful influence on many educators.

Introduction

MacIntyre converted to Roman Catholicism in the early 1980s, and now works against the background of what he calls an 'Augustinian Thomist approach to moral philosophy'. He has made a personal intellectual journey from Marxism to Catholicism and from Aristotle to Aquinas, and he is now one of the pre-eminent Thomist political philosophers. This article, *The Very Idea of a University: Aristotle, Newman and Us* (57, 4: 347–62), was given as a lecture at the University of Oxford in 2009 and in some ways was an extension of an article published in *Commonweal* in 2006, *The End of Education: The Fragmentation of the American University*. Essentially both articles ask the same question: 'What should be the distinctive calling of the American Catholic university or college here and now?' to which he answers, 'It should be to challenge its secular counterparts through recovering, both for them and for itself, a less fragmented conception of what an education beyond high school should be, by identifying what has gone badly wrong with even the best of secular universities. From a Catholic point of view the contemporary secular university is not at fault because it is not Catholic. It is at fault insofar as it is not a university.' MacIntyre notes that in the contemporary university, 'The fragmentation of enquiry and the fragmentation of understanding are taken for granted.'

In *God, Philosophy, Universities: A Selective History of the Catholic Philosophical Tradition* (2009), which was a series of lectures given at Notre Dame University, MacIntyre argues that not until John Henry Newman, who was an Aristotelian even before his conversion, was there a significant development in the Catholic philosophical tradition. He devotes a chapter to the thought of John Henry Newman, whose *The Idea of a University* deeply informs MacIntyre's thesis. In this book and the article, MacIntyre offers us an integrated overview of the unity and development of the Catholic philosophical tradition and argues that this philosophy can only flourish in educational institutions organized by it, not in contemporary universities organized as 'business Co-operations' aimed at selling a product fitted to student and corporate demand.

Related articles in this volume and the *Journal* are: *The Educative Importance of Ethos* (page 215 in this volume) and *Return to the crossroads: Maritain fifty years on* (43, 2: 162–78).

The Very Idea of a University: Aristotle, Newman, and Us

by *Alasdair MacIntyre,* University of Notre Dame, Indiana USA

I

The case that hostile critics have urged against Newman's *The Idea of a University* is impressive. J.M. Roberts wrote nearly twenty years ago that 'it is no longer possible to write a book with such a title ... no general doctrine of universities is possible' ('*The Idea of a University* revisited' in *Newman after a Hundred Years,* edd. Ian Ker and Alan G. Hill, Oxford: Clarendon Press, 1990, p. 222). And Bill Reddings later argued that Newman's conception of the university curriculum reflected a kind of literary culture that 'held together diverse specialities in a unity', a type of culture that no longer exists and that it is impossible to recreate (*The University in Ruins,* Cambridge, Mass.: Harvard University Press, 1996, p. 167). Those two critics could not have been more at odds with each other, Roberts being a distinguished member of the British University establishment, yet the two of them in agreement on Newman's irrelevance.

What is held to make Newman irrelevant to the concerns of those now at work in universities are three of his central affirmations, each entailing the denial of a conviction central to the functioning of contemporary universities. So why does that make Newman's claims irrelevant rather than just false? It is because, on the view taken by his critics, it is not only that Newman's idea of a university fails to hold true of contemporary universities, but that anyone who thought that it might hold true would have grossly misunderstood the nature and functioning of the contemporary university. To criticise contemporary universities from Newman's standpoint would be, on their view, like blaming a jet engine for not having the excellences of a windmill.

What then are the three matters on which what Newman says is taken to be at once false and irrelevant? The first is his conception of the unity of knowledge, or more accurately of the unity of understanding, of how each academic discipline contributes the knowledge of some particular aspect or part of the universe, so that in the search for understanding we need to study not only a number of different disciplines – physics, physiology, history, literature, mathematics, psychology – but also how each of these bears on the others, what the relationships between them are (*The Idea of a University,* ed. Martin J. Svaglic, Notre Dame, Indiana: University of Notre Dame Press, 1982, Discourse III, pp. 33–35 and Discourse

VI, p. 103). Newman was careful to emphasise that it is not just the study of a number of disciplines that educates (Discourse VI, p. 98). What educates is knowledge of several disciplines, such that one comes to understand both the indispensability of each for an overall understanding of the order of things and the limitations of each. The superficial generalist is as much the product of a defective education as the narrow specialist.

It is a commonplace that Newman in 1852 not only did not foresee the rise of the modem research university, first in Germany, then in the United States, but took it for granted that research was a task for institutions other than universities. What puts Newman in opposition to the research university, however, is not just this but, above all, his claim that intensive specialisation and narrowness of intellectual focus deform the mind, that the qualities characteristic of the minds of successful researchers are qualities incompatible with those of an educated mind. This claim follows from Newman's affirmation of his conception of the unity of knowledge, of the unity of understanding, together with his view of the effects of the academic division of labour. 'There can be no doubt,' Newman wrote, 'that every art is improved by confining the professor of it to that single study. But, *although the art itself is advanced by this concentration of mind in its service, the individual who is confined to it goes back*' (Discourse VII, p. 127).

That you may tend to injure and deform your mind by developing a narrowness of vision and a one-sidedness in judgment, if you devote yourself wholeheartedly to a life of scholarly research, is a thought that the protagonists of the twenty-first-century prestigious research university are scarcely capable of entertaining. We might exaggerate somewhat, if we formulated Newman's view in contemporary terms by saying that the possession of a Ph. D. or a D. Phil. is too often the mark of a miseducated mind, but we would come close enough to it to make it clear why Newman must seem not just irrelevant, but offensive to such protagonists.

Consider now a second way in which Newman is held to have disqualified himself from participation in our debates. He insists not only that theology is among the disciplines that must be taught in any university worthy of the name, but that it is the key discipline, that unless theology is given its due place in the curriculum, the relationships between disciplines will be distorted and misunderstood.

Since nobody in the twenty-first century thinks that an institution from which theology is absent cannot legitimately call itself a university, and since, even in universities where theology is taught, it is treated as simply one more specialised discipline among others, Newman's claims must sound eccentric to contemporary ears. We might be tempted to say that, for the vast majority of our academic contemporaries, it is their belief that universities are secular institutions that leads them to reject Newman's thesis about the place of theology in the curriculum. Yet Newman too held that universities are secular institutions. His claim is that it is *qua* secular institution that the university needs what he takes to be the secular discipline of theology. So what can this need be? Newman's answer returns us to his conception of the unity of understanding.

Without a recognition of theology as the key discipline, the university curriculum, so Newman argued, will disintegrate into a fragmented multiplicity of disciplines, each self-defining, each claiming autonomy in its own sphere. Some disciplines will of course continue to draw on each other, as physics does on mathematics, geology on chemistry. But there will be no conception of a whole to which each discipline contributes as a part. And of course this is just how it has become in the contemporary university, a condition one of whose symptoms is the great difficulty that university teachers generally have nowadays in arriving at agreement on what, if any, general education requirements should be imposed on undergraduates. University teachers are no longer members of an educated public constituted by agreements on what books every educated person needs to have read and what skills every educated person needs to possess. For now there is no such public inside or outside the university, as Bill Reddings rightly insisted. I am not suggesting that the principal cause of this condition is the absence of theology from the curriculum or its treatment as just one more specialised discipline. But it would have been Newman's view that the fragmentation of our curriculum is a condition that needs to be remedied and that only an acknowledgment of theology as the key unifying discipline can adequately remedy it.

Newman therefore with his judgments that the knowledge of God is a part of our secular knowledge and that such knowledge is the key to understanding affronts the secularised thinkers of our time, just as he affronted the secularising thinkers of his own. Part of what affronts them is that Newman was well aware that belief that God exists is contestable and that there are no knockdown arguments, equally compelling to every intelligent person, for the existence of God. But it is characteristic of contemporary unbelievers to believe that, only if they were offered some knockdown argument whereby belief in God would be incontestable, would they be rationally entitled to believe that God exists. To which the theist has to respond that any being whose existence was thus justified would not be God. It is not that there are not arguments sufficient to justify the theist's assertion of the existence of God, but that the soundness of those arguments will always be open to contestation, just because of the nature of God and of His relation to His creation.

Newman's idea of a university is then taken to be irrelevant to the contemporary university not only because of the overwhelmingly dominant place that the acquisition of specialised knowledge through research has in the contemporary university, and not only because no discipline could be accorded the place that theology has in Newman's scheme, but also because the claim that the knowledge of God is at once contestable and yet genuine and indispensable secular knowledge is at odds with the present day secular university's understanding of the secular.

A third respect in which it seems to many that Newman's views cannot be brought to bear on the contemporary university concerns how a university education is to be justified, both to those who are invited to become its students and to those whom it invites to sustain it financially, whether private and corporate donors or governments. Universities today would not survive, let alone flourish, if they were not able credibly to promise to their students a gateway to superior career possibilities and to donors and governments both a supply of appropriately skilled manpower and research that contributes to economic growth. Universities, that is to say, promise to be cost-effective enterprises. For Newman, by contrast, the activities that contribute to the teaching and learning of a university have goods internal to them that make those activities worthwhile in themselves. It may of course be the case that incidentally universities do contribute to career success and economic growth. But, on Newman's view, a university can succeed in both these respects and yet fail as a university. So there are three major issues that put Newman at odds with the contemporary research university's understanding of its mission: its pursuit of highly specialised knowledge, the secular university's understanding of what it is to be secular, and the university's self-justification by appeal to considerations of social utility. If we recognise that, given these three characteristics, no contemporary university could exemplify anything like Newman's idea of a university, should we simply agree with Roberts and Reddings in taking Newman's claims to be not only false, but also irrelevant?

II

I want to suggest three lines of thought which separately and jointly give us reason to take Newman's central claims seriously. Each of them begins from asking a set of Aristotelian questions and ends with an answer drawn from Newman. And about this we should not be surprised. For it was Newman who declared that 'while we are men, we cannot help, to a great extent, being Aristotelian' and that 'In many subject-matters to think correctly is to think like Aristotle' (Discourse V, p. 83). To think *like* Aristotle, for the questions from which I begin are perhaps not Aristotle's own, but they are questions which, if one presses an Aristotelian enquiry beyond a certain point, one is bound to ask. They are also – and Newman's remark on why he is an Aristotelian is very much to the point – questions that are inescapable for any sufficiently reflective human being, so that, even if Newman had never written *The Idea of a University*, we should have been compelled to raise them.

The first is this: What is it that we need to understand, if on some occasion the outcome of our practical deliberations has been perhaps disastrous, or at least very different from what we had expected? What are the different ways in which we may have gone astray? If our conception of practical reasoning is in general Aristotelian, there are several ways in which our deliberations may have been defective. Consider for example the kind of decision that will alter the course of someone's life, perhaps too the lives of others close to her or him, such choices as that to emigrate or not to emigrate *or* to change the land use of one's farm in some drastic way *or* the choice between participating in rebuilding one's town after some natural disaster and starting anew somewhere else.

Bad decisions may result from some failure to identify or rank order correctly the goods at stake in choosing this rather than that. And such failure may in turn derive from some misconception of what the agent's final good *qua* human being is. Or they may result from a failure to identify correctly the actions that in these particular circumstances would have to be undertaken to achieve the relevant goods. These two kinds of error will have been made in the course of formulating the premises of the agent's practical syllogisms. But they are not the only types of error of which we need to beware. For all such practical reasoning, whether successful or not, presupposes two sets of background assumptions about the natural and social contexts in which the reasoning and the actions that flow from that reasoning take place. Each of these types of assumption can also be a source of practical failure. What are they?

There are first of all assumptions about the present and future stability or otherwise of different aspects of our natural or social environments. So we all of us make assumptions, generally tacit, about the probability or improbability of the occurrence of earthquakes, volcanic eruptions, droughts, floods, disruptions in food supplies, famines, breakdowns in transportation, changes in the crime rate, breakdowns in tribal or family life, the strength or weakness of social and moral traditions, the functioning of the stock market and of the economy more generally – the list goes on and on. A second set of assumptions are about how others in the present or future will be likely to respond to our actions, so as either to further or to frustrate our intentions. Those – also generally tacit – assumptions concern not just the nature of their decision-making, but also the significance that our actions may have for their decision-making, among them their assumptions about our assumptions about them.

I have noticed in both cases that such assumptions are generally not spelled out. What is of crucial importance for the soundness of our practical reasoning is that we should be able to recognise when some of our assumptions do need to be made explicit and put in question and which type of assumption it is that we need to examine on this or that particular occasion. What would it be to be able to do this and to do it well? It would involve knowing both how to draw on the relevant findings of a range of disciplines and how to evaluate the reliability of those findings. So what kind of education would someone have to have received in order to do this? What kind of mind would such a one have?

It is in trying to answer these questions that we find ourselves returned to Newman's text. For the education of such a one will have to have included a more than superficial engagement with several disciplines, each with its own subject-matter and its own ways of viewing that subject-matter, as, for example, in understanding human beings and their activities we need to treat of them, says Newman, 'as physiologists, or as moral philosophers, or as writers of economics or of politics, or as theologians' (Discourse III, 3, p. 36). But Newman adds that, in evaluating each of these disciplinary contributions, 'the mind never views any part ... without recollecting that it is but a part' (Discourse VI, 6, p. 103), a part contributing to the understanding of a whole. If the mind fails to do this, it will be apt 'to give undue prominence to one' or more disciplines and 'to unsettle the boundary lines between science and science' (Discourse V, 1, p. 75), so that for example, it may attempt to understand the distribution of wealth in different parts of a city in purely economic terms, neglecting other social and moral dimensions, or it may treat some psychological disorder that involves lack of self-knowledge as though it were only a biochemical phenomenon.

Such confusions too often mark the public discourse of our present day culture. They make too many of us victims of the expertise of those trained to see things only in the narrow focus of their own discipline. Newman took it that what he called the constrained and contracted mind of the specialist characteristically expressed itself in opinionated and boring conversation (Discourse VI, 6, p. 104).

And so it still does. But such minds have now become more dangerous because more apt to set on foot large-scale consequences. And the range of disciplines that we may need in order to achieve the kind and degree of understanding that issue in sound practical reasoning has increased. Sometimes we need to correct what economists tell us by appealing to the historians, and sometimes of course vice versa. Sometimes we need to correct what neurophysiologists tell us by appealing to psychologists, and sometimes vice versa, and sometimes we may need as well or instead to go to novelists or dramatists. Note too that in many cases no evaluation of the claims made for this or that finding of specialised enquiry will be possible for those innocent of the relevant mathematics. We all of us therefore need to be schooled in a number of disciplines, just because each has its own methods, insights and standards. To be educated is, on this view, not only to know how to bring each discipline to bear in appropriate ways, but also how to respond to the unjustified claims made in the name of each. And for this we need not the contracted mind of the specialist, but a different sort of mind.

From this perspective Newman's enterprise begins to look somewhat different and the accusation that his conception of a university is irrelevant to universities as they now are misses the point. For perhaps the principal question that Newman was posing was not, as he supposed, 'What is a university?', but 'What is an educated mind?', a question which he answers in Aristotelian fashion by saying that everything has its own specific perfection, that there is a specific perfection of the intellect (Discourse V, 9, p. 92), and that the end of education is the achievement of that perfection, that 'true enlargement of mind which is the power of viewing many things as one whole, of referring them severally to their place in the universal system, of understanding their respective values, and determining their mutual dependence' (Discourse VI, 6, p. 107). To develop highly specialised knowledge only in one particular sphere, to focus one's mind on only one subject-matter, may certainly be valuable, but it will not enable the mind to achieve its specific perfection and is apt to prevent the mind from doing so.

The irrelevance to the contemporary university of Newman's prescriptions is thus cast in a new light. It is an indictment not of Newman, but of the contemporary university. For, if this irrelevance is as great as his critics claim, then whatever universities are achieving, they are not producing educated minds or, to put matters more justly, they are doing so only incidentally and accidentally. And, if they were to be able to rebut this accusation, it could only be because they had drastically revised their undergraduate curriculum, so that every student was introduced and somewhat more than introduced to, say, the calculus and the mathematics of probability, to historical and literary studies, to some parts of physics, certainly to thermodynamics, to the elements of biochemistry, and to ecological and evolutionary biology. Yet whatever disciplines we name in this catalogue, there always has to be something more, namely the communication of an understanding of the various ways in which the findings of those disciplines bear upon each other and so contribute to a larger understanding than any of them by themselves can provide. We should notice too that the teaching of this kind of curriculum will require a corresponding kind of education for teachers, since we shall need teachers of literature who are well informed about biochemistry and teachers of physics who are able to think historically, all of them being at home with the relevant mathematics.

III

To this proposal there will of course be a number of objections, of which here I consider only one, merely, that whether or not this is an account of what education is or should be, it is not or not yet Newman's account, and this in two different ways. First, in elucidating Newman's conception of understanding I began by considering some features of practical reasoning. But, it may be said, Newman's conception is of understanding as achieved by theoretical enquiry. So I may seem to have started in the wrong place. What matters, however, is that the conception of understanding at which we have arrived, although presupposed by successful practical reasoning, is itself a conception of the mind's theoretical grasp of the relations of parts and aspects to the whole. What this involves can be brought out by noting how questions that Newman takes to be central to theoretical understanding go characteristically unasked in the fragmented curriculum of the present day.

Consider Newman's suggestive discussion (Discourse III, 2, pp. 35–36) of how the different disciplines enable us to understand ourselves. We are, according to physics, composed of particles interacting with each other and with our environment. Chemistry tells us that we are sites of a variety of reactions; biology, as Newman was shortly to learn from Darwin, that we are in key part what we are because of the evolution of species. Sociology and economics characterise the structure of our roles and relationships; history informs us that we are what our past has made us and what we have made of our past. And theology views all these same features from a very different perspective. The crucial questions are: In what then does the unity of a human being consist? And what is it about human beings that enables them to ask this question about themselves? But these are questions, in Newman's idiom philosophical questions, which can only be asked by students who have a more than superficial grasp both of the relevant disciplines and of how they relate to each other. And they are questions that go unasked in the contemporary curriculum.

One respect in which this account of Newman's conception of multidisciplinary understanding does indeed fall short is the absence so far of any discussion of Newman's thesis that, if the curriculum is to have the unity that it needs to have, if it is to disclose the unity of the order of things, then the discipline of theology is indispensable. For it is theology that provides the curriculum with its unity and we will not understand the bearing of the other disciplines on each other adequately, if we do not understand theology's bearing on them and theirs on theology.

The theology of which Newman spoke was not specifically Catholic theology, but a theology shared with all theists, with all those for whom, as Newman put it, the word 'God' 'contains ... a theology in itself' (p. 27). God, as understood by theists, is 'an Individual, Self-Dependent, All-perfect, Unchangable Being; intelligent, living, personal and present ... who created and upholds the universe ... who is sovereign over, operative amidst, independent of, the appointments which He has made; One in whose hands are all things, who has a purpose in every event and a standard for every deed, and thus has relations of His own towards the subject-matter of each particular science which the book of knowledge unfolds, who has ... implicated Himself in all the history of creation, the constitution of nature, the course of the world, the origin of society, the fortunes of nations, the action of the human mind; and who thereby necessarily becomes the subject-matter of a science ... ' (Discourse II, 7, p. 27).

This surely states a doctrine unacceptable to the contemporary secular academic mind, although perhaps what that mind rejects in taking itself to reject this doctrine is not in fact this doctrine.

Whether that is so or not is a question that I shall approach indirectly by developing a second line of thought about what it is to understand. When we bring one or more of the particular disciplines to bear upon some event or state of affairs that we need to understand, say, the explanation of the incidence of bubonic plague in medieval Europe, and the part that it played in shaping social and economic life, or the varying causes of climate change during the earth's history, or the phenomena of neutron oscillation, the explanations at which we arrive are always partial and incomplete in that they always direct our attention to something more, to something needing further enquiry. Sometimes this is because certain questions are still left open, sometimes because that to which the explanation refers us as cause or causes itself stands in need of explanation, and sometimes because there is an appeal to principles or laws that have application in this particular sphere, but we do not as yet understand why those principles or laws must take the form that they do.

Moreover, as our enquiries proceed, we move towards unifying our various explanations, both those which lie wholly within one particular discipline and those which have a bearing on explanations in other disciplines. And this enables us to understand increasingly the place of this or that occurrence or state of affairs in the overall order of things. Yet our explanations are always imperfectly unified, just as they always remain in some respects incomplete, and so our enquiries never terminate, are never final. What they presuppose is twofold: first, that we are indeed directed towards a final, if unattainable end, that we do have a conception of what it would be to have achieved a kind of understanding that is perfected and completed – for it is only by contrast with this conception that we characterise our present explanations as partial, imperfect and incomplete – and secondly, and correspondingly, that the order of things, although indefinitely complex, has an intelligible unity that is gradually and increasingly disclosed by our enquiry and that will continue to be disclosed by those enquiries, no matter how far we carry them.

What is involved in having such a conception of the order of things as an intelligible unity, a conception that medieval Aristotelians, at least, would have confidently ascribed to Aristotle? It is to take it for granted that the further we carry our enquiries the nearer we come to understanding every part and aspect of the universe in relation to every other, just because of an indefinitely sustained underlying ordered unity. To move towards understanding on this view is to move towards achieving what scornful and sceptical critics have sometimes spoken of as a God's eye view of things, thinking thereby to discredit this conception of the achievement of understanding. But by so doing such critics have revealed an insightful grasp of what is at stake in accepting or rejecting this conception of understanding and indeed in accepting or rejecting the counterpart conception of an ordering power that is not itself a part or aspect of the finite order of things, but one without which the universe could not present itself to our minds as an intelligible unity, an ordering power that has the defining characteristics of the God of theism.

What this line of thought suggests is that about one thing at least Newman is right, namely that, if theology were not to be granted the place in the curriculum that he assigns to it, then the secular disciplines could not stand in the relationships to each other that he assigns to them. His defence of theology is integral to his conception of the unity of the order of things and to the unity of the curriculum. They stand or fall together. Take away theology and the curriculum will be frag-mented into a series of specialised disciplines, leaving at best the possibility of some kind of factitious unity imposed by social agreement. It turns out therefore that from Newman's point of view his attack upon specialisation in the curriculum and his attack on the removal of theology from the curriculum are one and the same attack. That there is an impressive philosophical case to be made *against* the theological conception of understanding that I am ascribing to Newman no one at work in a contemporary university is likely to be unaware. But the philosophical case *for* that conception has its own interest and it is important to distinguish the line of argument that leads to it from three other lines of argument with which it may easily be confused. First, it is not only different from, but incompatible with, the so-called argument for or from intelligent design, whether in Archdeacon Paley's eighteenth-century version or in more recent versions. For that bad argu-ment begins from an attempt to identify examples of natural phenomena whose complexity is such that, so it is alleged, they cannot be explained by the natural sciences. By contrast the line of thought that I have sketched begins not from contentions about the limits or failures of scientific enquiries, but rather from the continuing success of such enquiries and the justified confidence of those engaged in them. Newman's early reading of Hume had led him to be suspicious of the claims advanced by eighteenth-century proponents of intelligent design. I do not think that he would be any more sympathetic to their unfortunate contemporary heirs.

A second contrast is between R.G. Collingwood's account of the metaphysical presuppositions of scientific theorising and the account that I am defending, although I am certainly indebted to Collingwood. Collingwood understood that in different periods the intelligible unity of the order of nature had been conceived in different and incompatible ways, the post-Aristotelian and Ptolemaic conceptions of the late middle ages giving way to Galilean and Newtonian conceptions, and

244   *The Very Idea of a University: Aristotle, Newman and Us*

these in turn to quantum-mechanical and relativistic conceptions, each of which had, so Collingwood contended, its own distinctive metaphysical presuppositions and commitments. But on the view that I am taking the underlying presupposition of scientific enquiry is that, even although each of these particular attempts to characterise the intelligible unity of nature has either already failed or may at some point in the future fail, there is at a deeper level a unity yet to be discovered and an understanding yet to be achieved, so that we are committed to presupposing belief in an ordering power without which the concept of a continuing intelligible and unified order would be empty.

A third contrast is with the positions taken by Nicholas Maxwell in his *The Comprehensibility of the Universe* (Oxford: Clarendon Press, 1998). Maxwell treats the intelligibility and unity of the physical universe as something to which our commitment is inescapable, once we have understood the theoretical aims of physical enquiry (see especially pp. 180–81). And I am also indebted to his discussion of these issues. Moreover he provides impressive reasons for holding that the best conjecture as to why the physical universe has the intelligible unity that it has would be that God exists, if only the concept of an all good and all powerful God were not, on Maxwell's view, rendered wholly implausible by the facts of human and natural evil. The two crucial differences between my – and Newman's – line of thought on the one hand and Maxwell's on the other are: first, that Newman, like other theists, did not find the objection to theism posed by the problem of evil insuperable, and, secondly, that for Newman, like other theists, belief in God *cannot* be a conjecture and is in relation to scientific enquiry, we might be tempted to say, an inescapable presupposition.

Inescapable? That must surely not be so. Newman himself noted of natural science that a 'vast multitude of its teachers ... have been either unbelievers or skeptics' (Discourse IX, p. 167) and periodic surveys of members of the American Academy of Science during the twentieth century have shown that the numbers of believers in God among them, never large, steadily dwindled to about five percent. But what then is the antitheist's alternative to Newman's position? It is that there is some noncircular inductivist justification for inferring from the characteristics of the universe to date to the unity and continuing intelligibility of the universe. That scientific enquirers who are antitheists badly need just such a justification, if their claims are to be sustained, is clear. That such a justification can be provided remains far from clear. And the onus for providing it is on the antitheist.

IV

I turn now to the third area of contention between Newman and the protagonists of the contemporary university. The contemporary university, as I noted earlier, boasts that it is socially useful and often justifies itself by citing as an example of its usefulness the provision of skilled manpower. By contrast, Newman's view was that what matters about an educated individual is not primarily any set of useful skills that she or he may happen to possess, but her or his capacity for judgment, judgment both in putting these skills to work and in acting 'as a friend, as a companion, as a citizen', and in domestic life and in the pursuits of leisure (Discourse VII, 8, p. 129). Newman is quoting from the argument advanced by John Davison – one of the reforming Fellows of Oriel in the early nineteenth century – in defence of a curriculum that introduces the student to 'religion (in its evidence and interpretation), ethics, history, eloquence, poetry, theories of general speculation, the fine arts, and works of wit', studies which, so Davison had claimed, are 'such as give a direct play and exercise to the faculty of judgment' and thus educate 'the active and inventive powers' (Discourse VII, 9, p. 132). The question that readers will want to put to Davison and Newman is: What then are the marks of judgment? What is it to possess or to fail to possess it? And of course in putting this question to Davison and Newman, we are close to asking of Aristotle, 'What is *phronēsis*?' and of Aquinas 'What is *prudentia*?' Let me consider then just one aspect of judgment, one that throws additional light on Newman's proposed curriculum, and suggests that without something like that curriculum we will not only be defective practical reasoners, but will even be apt not to know what we are doing.

Human action always has several dimensions. 'What are you doing?' we ask. 'Solving an equation; predicting next week's stock prices; pleasing my employer; working late in the office; absenting myself from dinner with my family; alienating my oldest child.' Or perhaps 'Digging a hole; building a condominium tower; constructing a new competitor for scarce water resources; ignoring some of the relevant geological facts; endangering lives in twenty years time.' Even examples as sketchy as these bring out some salient features of action: first, that what we are not doing or are failing to do by doing what we do may be as important as what we do; secondly, that ignorance of relevant facts from a variety of disciplines may make us unable to recognise aspects of what we are doing; and thirdly that, by focusing on particular aspects of what we are doing we may conceal from ourselves other aspects. There always may of course be aspects of our actions of which we remain unaware through no fault or defect of our own and some of them may be such that we have no need to be aware of them. But the range of facts of which we may at some point badly need to be aware, if we are to know what we are doing, is clearly wide and requires, as we have already emphasised, some knowledge of a number of disciplines.

Evidently of course such academic knowledge, although necessary, is insufficient for an agent to be able to answer the question 'What are you doing?' She or he needs also to know how to deploy that knowledge when and as it is required and this ability can be developed only through engagement in a range of practices. Yet, lacking an education that has introduced agents to a sufficient number of disciplines, they will be unlikely to develop that ability. And they will also need another characteristic that cannot be acquired through academic study, that of valuing the quality of knowing what they are doing and of valuing that quality in others. One can of course know what one is doing and nonetheless do the wrong thing. But even to begin to say what is involved in judging and acting rightly would be to open up questions too large for this occasion. What has already been said is sufficient to establish the connection between Newman's account of the curriculum and his conviction that what it is to have an educated mind is one thing, what it is to have professional skills something else, even if it is important for the exercise of professional skills that those who exercise them have educated minds.

If we are to take this line of argument further, we must do so in two directions, one of which involves us in rejecting an assumption of Newman's, an assumption shared with most, if not quite all, of his educated contemporaries. It is that the type of university education that he commends is suitable only for a small and privileged minority. Yet, if in fact in the contemporary world this kind of education is needed in order to know what one is doing, then everyone needs it and not only the makers of large-scale social and economic decisions. Indeed it is crucial for plain persons that they should have this type of education, so that they can begin to recognise when those who exercise power over their lives no longer know what they are doing. But the question of how such an education might be made widely available is yet another that I put on one side. I do so in order to make a claim whose truth or falsity is of crucial significance in the debate between the followers of Newman and the protagonists of the contemporary research university.

V

That claim is that a surprising number of the major disorders of the latter part of the twentieth century and of the first decade of the twenty-first century have been brought about by some of the most distinguished graduates of some of the most distinguished universities in the world and this as the result of an inadequate general education, at both graduate and especially undergraduate levels, that has made it possible for those graduates to act decisively and deliberately without knowing what they were doing. Examples of such disasters include: the Vietnam War, the policies of the United States towards Iran for more than half a century, and the present world economic crisis. Of course I cannot here argue adequately for such a contentious claim. But I can illustrate it by considering some salient features of the genesis of the present economic crisis.

Too many people have already forgotten the great forerunner of this crisis, the collapse of the hedge fund, Long-Term Capital Management, in 1997, a collapse so massive that for a short time it threatened the entire financial system. Long-Term Capital Management had on their board two Nobel Prize winning economists, who made use for the first time of certain complex mathematical models that, so they confidently believed, enabled them to enter into large-scale derivative contracts with measurable risk and without significant danger. And so far as both the mathematics and the economic theory was concerned they knew very well what they were doing (see Roger Loewenstein, *When Genius Failed: The Rise and Fall of Long-Term Capital Management*, New York: Random House, 2000). What they lacked was historical knowledge of two different kinds of contingency: knowledge in depth of the histories of risk-taking firms and of the vicissitudes encountered in those histories and knowledge of the politics of the different cultures within which markets operate, so that, most notably, they misinterpreted events in Russia and were taken wholly by surprise when the Russian 'government simply decided would rather use its rubles to pay Russian workers than Western bondholders' (Loewenstein, p. 144).

The collapse of Long-Term Capital Management had about it something of the character of a farce, of a story of experts ludicrously victimised by their own expertise. Its successor, our present crisis, has instead some of the characteristics of a tragedy, a tale of characters who self-confidently take themselves to be farsighted walking, as if blindly, over a cliff, and in their *hubris* taking all too many others with them. For it was cohorts drawn from the most highly educated among us who trusted in sophisticated mathematics whose applications the vast majority of them did not understand, who relied upon conceptions of risk that they had never adequately analysed, who went down historically well-marked roads not knowing that those roads had been already travelled more than once, and who lacked the dramatic imagination that could have told them just what kind of a play it was in which they had allotted themselves roles. They lacked, that is, just what Davison's – and Newman's – curriculum might have given them. It is small wonder then that they were also oblivious to what they might have learned from Newman's Aristotelian contemporary, Karl Marx.

VI

What we have to learn then from Newman is first of all that undergraduate education has its own distinctive ends, that it should never be regarded as a prologue to or a preparation for graduate or professional education, and that its ends must not be subordinated to the ends of the necessarily specialised activities of the researcher. But it is not just that undergraduate education has its own ends. It is also that undergraduate education, when well conducted, is in key part an education in how to think about the ends of a variety of human activities and, that is to say, in how to evaluate, among others, such activities as those of the specialist and the researcher, the activities of those dedicated to the ends which the contemporary research university serves. The danger is therefore that in research universities the ability to think about ends, including the ends of the university, will be lost and with it the ability to engage in radical self-criticism, so that the leadership of those universities will become complacent in their wrongheadedness. How unsurprising it is then that so often from their point of view Newman's lectures should now appear not only false, but irrelevant.

18 John Dewey, Gothic and Modern

J. S. Kaminsky

Author

James. S. Kaminsky is Mildred Cheshire Fraley Distinguished Professor in the Department of Educational Foundations, Leadership, and Technology at Auburn University, Alabama, USA. He has focused much of his research on the history of educational philosophy, post-modern theory in educational administration and neo-pragmatism in educational thought. He has published widely in *Educational Theory*, *The Journal of Educational Administration*, *The Journal of Educational Thought* and *The Australian Journal of Education*, among others. Previously, he was executive editor of *Education Philosophy and Theory*.

Introduction

The final article (58: 3, 249–266) in our collection brings us full circle. Volume 1, Issue 1 (p. 69) of the *British Journal of Educational Studies* published in 1952 contained an obituary to John Dewey written by William Boyd. Dewey (1859–1952) had died from pneumonia that resulted from breaking a hip in a fall while playing with his adopted young son. Some might argue that the tone of Boyd's 1952 article was 'typically British' – especially in the concluding paragraph:

> As a lecturer, it is true, he was rather dull and ordinary. As a writer he tended to be too abstract in exposition to make ready appeal to the common reader. As a man to meet he was not specially impressive till, with better acquaintance, his fine human qualities had time to show themselves. What then was the secret of his extraordinary influence on two generations? Surely the strength and integrity of his thinking. At a time when the old philosophies of Europe were in decline he grasped the clue of the practical man's pragmatic faith and with its help found the kind of certainty that a changing civilization has needed to educate for the future.

Although the obituary notes that 'there has been some falling off in the influence of Dewey since the Second World War, both in America and Europe' perhaps because 'educators in this country are giving less thought to Dewey because they have made his essential ideas their own, with the changes necessary to adapt them to our own conditions'. Articles discussing Dewey and his work, or which draw upon his thinking, have appeared in the *Journal* during the ensuing sixty years of publication: particularly in the last decade. Readers also may be interested in: *John Dewey in Retrospect: An American reconsideration* (8, 2: 99–111); *How is Education Possible? Pragmatism, Communication and the Social Organisation of Education* (54, 2: 160–74); *Towards an Educationally Meaningful Curriculum: Epistemic Holism and Knowledge Integration Revisited* (55, 1: 3–20); *Civic Republicanism and Contestatory Deliberation: Framing Pupil Discourse within Citizenship Education* (57, 1: 55–69); *Education, Contestation and Confusions of Sense and Concept* (58, 1: 89–104).

The following novel and perhaps provocative article takes as its premise 'that it would be interesting to think about Dewey's life and works from outside the confines of traditional descriptions that cast him as a prodigal liberal or fellow traveller' and 'suggests a more robust and complex Dewey: an American Gothic and, simultaneously, modern Dewey'. It argues to understand Dewey's thought only as that of 'a prodigal liberal or a fellow traveller' fails to capture the complexity of his work. Kaminsky asserts that:

Dewey's work was driven by an oscillation between Gothic (magical transformation) and modern (instrumental transformations). In his work he was inventing America the way he would like it to be, not the way it was. He was busy inventing a country in which freedom of speech, freedom from want, freedom from religious persecution, and freedom from fear would be commonplace. Dewey was paying attention to the country's promise, not the flaws and shortcomings of which there were many.

John Dewey, Gothic and Modern

by James S. Kaminsky, Auburn University, USA

1. Introduction

Sometimes when introducing a friend or an old acquaintance, an individual we have known for many years, in several roles, and in many places – John Dewey in this case – it is best to begin in a roundabout way. This roundabout manner of introduction, this 'magical realist' opening, works particularly well when it is important to call attention to some new adventure, accomplishment, or aspect of a personality that has gone unnoticed or unappreciated. This winding manner of beginning is similar to telling a story; each retelling is partially discursive and partially poetic. Each retelling suggests an opportunity for thinking and talking about that person or event differently. The suggestion is that it would be interesting to think about Dewey's life and works from outside the confines of traditional descriptions that cast him as a prodigal liberal or fellow traveller. This essay suggests a more robust and complex Dewey: an American Gothic and, simultaneously, modern Dewey.[1]

The magical realist perspective of this paper is somewhat unique in a post-everything world. Magical realism is modern but not quite post-modern. It constructs an 'ex-centric' sketch of John Dewey's thought through a device Franz Roh created called 'magical realism' (Roh, [1925] 1995, p. 25). Magical realism uses 'hallucinatory scenes and events, fantastic/phantasmagoric characters' to construct an ex-centric discourse (Zamora and Faris, 1995, p. 6). The preceding sounds post-modern except for the fact that 'magical realism' remains mortgaged to a 'soft or sloppy' – take your pick – sense of realism in which the authority of the author, time, place, and event are not forsaken within the relationship of audience and text (*ibid.*, p. 3).

Magical realism (the genre) is a matter of learning to read 'ex-centrically'. To write ex-centrically implies 'dis-placing discourse' (removing discourse from its expected context). 'Ex-centric texts' are created by approaching the 'given/ expected reality' from the perspective of other 'modalities' (dance, painting, poetics, the novel, music and so on) when they are understood as explorations of 'being' and 'not being' at home in the world. Arguably, Gabriel Garcia Márquez's *One Hundred Years of Solitude* (1970); John Fowles' *The French Lieutenant's Woman* (1969); Salman Rushdie's *Midnight's Children* (2006), Angela Carter's *Nights at the Circus* (1985) and Yann Martel's *Life of Pi* (2001) might be thought of as examples of magical realist investigations of 'being' and 'not being' at home in the world at different places in time and history.

The argument is that magic realist writing achieves this end by first appropriating the techniques of the 'center'-al line and then using magical realism's displacements 'realistically'; that is, to create an alternative authenticity to adjust the 'normativity' of the present (D'Haen, 1995, p. 195). Reading 'ex-centrically' allows the reader to displace the 'normativity' that mortgages Dewey's intellectual work to 'experience' alone. The 'ex-centric' distance between Gothic and modern world calls attention to the importance of 'inexperience' in Dewey's thought. This work encourages the reader to dwell on the importance of 'inexperience' as a cognitive catalyst for personal and social composition.

2. American Gothic

The magical realist introduction to John Dewey chosen here begins with a version of Gothic fiction, a Latin Gothic. This Latin Gothic is evident in *One Hundred Years of Solitude* (Márquez, 1970) and *The Lost Steps* (Carpentier, 1956). The books are different in many ways; however, both contain a Latin Gothic narrative. In a manner analogous to Gothic fiction in general, both share a shadowy setting filled with bizarre and violent transformational events in attendant conditions of decay and decline. Examining the modern Latin Gothic evident in *One Hundred Years of Solitude* and *The Lost Steps* provides some clarification of Latin Gothic's intellectual orientation. Both are set in Latin America; nevertheless, they are very different stories. *One Hundred Years of Solitude* is about an extended family struggling to stay together, '"Look what we've come to," she [Úrsula] would tell him ... "Look at the empty house, our children scattered all over the world, and the two of us alone again, the same as in the beginning"' (Márquez, 1970, p. 108). *The Lost Steps* is about a man struggling to escape his responsibilities. They are very different, stylistically. *One Hundred Years of Solitude* uses magical realism to incorporate enchantment into an otherwise ordinary setting. 'This time ... they [the gypsies] brought a flying carpet. ... The people at once dug up their last gold pieces to take advantage of a quick flight over the houses of the village' (Márquez, 1970, p. 31). *The Lost Steps* uses the technique of contrasting the marvellous and real to make the ordinary fantastic. 'It was as though a subterranean world had suddenly come alive, dredging up from its depths a myriad of strange forms of animal life. Out of the gurgling waterless pipe came queer lice, moving gray wafers ... ' (Carpentier, 1956, p. 55). Also obvious is the fact that the narrator in *The Lost Steps* is running towards the primitive world that José Arcadio Buendía is fleeing. They do, however, have similar underlying themes. Beyond the fatalistic tendencies, there is an underlying art that holds the characters' various presents together – magic for *One Hundred Years of Solitude* and music for *The Lost Steps.* Both magic and music are degraded and almost eliminated and then both reappear at the final undoing of each novel's characters. Similarly, in Dewey's life both intuition and emotion are degraded and almost eliminated in the gaze of science and technology, then both reappear in the final act as the Gothic and modern merge in Dewey's philosophical thought (e.g., 1934a).

Once the Gothic nature of Dewey's character is recognised it is hard to portray him simply as an effete liberal or a fellow traveller (cf. Hook, 1987b). Many of the aspects of this Latin Gothic run parallel to its American cousin. The interesting aspect of its American cousin is that implicit within both is a modern and primitive world. Of course, the primitive referred to here is not the medieval world of gargoyles, cathedrals, monastic orders, the Black Death and the 100 Years War. Nor is the modernity referred to here that of air travel, digital computers and cyberspace; however it is modern. In the modern aspect of American Gothic one finds the public identifying with the steam engine, dynamo and life in the metropolis. The primitive element of American Gothic is committed to the horse, candle and pastoral life on the farm. The modern and primitive are also evident in Latin Gothic. In *One Hundred Years of Solitude* (Márquez, 1970) and *The Lost Steps* (Carpentier, 1956), the stories' narratives present characters that are simultaneously fleeing and approaching a primitive world that events are violently transforming. American versions of Gothic emphasise a similar narrative, a narrative in which its characters are both approaching and fleeing a primitive world. Coming to understand Dewey as a simultaneously Gothic and modern American character fleeing and approaching a primitive world provides some different tropes that grant him a more complex and vigorous character.

In 1930, Grant Wood encapsulated the North American version of his contradictory Gothic world in his painting *American Gothic*. The painting's dynamic has several stylistic elements: a hard cold realism tempered by an honest, direct, earthy quality and an honest sympathy for those who had little or nothing of the American dream. It also portrays two individuals who are part of a world that never will be the same as the primitive world of their childhood. Surrounded by the frame that encompasses Wood's painting stands a joyless, hard, farmer/preacher and his equally joyless spouse/daughter; they stand stiff, impassive and emotionless in front of a farmhouse with a large cathedral window. The implicit presence of the Great Depression is evident in their dress and demeanour; it provides the attendant conditions of decay and decline. It is implied by the painting's Gothic theme. The farmer-preacher and joyless wife-daughter are hard-edged individuals, convinced of the seriousness of life and filled with the certainty that the events of their time will betray the efforts of their lives. The scene portrays a poignant primitive ethos in the same way that its bright colours and hard-edged draftsmanship portray modernity's hopeful ethos, everywhere evident in the painting's Bauhaus-like simplicity and design.

In its own way, the painting's Gothic theme is a summary of the nation's attempt to both flee and approach the primitive world of turn-of-the-century America. It reflects the profound cultural 'disconnection' the people of the United States experienced in the period during and preceding the Great Depression. It was a period that vacillated between a world that had been lost and one that was yet to be constructed (Kloppenberg, 1986, pp. 7–8). Dewey, first and foremost, was an inhabitant of the pastoral world of his childhood Vermont (Dykhuizen, 1959). Be that as it may, like the narrator in *The Lost Steps*, Dewey was caught by the city. He was a creature of Chicago and New York. The narrator of *The Lost Steps* noted, 'The city would not let me go. Its streets wove a web around me like a net, a seine, that had been dropped over me' (Carpentier, 1956, p. 257). Dewey's situation was very similar. The city mesmerised him, encapsulating everything that modernity made possible. For Dewey the city was awe-inspiring; having known Chicago, he could not stay in the wilds of Minnesota (Westbrook, 1991, p. 84). The city was the unlimited potential of the dynamo, steam engine and radio. Dewey also realised that it, the metropolis, was not unproblematic. He understood the city was its own nemesis. Dewey recognised that the city was as grotesque as it was marvellously real. Out of the 'waterless pipe' in Dewey's cities, Chicago and New York, came literature, drama, jazz, science and technological marvels, as well as drunkenness, prostitution, influenza, typhus, smallpox, measles, and the hopelessness and despair of slave-like labour (cf. Westbrook, 1991, p. 83).

It was the art of philosophy that held Dewey's world together. It helped him make sense of the world and provided the means through which he attempted to solve the city's contradictions. The problem of how to both flee and approach the present for Dewey revolves around how the nation might somehow escape the Gothic world and remain part of it (its pastoral values and worldview) while simultaneously approaching modernity's promise and becoming its resident. It is the problem Dewey first addressed directly in 'The school and social progress,' one of the small essays that make up his work *School and Society and the Child and the Curriculum* (Dewey, [1899] 1990). Later in *The Public and Its Problems* (1927) he addressed the same question.

The city was the source of irrepressible anxiety for America's Victorian intellectual establishment.[2] The city's 'modernists demanded the new in life and art: new forms, new sexual values, new freedoms, new feelings unhindered by old rules' (Crunden, 1993, p. xii). America's urban Victorians were horrified. The city's modernists were immigrants among landed gentry, homosexuals in a heterosexual society, the dispossessed in a land of established wealth, Blacks in a white culture, Catholics in a Protestant society, agnostics in a Christian country, Southerners in a Yankee society, and women in a man's world. They were outsiders. They were all Oscar Wilde in one sense or another. Their demands for the 'new' emphasized the discontinuities and frustrations of their lives and experience. They preferred European or Continental to the domestic, the arts to sciences, the unknown to the known, and the exotic to the familiar. They were strangers in a strange land. They were the objects of the nation's intolerance.

The answer to the modernist anxiety for Dewey was to be found somewhere in a 'once and future' place, not the present. Dewey knew that,

> systematic hatred and suspicion of any human group, 'racial,' sectarian, political ... Negroes, Catholics, and Jews is no new thing in our life ... But for this very reason, the task of those who retain belief in democracy is to revive and maintain in full vigor the original conviction of the intrinsic moral nature of democracy ... We have yet to realize that it is a way of personal life

and one which provides a moral standard for personal conduct. (Dewey, 1939, pp. 98–99, 101)

Education – public education – was to Dewey's mind a central necessity for ridding the nation of intolerance and 'working out the American project' (Ryan, 1995, p. 364). As Dewey noted, writing about schools for the public,

> We must conceive of them in their social significance, as types of the processes by which society keeps itself going, as agencies for bringing home to the child some of the primal necessities of community life, and as ways in which these needs have been met by the growing insight and ingenuity of man; in short, as instrumentalities through which the school itself shall be made a genuine form of active community life, instead of a place set apart in which to learn lessons. (Dewey, [1899] 1990, p. 14)

The public school was the place where the 'American' community would be contrived. 'A liberal education, therefore, had to be one in which children from different backgrounds could talk about the achievements of their traditions and their contribution to American life' (Ryan, 1995, p. 364).

3. Chicago Gothic

While in Chicago under the tutelage of Jane Addams and the people he came to know at Hull House, Dewey discovered specific examples of how the city indifferently diminished the lives of honest and not so honest hard-working people in the same way that it seemed to randomly shower beneficence upon the lives of those who had wealth. Dewey fretted over the direction of the republic's culture, purpose, goals, collective identity and values. Dewey, similar to Thorstein Veblen, demonstrated a certain concern over the manner in which the new republic's conspicuous consumption was dissolving the values of a simpler time (Ryan, 1995, p. 237) and the distinctions it was creating between labour and leisure classes. Dewey noted,

> Probably the most deep-seated antithesis which has shown itself in educational history is that between education in preparation for useful labor and education for a life of leisure. The bare terms 'use-ful labor' and 'leisure' confirm the statement already made that the segregation and conflict of values are not self-inclosed, but reflect a division within social life. (Dewey, 1916a, p. 250)

And, of course, Dewey was not out of touch with the modernist literature of the period. Dewey, James and Dreiser were all looking at and greeting the triumph of corporate capitalism in just the right manner (Livingston, 1994). Theodore Dreiser described the world of Gothic America – the daring and the damned – in *Sister Carrie* (1900) and *An American Tragedy* (1925). In *The Financier* (1912) and *The Titan* (1914), Dreiser noted that life's reward was to those who dared. Failure was merely part of the dross of ordinary life. In the dramatic opening chapter of *The Financier*, Dreiser, through the character Frank Algernon Cowperwood, describes the desperate and hopeless struggle of a squid contained in a small tank, relentlessly stalked by a lobster. Eventually, the lobster takes the squid and the squid's last desperate struggle is reduced to an amusement for those individuals near the tank. The irony is, of course, that the lobster is condemned to a similar fate. Dewey was persuaded. Yet, his abiding sense of Christian charity would not allow his art and especially his philosophy of education to remain socially unconscious and indifferent to the fate of those who toiled and struggled without hope (Dewey, 1916a, 1920, 1934b).

The conclusion of the scene between the squid and lobster is desperately and exquisitely Gothic. In the same way that the ultimate meaning of the struggle for life between the lobster and the squid was denied to them, modernists realised that the ultimate meaning of their lives and struggles was also denied to them. Dewey saw in Dreiser's novels and in the world he passed on the boulevard, a world in need of redemption; even if, unlike Marx, he was at a loss to state what a redeemed world would be like. It was a worldview that had a place for charity, kindness and education and no place for violence and revolution (Dewey, 1920, 1927, 1935).

Dewey knew that if the art of his philosophy – the art that held his world together – was to continue, then his work had to be conducted in terms of the actual problems being faced by men and women in this world. In Dewey's words, 'The popular impression that pragmatic philosophy means that philosophy shall develop ideas relevant to the actual crises of life, ideas influential in dealing with them and tested by the assistance they afford, is correct' (Dewey, [1917] 1985, p. 43). It became apparent to Dewey that the art of philosophers had to be culturally useful in the same way as the work of poets, engineers, architects and playwrights (Rorty, 1991, p. 71; 1998; Westbrook, 1991, pp. 117–49).

Within modernity's democracy of things the city's culture, community, work, leisure, identity, values and people had become commodities to be bought, sold, consumed and eventually discarded. Thrift, work, patience, denial, virtue and the loyalty of simpler times all seemed to be lost in the country's desperate pursuit of tomorrow. The United States had become a place where the most important thing was what one consumed not what one produced or who one was. It seemed to Dewey that in the nation's pursuit of a democracy of things the virtues of a simpler time were being lost. Be that as it may, he remained an aggressive nationalist who was convinced that the great community public education was to create would be thoroughly American (Ryan, 1995, p. 153).

However, he still had Christian faith in the virtues of simpler time. Akin to the cathedral window in Grant Wood's painting, the bright Gothic of Dewey's Christian faith and charity was at the core of his social thought (Rockefeller, 1991, pp. 125–68). The city, of course, was the contradiction of his Christian faith and charity. The country's morality for Dewey was the symbol of simpler virtues and conduct. The country was the simple life of his childhood in Vermont. It was a world in which people were more concerned about their social responsibilities and less concerned about their salvation or damnation. Theological dread of the city was a luxury of modern life; pastoral Americans did not have the time or energy for the city's anxieties. They loved their God and expressed their faith in acts of Christian charity. Christian charity and therein social reform was led by organisations such as: the Massachusetts Board of State Charities, the Settlement House Movement and the Salvation Army (Silver, 1983a). Social reform in the United States was and would remain for Dewey a matter of conscience and Christian charity, not 'direct action'.

Dewey's politics were not Marxist, nihilist, or anarchist – they were pragmatic in the best sense (Hook, 1987a). And for achieving solidarity he was a nationalist, but hardly a mindless nationalist. He acknowledged nationalism's genocidal potential, the environmental devastation of its history and its economic colonialism. Post-modern scholars have argued that representative democracy is alienating, exclusive, boring, desecrating, and fraudulent. Dewey could not have disagreed more. He recognised that representative politics were an effective means of forcing 'establishment' or 'anti-establishment' figures to take ordinary people seriously. He was an American democrat, Gothic (a pastoral sense of associated living) and modern (an urban sense of a cosmopolitan world) at the same time. Dewey would have agreed with Reinhold Niebuhr when he wrote, 'Men's capacity for justice makes democracy possible; but men's inclination to injustice makes democracy necessary' (Niebuhr, 1944, pp. xii–xv).

'Moral democracy', for Dewey, 'called not only for the pursuit of worthwhile ends but for the pursuit of these ends in ways that enlisted the freely cooperative participation of all concerned' (Westbrook, 1991, pp. 164–65). His version of political and social reform marked an increased willingness to let people alone and allow them to live their lives outside of this or that political kitsch. It is a version of social democracy that is simultaneously Gothic and modern. The Gothic facet of his politics cast social reform in moral and ethical terms. It was an attempt for the city's inhabitants to get right with each other, if they could not get right with God (Dewey, 1934b). Its modern facet cast social reform as a matter of personal not divine responsibility. For Dewey, whatever deliverance humankind could accomplish would be what humankind could achieve in this world, not the next (Diggins, 1994).

4. Dewey Modern and Gothic

Central to American Gothic was the movement from religion (faith) to science (experience), philosophy (reason) to literature (narrative and poetry), and from feudalism (land) to capitalism (industry). Modernists who surrounded Dewey in Chicago and New York – William James, Frank Norris, Jane Addams, Charlotte Perkins Gilman, Emma Goldman, Alfred Stieglitz, Mabel Dodge and Walter and Louise Arensberg – understood something very similar (Crunden, 1993; Diggins, 1994). The United States was transformed by modernity's commitment to new sexual mores, moving pictures, modern dance, jazz, individualism and greed (Crunden, 1993). The period changed its sympathies; its arts played a significant part in generating those changes. Modernists knew life was a function of each individual's ability to be 'daring'. In the pages of the period's most popular fiction modern life played itself out somewhere between those whose lives were foredoomed to economic and personal disaster in the city's sweatshops and stockyards and those Robber Barons who dared to be more. Dewey, the primitive, could not muster the quirky, passionate, and idiographic passion of either a Santayana or a Russell (Ryan, 1995, p. 368). It left his philosophy and his philosophy of education strangely in and out of step with the day.

In the simplest terms, American modernism is a declaration of intellectual and cultural independence from the authoritarian traditions – cultural and political (Kloppenberg, 1986). Charles Darwin, Karl Marx and Sigmund Freud among others challenged authoritarian concept of virtually every aspect of public life informed by the Western intellectual tradition.[3] They painted an intellectually world-shattering backdrop that is useful for generating tropes that are helpful in coming to understand the intellectual labours Dewey shouldered and those he did not.

Darwin dissolved the species chauvinism that the human species was something special (Darwin, 1860). Humanity was not separated from the animals of the field and birds of the air by the eye of God. Darwin asserted the unspeakable: The unity of all life. 'Here then is Darwin's dangerous idea: the algorithmic level is the level that best accounts for the speed of the antelope, the wing of the eagle, the shape of the orchid, the diversity of species, and all the other occasions for wonder in the world of the nature' (Dennett, 1995 p. 59). Darwin persuasively constructed a descriptive case for the unity of all life and the method of its differentiation, evolution, using materials gathered from his voyage on the HMS *Beagle*. Darwin argued that all life had crawled out of the primordial ooze together, humanity being no exception (Dawkins, 1976, 1996, 1999). The Great Chain of Being fell to earth with unnerving consequences. Dewey embraced evolutionary theory (Feuer, 1958).

Dewey was thoroughly modern when it came to the cultural heroes of the day. Scientists certainly were among the cultural heroes of the time. Dewey could only agree. He was taken by science and was complete persuaded by one of its most powerful theories: evolution. The work of the scientist Charles Darwin was one of the most important forces in Dewey's intellectual life during his college years and afterwards (Dykhuizen, 1959; Feuer, 1958). He read the work of Darwin again and again.

A convinced Darwinian, Herbert Spencer profoundly influenced Dewey's educational thought (Kaminsky, 1993, pp. 36–37). 'Fascinated and outraged with Spencer's work, Dewey, like William James, spent years engaging him and disentangling evolutionary theory from Spencer's theory of mind and his social and economic politics' (Kaminsky, 1993, p. 37). Dewey's solidarity with evolutionary science was obvious in his philosophical discussions of education (Dewey, 1916b, pp. 1–22). He and Spencer were at one when it came to discounting traditional concepts of education. Spencer was the first to translate science's evolution ethos into education. His translation is found in *Education: intellectual, moral and physical* (1861). For Spencer, 'real' education was not a matter of enlightenment, aristocratic manners, or theological propriety; it was about survival. In *Democracy and Education*, Dewey echoes Spencer writing,

> Reproduction of other forms of life goes on in continuous sequence. And though as the geological record shows, not merely individuals but also species die out, the life process continues in increasingly complex forms. As some species die out, forms better adapted to utilize the obstacles against which they struggled in vain come into being. ... Education, in its broadest sense, is the means of this social continuity of life. (p. 2)

Education to Spencer and Dewey was not about some version of effete Enlightenment; it was a Darwinian survival. It was about the human struggle for continuation. The idea was thoroughly modern, but it was painted against the Gothic background of fang and claw. It was an idea that would show up in the opening chapters of *Democracy and Education* (Dewey, 1916b). Here education was the primitive world's contradiction and modernity's possibility. The lessons of worldly experience, not intelligence, in Dewey's view were the key to survival – just as education was the key to what it was to be human.[4] It was a concept that was consistent with the confidence of the time before World War I. It was a view of education that was wildly popular in the United States and England (Kaminsky, 1993, pp. 36–37). It was Dewey's version of a Promethean reconstruction of society.

Solidarity with the American people for Dewey was a matter of Christian conscience and social democratic principle (Rockefeller, 1991). Christian conscience and social democratic principle were the same core standards that drove the 1890s social reform movement (Silver, 1983b). Unlike Marx, the social obligation Dewey believed in was moral, not political. He argued in a manner similar to Britain's Samuel Alexander (Alexander, [1933] 1966), Australia's John Anderson (see Baker, 1986) for an empirical metaphysics (Dewey, 1925) and a worldly ethics (Dewey, 1929) that were grounded in the concerns of this world, this nation, this city and these people. Dewey argued for an empirical ethics to guide those who were unchurched and unschooled since childhood and an empirical metaphysics (science) to improve their lives. Dewey notes in *Human Nature and Conduct*:

> Common-sense in short never loses sight wholly of the two facts which limit and define a moral situation. One is that consequences fix the moral quality of an act. The other is that upon the whole, or in the long run but not unqualified, consequences are what they are because of the nature of desire and disposition. Hence there is a natural contempt for the morality of the 'good' man who does not show his goodness in the results of his habitual acts. (1922, pp. 43–44)

Be that as it may, he never abandoned his Gothic faith and belief in Christian charity – although he had more than some problems with the Christian church (Rockefeller, 1991). Because of his Gothic faith, social reform in his mind would always remain a moral – not a political – obligation (Rockefeller, 1991, pp. 126–68).

Social reform was a matter of integrating the idea of Christian charity into the process of secular democratic action (Rockefeller, 1991, p. 169). Dewey was convinced of the importance of worldly contributions to social reform. His modern faith in secular social action is found in *Democracy and Education* (Dewey, 1916b), *Freedom and Culture* (Dewey, 1939), *The Public and Its Problems* (Dewey, 1927) and similar shorter pieces of writing (see Dewey and Boydston, 1976, passim). But public education was at the core of it all. The point is that public education for Dewey was a matter of showing each person the language of solidarity's possibility and their social self-invention. If education is to be measured against anything, it is to be measured against the possibility of achieving our world and ourselves.[5]

In the modern period Marx contributed to – if he did not almost invent – the assault upon capitalism, aristocratic authority and privilege that separated the primitive and modern world (Marx, 1954). He set Hegel's metaphysical description of the world on its head and explained the period's chaotic present in terms of predatory economic relations. Nationalism was no longer merely a matter of domestic solidarity, it was economic war waged by the strong on the weak. World War I was, of course, an obvious example of the aristocratic economic and political frenzy to which Marx alluded (Tuchman, 1966). Marx's work, of course, profoundly affected Dewey (Hook, 1987a). In one sense, his educational philosophy in *Democracy and Education* (Dewey, 1916b) is a theory of the educational reconstruction of class in the United States. Marx's influence on Dewey's philosophy of education is obvious. The left politics of *Democracy and Education* (Dewey, 1916a) is class conscious but detached and wistful. As Dewey writes: 'Nothing is more tragic than failure to discover one's true business in life, or to find that one has drifted or been forced by circumstance into an uncongenial calling' (Dewey, 1916b, p. 308). Dewey's prose certainly does not measure up to the left's call for direct action.

Unlike Marx, Dewey never understood the inflexibility of large institutions (Ryan, 1995, p. 368). As a result he could never appreciate the economic miracle Franklin Delano Roosevelt had performed during the Great Depression nor could he appreciate what progressive educators were attempting to do. He could appreciate the 'schools of tomorrow'; however, he could not understand what it would take to make them a reality (Ryan, 1995, pp. 142–53). In a manner similar to José Arcadio Buendía who could not understand what it would take to make his world scientific, Dewey could not understand the effort it would take to make his world and the schools he loved economically, politically and socially modern. As a result a book like *Liberalism and Social Action* (Dewey, 1935) would end, arguably, just where it should have begun (Ryan, 1995, p. 369). In closing *Liberalism and Social Action* Dewey wrote:

It would be fantastic folly to ignore or to belittle the obstacles that stand in the way. But what has taken place, also against great odds, in the scientific and industrial revolutions, is an accomplished fact; the way is marked out. It may be that the way will remain untrodden. If so, the future holds the menace of confusion moving into chaos, a chaos that will be externally masked for a time by an organization of force, coercive and violent. In which the liberties of men will all but disappear ... The business of liberalism is to bend every energy and exhibit every courage so that these precious goods may not even be temporarily lost but be intensified and expanded here and now. (1935, p. 93)

This was a weak finish to what was, at the time, an important book.

Dewey's modernist declaration of intellectual and cultural independence from the authoritarian traditions, cultural and political, did not extend to matters of sexuality. It seems an odd exception given the fact that Dewey defined democracy as a mode of associated living in which democracy was measured against the length and breadth of associated living. Unlike Anais Nin, Gertrude Stein and Alice B. Toklas, Dewey was not terribly interested in ridding women of the fondness for subordination, modest dress, effete manners and passive sexuality. His concern for women's rights seems confined to a concern for equal educational opportunity and women's suffrage. The private world of women seemed a matter of small concern for Dewey. The explanation of course can be found in Dewey's concept of the social obligations of a Gothic social order.

John Dewey would never look back on his own life and write a *Blackberry Winter* (Mead, 1972) – the autobiographical book that showcased Margaret Mead's attempt to come to terms with sexuality in American culture and her own life. As Ryan notes, 'Dewey was oddly untouched by Freud' (Ryan, 1995, p. 368). Freud finished his essays on meta-psychology during World War I (Freud and Rieff, 2008). Western intellectuals discovered that they were driven by sexuality and had lost their mind to the dark forces of the subconscious. Freud's assault upon the tower of reason outlined the significance of the human subconscious's shadowy and irrational side. It was deliciously eerie. Against the context of the pointless mayhem and slaughter of World War I the idea of humankind directed by irrational and, perhaps, anti-human (evil) subconscious was more than plausible.

Dewey was disconnected if not almost silent about the issues of sex, intimacy, temperament, and the modernity's culture of narcissism. His work always presented a stern Gothic face in public, at least as far as the 'fairer sex' was concerned. Dewey's unconsummated affair with Anzia Yezierska demonstrates the contradictions between his modernist commitment to reason and his emotional ties to a Gothic social order (Dewey and Boydston, 1977). One needs to return to Grant Wood's painting *American Gothic* to understand Dewey's Gothic romanticism. His conflicted sense of love, sexuality and passion forced him to simultaneously flee (the bonds of his marriage to Alice Chipman) and approach (his romantic encounter with Anzia Yezierska) a modern world that events are violently transforming. The farmer-preacher and joyless wife-daughter are hard-edged individuals, convinced of the seriousness of life and filled with the certainty that the events of their time will betray the efforts of their lives. The farmer-preacher represents the serious, unsmiling philosopher. His lined face, stern moustache and flowing grey hair masked his romanticism that he understood, as reason's undoing.

The publication of Dewey's poems – written for a graduate student while married to Alice Chipman – reveal his conflicted emotional answer to the needs of the heart (Dewey and Boydston, 1977). Love and sexuality were immediate and intrinsically private emotions – the stern farmer-preacher who would never publicly reveal the passions of his heart. Dewey shows his concept of the immediate and intrinsically private emotion of love in this poem:

> In its beginning an emotion flies straight to its object. Love tends to cherish the loved object as hate tends to destroy the thing hated ... The emotion of love may seek and find material that is other than the directly loved one, but that is congenial and cognate through the emotion that draws things into affinity ... Consult the poets, and we find that love finds its expression in rushing torrents, still pools, in the suspense that awaits a storm, a bird poised in flight, a remote star or the fickle moon. (Dewey, 1934a, p. 76)

Such immediacy and passion was more than evident in Dewey's emotional and romantic involvement with the graduate student, Anzia Yezierska. She audited his class in social and political philosophy. He met the strikingly beautiful Anzia in October of 1917 (Dewey and Boydston, 1977). She worked as Dewey's interpreter in a group of graduate students conducting a study of the living conditions of the Polish community in 1918. Dewey writes poetically of their relationship this way:

> By the sweetness of every chance caress,
> By the words of love we swore,
> By the quick magic of each vagrant tress,
> And every sigh that from sealed lips did pour,
> By every intercepted glance
> That spoke the untold take,
> By every touch of hands that did enhance
> Desire till distance lost its stern avail,
> By the drops of blood that trait'rous started
> In warm wonder whene'er we met,
> By every ling'ring kiss with which we parted,
> By every sacred tear that wet
> Th' innocence of our unopened scroll of love,
> By every laughing joy that illumined
> With the flow of all the stars above
> That scroll when its pages opened.
>
> (Dewey and Boydston, 1977, p. xxxviii)

His poem, *Two weeks*, demonstrates his Gothic inability to abandon the role of stern farmer-preacher and act to consummate their involvement.

> Riches, possessions hold me? Nay,
> Not rightly have you guessed

The things that block the way,
Nor into what ties I've slowly grown
By which I am possest.
For I do not own.
Who makes, has. Such the old old law.
Owned then am I by what I felt and saw
But most by them with whom I've loved, and fought,
Till within me has been wrought
My power to reach, to see and understand.
Such is the tie, such the iron band.

And Anzia's response to him as wife-daughter is displayed in the stories and books she wrote. Boydston writes: 'She often depicts a Dewey-figure as the Anglo-Saxon or Gentile struggling to overcome the Puritanism that made him "cold in the heart, clear in the head"' (Dewey and Boydston, 1977, p. xlii).

Love and sexuality, the romantic intuition, could not be reduced to some crude psycho/biological urge. To be moved by Freud was unacceptable. To place the immanent and irrational emotion of passion within unreason's coherence was too great a loss. In a way, recognising Dewey's Gothic romanticism explains the huge stillness in his work about the private, the intimate, and human sexuality. Love was a function of the fact he believed that love was an aesthetic created by the convergence of two lives. The idea that human love was an epiphenomenon of subliminal psychological and biological sexual urges was just too modern and intellectually crude for Dewey's taste.

5. Conclusion

Again, central to American Gothic was the movement from religion (faith) to science (experience), philosophy (reason) to literature (narrative and poetry), and from feudalism (land) to capitalism (industry). Modernists of the period adopted scientists as one of their cultural heroes. Dewey added his work to their voices. But he could not give up his Gothic faith in God and a pastoral social order. Dewey like José Arcadio Buendía was among the first to reject the Gothic ethos to find the world that only 'science' could provide. However, like Buendía he could not quite give up the magical Gothic world of his childhood. Dewey could not abandon the idea of faith, faith in the Christian sense of the hoped for and believed in (Dewey, 1934b). As Rockefeller notes, even in his later years the idea of the stern and severe God acquired in his youth was still active in his thought (Rockefeller, 1991). It was the hope for a new God that appeared in a *Common Faith* (1934b). Dewey phrased it this way in his poem *Paradise Lost and Regained*:

Now listening you may hear the welcome tale
Of liberation from illusion's veil:–
When chosen is the better from the worse
'Mid mingled flowing good and ill

A new created God dispels the curse;
And from the doubled mixture grows a single will
That this world which subtly mingled is
Shall ever better come to be, till man knows
That such growth of better is his sole bliss,
Lovelier too than lovely mystic rose
That fall of man, dividing bad from good,
Has caused to grow in its far solitude
Of Trinity, holy all its lonely days,
With but themselves alone to see and praise.

(Dewey and Boydston, 1977, pp. 59–60)

What was left to all modernists, Dewey included, was the here and now; it was all there was.

> A sense of possibilities that are unrealized and that might be realized are when they are put in contrast with actual conditions, the most penetrating 'criticism' of the latter that can be made. It is by a sense of possibilities opening before us that we become aware of constrictions that hem us in and of burdens that oppress. (Dewey, [1934] 1958, p. 346)

For Dewey, the modernist, the here and now had to be enough. As Dewey noted, 'Philosophy recovers itself when it ceases to be a device for dealing with the problems of philosophers and becomes a method, cultivated by philosophers, for dealing with the problems of men' (Dewey, [1917] 1985, p. 46). Dewey's philosophy and philosophy of education promised to liberate humankind from ignorance and irrationality in the name of the Promethean excitement generated by the apparently unlimited potential of mechanical energy and the dynamo (Livingston, 1994). However, it did so with a certain confidence in modern science and the objective knowledge it held in its fingertips. He wrote his philosophy within the assumed primacy of industrial production and the omnipresence of class struggle. It also assumed the problems of men were industrialism, urbanisation, technology, nationalism (American, Russian, Japanese and German), alienation, poverty and anomie.

Dewey's work was driven by an oscillation between Gothic (magical transformation) and modern (instrumental transformations). In his work he was inventing America the way he would like it to be, not the way it was. He was busy inventing a country in which freedom of speech, freedom from want, freedom from religious persecution, and freedom from fear would be commonplace. Dewey was paying attention to the country's promise, not the flaws and shortcomings of which there were many. The world he foreshadowed wrapped its natural forms around the smooth curves and rectilinear lines of science and the emotional comfort of a Gothic faith – the result was life as Art Nouveau (Livingston, 1994). Life to Dewey's mind is an eternal contest of 'modern' engagements and intermissions inspired by a sense of Gothic imagination (Kloppenberg, 1986, pp. 349–80).

264 John Dewey, Gothic and Modern

And as the character José Arcadio Buendía reminds us, having a life is something people accomplish, not something they have within them. Life is a game, a serious game, which can be won or lost. Like the character José Arcadio Buendía, Dewey rejected the magical power of the Gothic past to find a modern world that only 'science' could provide. The characters in *One Hundred Years of Solitude* created their own worlds, fleeing the one they were born in and pursuing the one they did not create and did not know while holding fast to a Gothic faith in what had gone before. Having a life for Dewey then is the catalyst of 'inexperience' between Gothic tradition (the way things and we were) and modern (the way things and we might be). 'Inexperience' is the handmaiden of reality's composition – personal and social. In 'inexperience' Gothic emotion and intuition reappear in science and technology, as 'Art Nuevo' – science and technology aesthetically blended in service to the problems of mankind. The education of 'inexperience' for Dewey is the predicate for the art of being-in-the-world's composition.

References

Alexander, S. ([1933] 1966) *Space, Time, and Deity: the Gifford Lectures at Glasgow 1916–1918* (New York, Dover Publications).
Baker, A. J. (1986) *Australian Realism: the Systematic Philosophy of John Anderson* (Cambridge/New York, Cambridge University Press).
Carpentier, A. (1956) *The Lost Steps* (Trans. H. D. Onis) (New York, Knopf).
Carter, A. (1985) *Nights at the Circus* (1st American edn.) (New York, Viking).
Crunden, R. M. (1993) *American Salons: Encounters with European Modernism, 1885–1917* (New York, Oxford University Press).
D'Haen, T. L. (1995) Magical realism and postmodernism: decentering privileged center. In L. P. Zamora and W. B. Faris (Eds) *Magical Realism* (Durham, NC, Duke University Press).
Darwin, C. (1860) *On the Origin of Species by Means of Natural Selection, or the Preservation of Favoured Races in the Struggle for Life* (New York, D. Appleton and Co.).
Dawkins, R. (1976) *The Selfish Gene* (New York, Oxford University Press).
——(1996) *The Blind Watchmaker* (New York, W. W. Norton and Co.).
——(1999) *The Extended Phenotype: the Long Reach of the Gene* (New York, Oxford University Press).
Dennett, D. C. (1995) *Darwin's Dangerous Idea: Evolution and the Meanings of Life* (New York, Simon and Schuster).
Dewey, J. ([1899] 1990) *The School and Society and the Child and the Curriculum* (Chicago, University of Chicago Press).
——(1916a) *Democracy and Education* (New York, The Free Press).
——(1916b) *Democracy and Education: an Introduction to the Philosophy of Education* (New York, Macmillan).
——([1917] 1985) The need for a recovery in philosophy. In J. A. Boydston (Ed.) *John Dewey: the Middle Works, 1899–1924, V. 10* (Carbondale, Southern Illinois University Press).
——(1920) *Reconstruction in Philosophy* (New York, H. Holt and Co.).
——(1922) *Human Nature and Conduct; an Introduction to Social Psychology* (New York, Holt).

——(1925) *Experience and Nature* (Chicago / London, Open Court).

——(1927) *The Public and Its Problems* (New York, H. Holt and Co.).

——(1929) *The Quest for Certainty* (New York, Minton, Balch and Co.).

——([1934] 1958) *Art as Experience* (New York, Capricorn Books, G. P. Putnam's Sons).

——(1934a) *Art as Experience* (New York, Minton).

——(1934b) *A Common Faith* (New Haven, Yale University Press).

——(1935) *Liberalism and Social Action* (New York, G. P. Putnam's Sons).

——(1939) *Freedom and Culture* (New York, G. P. Putnam's Sons).

Dewey, J. and Boydston, J. A. (1976) *The Middle Works, 1899–1924* (Carbondale, Southern Illinois University Press).

——(1977) *The Poems of John Dewey* (Carbondale, Southern Illinois University Press).

Diggins, J. P. (1994) *The Promise of Pragmatism* (Chicago, University of Chicago Press).

Dreiser, T. (1900) *Sister Carrie* (New York, Doubleday, Page and Co).

——(1912) *The Financier: a Novel* (New York, Harper and Brothers).

——(1914) *The Titan* (New York, John Lane).

——(1925) *An American Tragedy* (New York, Boni and Liveright).

Dykhuizen, G. (1959) John Dewey: the Vermont years, *Journal of the History of Ideas*, 20.

Feuer, L. S. (1958) John Dewey's reading at college, *Journal of the History of Ideas*, 19.

——(1959) John Dewey and the back to the people movement, *Journal of the History of Ideas*, 20.

Fowles, J. (1969) *The French Lieutenant's Woman* (London, Cape).

Freud, S. and Rieff, P. (2008) *General Psychological Theory: Papers on Metapsychology* (1st Touchstone paperback edn.) (New York, Touchstone).

Hook, S. (1987a) *Out of Step: an Unquiet Life in the 20th Century* (1st edn.) (New York, Harper and Row).

——(1987b) *Out of Step: an Unquiet Life in the 20th Century* (New York, Carroll and Graf).

Kaminsky, J. S. (1993) *A New History of Educational Philosophy* (Westport, CO, Greenwood Press).

Kloppenberg, J. T. (1986) *Uncertain Victory: Social Democracy and Progressivism in European and American Thought, 1870–1920* (New York, Oxford University Press).

Livingston, J. (1994) *Pragmatism and the Political Economy of Cultural Revolution, 1850–1940* (Chapel Hill, University of North Carolina Press).

Márquez, G. G. (1970) *One Hundred Years of Solitude* (1st edn.) (New York, Harper and Row).

Martel, Y. (2001) *Life of Pi: a Novel* (1st U.S. edn.) (New York, Harcourt).

Marx, K. (1954) *Capital* (Moscow, Progress Publishers).

Mead, M. (1972) *Blackberry Winter; My Earlier Years* (New York, Morrow).

Niebuhr, R. (1944) *The Children of Light and the Children of Darkness* (New York, C. Scribner's Sons).

Rockefeller, S. C. (1991) *John Dewey: Religious Faith and Democratic Humanism* (New York, Columbia University Press).

Roh, F. ([1925] 1995) Magical realism: post-expressionism. In L. P. Zamora and W. B. Faris (Eds) *Magical Realism* (Durham, NC, Duke University Press).

Rorty, R. (1991) *Objectivity, Relativism, and Truth* (Cambridge / New York, Cambridge University Press).

——(1998) *Achieving Our Country: Leftist Thought in Twentieth-Century America* (Cambridge, MA, Harvard University Press).

Rushdie, S. (2006) *Midnight's Children: a Novel* (25th anniversary edn.) (New York, Random House Trade Paperbacks).

Ryan, A. (1995) *John Dewey and the High Tide of American Liberalism* (1st edn.) (New York, W.W. Norton).

Seaman, L.C.B. (1973) *Victorian England* (London, Methuen).

Silver, H. (1983a) *Education as History* (London, Methuen).

——(1983b) *Education as History: Interpreting Nineteenth- and Twentieth-Century Education* (London/New York, Methuen).

Spencer, H. (1861) *Education: Intellectual, Moral, and Physical* (London, Williams and Norgate).

Tuchman, B.W. (1966) *The Proud Tower; a Portrait of the World before the War, 1890–1914* (New York, Macmillan).

Westbrook, R. B. (1991) *John Dewey and American Democracy* (Ithaca, NY, Cornell University Press).

Zamora, L. P. and Faris, W. B. (1995) *Magical Realism: Theory, History, Community* (Durham, NC, Duke University Press).

Notes

1 Anyone interested in Dewey's romance with modernity would be well rewarded by reading Alan Ryan's *John Dewey* (1995).
2 In a very strict sense the Victorians were English and London was the epicentre of the Victorian experience. But writing of the Victorian period in such a narrow stipulated sense is misleading. Intellectually speaking the work of Darwin, Tennyson, Gladstone, Dickens and Browning among others defined high moral purpose that marked the Victorians and the Victorian period. The Victorian worldview was characteristic of the intellectual establishment of the United States in the same way that Victorians and the Victorian period influenced the entire English-speaking world.
    Victorian bureaucrats who governed and administered the Empire throughout the century and beyond extended its reach across the globe (Seaman, 1973). Furthermore, chronologically speaking, it was an incredibly elastic period. The Victorian period did not begin in 1837 nor end in 1901. A woman of 50 in 1865 no less a man who reached said age in 1921 could certainly be described as a Victorian. In one sense, it was the Festival of Britain in 1951 that marked the close of the Victorian period (Seaman, 1973; Silver, 1983b).
3 The Victorian period generated a phalanx of intellectual giants. My selection of these three individuals is, obviously, somewhat arbitrary. The strongest argument for their selection is that each of them had an immense impact upon the Victorian Zeitgeist. And of course, the argument for selecting the Victorian period for the chronological setting of this article is that it roughly overlaps the period of John Dewey's life.
4 The debate over the centrality of intelligence to the educational endeavour was a contest Dewey lost to Lewis Terman whose work on IQ became essential to educational thought in the modern period.
5 It really is quite wrong to think that Dewey thought that education is its own excuse. Although there is the famous aphorism in Dewey's work implying that the criteria of education is growth and only growth, the aphorism is quite misleading. Dewey always assessed education against its contribution to the well-being of all the individuals that were part of the social compact and the contribution education made to discovering democracy's 'undiscovered country' (Feuer, 1959).

An Appreciation of Roy Niblett CBE[1]

James Arthur

In April 2005 I had an appointment with William Roy Niblett at his nursing home in Gloucester. Unfortunately, on the morning of my visit I was called by a nurse from the home to say that Roy was not well enough to receive me. I learnt a few weeks later that Roy had died aged 98. At that point I did not know the extent of Roy's involvement with the *British Journal of Educational Studies* of which I had recently been elected Editor. My involvement with Roy had emerged from an invitation to give a paper to the Higher Education Foundation Conference in 2005 and Roy had been sent my draft paper and commented upon it. He wrote to me and then we phoned each other and discussed the shape of my paper for the Conference. Roy was keen to advise me and his advice was most welcome. At the time I had no idea he was 98 years old, but I do remember that he was still intellectually sharp and offered excellent advice and encouragement. It was only after I had been Editor of the *British Journal of Educational Studies* for some time that I realised the full extent of Roy's involvement in the *Journal*'s establishment and the regrettable fact that the *Journal* had not published an appreciation of him after his death. This editorial is therefore devoted to the memory of Roy the man and his achievements in the field of education.

Roy was born on 25 July 1906 and was educated at the Merchant Venturers' School in Bristol before graduating with first-class honours in English from the University of Bristol. He moved to the University of Oxford to complete a MLitt course and commented that he found the teaching inferior to that at Bristol, but the friendships were closer and the horizons wider. He became an English teacher at Doncaster Grammar School in 1930. In 1934 he moved to King's College, Newcastle, then part of Durham University, as lecturer in education, and in 1945 he became Professor of Education at the then University College of Hull. By October 1947 he had become Professor of Education and Director of the newly established Institute of Education in the University of Leeds. In 1959 he became the Dean of the University of London, Institute of Education. Roy published extensively during these years and was a member of the University Grants Committee from 1949–59 and of the National Advisory Council on Training and Supply of Teachers from 1950–61. He also served on many other educational foundations and associations as well as making time for a large number of informal educational networks and discussion groups. He was the first holder of a university chair in higher education and he played a key role in the establishment of the Higher Education Foundation and helped establish the Society for Research into Higher Education in the 1960s.

Roy was centrally involved with the establishment of the *British Journal of Educational Studies* in 1952, which was the journal of the Standing Conference on Studies in Education that had been formed the previous year. The Standing Conference was founded and chaired by Roy, who was then a Professor of Education at the University of Leeds. To edit the *Journal* he selected Arthur Beales, who was at the time a lecturer in the History of Education at King's College, London.

Roy Niblett was a committed Christian throughout his life and thought that education should be concerned with fundamental questions about the value and purpose of human life. From reading Niblett's personal papers, now deposited in the University of Bristol, it is clear that his deeply held religious beliefs, grounded in nonconformity, were a central element throughout his whole life. He was shaped intellectually in the inter-war era of liberal biblical and theological scholarship, particularly among those with a common concern for the application of Christian faith and ethics to society. He believed that education should not be reduced to a purely instrumental and utilitarian preparation for life and he feared that society was in danger of lacking any sense of a goal, and so he emphasised in education metaphysical beliefs in general and Christian beliefs in particular. In professional terms, he was first and foremost a teacher and trained teachers – in this sense he was both a thinker and practitioner. His publications were responses to a wide variety of educational problems that arose in the early days of education's emergence as a separate discipline.

When Roy was Professor of Education at Leeds in 1948, he campaigned to get the University to establish its Institute of Education. He successfully used all his Christian connections to lobby the Senate to this end. He organised annual Foundation Conferences between 1947 and 1960 for those sympathetic to Christian presuppositions in education, and a broad range of people, including educationalists, headteachers, and chief education officers, attended them. He edited a series, *Educational Issues of Today*, which grew out of the conferences, and in the editorial note to each book he wrote 'Christianity has insights to offer for which there is no substitute'. He was also a key member of the Institute for Christian Education and wrote in its journal *Religion and Education*. Roy wanted Christians and humanists to work together.

On his retirement from the Institute of Education, University of London he remained active in educational matters until his death. His contacts and networks were wide-ranging and I am proud to say included me at the very end through my involvement with the Higher Education Foundation (HEF), which Roy established in 1980.

Note

1 This appreciation of Roy Niblett first appeared as the *BJES* Editorial in December 2011.

Index

Please note that page numbers relating to Notes will have the letter 'n' following the page number.